Shojo Beat

DAYTIME SHOOTING STAR

Story & Art by
Mika Yamamori

CONTENTS

STORY THUS FAR

Suzume Yosano is a first-year in high school. Born in the country, she grew up living a free and easy life. Due to family circumstances, she was forced to transfer to a school in Tokyo. Lost on her first day in the city, she is found by a man who later turns out to be her homeroom teacher, Mr. Shishio. Suzume gradually develops feelings for him.

Unable to suppress her feelings, Suzume declares her love to him! Shishio turns her down, but soon after he admits to Suzume that he returns her feelings. Their relationship is full of highs and lows, and despite her best efforts, Suzume can't seem to get closer to Shishio. Meanwhile, something weighs heavily on Shishio's mind.

Urged on by Yuyuka, Suzume attempts to get Shishio to clarify their relationship. However, before she can get the words out, Shishio expresses his desire to return to just being teacher and student. As if that wasn't bad enough, he tells Suzume that he never loved her—a revelation that causes Suzume to burst into tears.

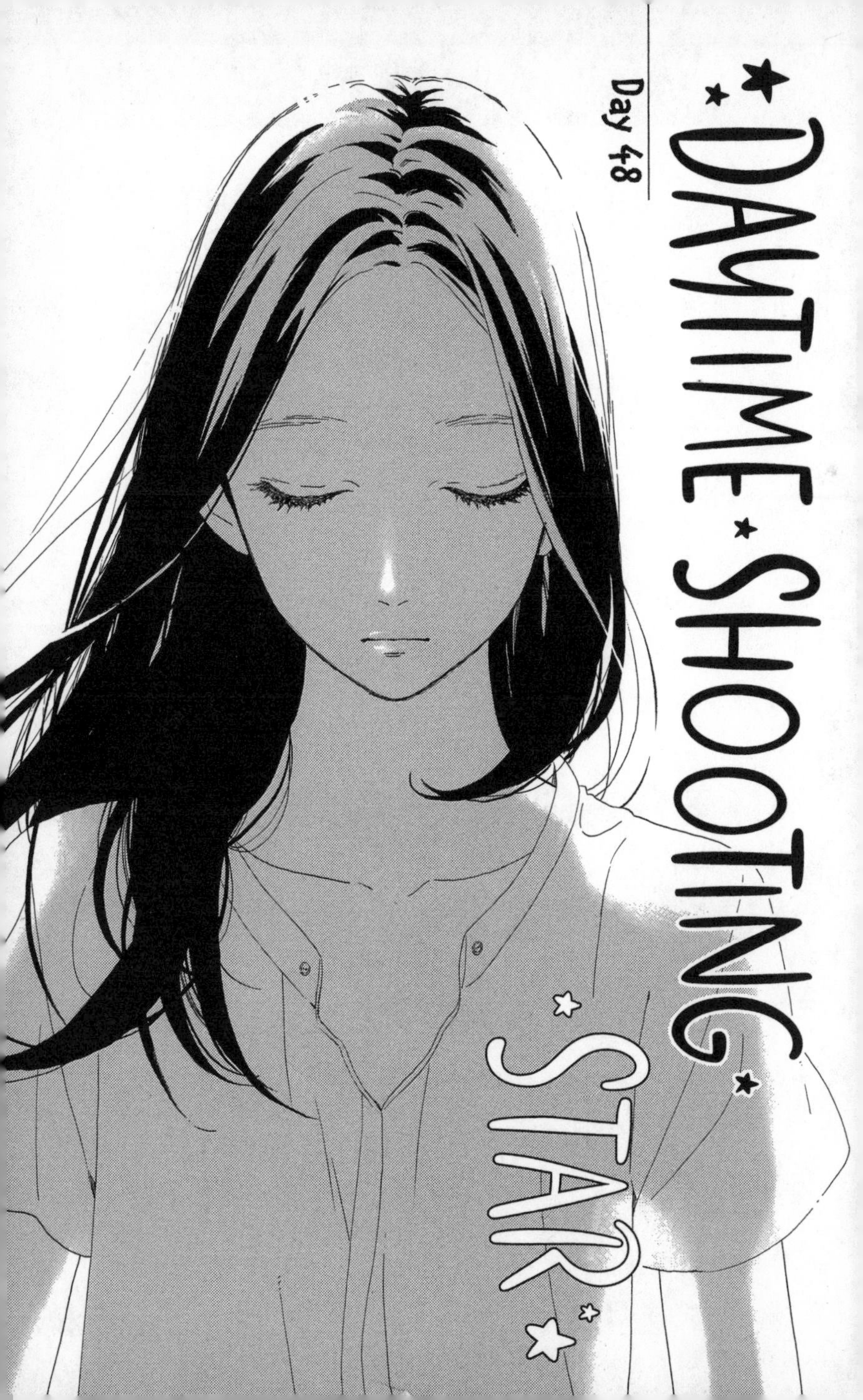
DAYTIME SHOOTING STAR
Day 48

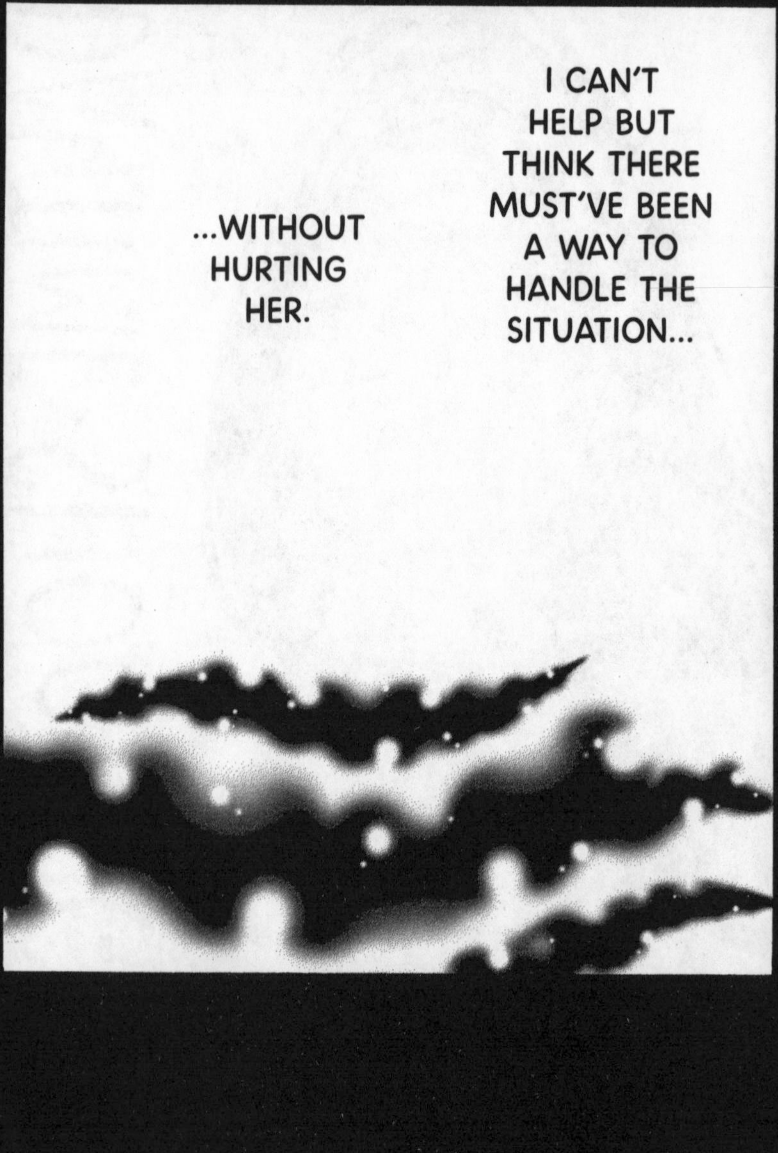

I CAN'T HELP BUT THINK THERE MUST'VE BEEN A WAY TO HANDLE THE SITUATION...

...WITHOUT HURTING HER.

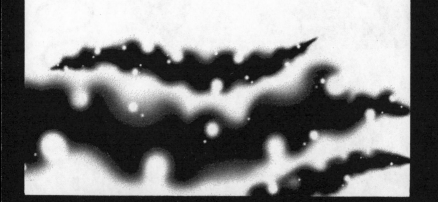

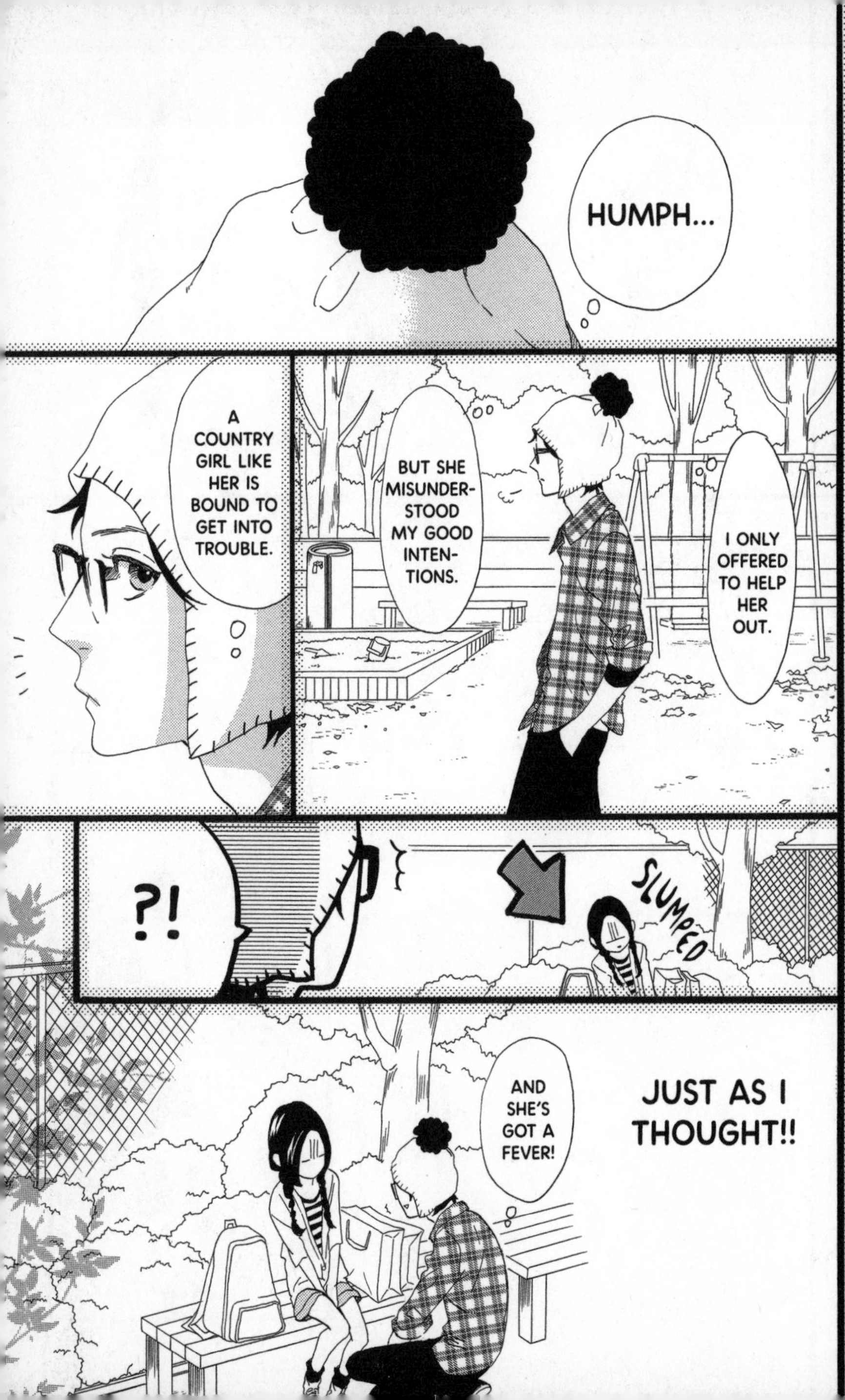
HUMPH...
I ONLY OFFERED TO HELP HER OUT.
BUT SHE MISUNDERSTOOD MY GOOD INTENTIONS.
A COUNTRY GIRL LIKE HER IS BOUND TO GET INTO TROUBLE.
SLUMPED
?!
JUST AS I THOUGHT!!
AND SHE'S GOT A FEVER!

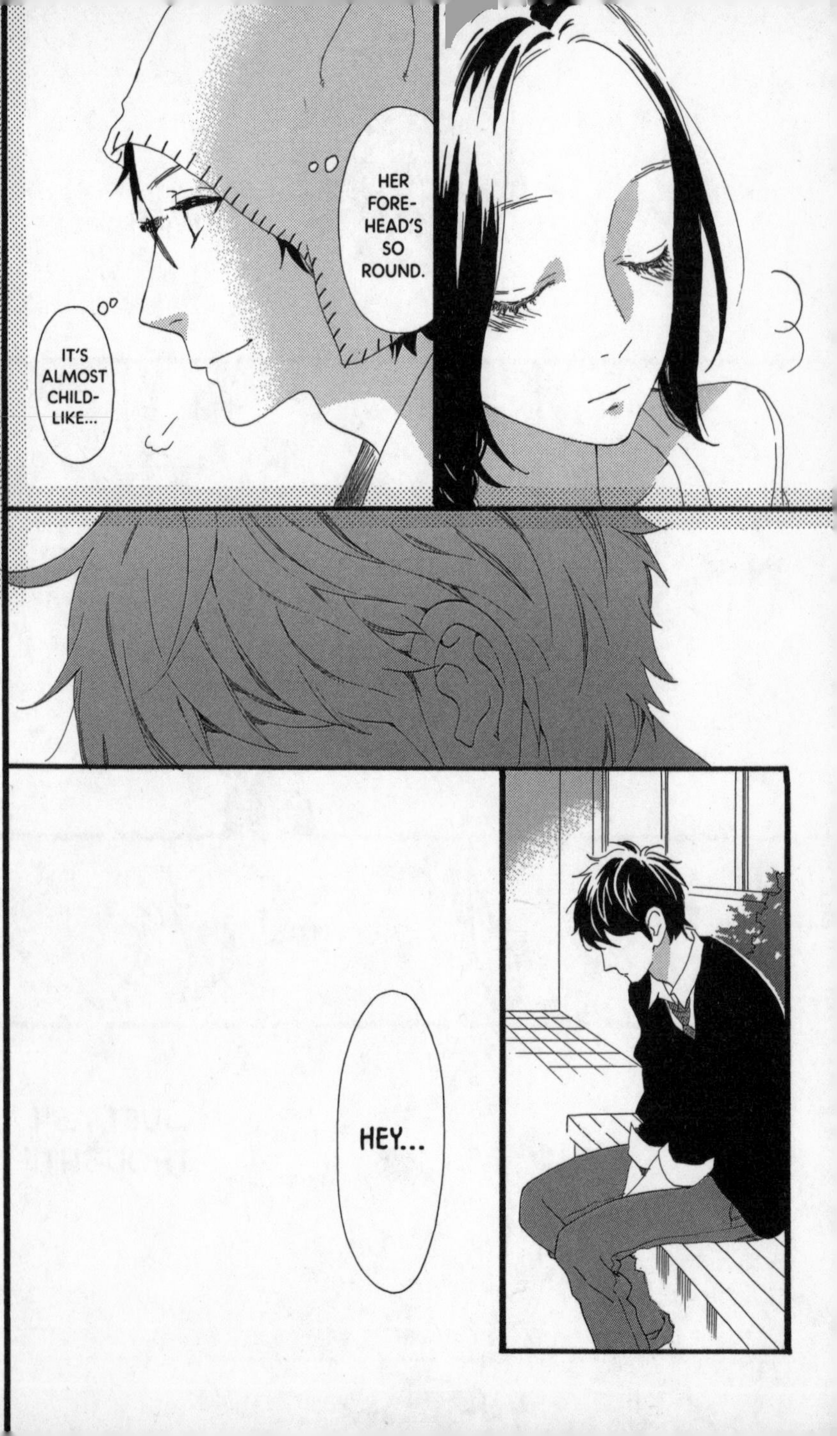
HER FORE-HEAD'S SO ROUND.
IT'S ALMOST CHILD-LIKE...
HEY...

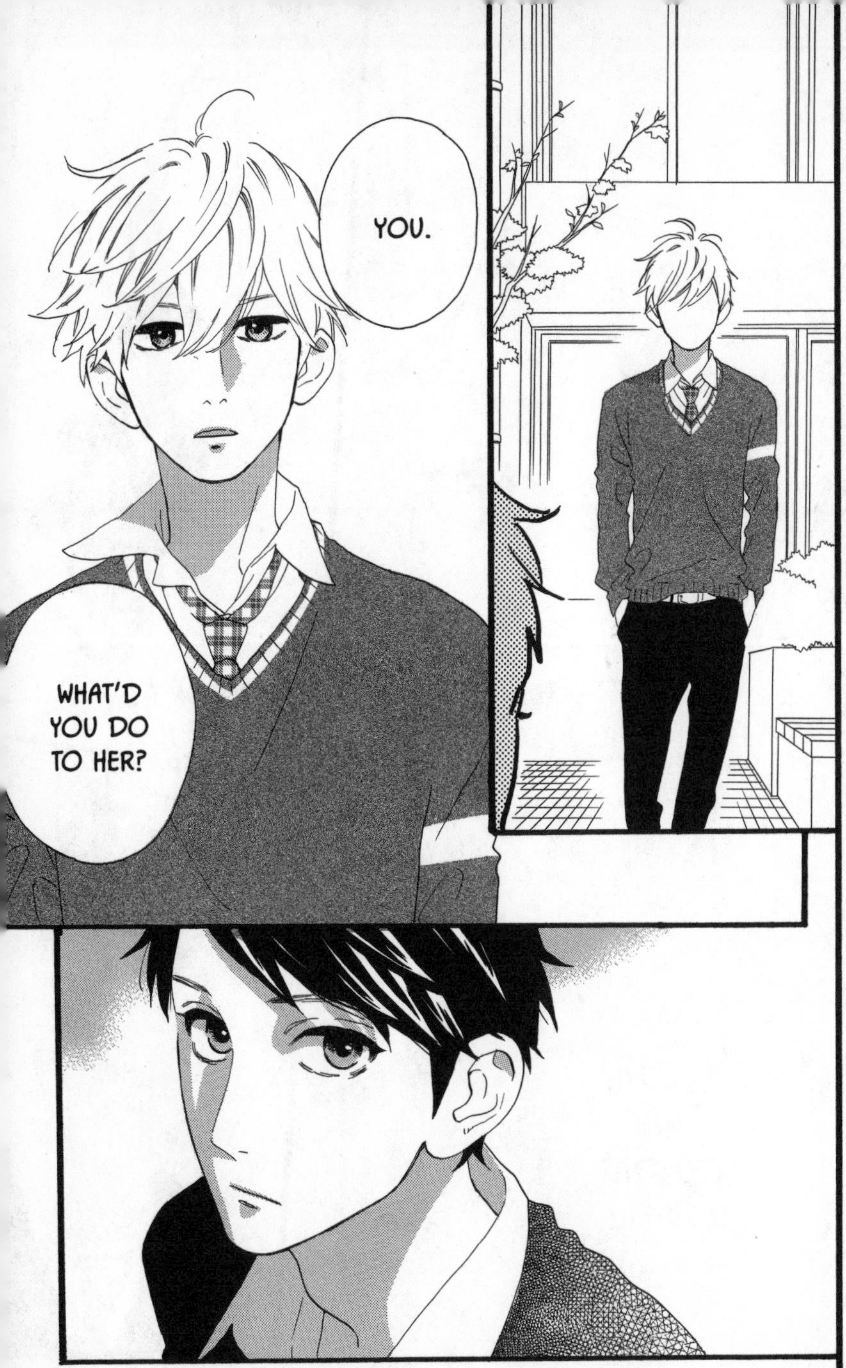
YOU.
WHAT'D YOU DO TO HER?

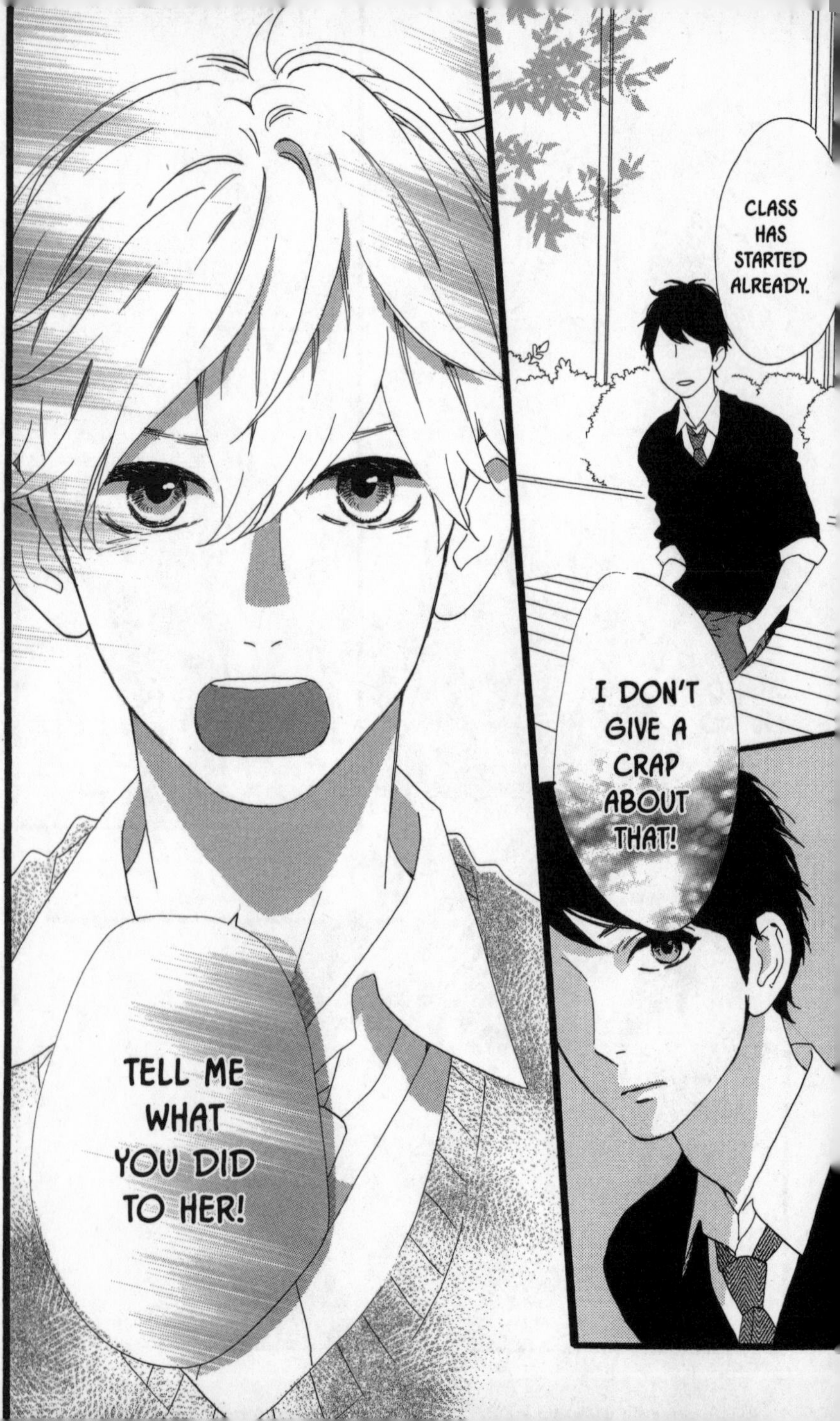
CLASS HAS STARTED ALREADY.
I DON'T GIVE A CRAP ABOUT THAT!
TELL ME WHAT YOU DID TO HER!

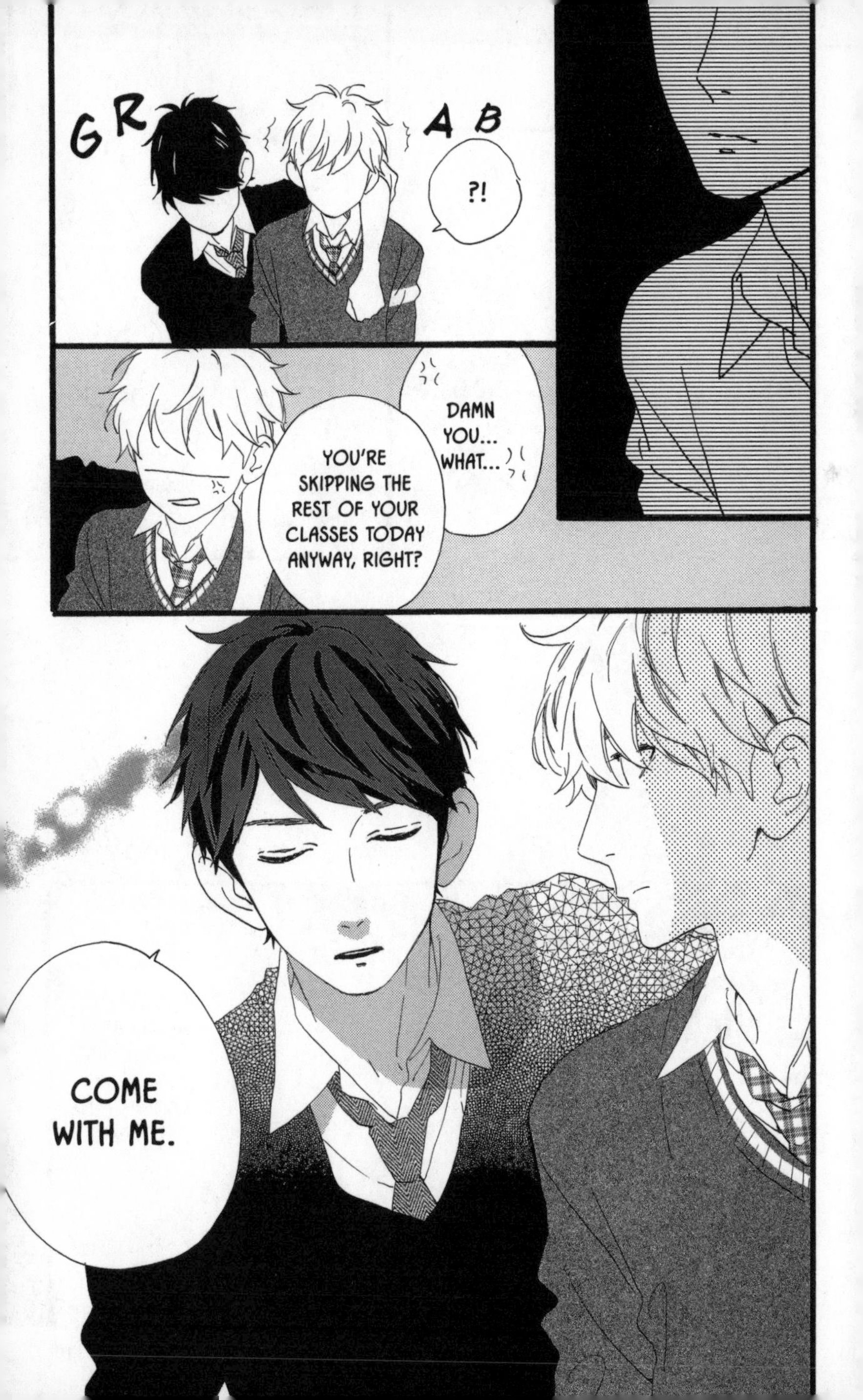
GRAB
?!
DAMN YOU... WHAT...
YOU'RE SKIPPING THE REST OF YOUR CLASSES TODAY ANYWAY, RIGHT?
COME WITH ME.

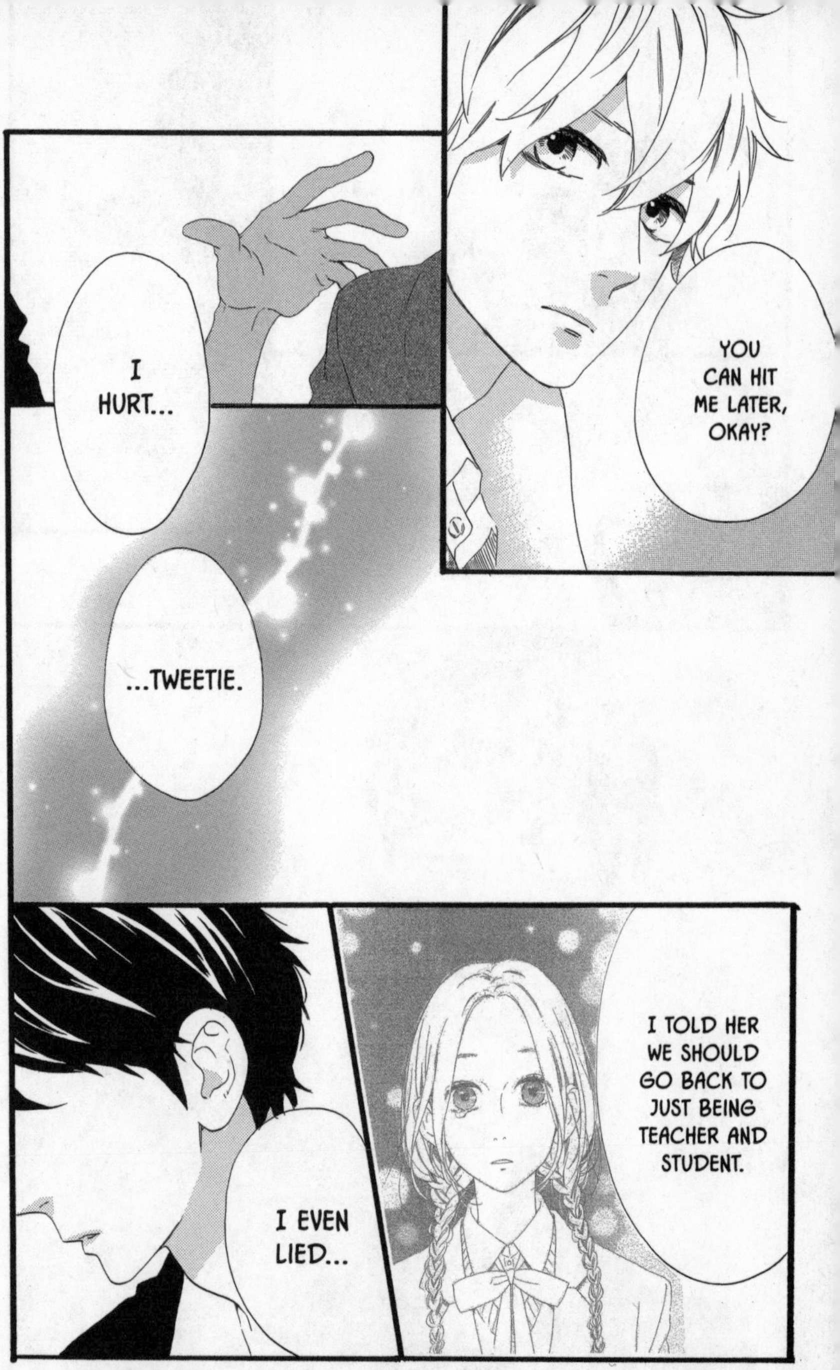
YOU CAN HIT ME LATER, OKAY?
I HURT...
...TWEETIE.
I TOLD HER WE SHOULD GO BACK TO JUST BEING TEACHER AND STUDENT.
I EVEN LIED...

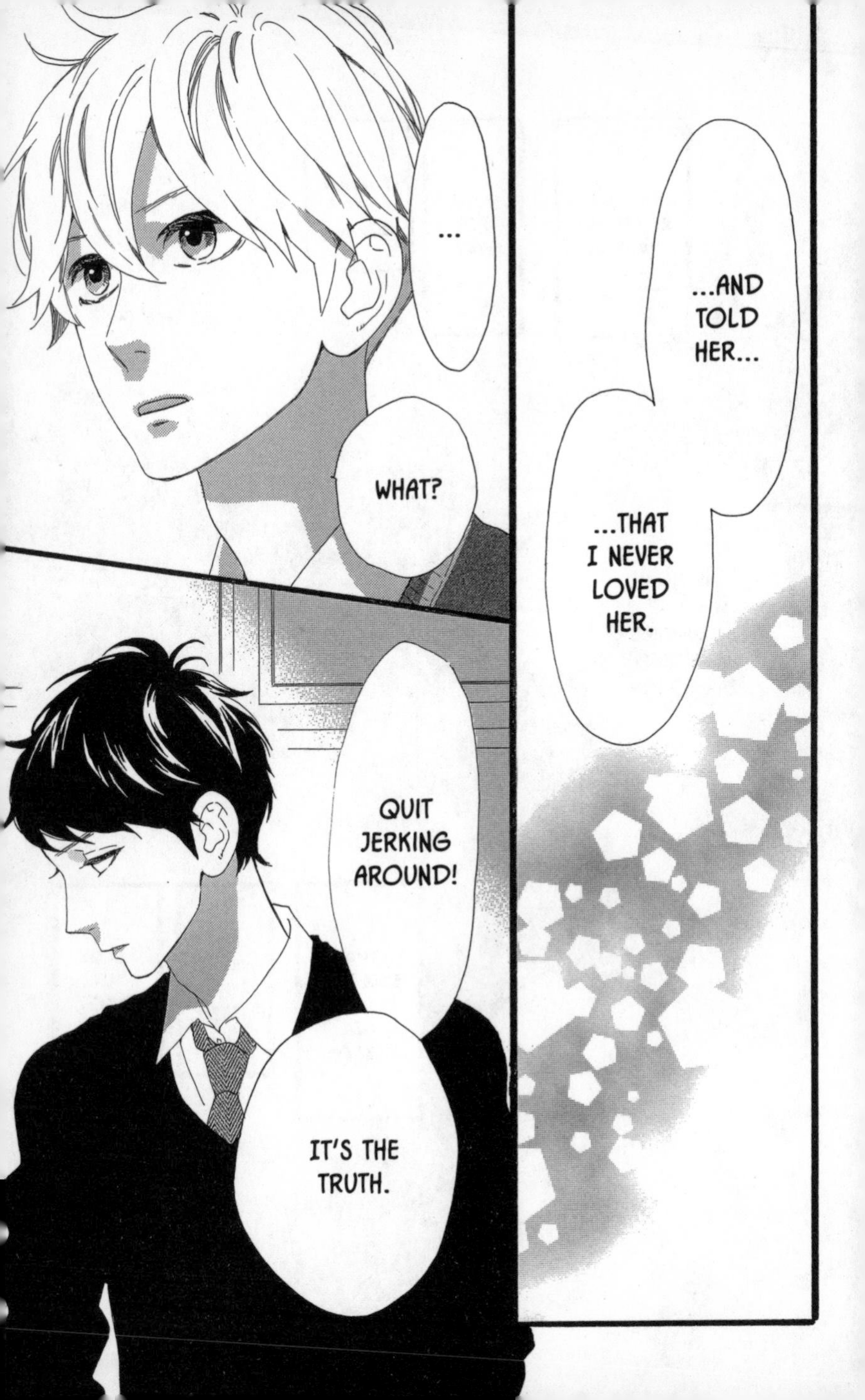
...AND TOLD HER...
...THAT I NEVER LOVED HER.
...
WHAT?
QUIT JERKING AROUND!
IT'S THE TRUTH.

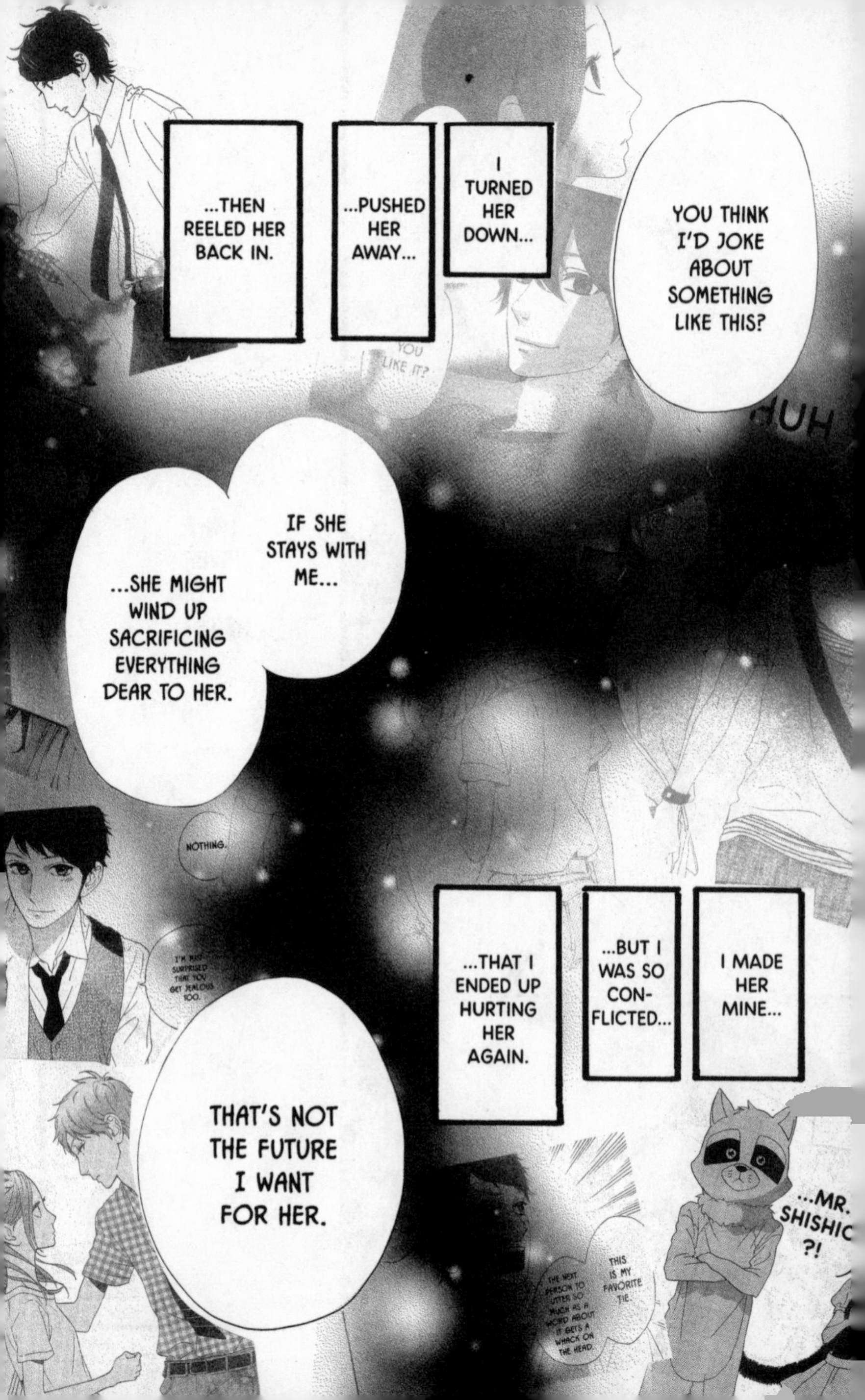
YOU THINK I'D JOKE ABOUT SOMETHING LIKE THIS?
DUH
I TURNED HER DOWN...
...PUSHED HER AWAY...
...THEN REELED HER BACK IN.
YOU LIKE IT?
IF SHE STAYS WITH ME...
...SHE MIGHT WIND UP SACRIFICING EVERYTHING DEAR TO HER.
NOTHING.
I MADE HER MINE...
...BUT I WAS SO CON-FLICTED...
...THAT I ENDED UP HURTING HER AGAIN.
I'M JUST SURPRISED THAT YOU GET JEALOUS TOO.
...MR. SHISHIC ?!
THIS IS MY FAVORITE TIE.
THE NEXT PERSON TO UTTER SO MUCH AS A WORD ABOUT IT GETS A WHACK ON THE HEAD.
THAT'S NOT THE FUTURE I WANT FOR HER.

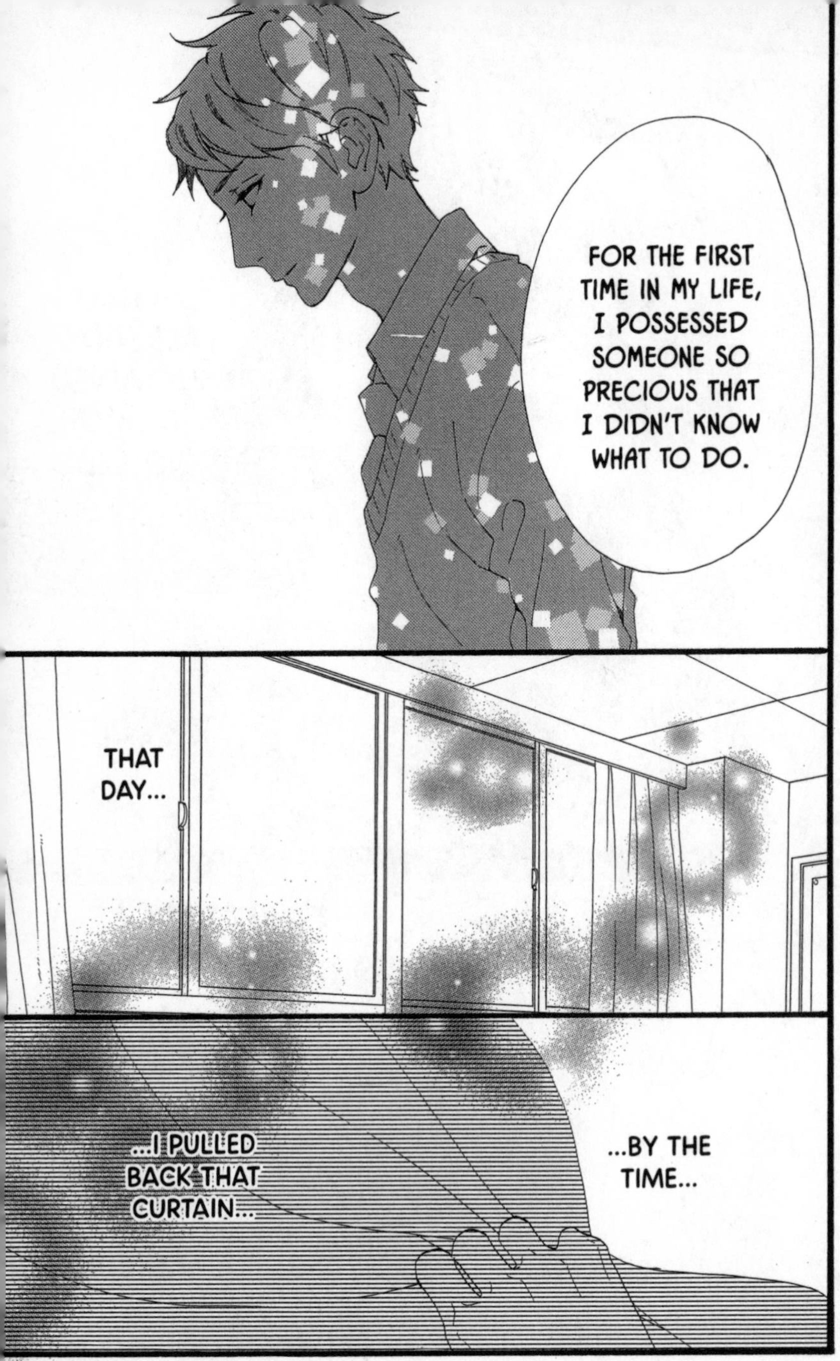
FOR THE FIRST TIME IN MY LIFE, I POSSESSED SOMEONE SO PRECIOUS THAT I DIDN'T KNOW WHAT TO DO.
THAT DAY...
...BY THE TIME...
...I PULLED BACK THAT CURTAIN...

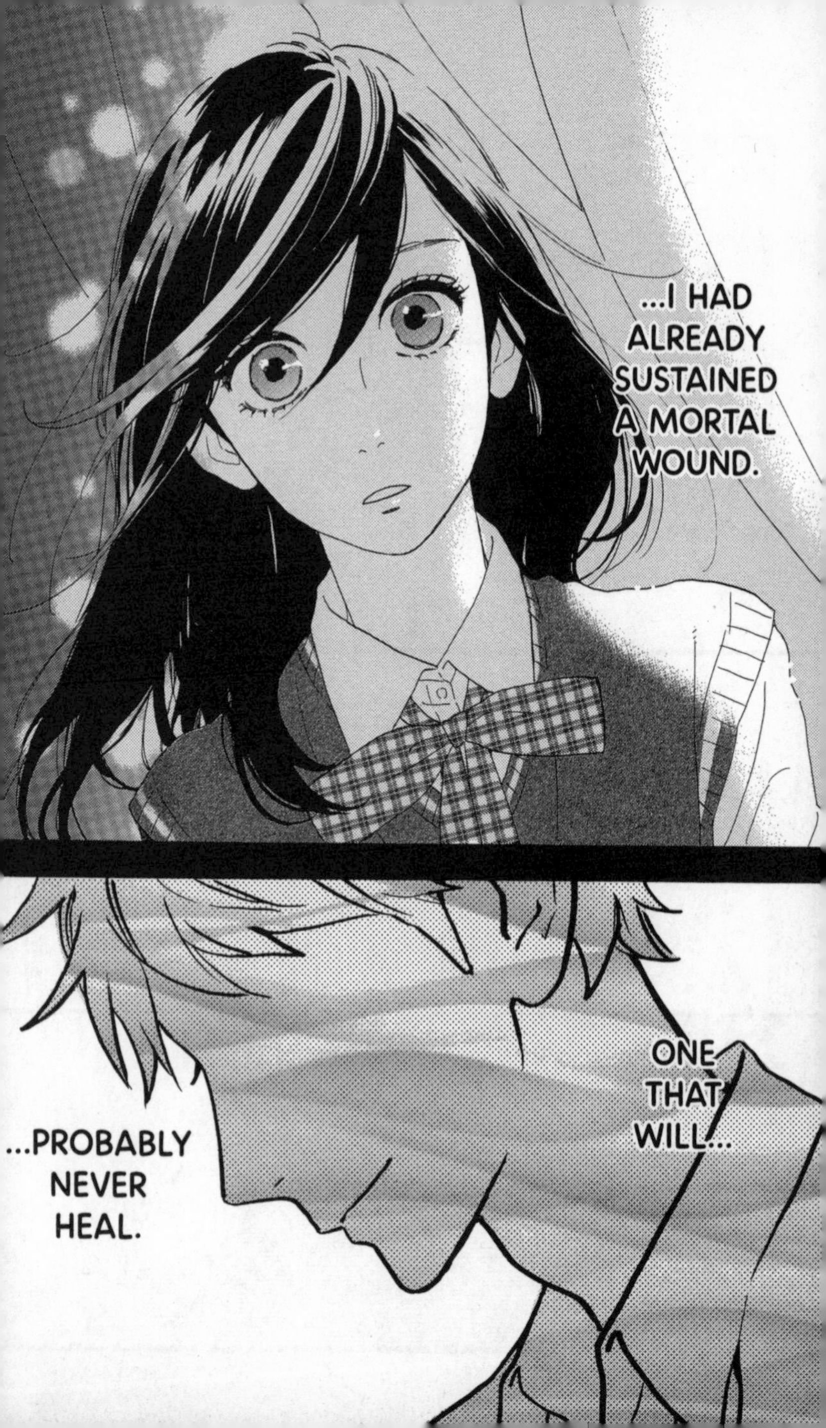
...I HAD ALREADY SUSTAINED A MORTAL WOUND.
ONE THAT WILL...
...PROBABLY NEVER HEAL.

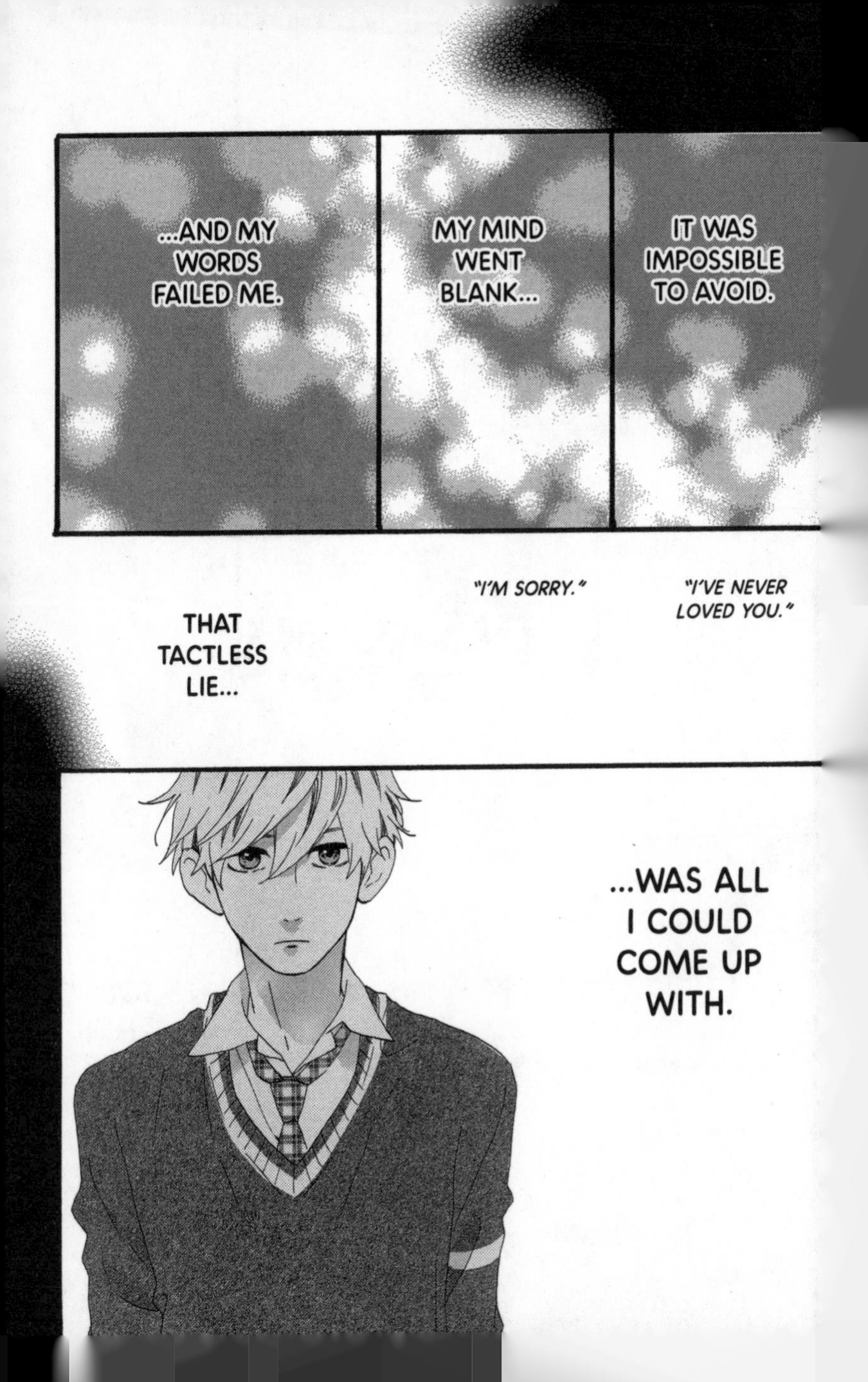
IT WAS IMPOSSIBLE TO AVOID.
MY MIND WENT BLANK...
...AND MY WORDS FAILED ME.
"I'VE NEVER LOVED YOU."
"I'M SORRY."
THAT TACTLESS LIE...
...WAS ALL I COULD COME UP WITH.

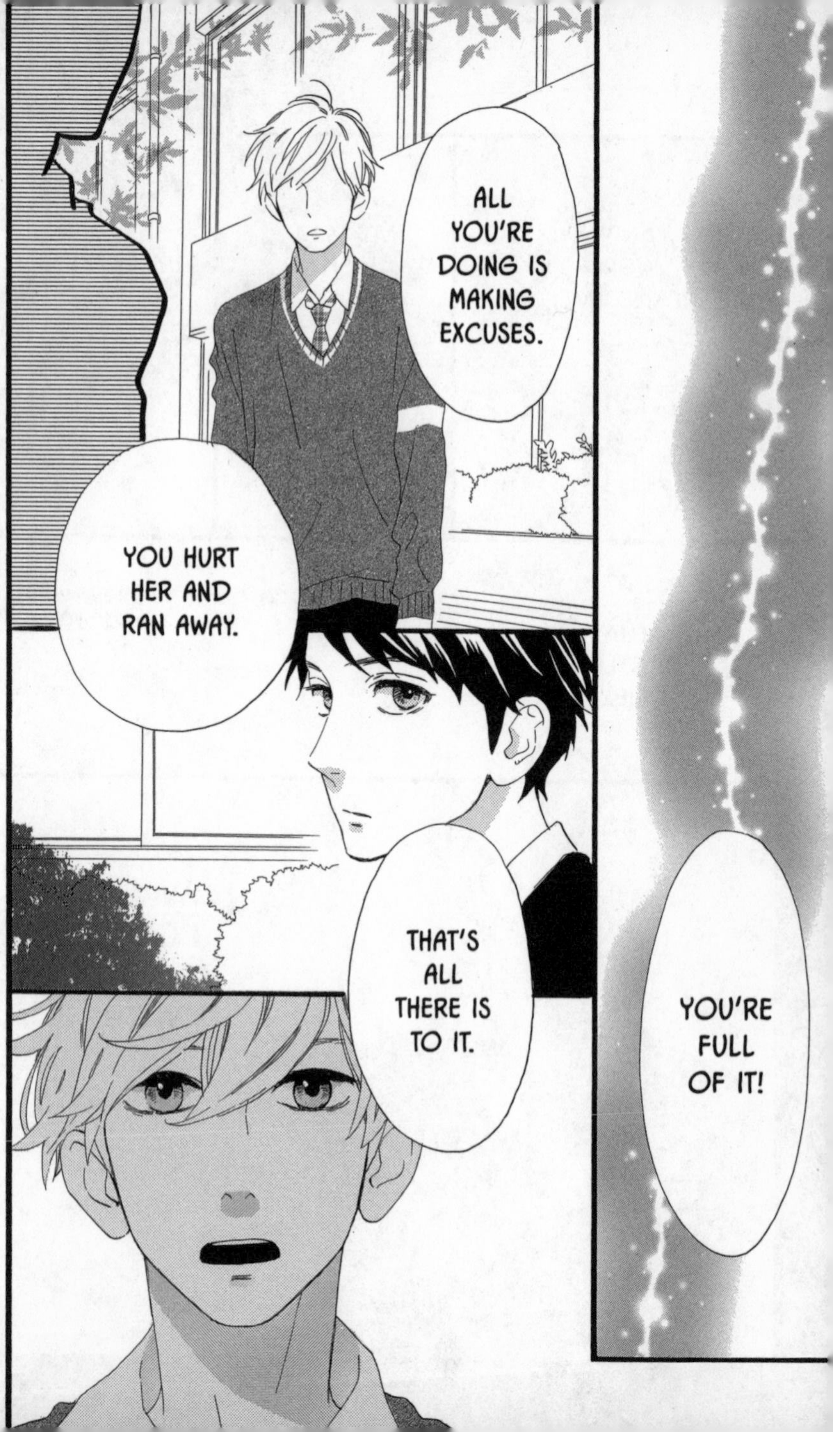
YOU'RE FULL OF IT!
ALL YOU'RE DOING IS MAKING EXCUSES.
YOU HURT HER AND RAN AWAY.
THAT'S ALL THERE IS TO IT.

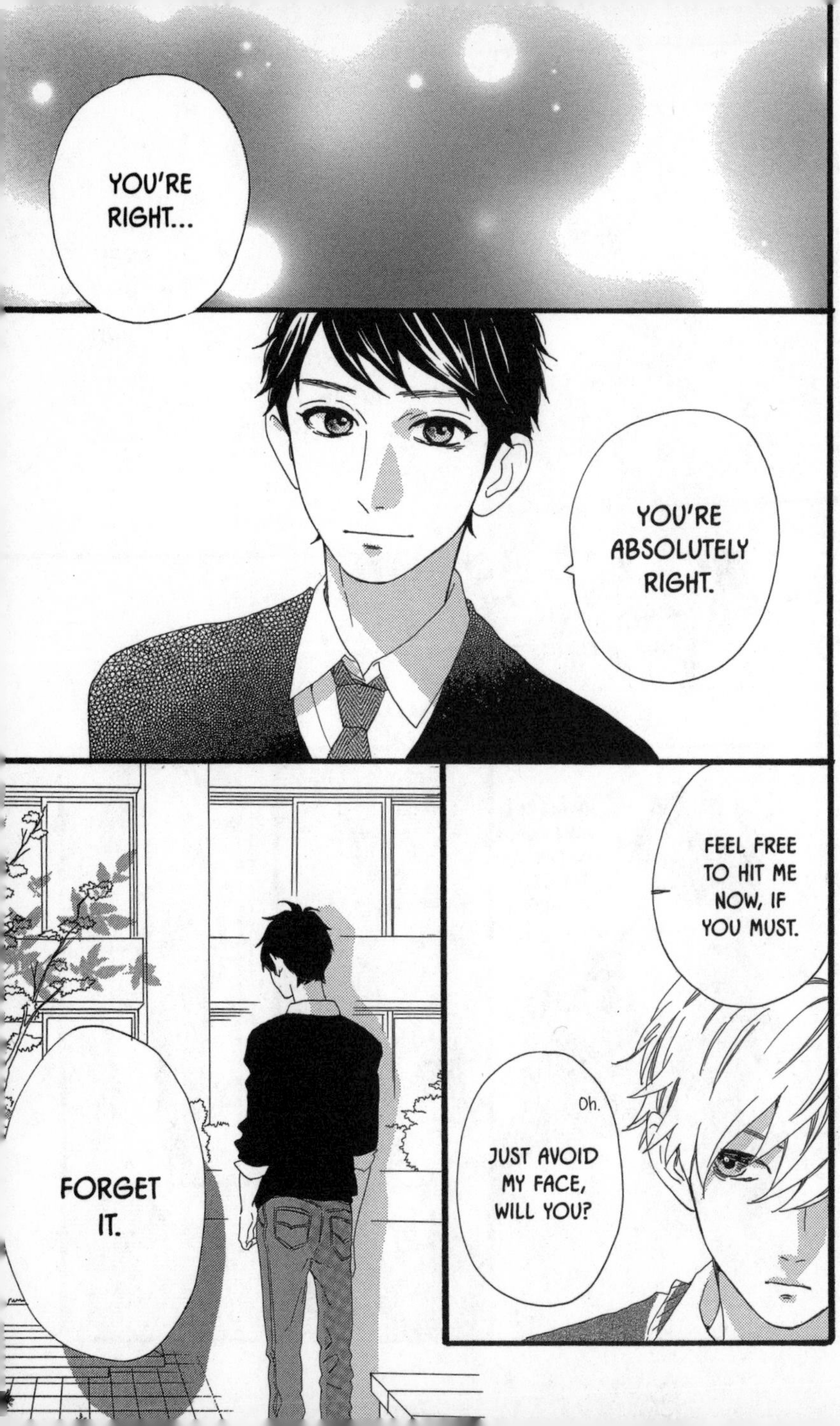
YOU'RE RIGHT...
YOU'RE ABSOLUTELY RIGHT.
FEEL FREE TO HIT ME NOW, IF YOU MUST.
Oh.
JUST AVOID MY FACE, WILL YOU?
FORGET IT.

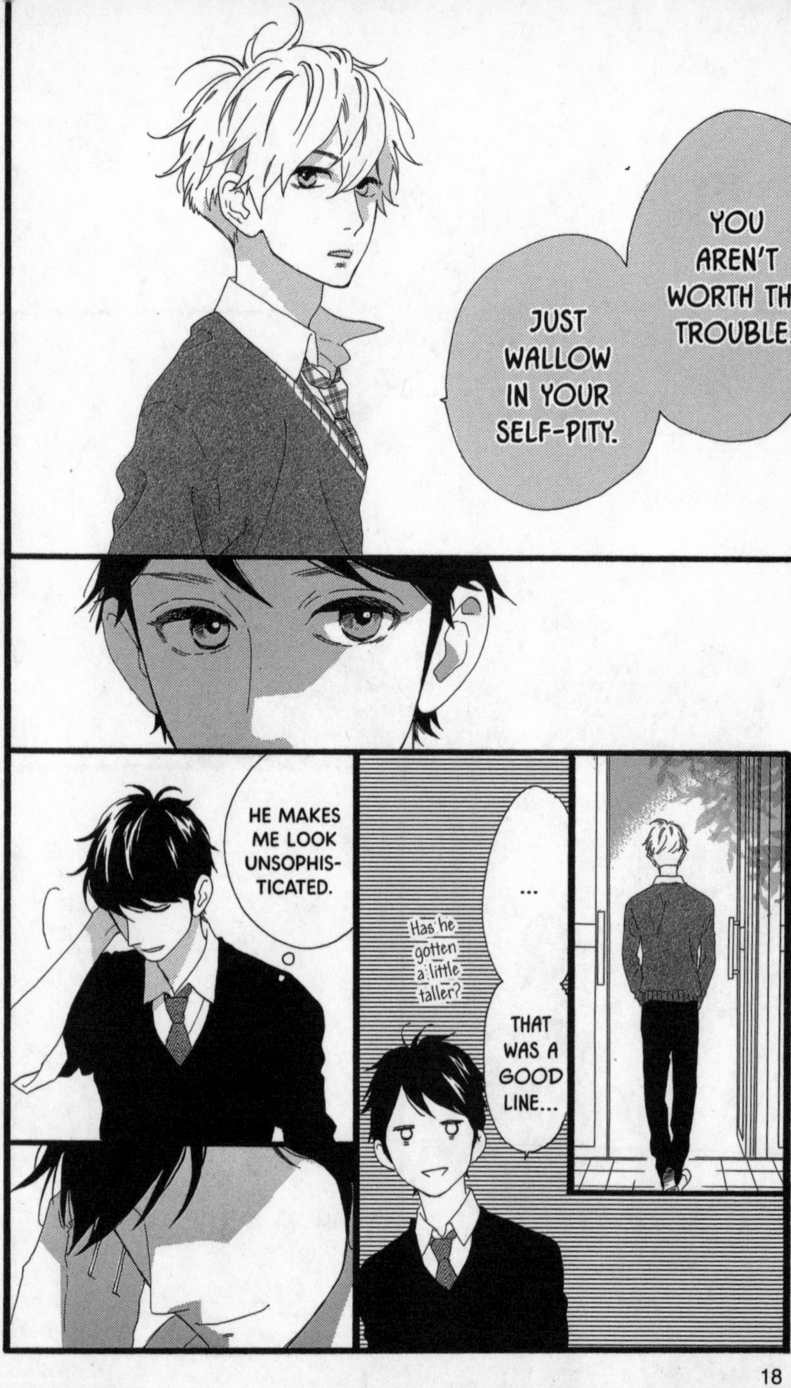
YOU AREN'T WORTH THE TROUBLE.
JUST WALLOW IN YOUR SELF-PITY.
... THAT WAS A GOOD LINE...
Has he gotten a little taller?
HE MAKES ME LOOK UNSOPHIS-TICATED.

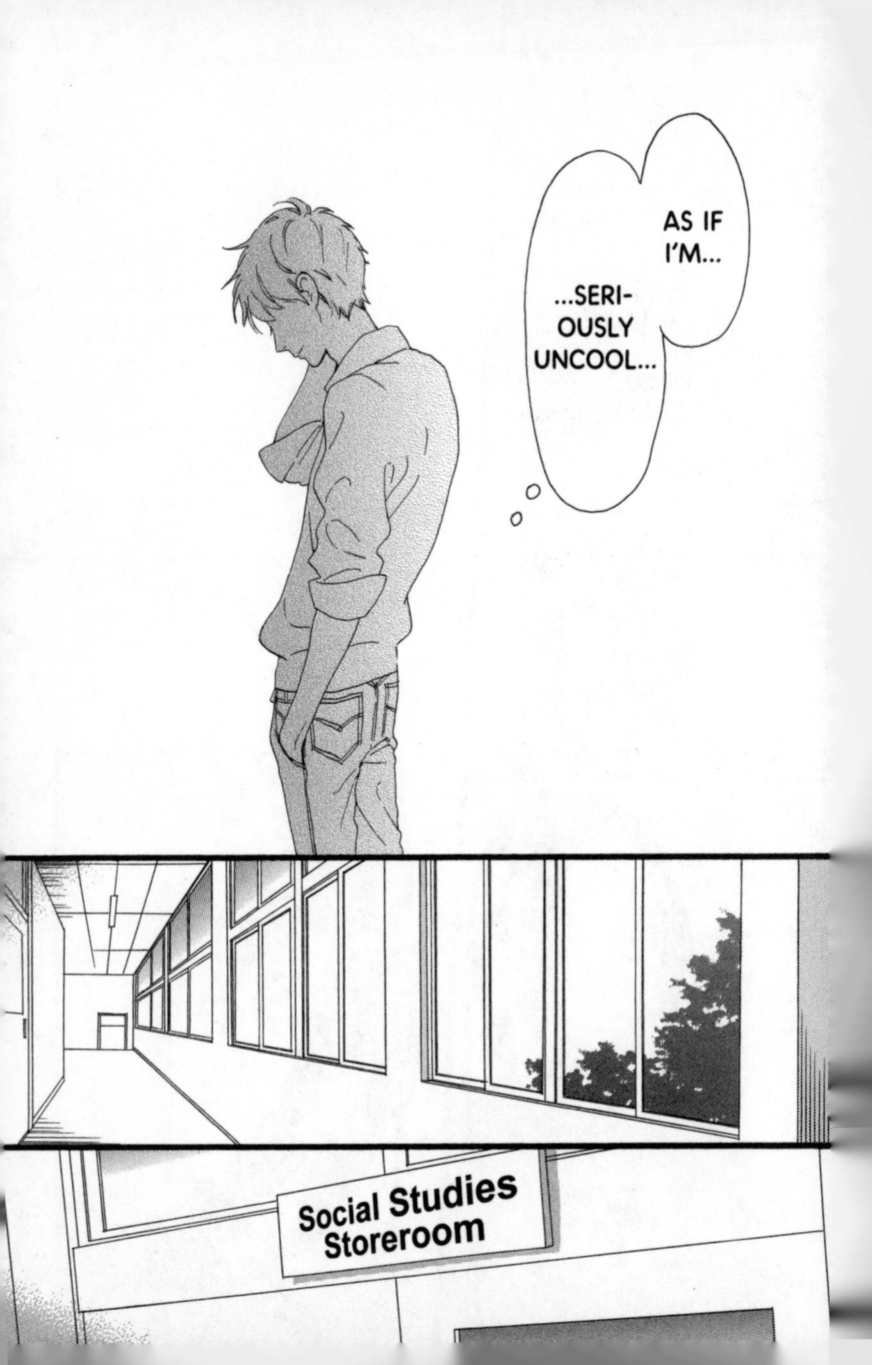
AS IF I'M...
...SERI-OUSLY UNCOOL...
Social Studies Storeroom

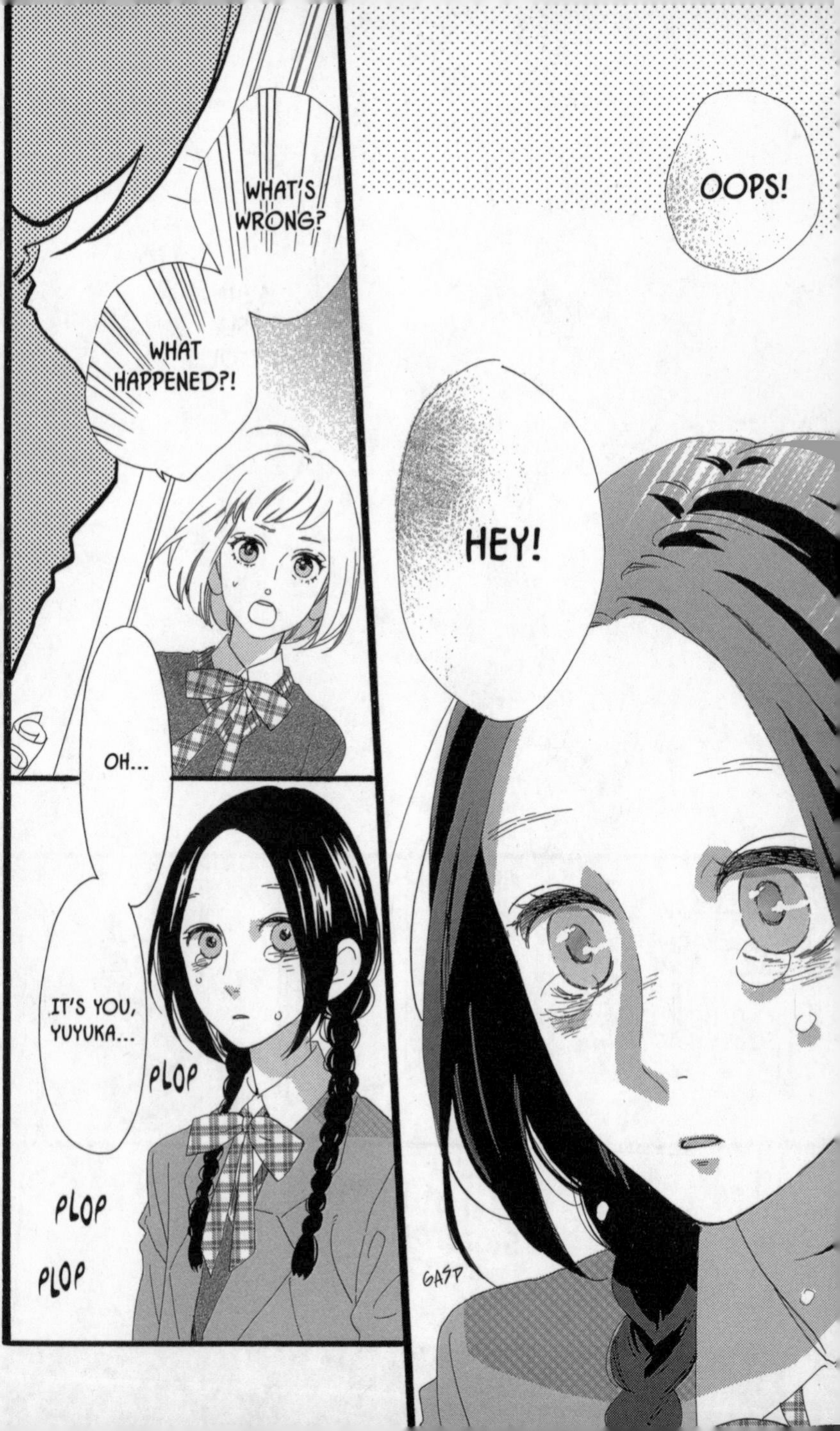
OOPS!
HEY!
GASP
WHAT'S WRONG?
WHAT HAPPENED?!
OH...
IT'S YOU, YUYUKA...
PLOP
PLOP
PLOP

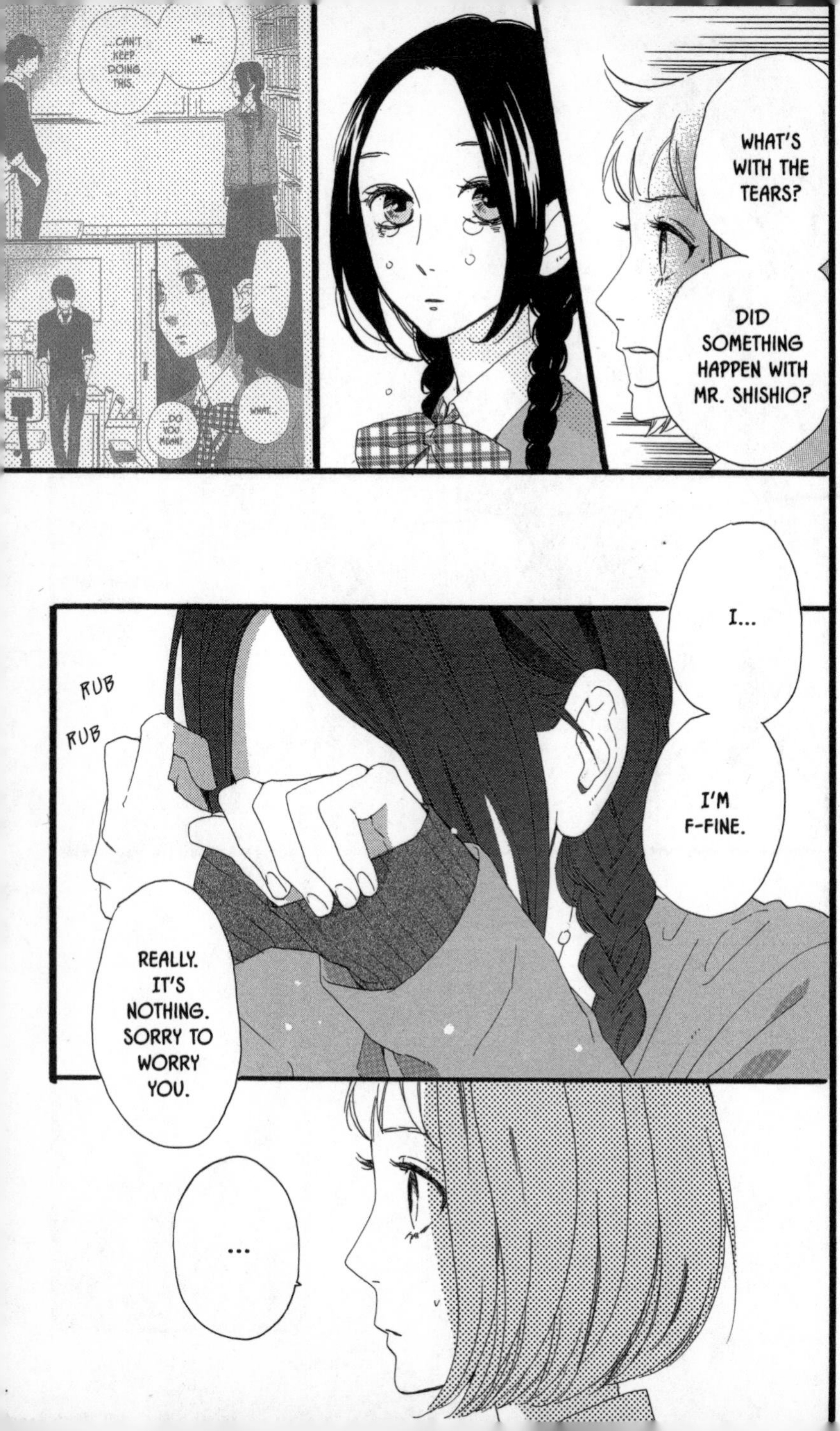
WHAT'S WITH THE TEARS?
DID SOMETHING HAPPEN WITH MR. SHISHIO?
WE...
...CAN'T KEEP DOING THIS.
WHAT...
...DO YOU MEAN?
I...
I'M F-FINE.
RUB
RUB
REALLY. IT'S NOTHING. SORRY TO WORRY YOU.
...

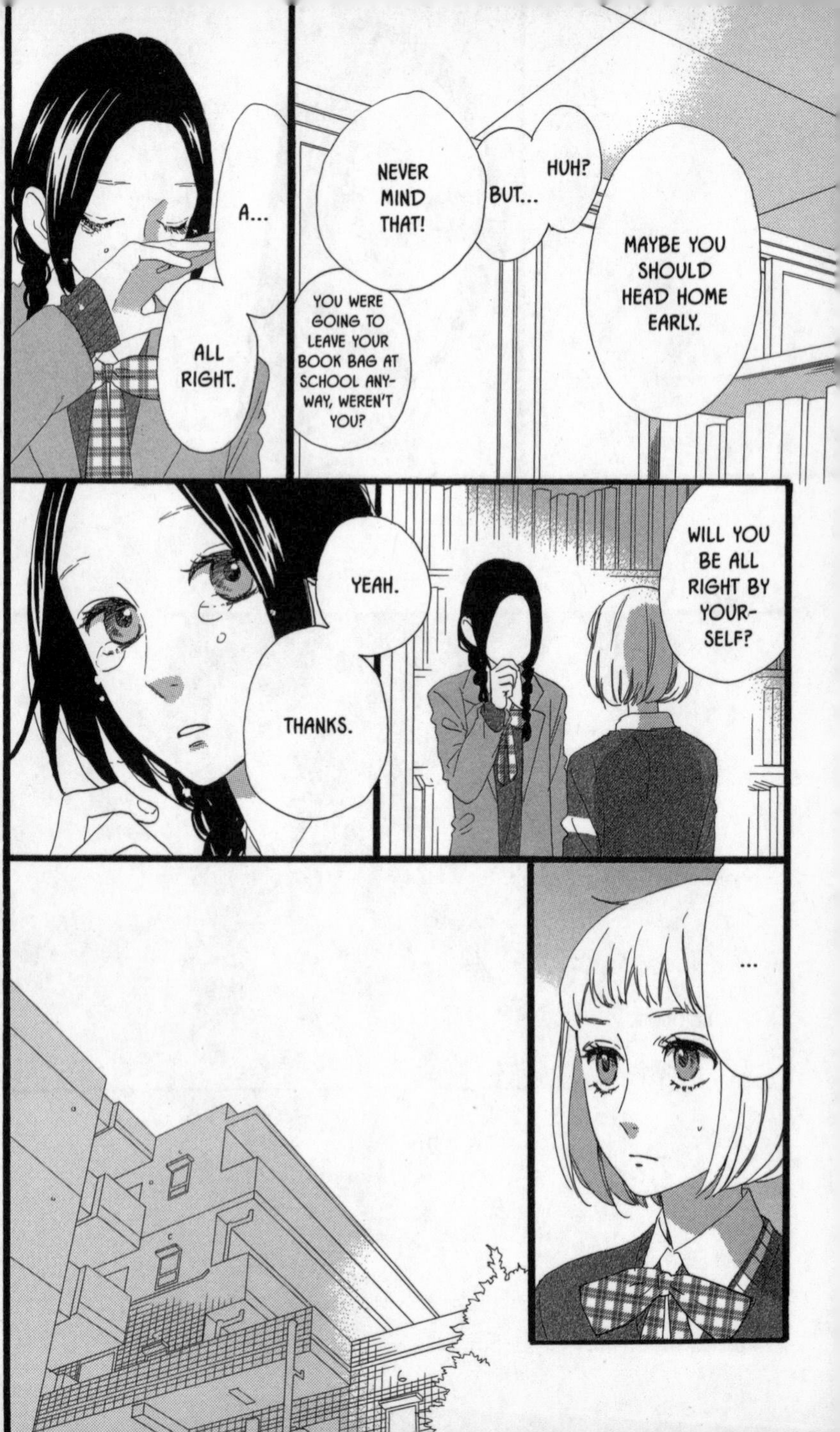
MAYBE YOU SHOULD HEAD HOME EARLY.
HUH?
BUT...
NEVER MIND THAT!
YOU WERE GOING TO LEAVE YOUR BOOK BAG AT SCHOOL ANY-WAY, WEREN'T YOU?
A...
ALL RIGHT.
WILL YOU BE ALL RIGHT BY YOUR-SELF?
YEAH.
THANKS.
...

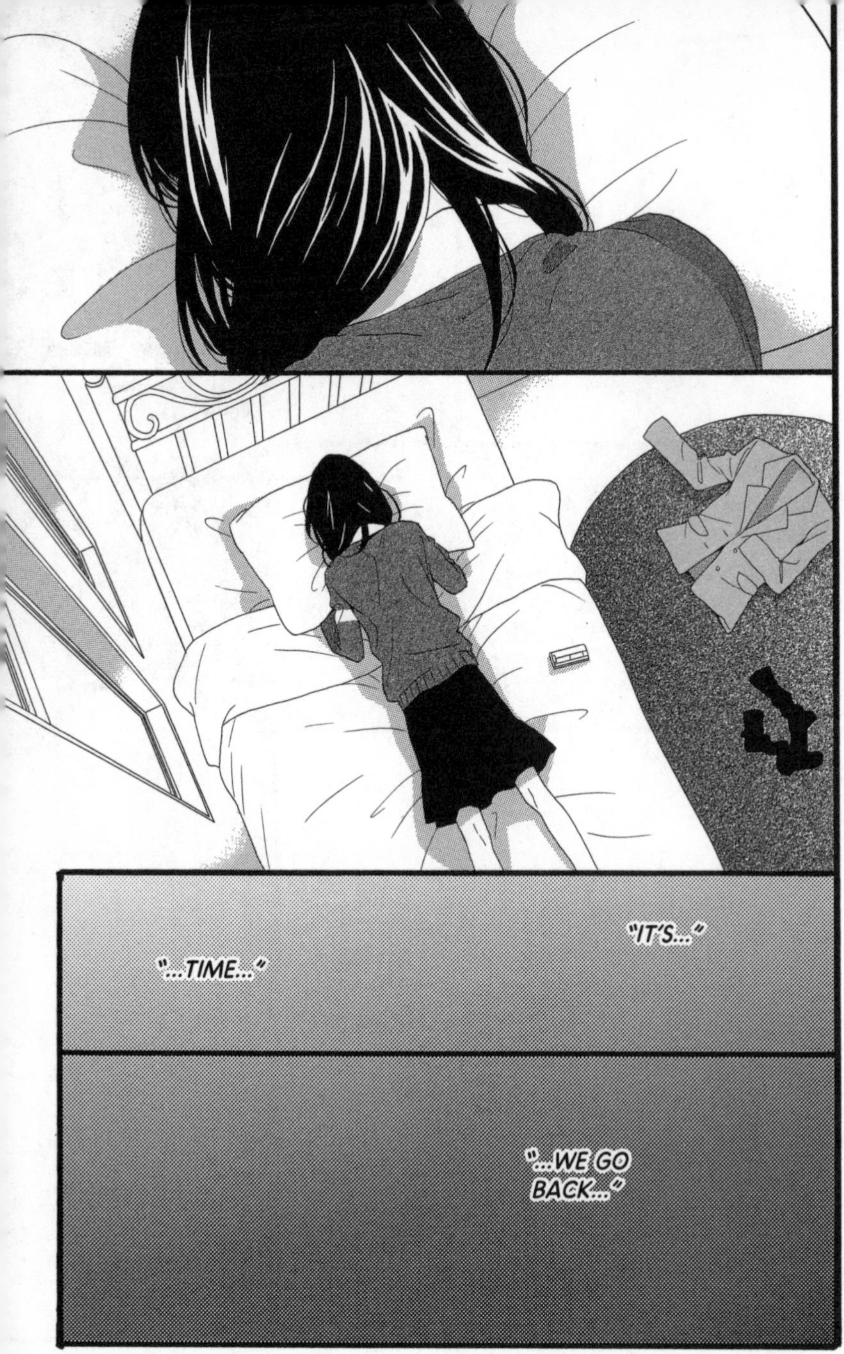
"IT'S..."
"...TIME..."
"...WE GO BACK..."

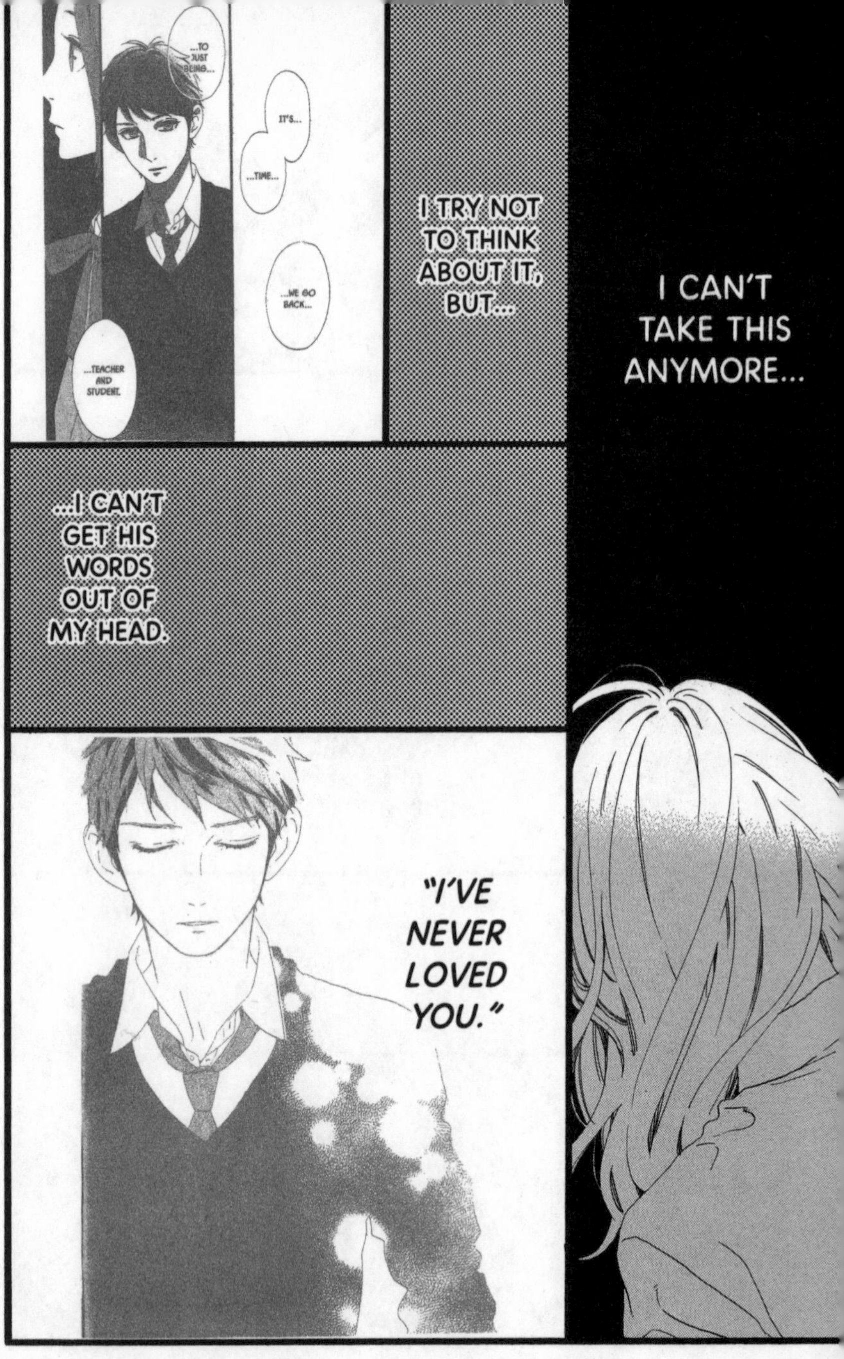
I CAN'T TAKE THIS ANYMORE...
I TRY NOT TO THINK ABOUT IT, BUT...
IT'S...
...TIME...
...WE GO BACK...
...TO JUST BEING...
...TEACHER AND STUDENT.
...I CAN'T GET HIS WORDS OUT OF MY HEAD.
"I'VE NEVER LOVED YOU."

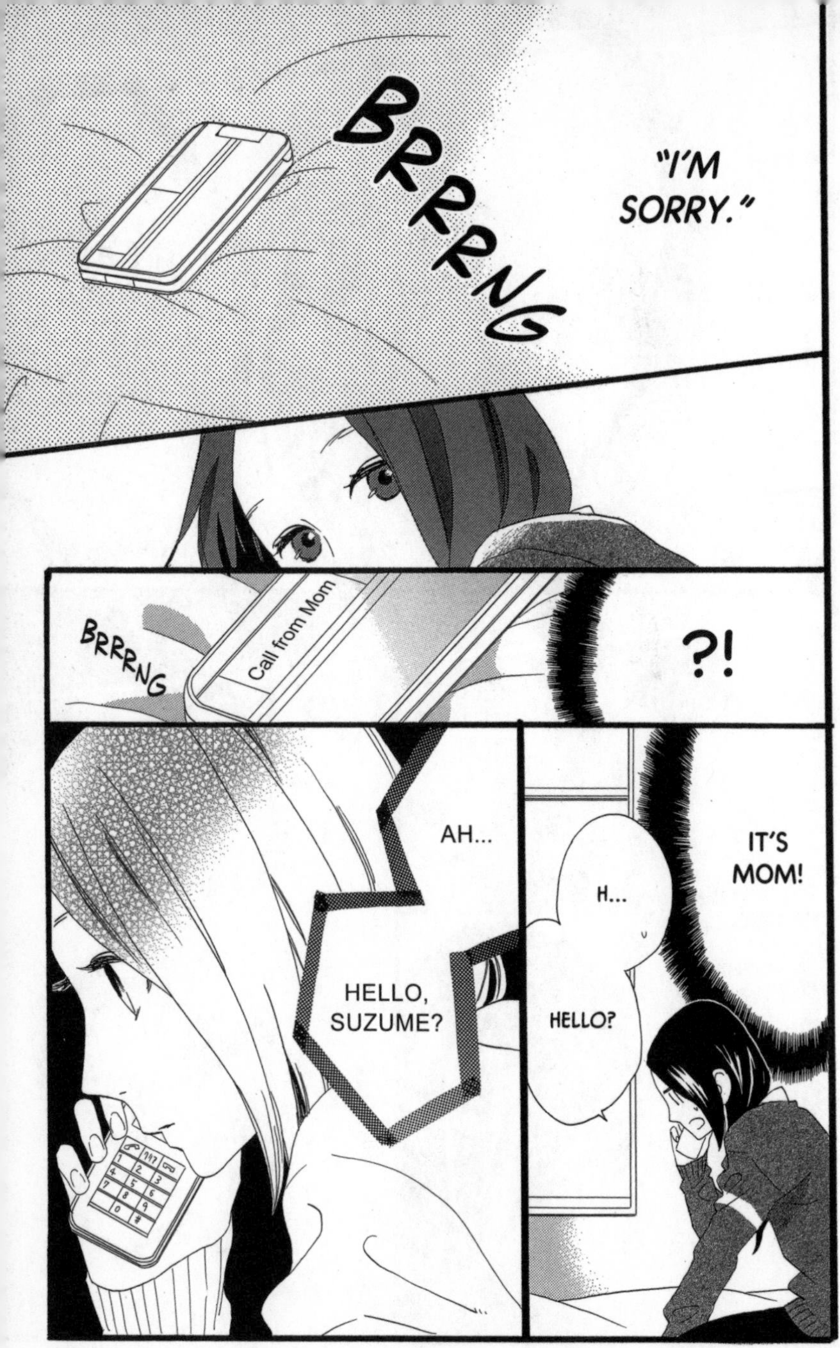
"I'M SORRY."
BRRRNG
?!
Call from Mom
BRRRNG
IT'S MOM!
H... HELLO?
AH...
HELLO, SUZUME?

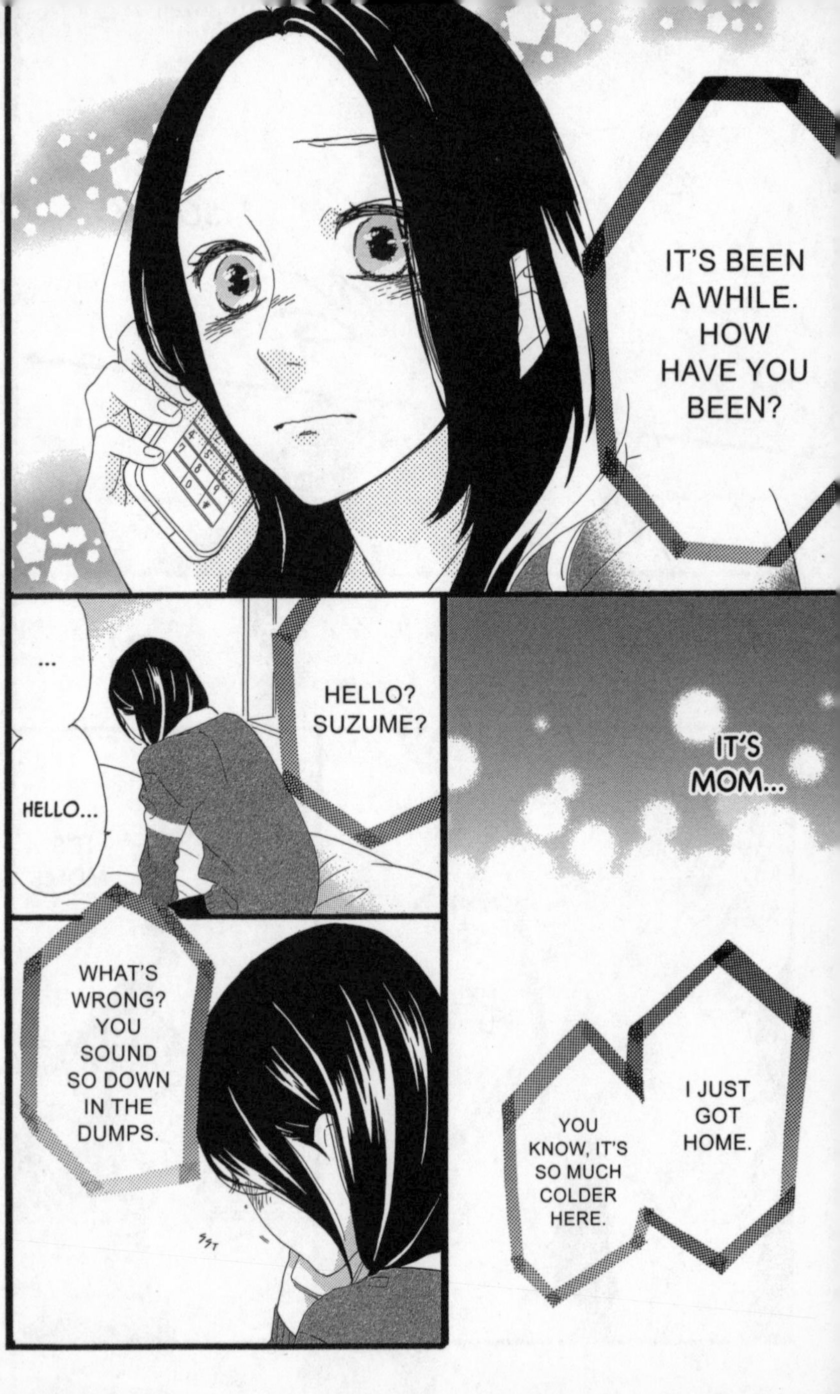
IT'S BEEN A WHILE. HOW HAVE YOU BEEN?
IT'S MOM...
I JUST GOT HOME.
YOU KNOW, IT'S SO MUCH COLDER HERE.
HELLO? SUZUME?
...
HELLO...
WHAT'S WRONG? YOU SOUND SO DOWN IN THE DUMPS.
SST

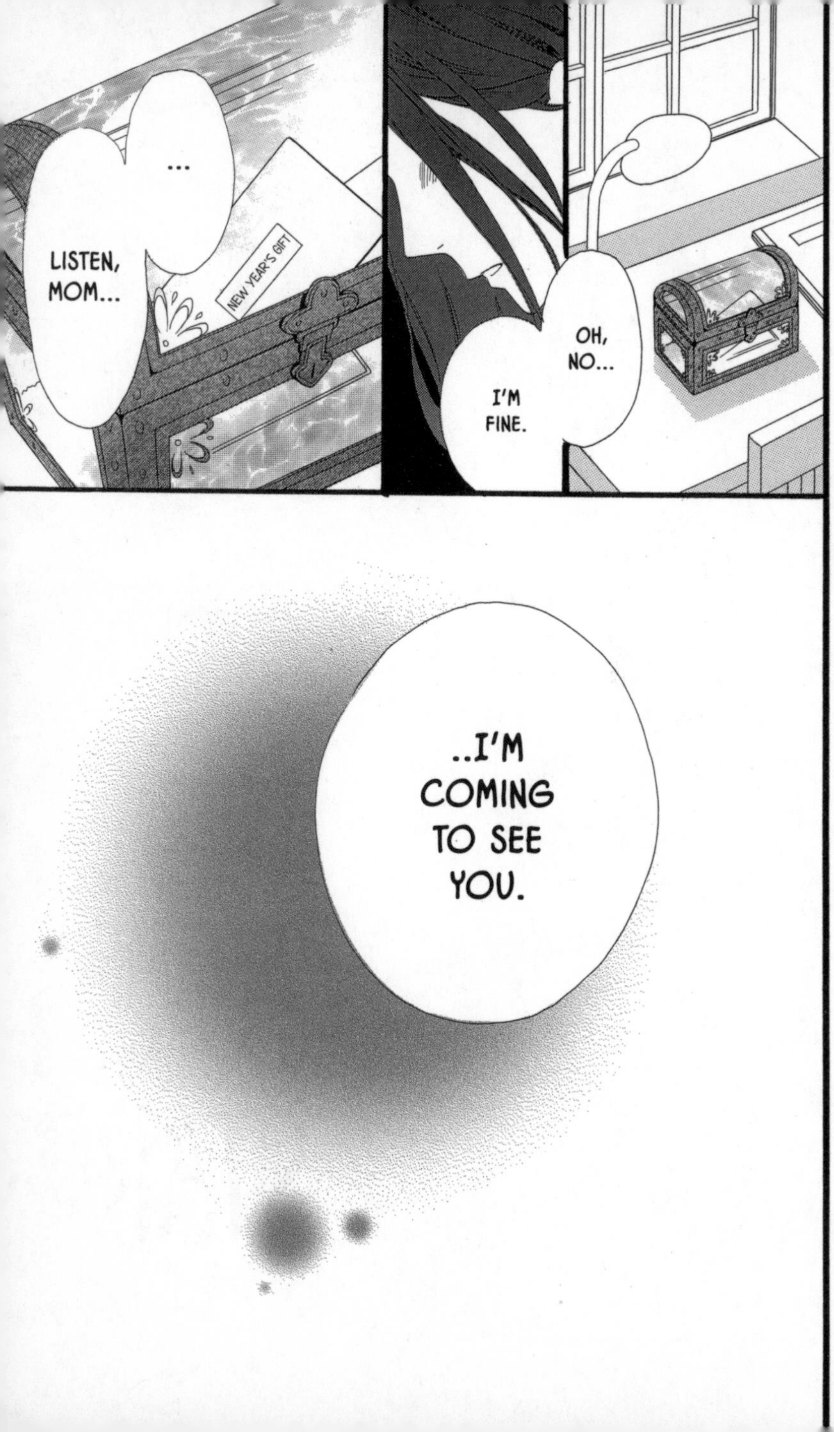
OH, NO...
I'M FINE.
...
NEW YEAR'S GIFT
LISTEN, MOM...
..I'M COMING TO SEE YOU.

DAYTIME SHOOTING STAR

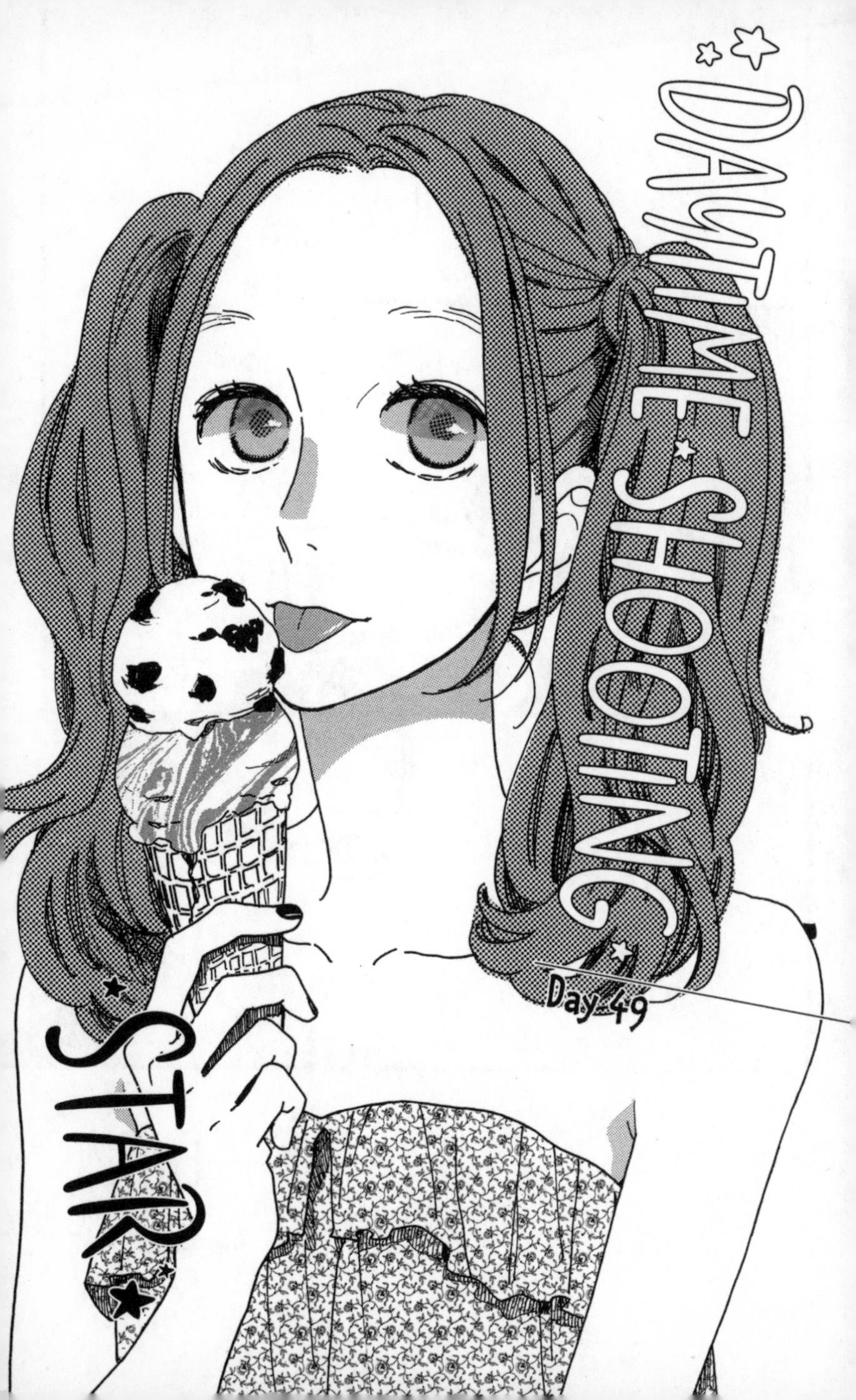
DAYTIME SHOOTING STAR
Day 49

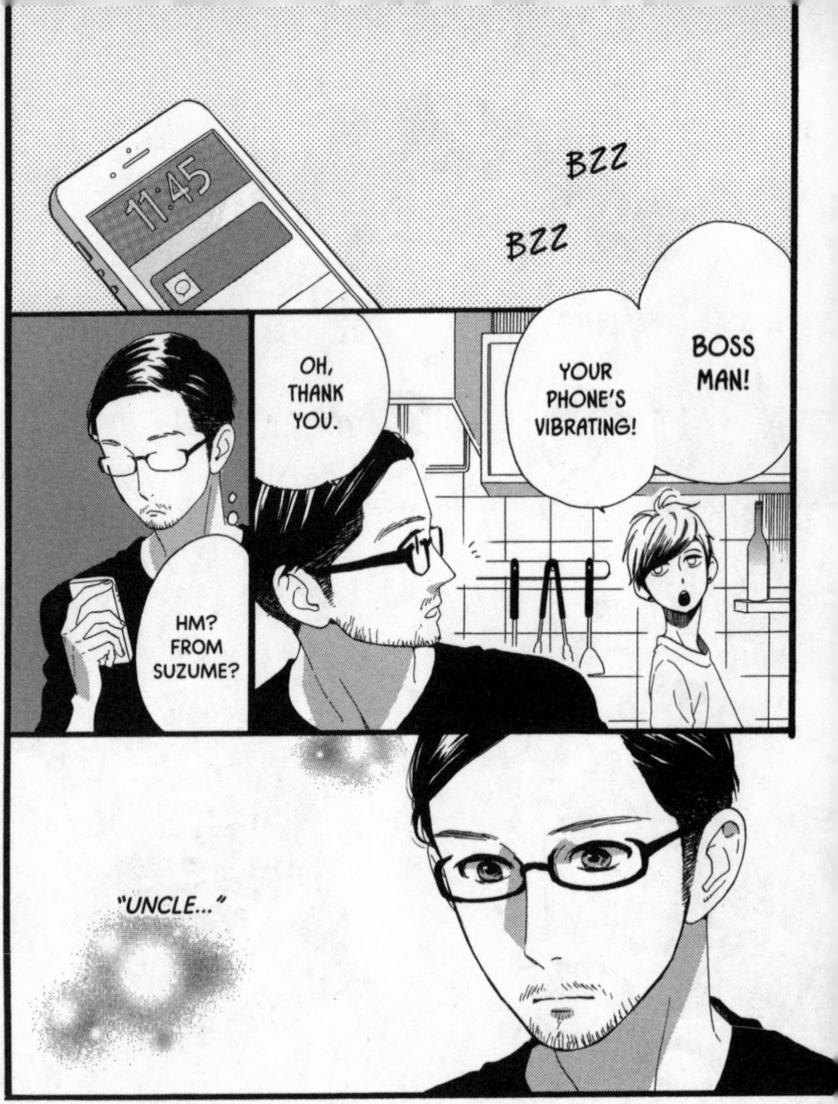
BZZ
BZZ
BOSS MAN!
YOUR PHONE'S VIBRATING!
OH, THANK YOU.
HM? FROM SUZUME?
"UNCLE..."

DAYTIME SHOOTING STAR

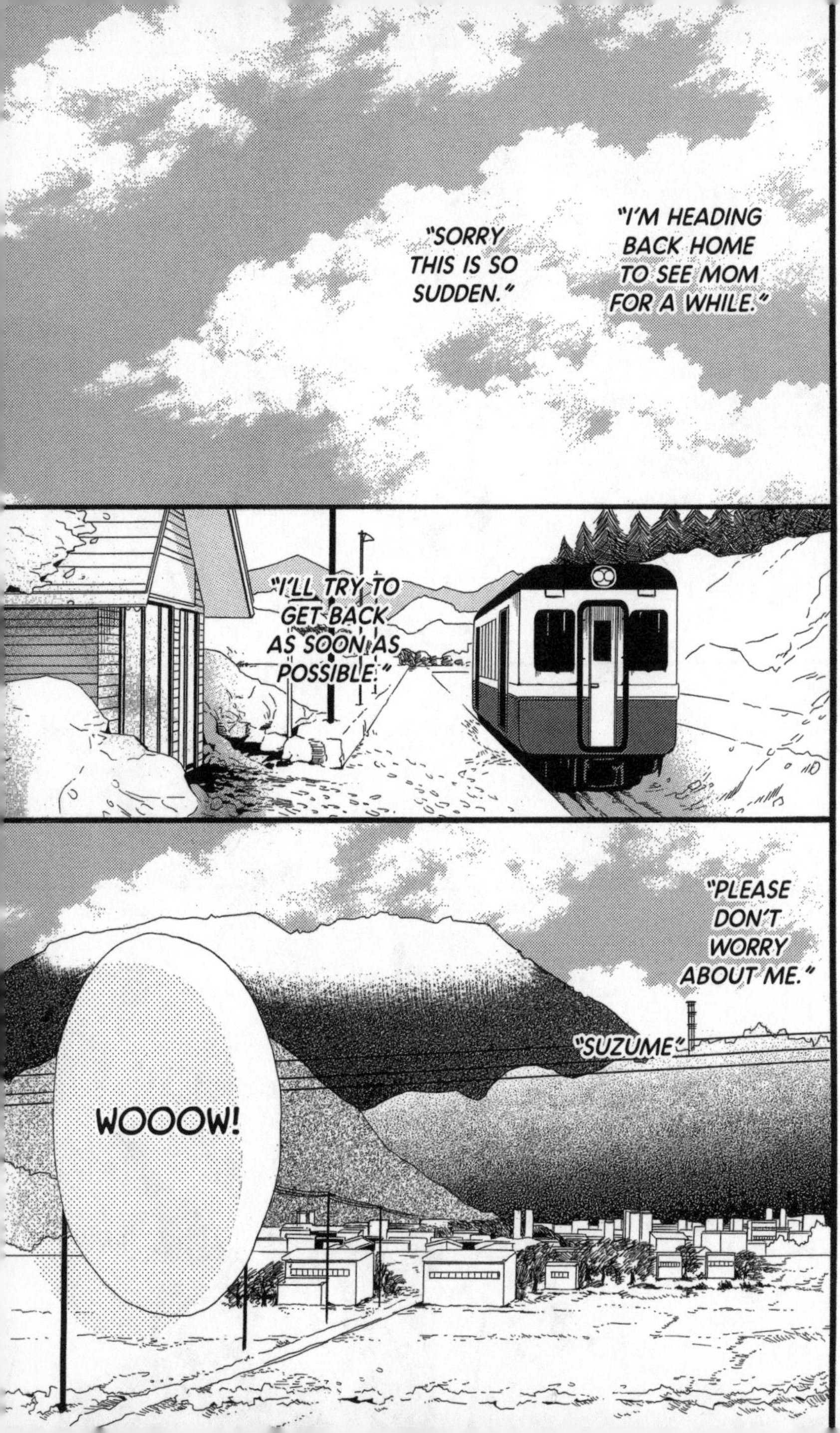
"I'M HEADING BACK HOME TO SEE MOM FOR A WHILE."
"SORRY THIS IS SO SUDDEN."
"I'LL TRY TO GET BACK AS SOON AS POSSIBLE."
"PLEASE DON'T WORRY ABOUT ME."
"SUZUME"
WOOOW!

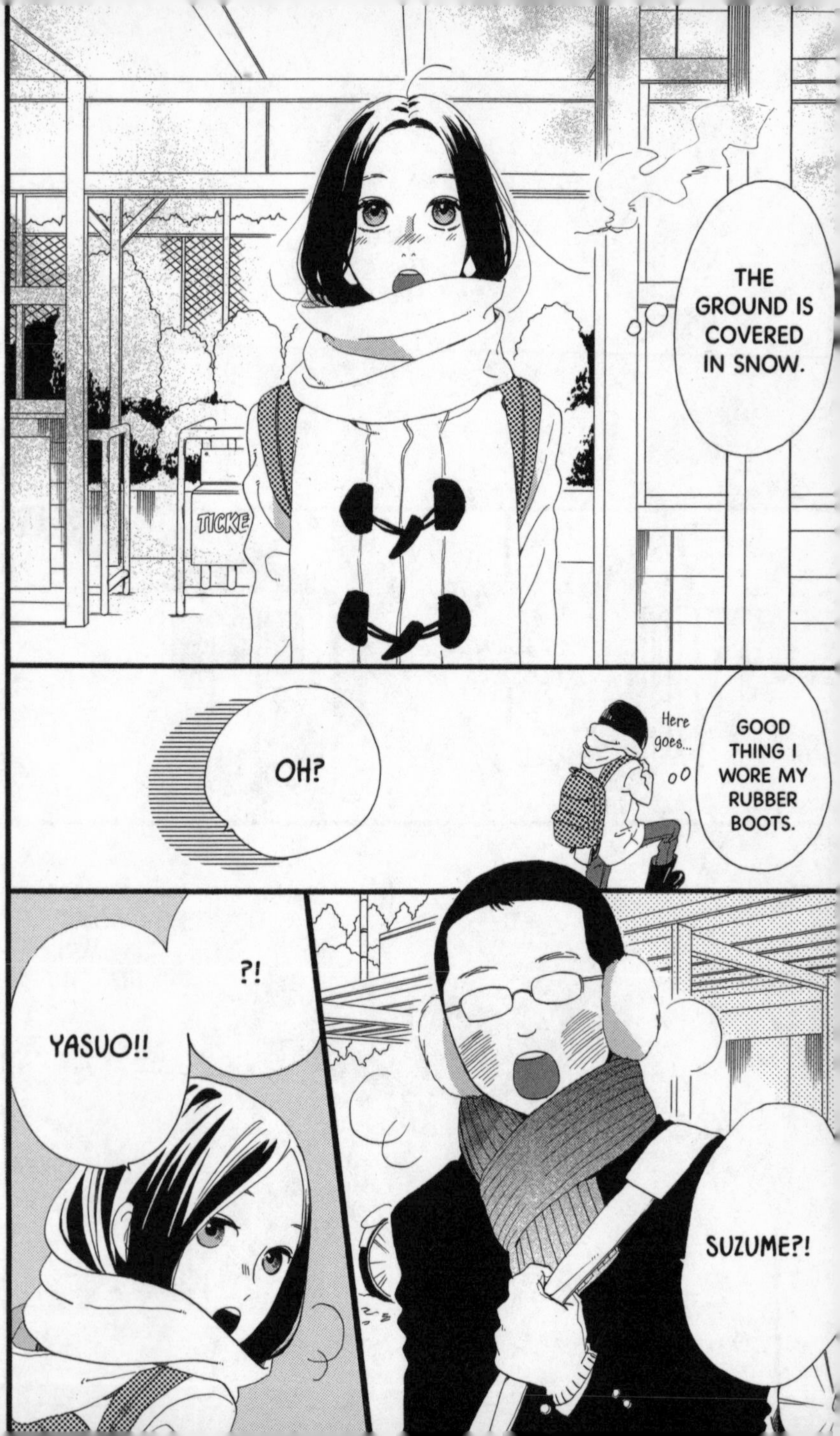
THE GROUND IS COVERED IN SNOW.
GOOD THING I WORE MY RUBBER BOOTS.
Here goes...
OH?
SUZUME?!
?!
YASUO!!

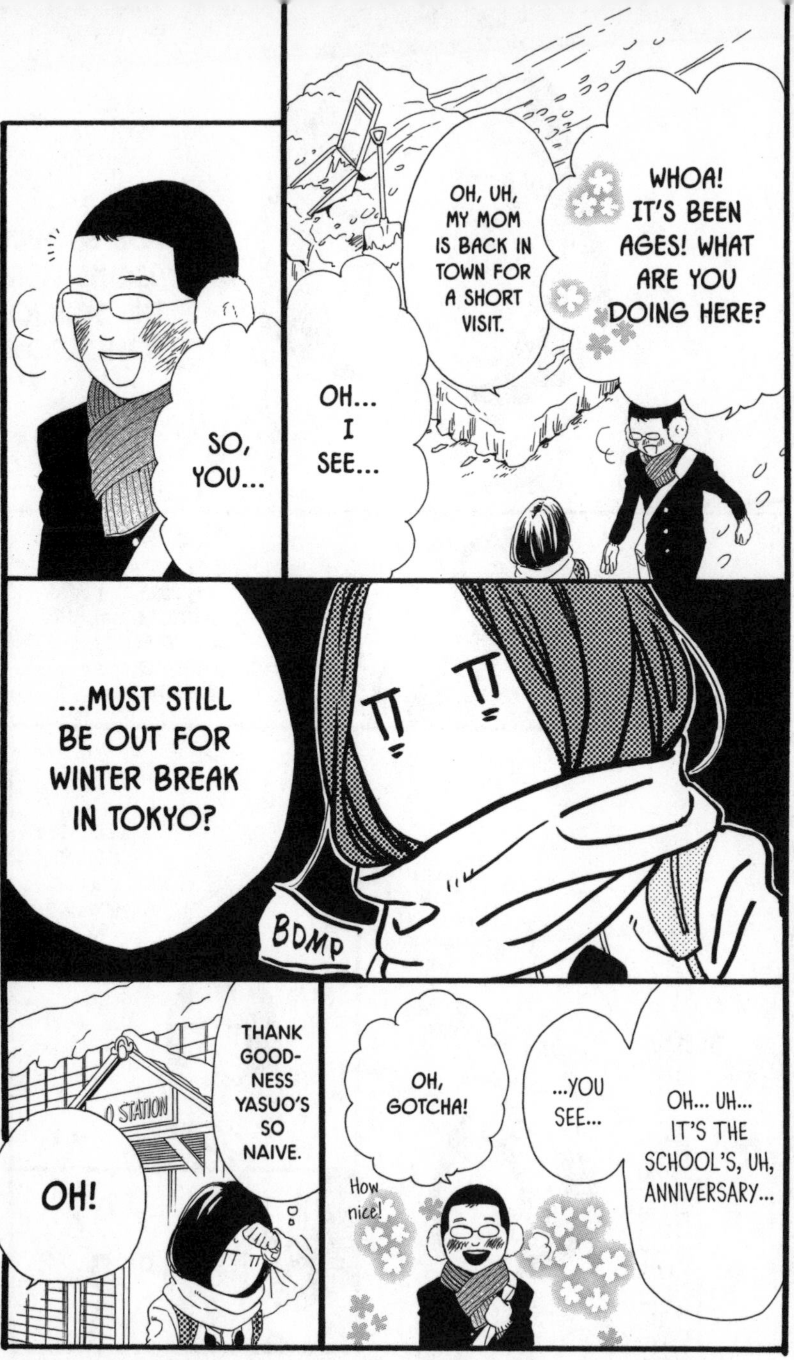
WHOA! IT'S BEEN AGES! WHAT ARE YOU DOING HERE?
OH, UH, MY MOM IS BACK IN TOWN FOR A SHORT VISIT.
OH... I SEE...
SO, YOU...
...MUST STILL BE OUT FOR WINTER BREAK IN TOKYO?
BDMP
OH... UH... IT'S THE SCHOOL'S, UH, ANNIVERSARY...
...YOU SEE...
OH, GOTCHA!
How nice!
THANK GOODNESS YASUO'S SO NAIVE.
O STATION
OH!

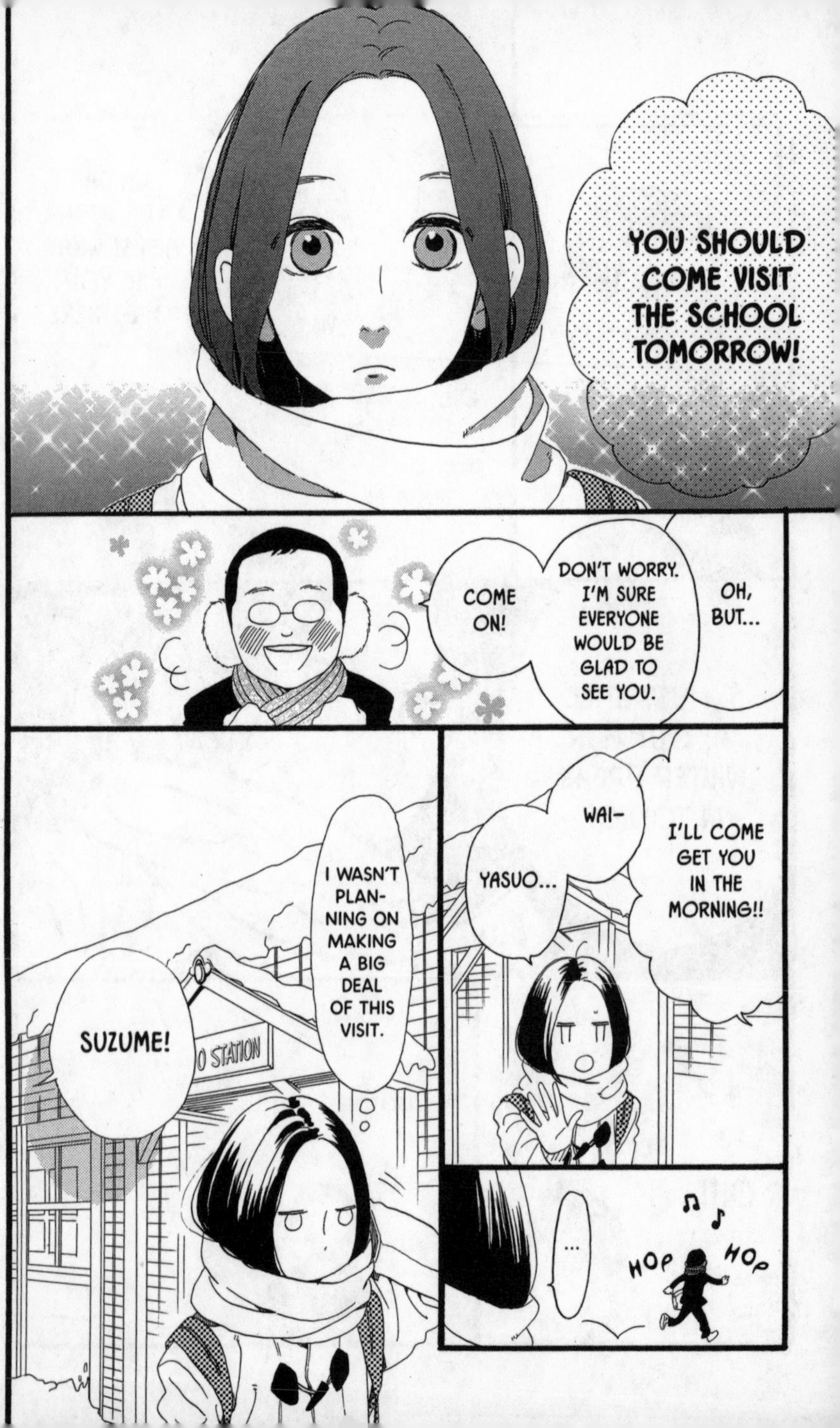
YOU SHOULD COME VISIT THE SCHOOL TOMORROW!
OH, BUT...
DON'T WORRY. I'M SURE EVERYONE WOULD BE GLAD TO SEE YOU.
COME ON!
I'LL COME GET YOU IN THE MORNING!!
WAI-
YASUO...
HOP HOP
...
I WASN'T PLAN-NING ON MAKING A BIG DEAL OF THIS VISIT.
SUZUME!
O STATION

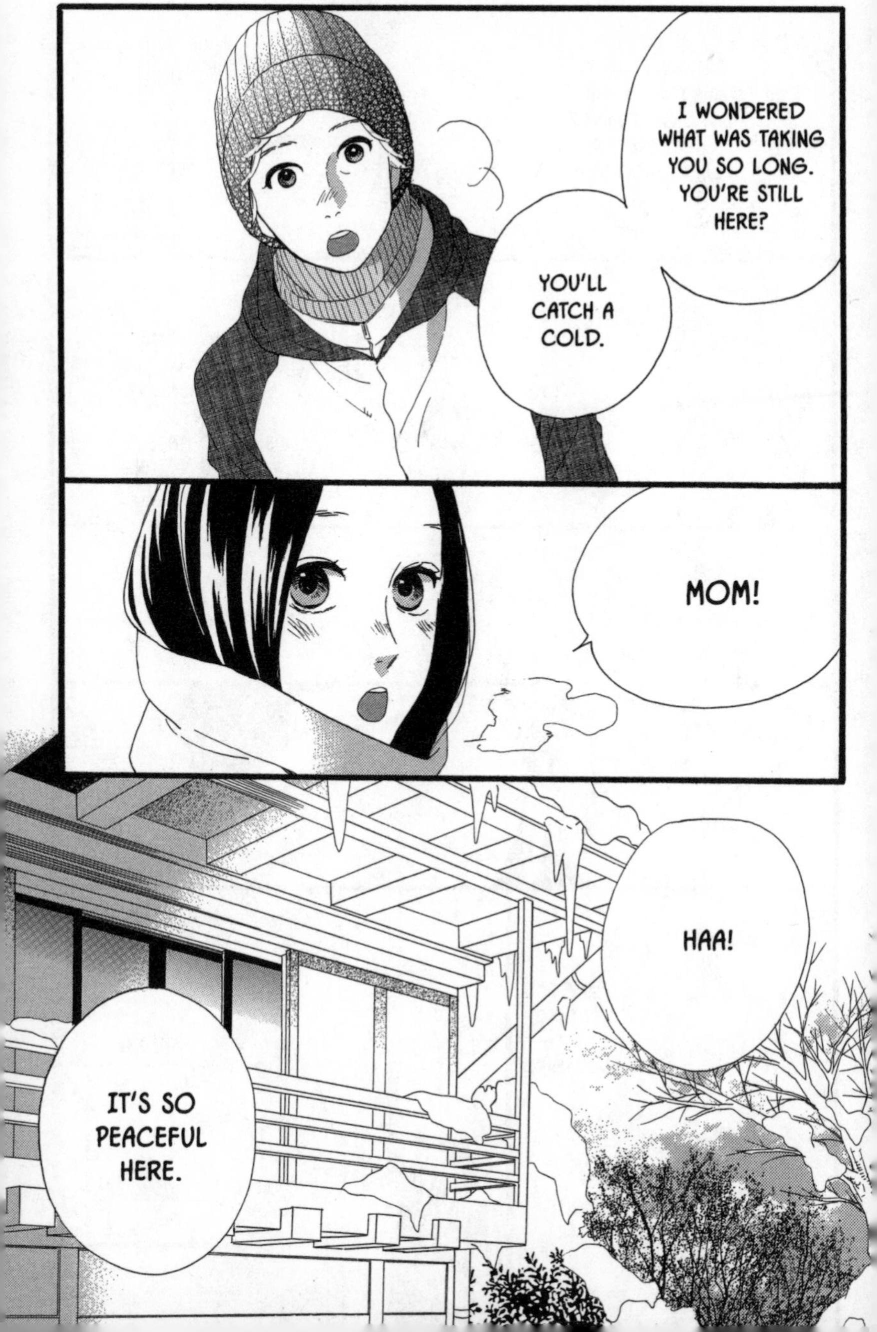
I WONDERED WHAT WAS TAKING YOU SO LONG. YOU'RE STILL HERE?
YOU'LL CATCH A COLD.
MOM!
HAA!
IT'S SO PEACEFUL HERE.

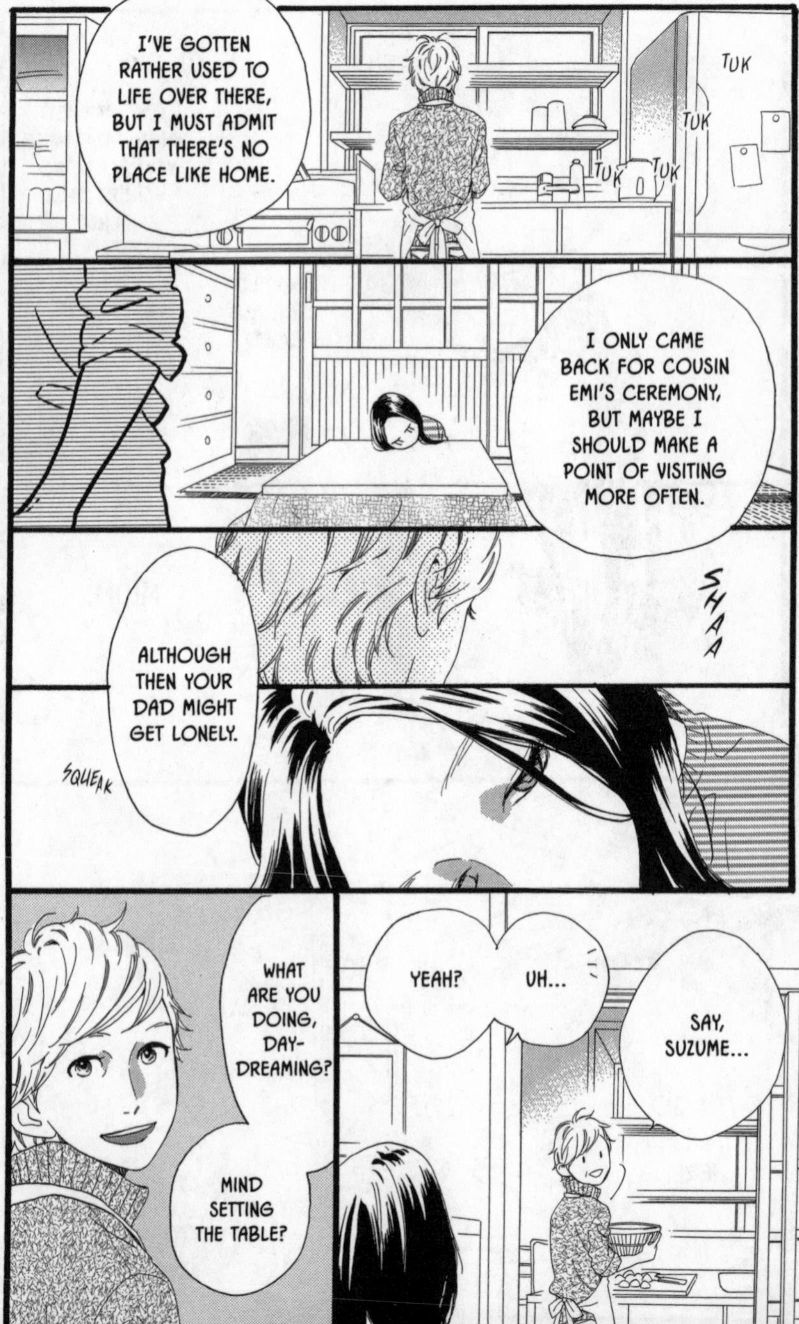
TUK
TUK
TUK
TUK
I'VE GOTTEN RATHER USED TO LIFE OVER THERE, BUT I MUST ADMIT THAT THERE'S NO PLACE LIKE HOME.
I ONLY CAME BACK FOR COUSIN EMI'S CEREMONY, BUT MAYBE I SHOULD MAKE A POINT OF VISITING MORE OFTEN.
SHAA
ALTHOUGH THEN YOUR DAD MIGHT GET LONELY.
SQUEAK
SAY, SUZUME...
UH...
YEAH?
WHAT ARE YOU DOING, DAY-DREAMING?
MIND SETTING THE TABLE?

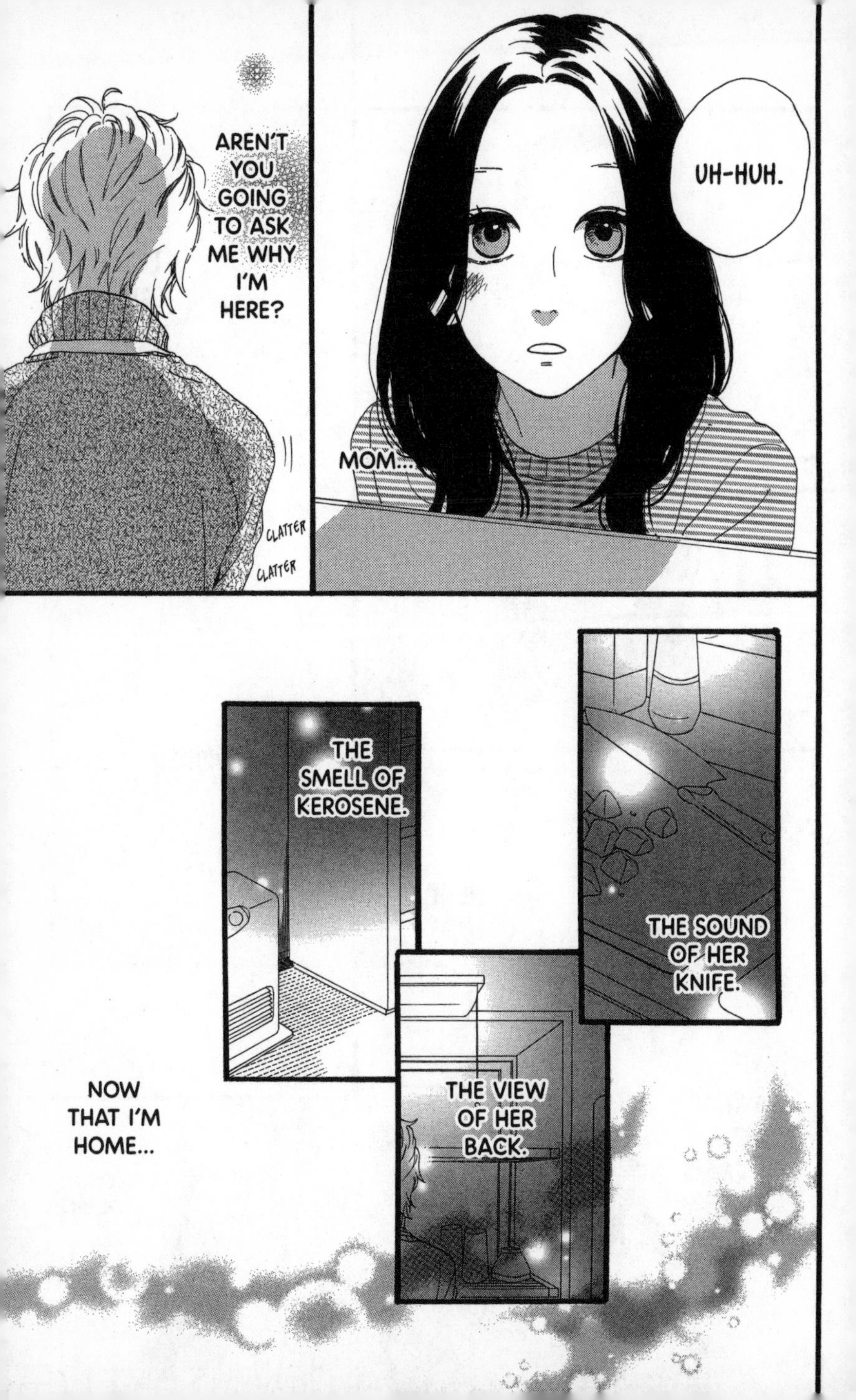
UH-HUH.
MOM...
AREN'T YOU GOING TO ASK ME WHY I'M HERE?
CLATTER
CLATTER
THE SOUND OF HER KNIFE.
THE SMELL OF KEROSENE.
THE VIEW OF HER BACK.
NOW THAT I'M HOME...

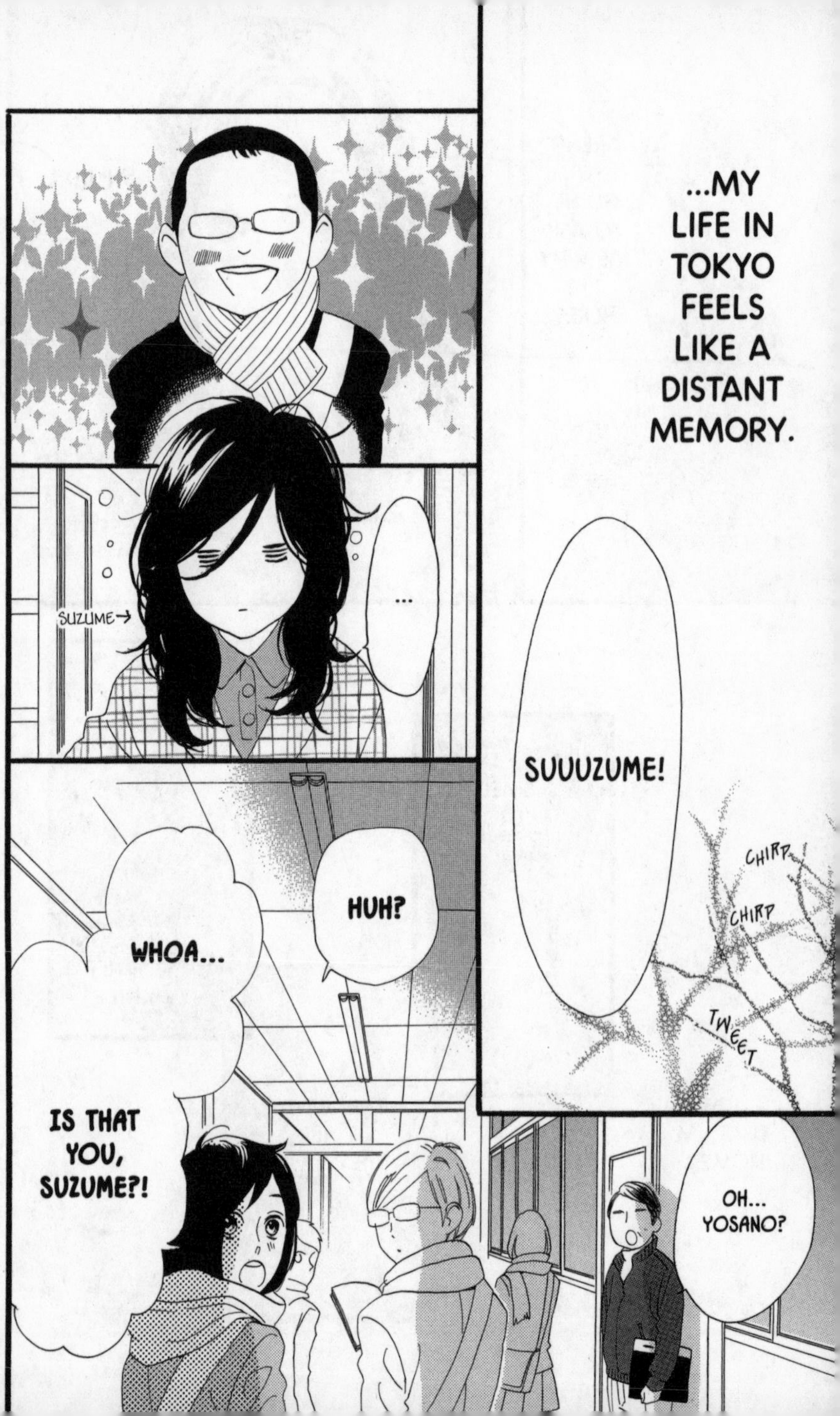
...MY LIFE IN TOKYO FEELS LIKE A DISTANT MEMORY.
SUUUZUME!
CHIRP
CHIRP
TWEET
SUZUME→
...
HUH?
WHOA...
IS THAT YOU, SUZUME?!
OH... YOSANO?

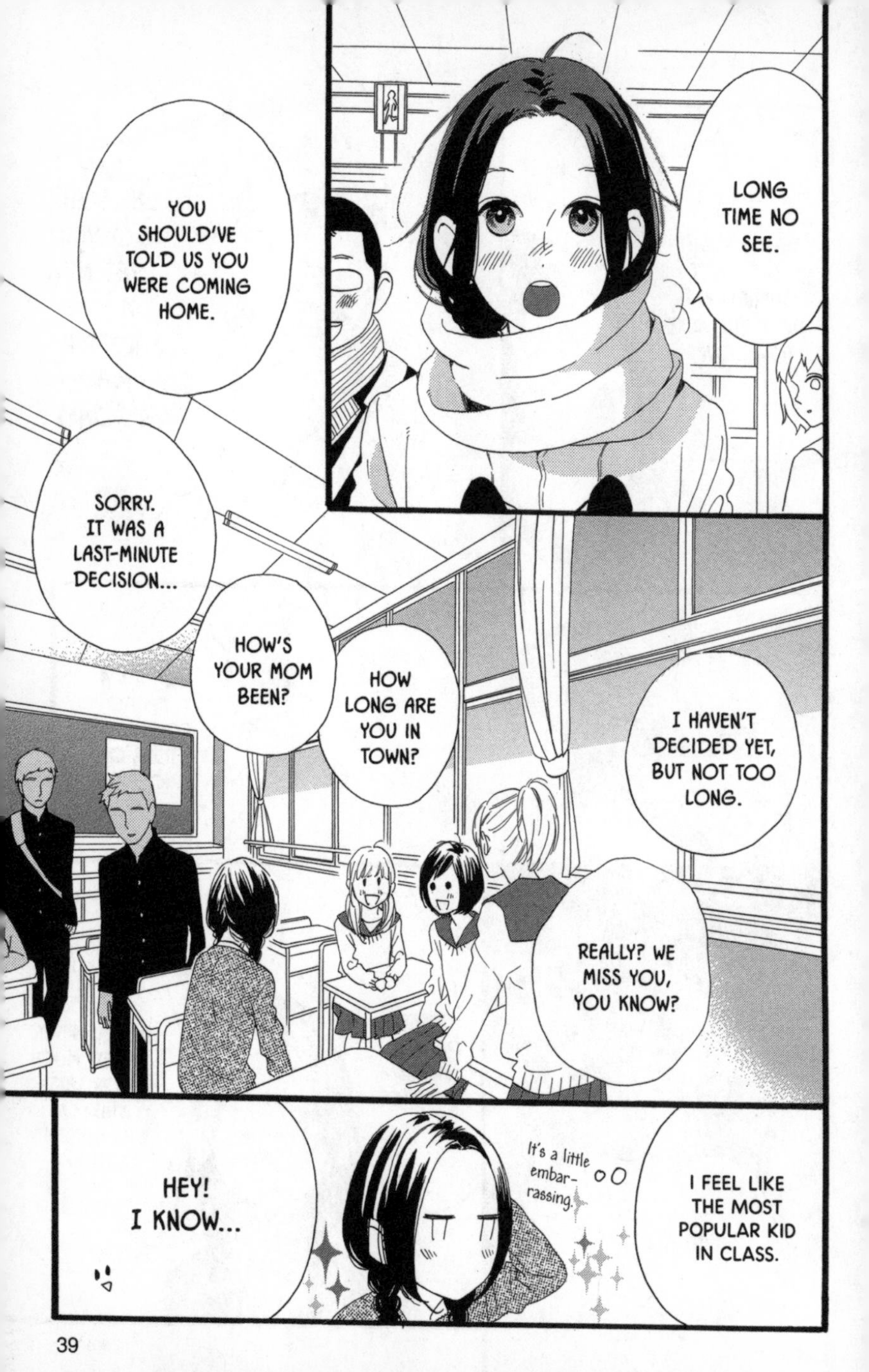
LONG TIME NO SEE.
YOU SHOULD'VE TOLD US YOU WERE COMING HOME.
SORRY. IT WAS A LAST-MINUTE DECISION...
HOW'S YOUR MOM BEEN?
HOW LONG ARE YOU IN TOWN?
I HAVEN'T DECIDED YET, BUT NOT TOO LONG.
REALLY? WE MISS YOU, YOU KNOW?
I FEEL LIKE THE MOST POPULAR KID IN CLASS.
It's a little embarrassing.
HEY! I KNOW...

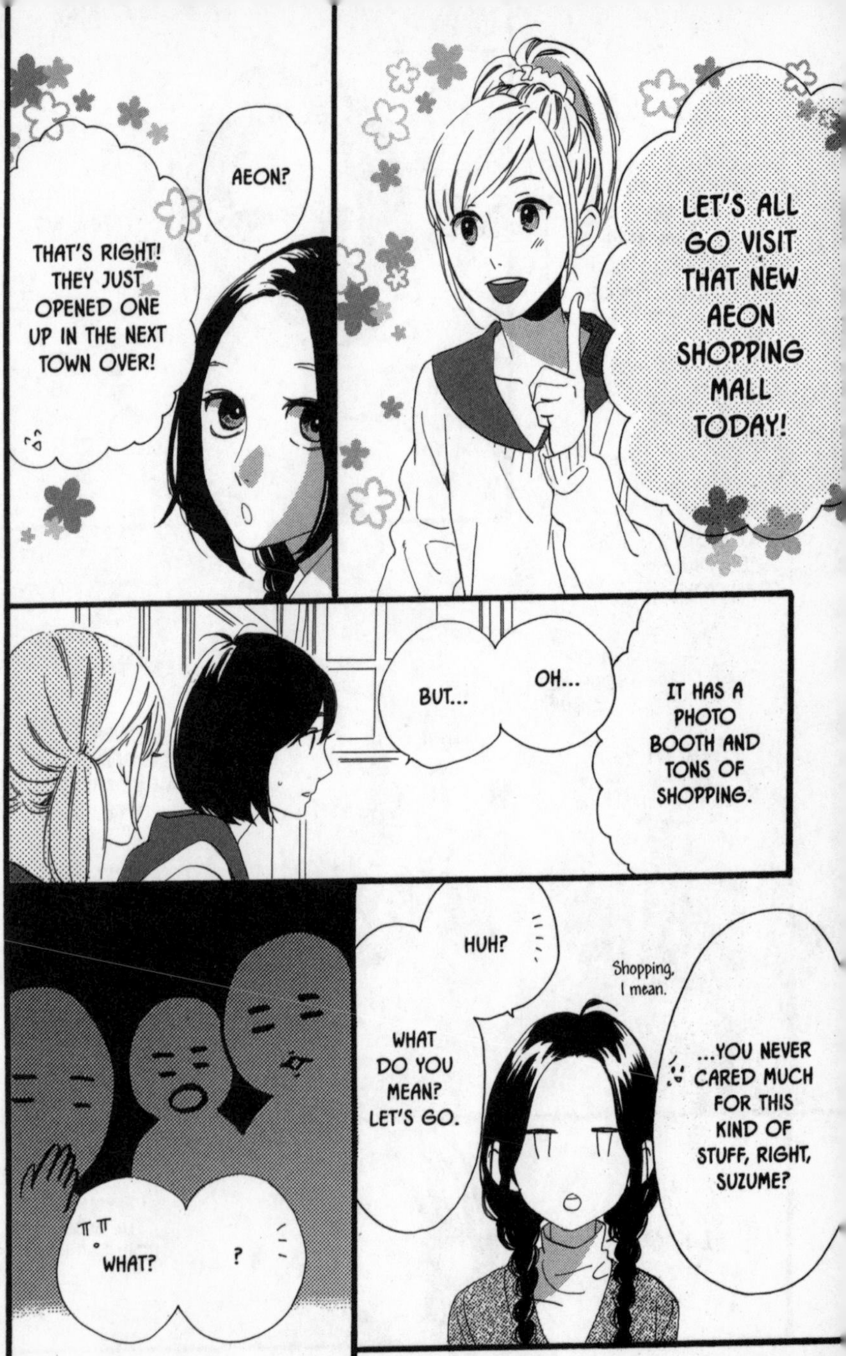
LET'S ALL GO VISIT THAT NEW AEON SHOPPING MALL TODAY!
AEON?
THAT'S RIGHT! THEY JUST OPENED ONE UP IN THE NEXT TOWN OVER!
IT HAS A PHOTO BOOTH AND TONS OF SHOPPING.
OH...
BUT...
...YOU NEVER CARED MUCH FOR THIS KIND OF STUFF, RIGHT, SUZUME?
Shopping, I mean.
HUH?
WHAT DO YOU MEAN? LET'S GO.
?
WHAT?

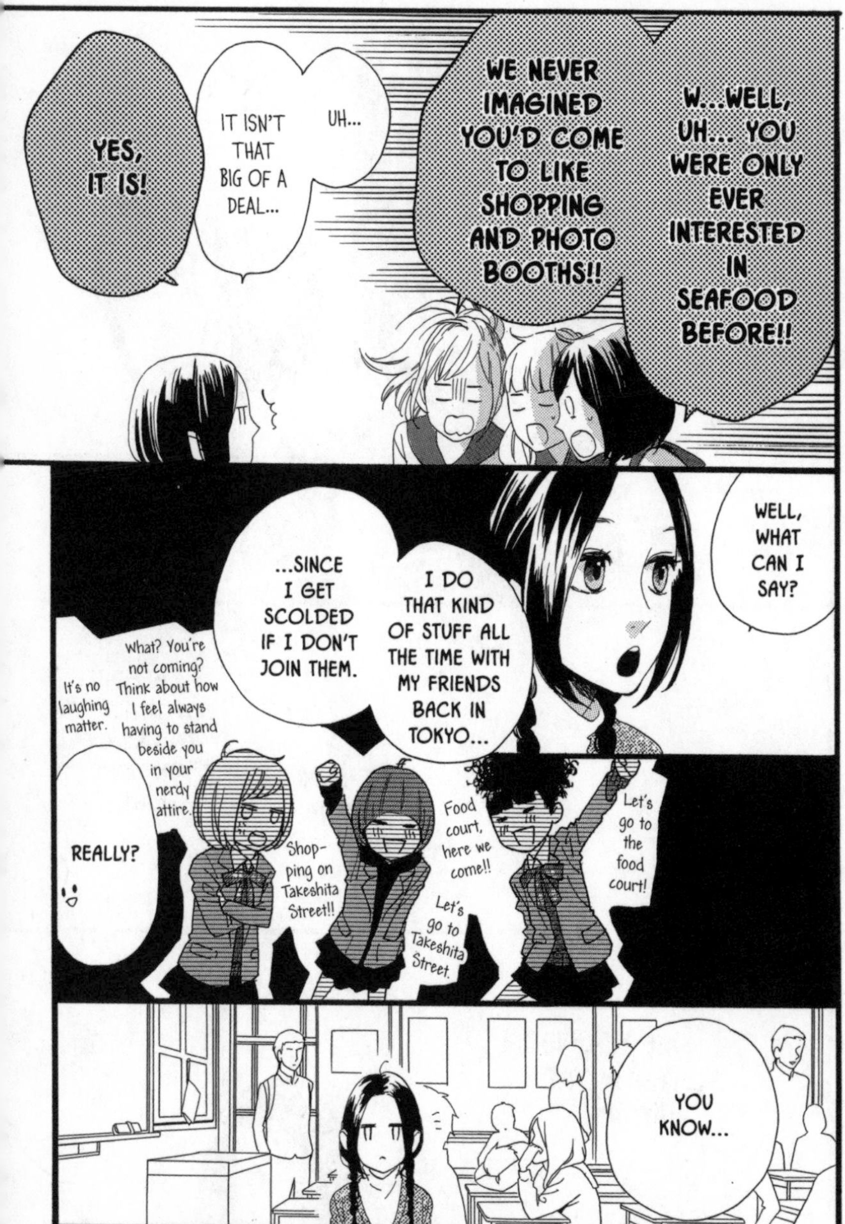
W...WELL, UH... YOU WERE ONLY EVER INTERESTED IN SEAFOOD BEFORE!!
WE NEVER IMAGINED YOU'D COME TO LIKE SHOPPING AND PHOTO BOOTHS!!
UH...
IT ISN'T THAT BIG OF A DEAL...
YES, IT IS!
WELL, WHAT CAN I SAY?
I DO THAT KIND OF STUFF ALL THE TIME WITH MY FRIENDS BACK IN TOKYO...
...SINCE I GET SCOLDED IF I DON'T JOIN THEM.
Let's go to the food court!
Food court, here we come!!
Let's go to Takeshita Street.
Shop-ping on Takeshita Street!!
What? You're not coming? Think about how I feel always having to stand beside you in your nerdy attire.
It's no laughing matter.
REALLY?
YOU KNOW...

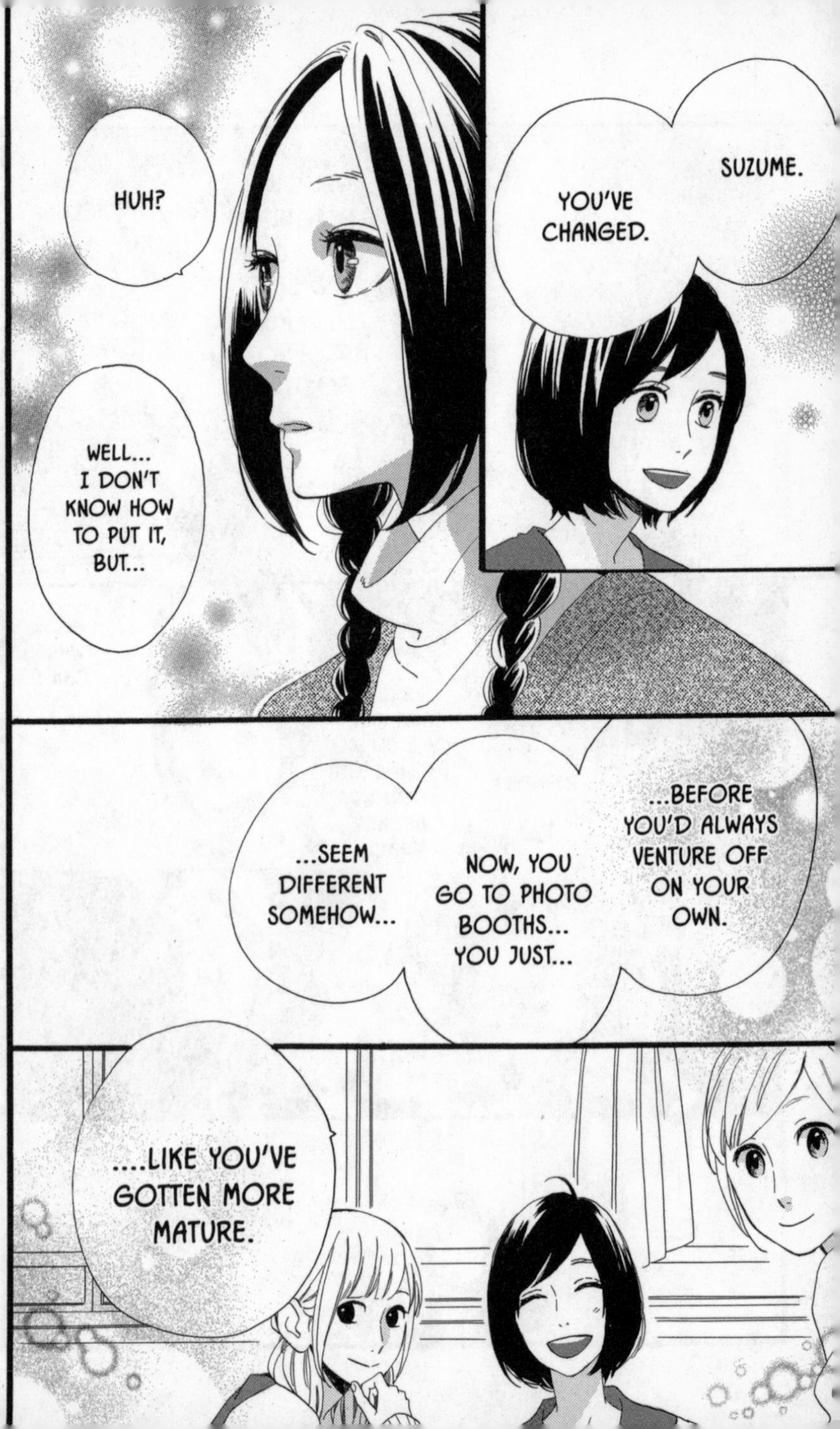
SUZUME.
YOU'VE CHANGED.
HUH?
WELL... I DON'T KNOW HOW TO PUT IT, BUT...
...BEFORE YOU'D ALWAYS VENTURE OFF ON YOUR OWN.
NOW, YOU GO TO PHOTO BOOTHS... YOU JUST...
...SEEM DIFFERENT SOMEHOW...
....LIKE YOU'VE GOTTEN MORE MATURE.

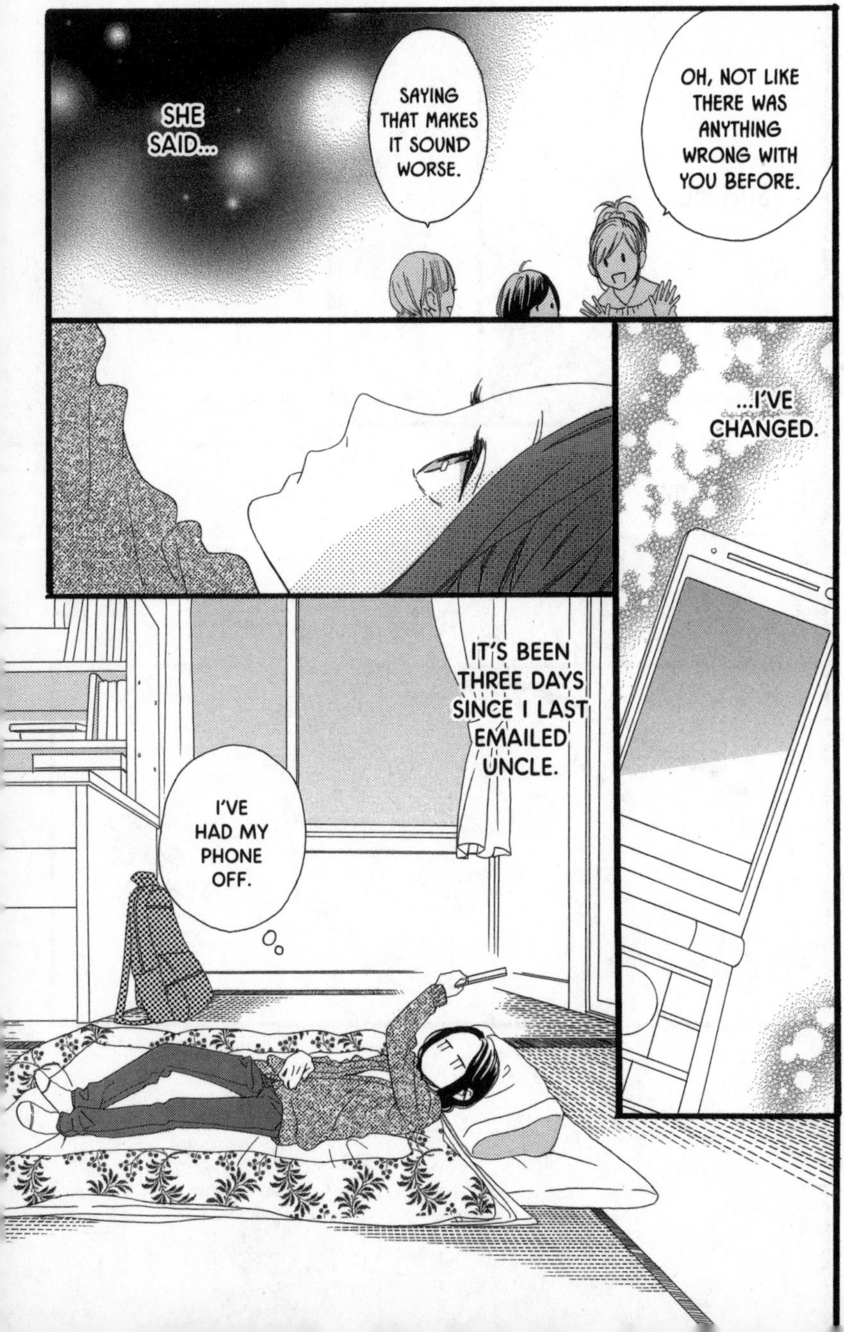
OH, NOT LIKE THERE WAS ANYTHING WRONG WITH YOU BEFORE.
SAYING THAT MAKES IT SOUND WORSE.
SHE SAID...
...I'VE CHANGED.
IT'S BEEN THREE DAYS SINCE I LAST EMAILED UNCLE.
I'VE HAD MY PHONE OFF.

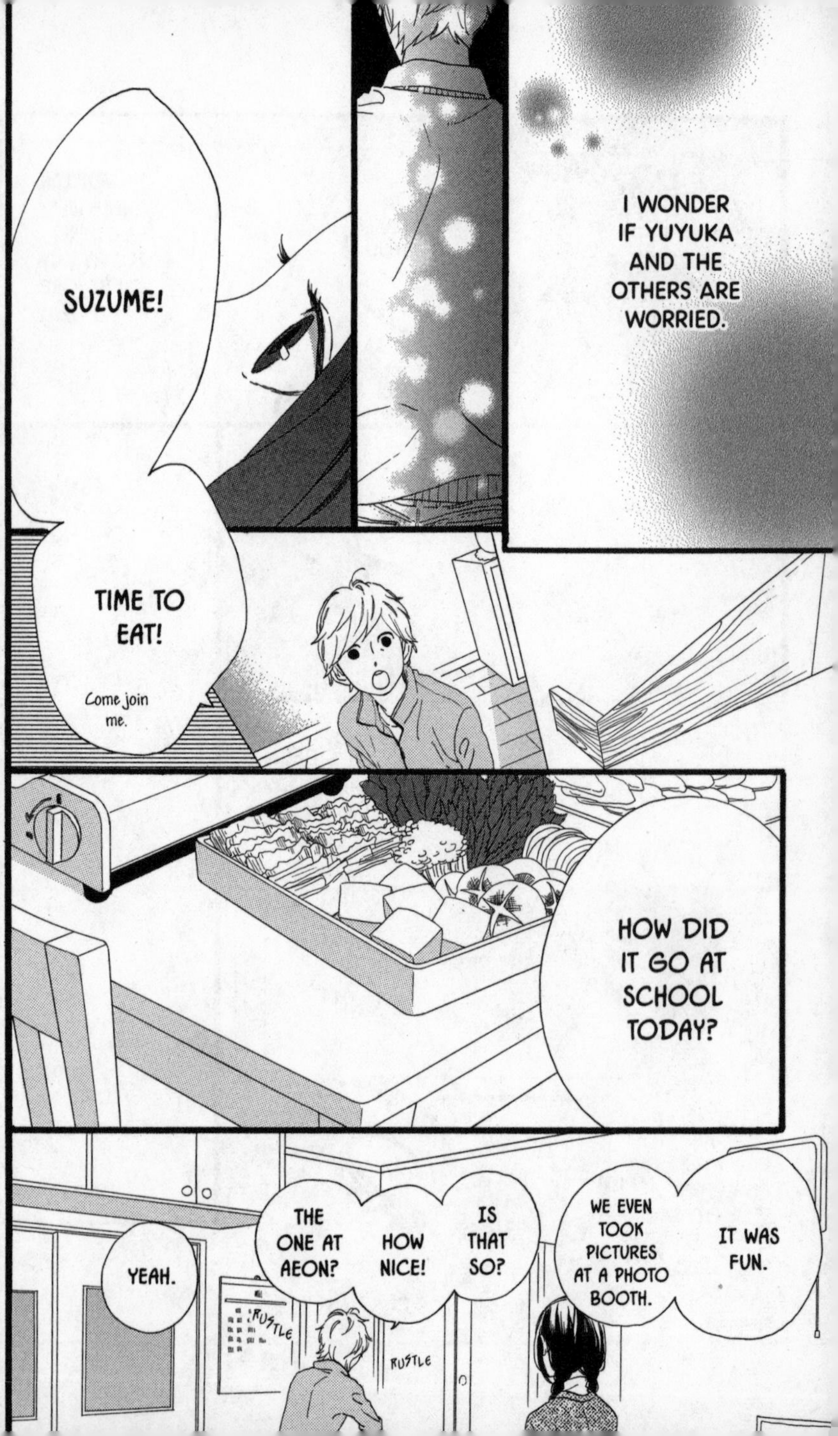
I WONDER IF YUYUKA AND THE OTHERS ARE WORRIED.
SUZUME!
TIME TO EAT!
Come join me.
HOW DID IT GO AT SCHOOL TODAY?
IT WAS FUN.
WE EVEN TOOK PICTURES AT A PHOTO BOOTH.
IS THAT SO?
HOW NICE!
THE ONE AT AEON?
YEAH.
RUSTLE
RUSTLE

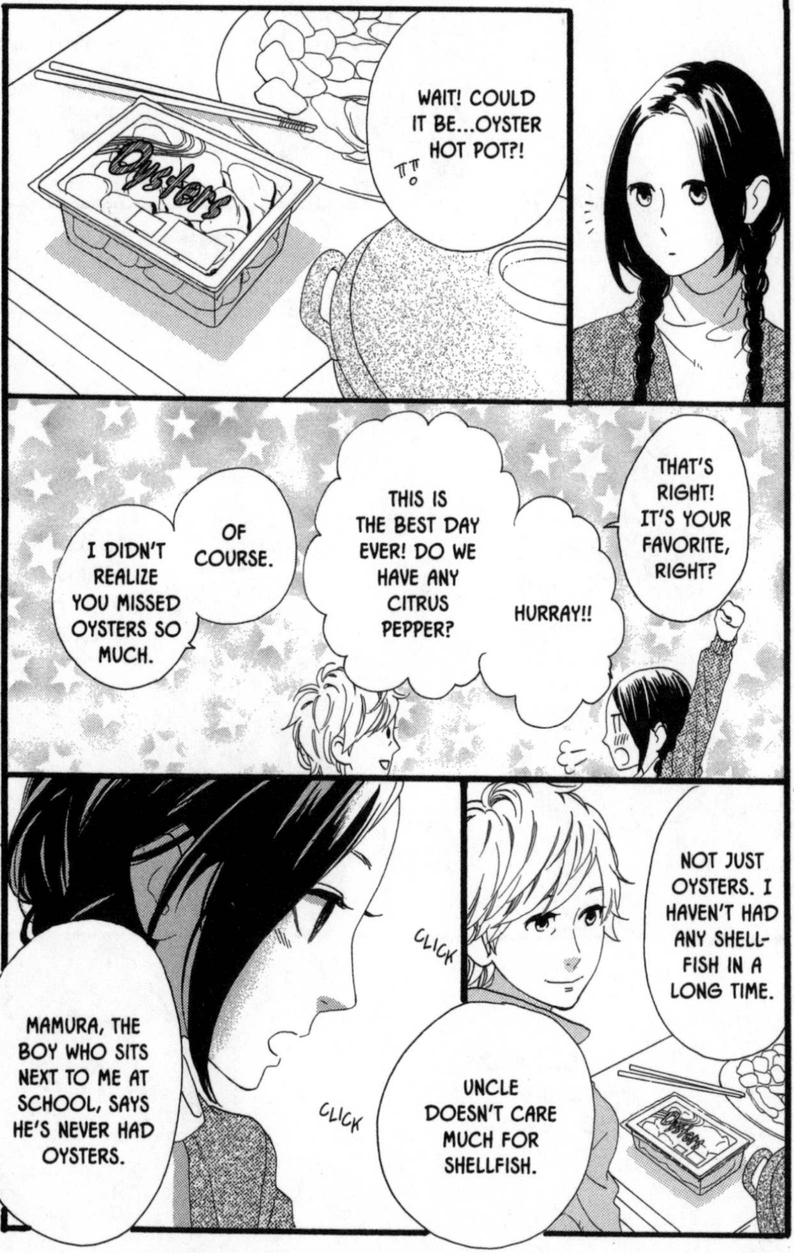
Oysters
WAIT! COULD IT BE...OYSTER HOT POT?!
THAT'S RIGHT! IT'S YOUR FAVORITE, RIGHT?
HURRAY!!
THIS IS THE BEST DAY EVER! DO WE HAVE ANY CITRUS PEPPER?
OF COURSE.
I DIDN'T REALIZE YOU MISSED OYSTERS SO MUCH.
NOT JUST OYSTERS. I HAVEN'T HAD ANY SHELLFISH IN A LONG TIME.
UNCLE DOESN'T CARE MUCH FOR SHELLFISH.
CLICK
CLICK
MAMURA, THE BOY WHO SITS NEXT TO ME AT SCHOOL, SAYS HE'S NEVER HAD OYSTERS.

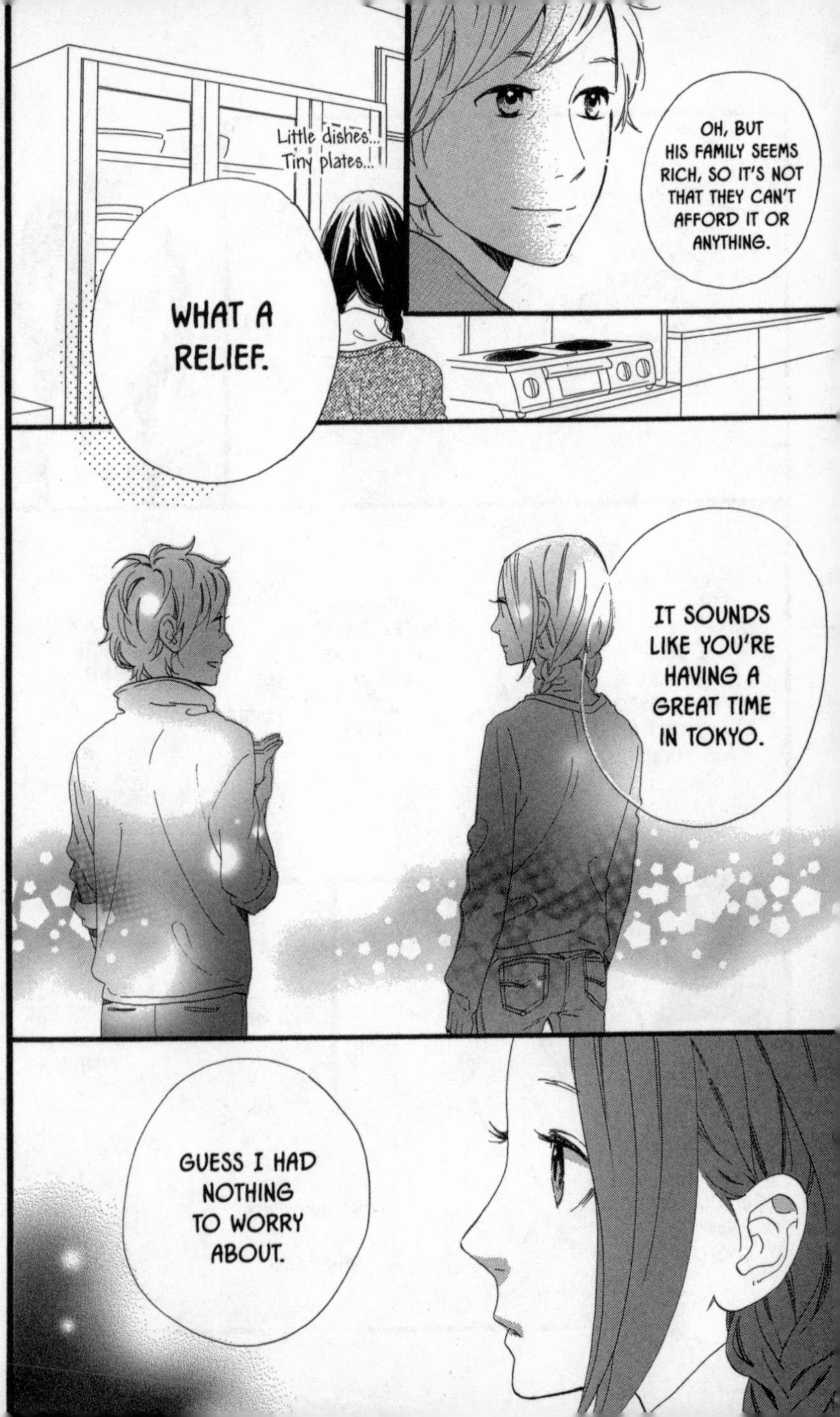
OH, BUT HIS FAMILY SEEMS RICH, SO IT'S NOT THAT THEY CAN'T AFFORD IT OR ANYTHING.
Little dishes... Tiny plates...
WHAT A RELIEF.
IT SOUNDS LIKE YOU'RE HAVING A GREAT TIME IN TOKYO.
GUESS I HAD NOTHING TO WORRY ABOUT.

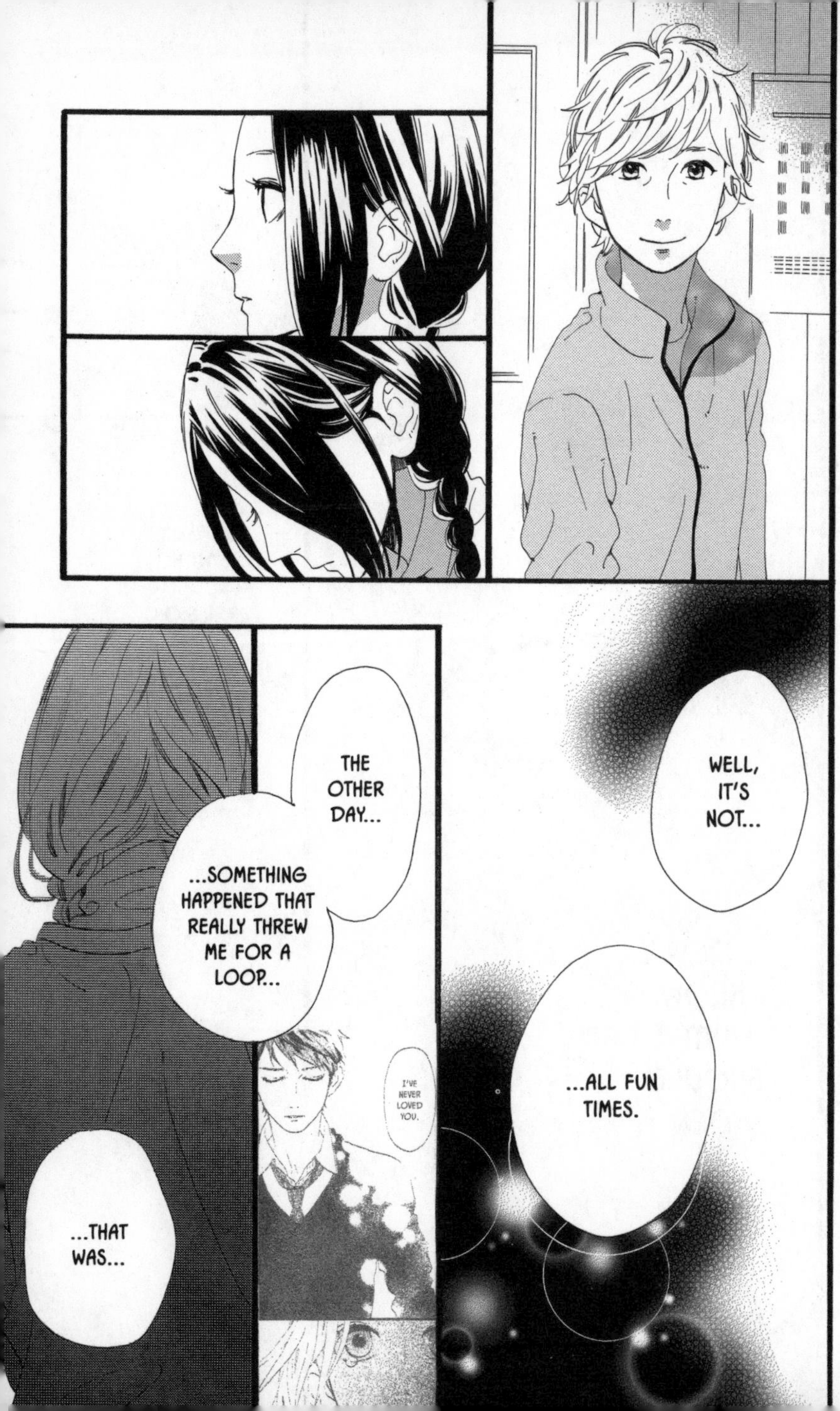
WELL, IT'S NOT...
...ALL FUN TIMES.
THE OTHER DAY...
...SOMETHING HAPPENED THAT REALLY THREW ME FOR A LOOP...
I'VE NEVER LOVED YOU.
...THAT WAS...

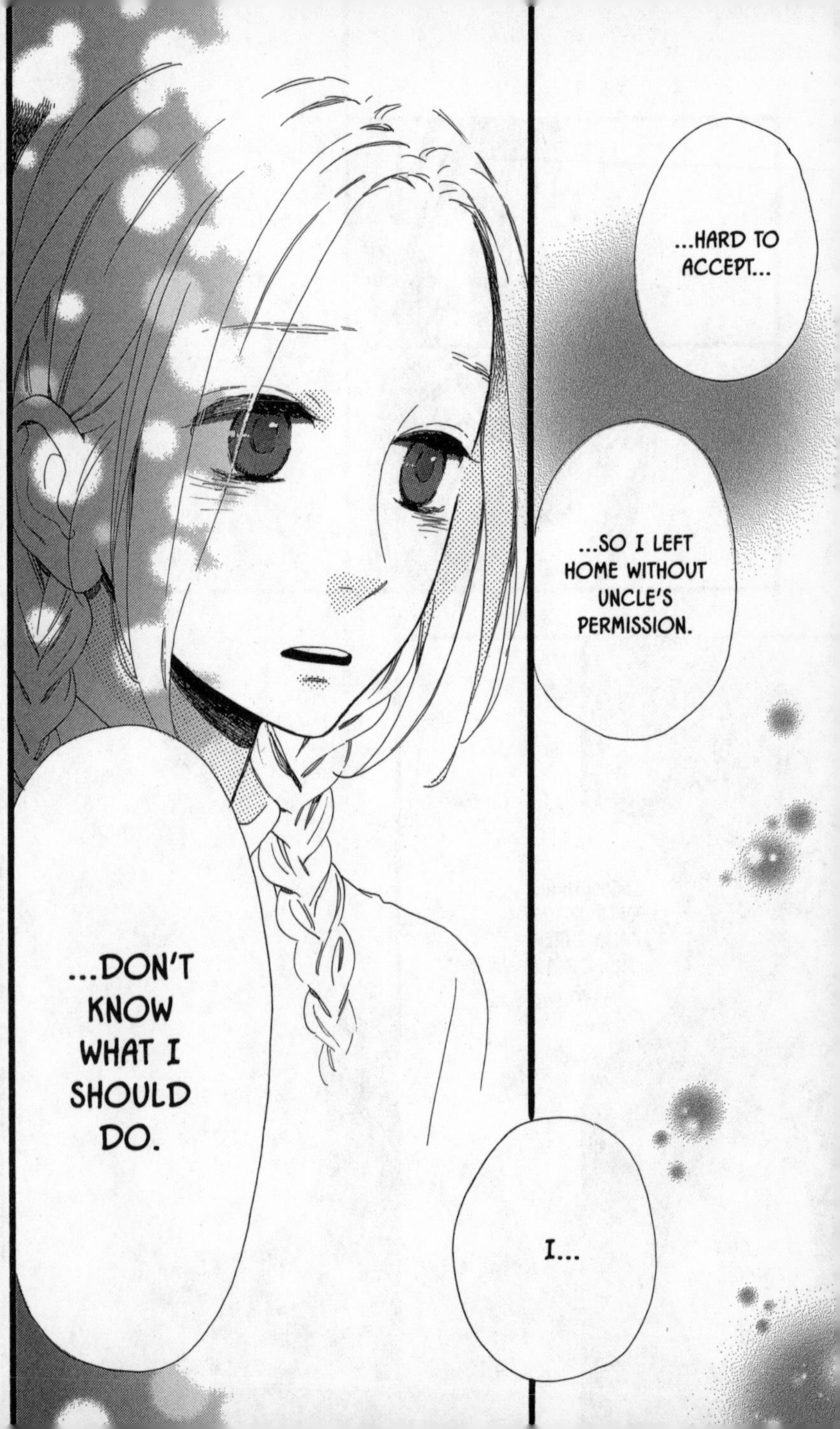
...HARD TO ACCEPT...
...SO I LEFT HOME WITHOUT UNCLE'S PERMISSION.
I...
...DON'T KNOW WHAT I SHOULD DO.

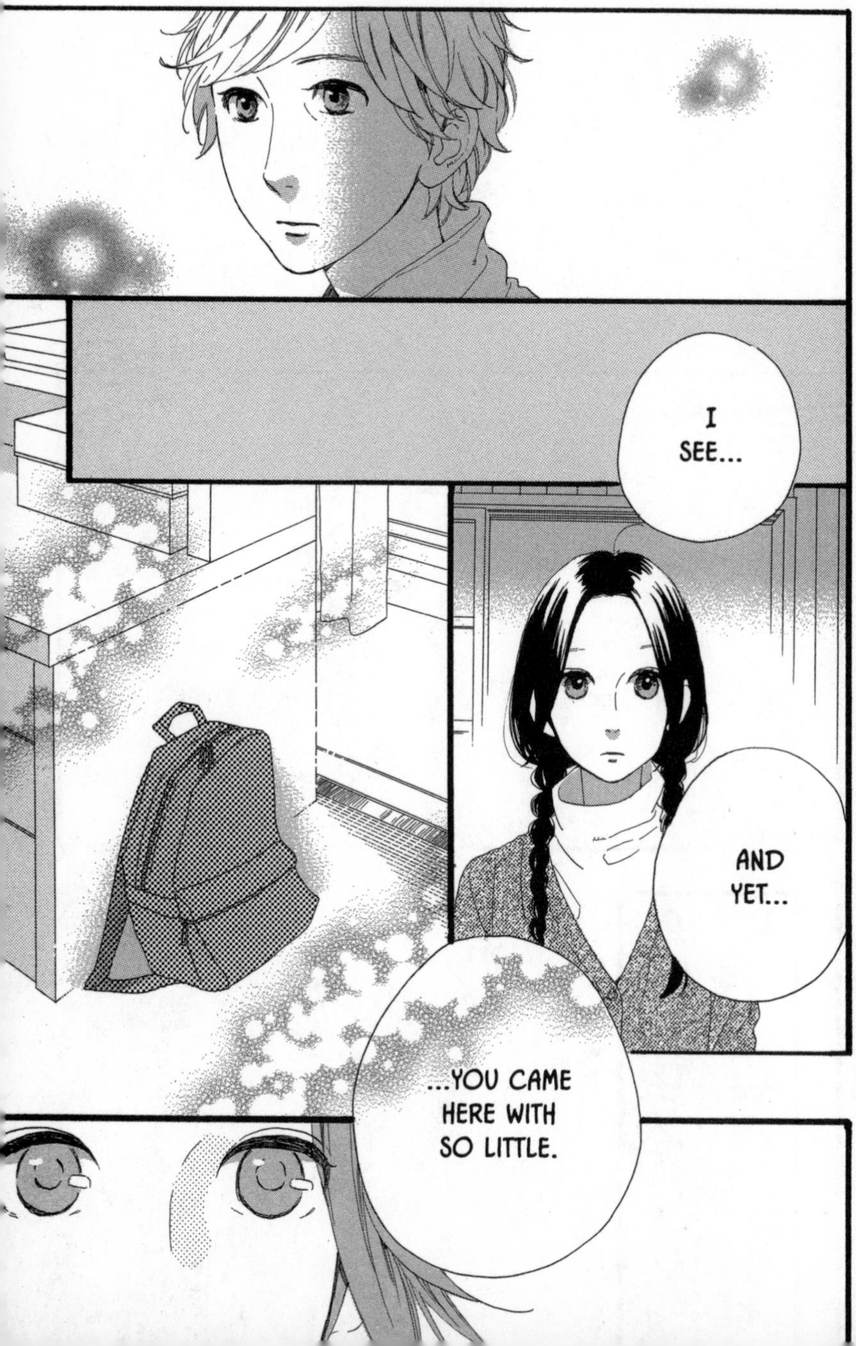
I SEE...
AND YET...
...YOU CAME HERE WITH SO LITTLE.

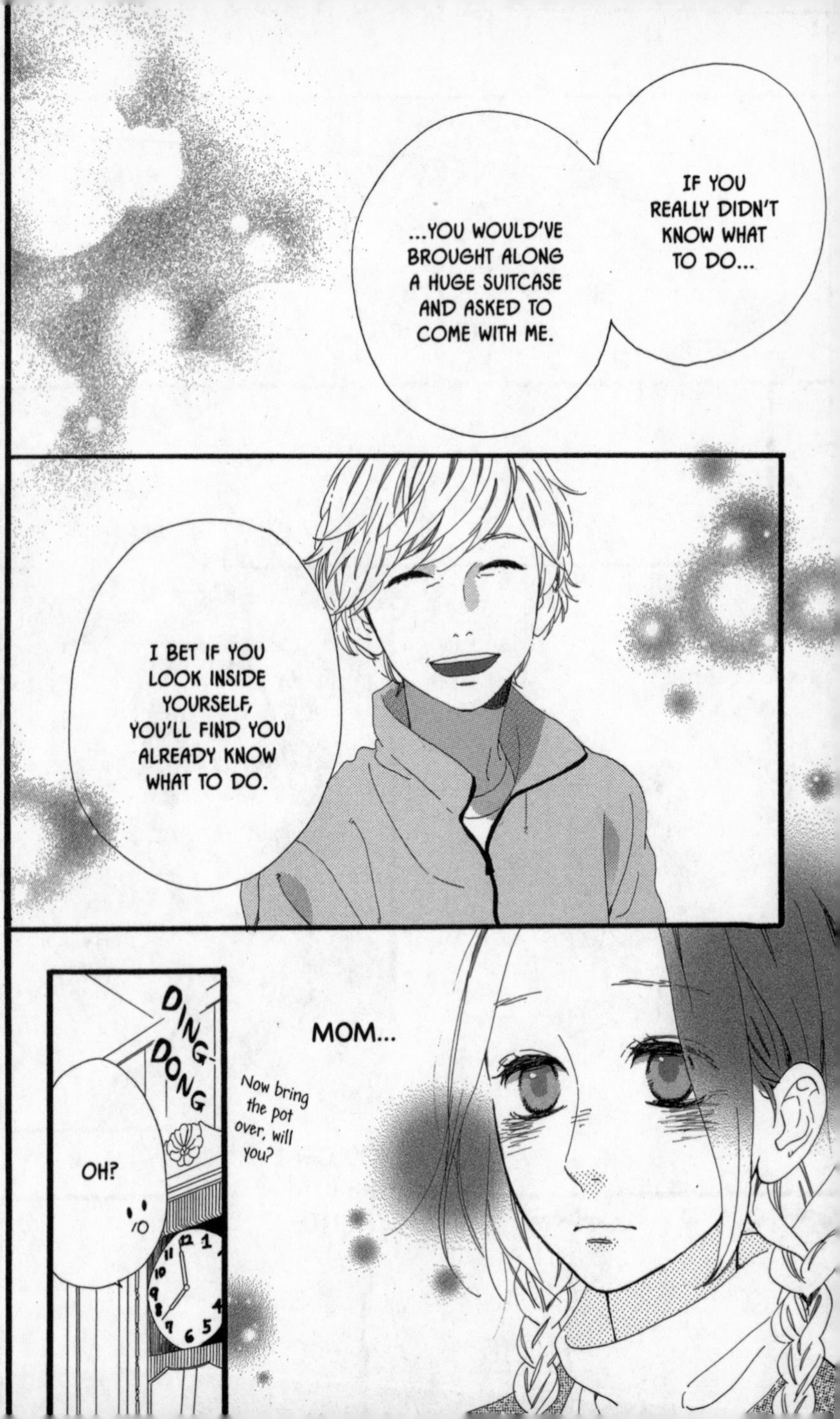
IF YOU REALLY DIDN'T KNOW WHAT TO DO...
...YOU WOULD'VE BROUGHT ALONG A HUGE SUITCASE AND ASKED TO COME WITH ME.
I BET IF YOU LOOK INSIDE YOURSELF, YOU'LL FIND YOU ALREADY KNOW WHAT TO DO.
MOM...
Now bring the pot over, will you?
DING DONG
OH?

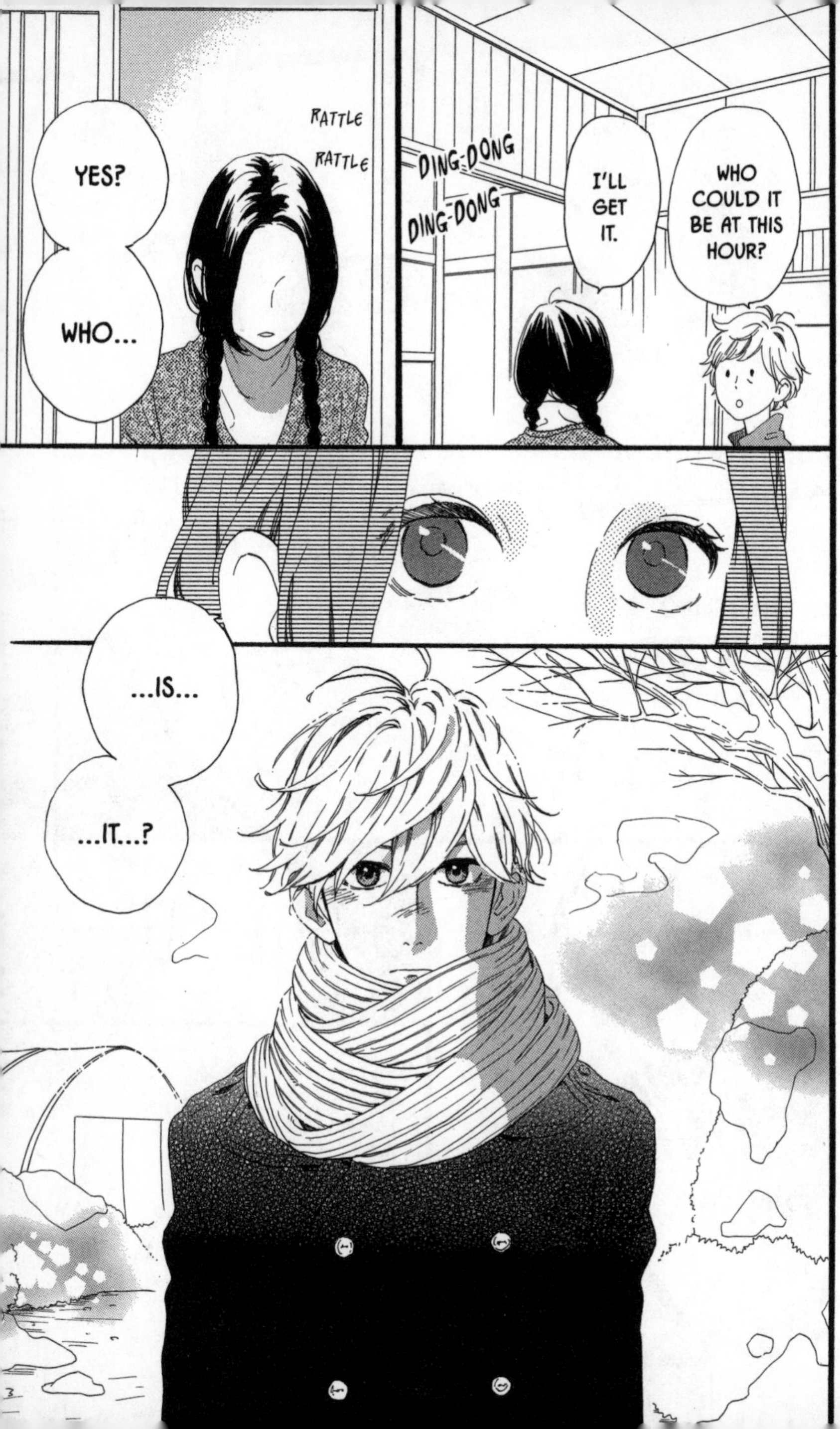
WHO COULD IT BE AT THIS HOUR?
I'LL GET IT.
DING-DONG
DING-DONG
RATTLE
RATTLE
YES?
WHO...
...IS...
...IT...?

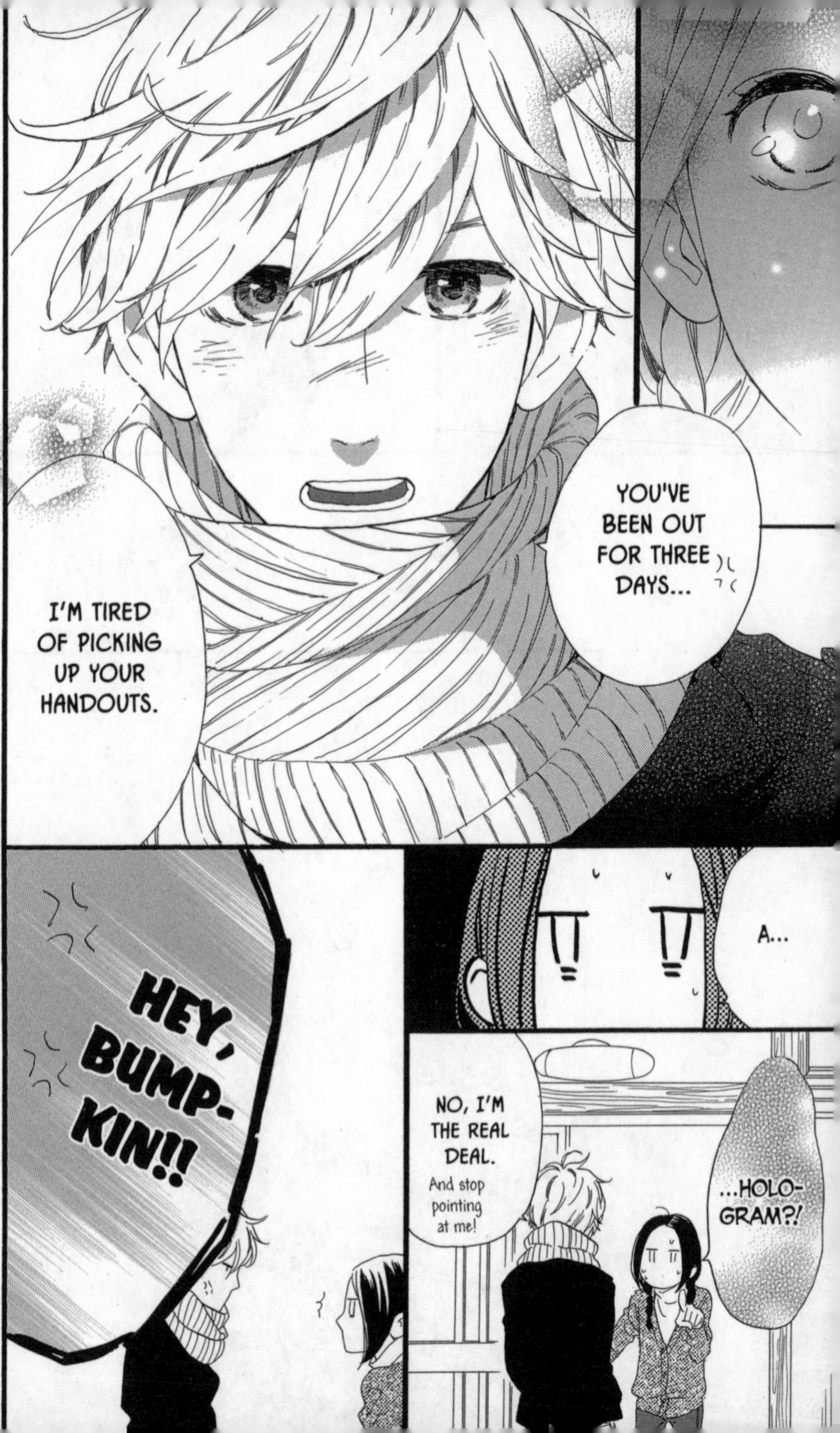
YOU'VE BEEN OUT FOR THREE DAYS...
I'M TIRED OF PICKING UP YOUR HANDOUTS.
A...
...HOLOGRAM?!
NO, I'M THE REAL DEAL.
And stop pointing at me!
HEY, BUMPKIN!!

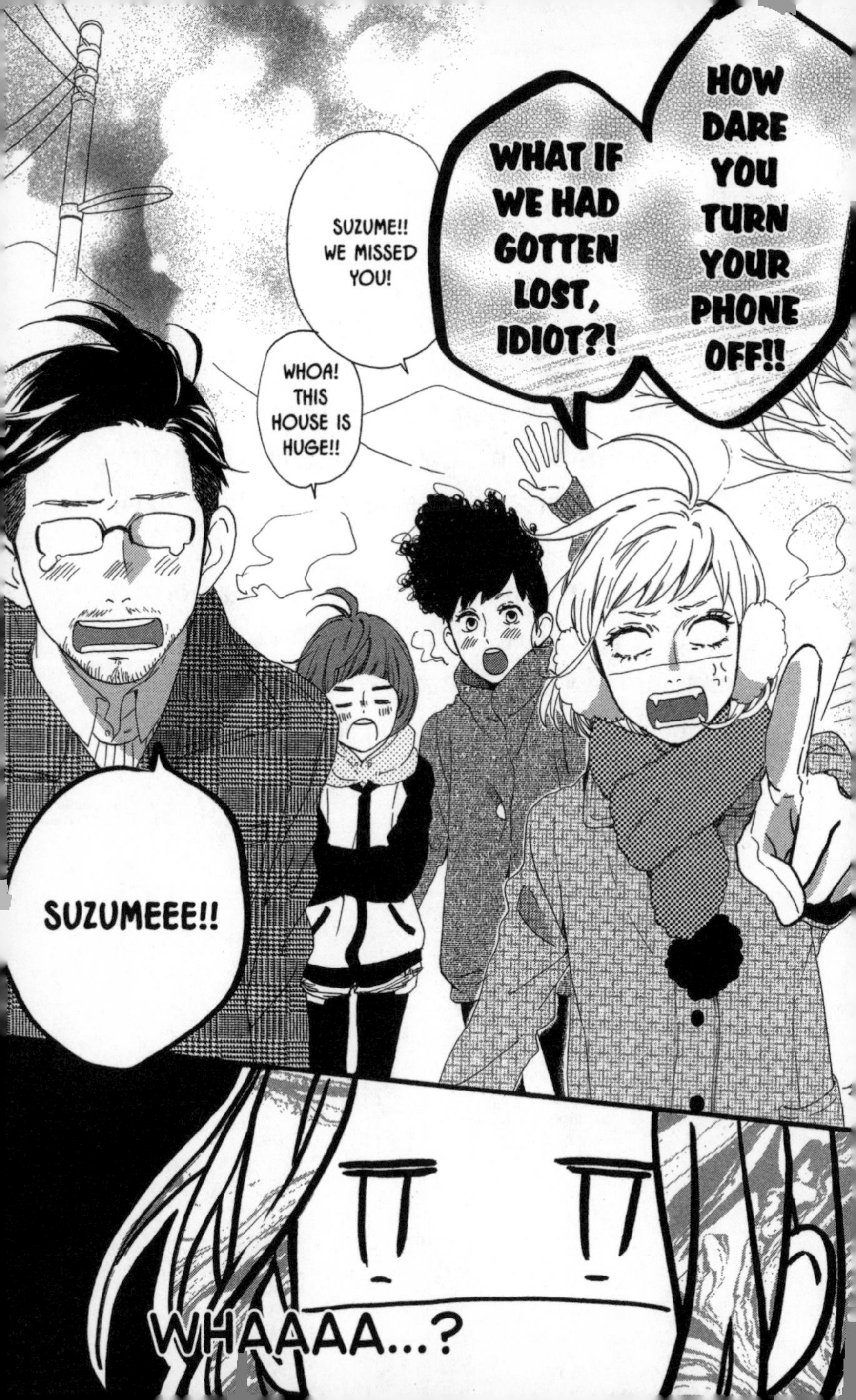
HOW DARE YOU TURN YOUR PHONE OFF!!
WHAT IF WE HAD GOTTEN LOST, IDIOT?!
SUZUME!! WE MISSED YOU!
WHOA! THIS HOUSE IS HUGE!!
SUZUMEEE!!
WHAAAAA...?

And so...

We've reached volume 8 of *Daytime Shooting Star*!
I bet you're thinking, "Huh? Didn't volume 7 just
come out?" You're right. Volume 7 released just
three months ago in Japan!! And the next volume
will be out in three months' time too!! I hope you'll
read that one also!

It might be hard to believe but...I've run out of
things to write here... If there's anything you'd like
me to draw for you, please send in your requests.
I'm looking forward to hearing your reactions to
Daytime Shooting Star volume 8!

UGH

UGH

Autumn, the
season of
tasty things...

I've grown
rounder,
especially in
the face.

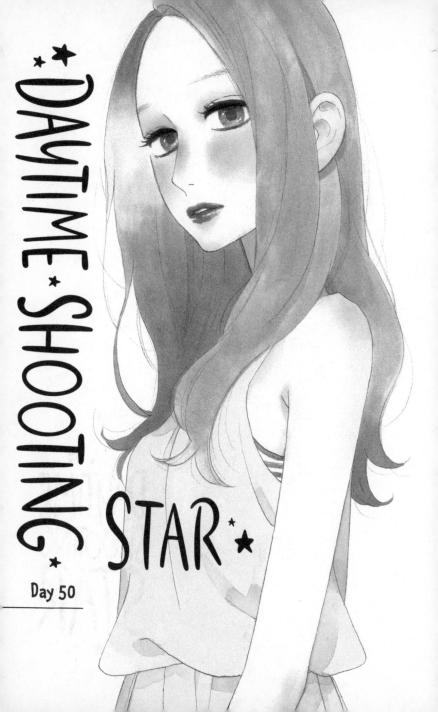

DAYTIME SHOOTING STAR

Day 50

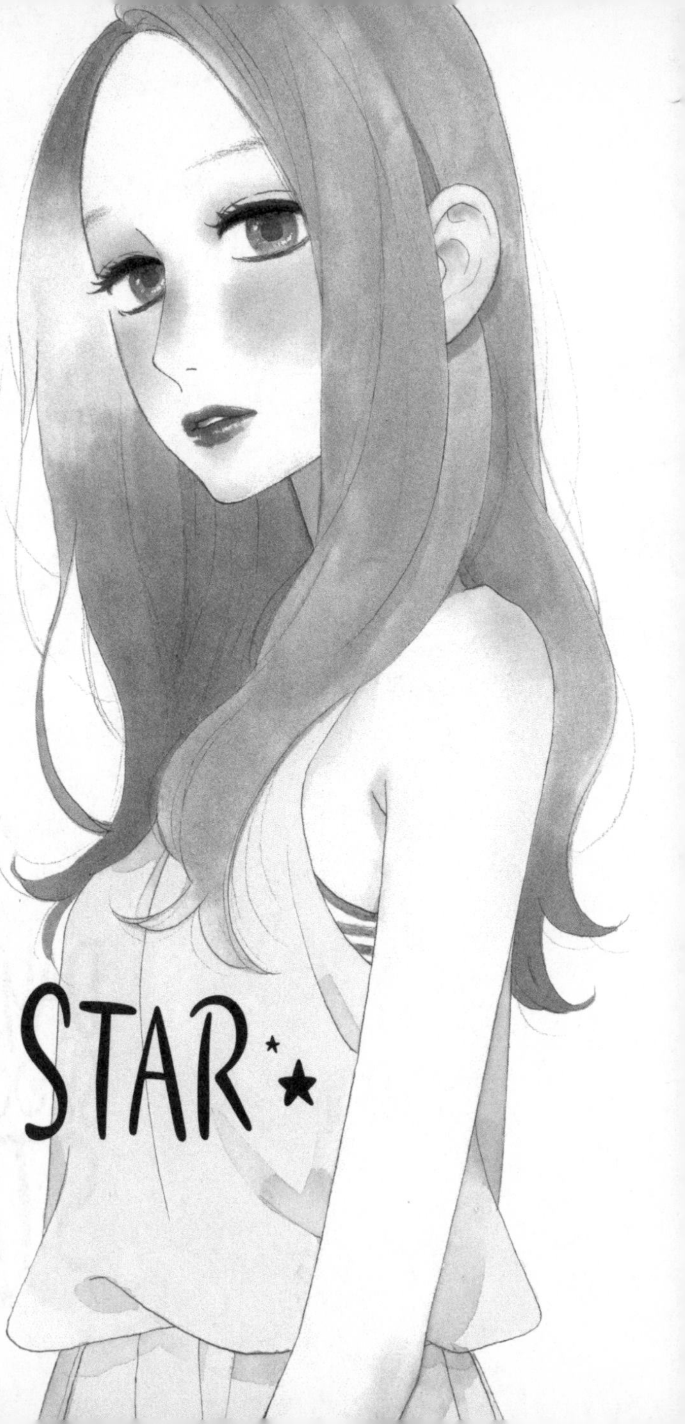

DAYTIME
SHOOTING
STAR

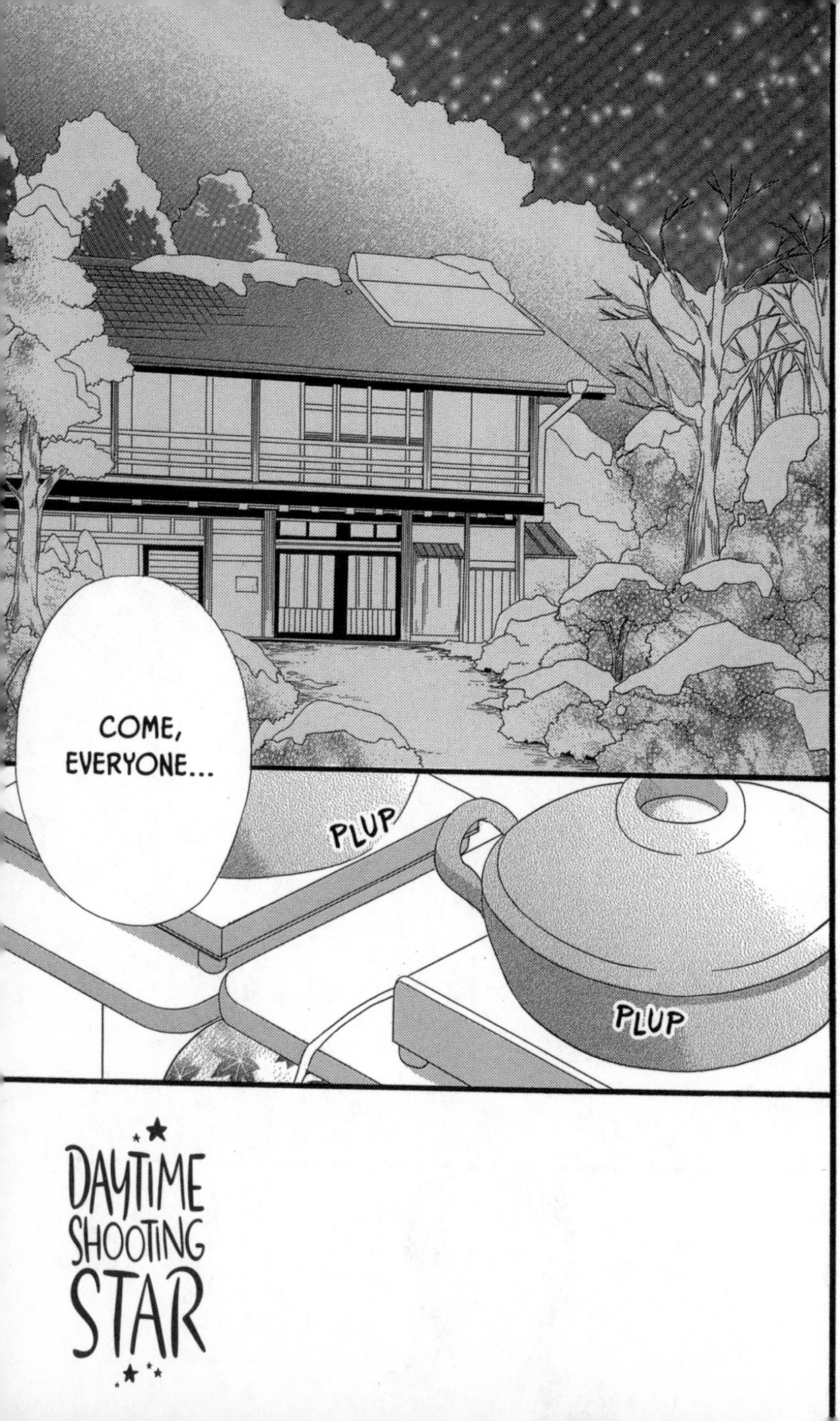
COME, EVERYONE...
PLUP
PLUP
DAYTIME SHOOTING STAR

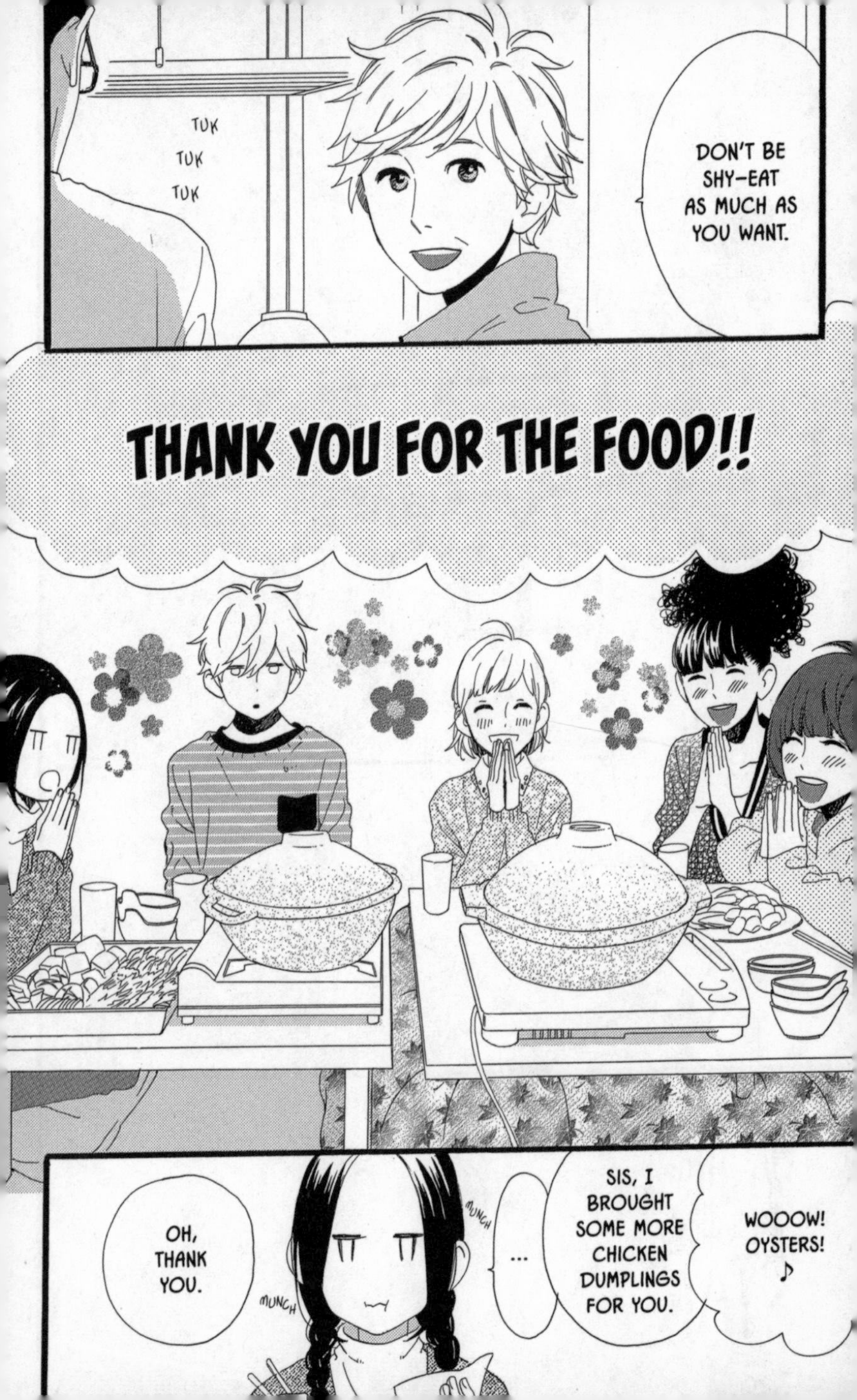
DON'T BE SHY—EAT AS MUCH AS YOU WANT.
TUK
TUK
TUK
THANK YOU FOR THE FOOD!!
WOOOW! OYSTERS! ♪
SIS, I BROUGHT SOME MORE CHICKEN DUMPLINGS FOR YOU.
...
MUNCH
MUNCH
OH, THANK YOU.

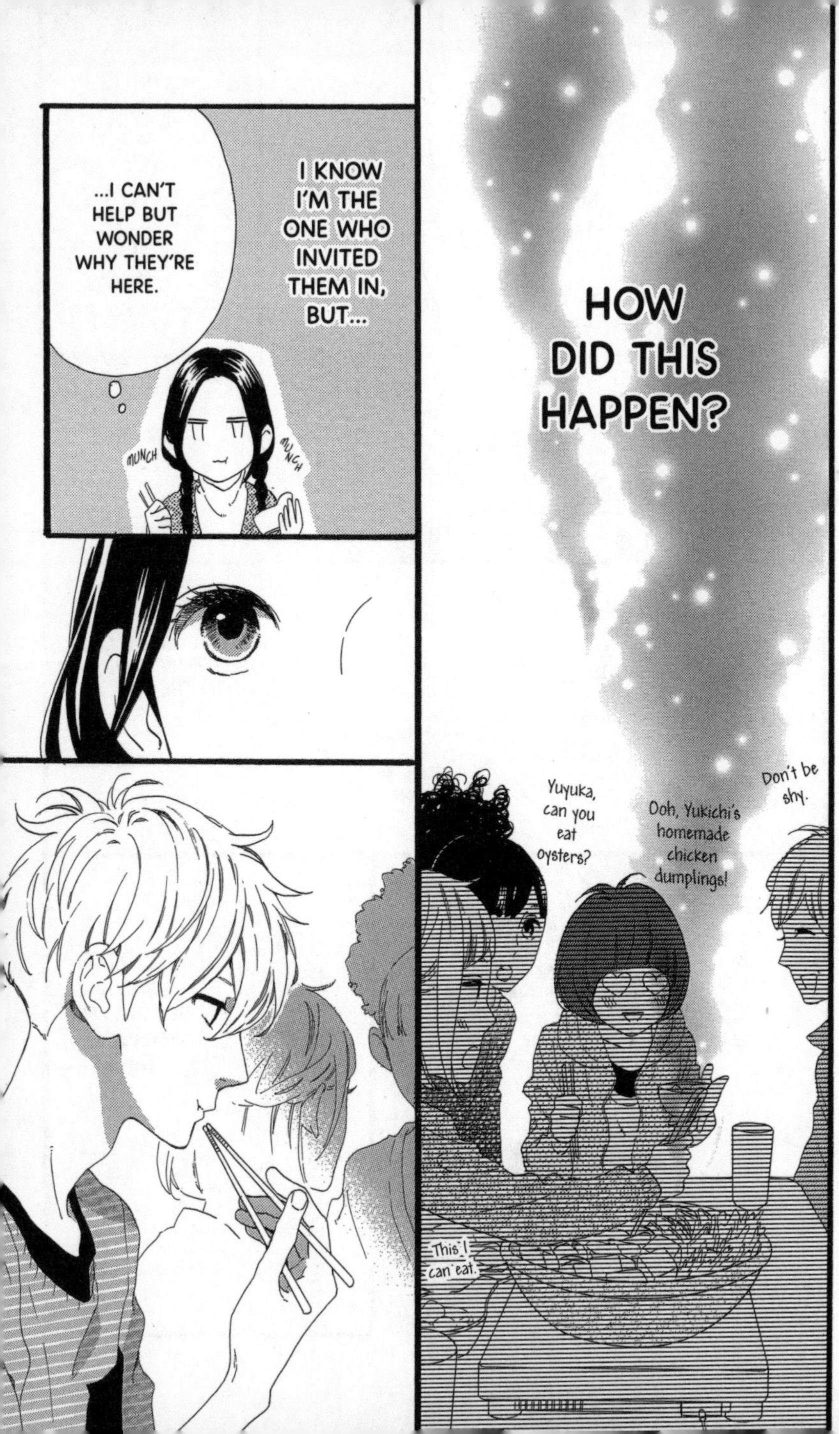
HOW DID THIS HAPPEN?
Don't be shy.
Ooh, Yukichi's homemade chicken dumplings!
Yuyuka, can you eat oysters?
This I can eat.
I KNOW I'M THE ONE WHO INVITED THEM IN, BUT...
...I CAN'T HELP BUT WONDER WHY THEY'RE HERE.
MUNCH
MUNCH

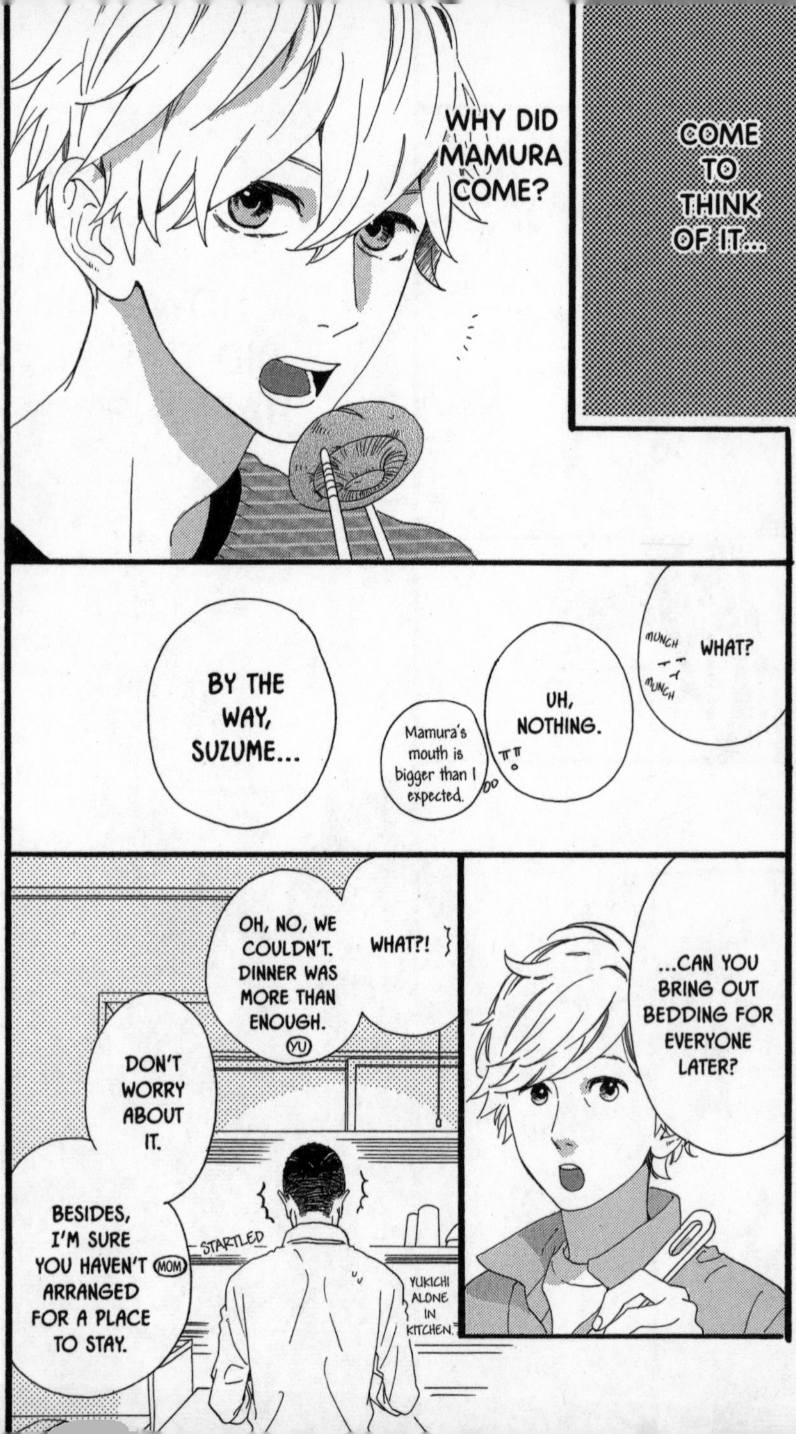
COME TO THINK OF IT...
WHY DID MAMURA COME?
MUNCH MUNCH
WHAT?
UH, NOTHING.
Mamura's mouth is bigger than I expected.
BY THE WAY, SUZUME...
...CAN YOU BRING OUT BEDDING FOR EVERYONE LATER?
WHAT?!
OH, NO, WE COULDN'T. DINNER WAS MORE THAN ENOUGH.
YU
DON'T WORRY ABOUT IT.
BESIDES, I'M SURE YOU HAVEN'T ARRANGED FOR A PLACE TO STAY.
MOM
STARTLED
YUKICHI ALONE IN KITCHEN.

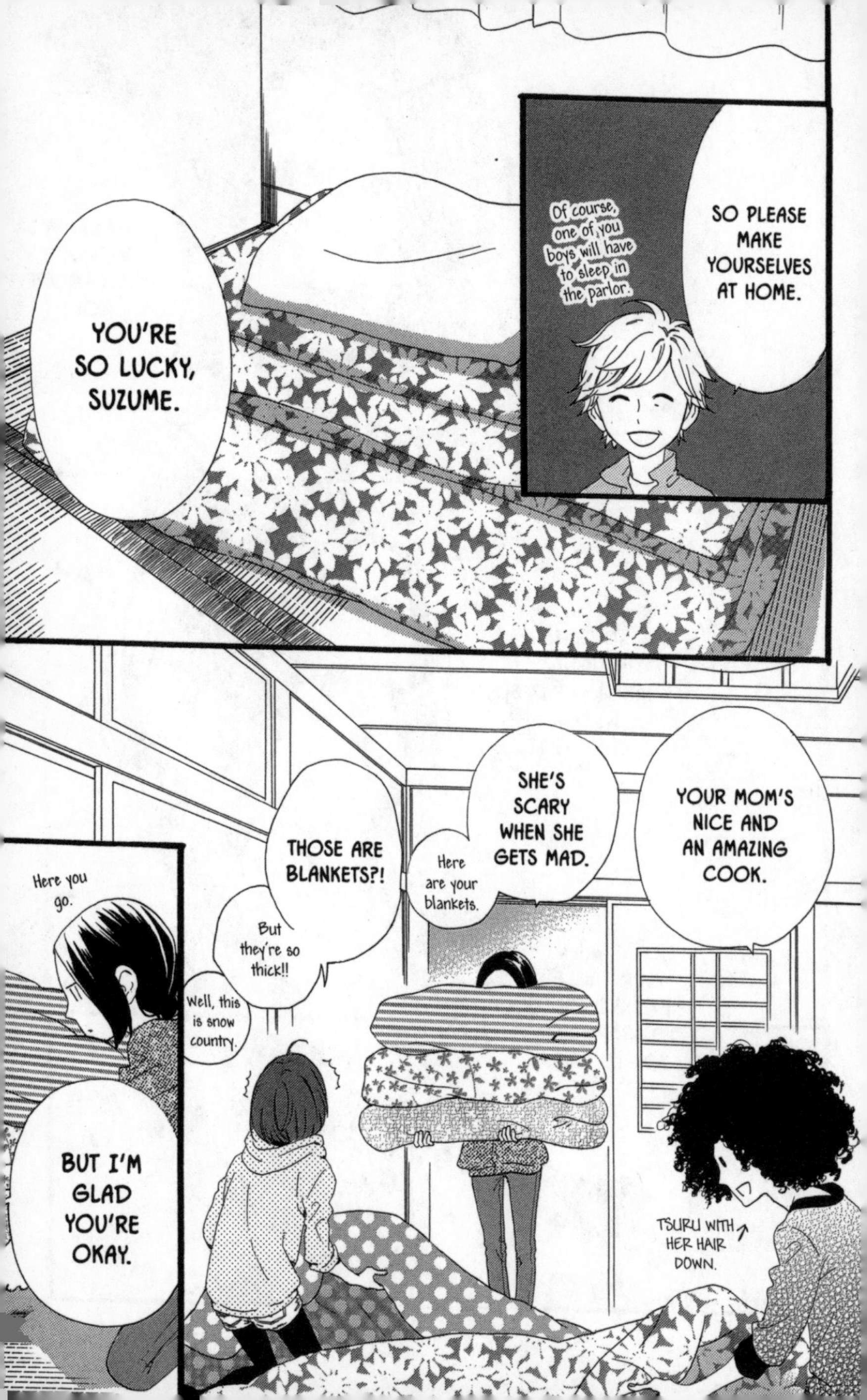
SO PLEASE MAKE YOURSELVES AT HOME.
Of course, one of you boys will have to sleep in the parlor.
YOU'RE SO LUCKY, SUZUME.
YOUR MOM'S NICE AND AN AMAZING COOK.
SHE'S SCARY WHEN SHE GETS MAD.
Here are your blankets.
THOSE ARE BLANKETS?!
But they're so thick!!
Well, this is snow country.
TSURU WITH HER HAIR DOWN.
Here you go.
BUT I'M GLAD YOU'RE OKAY.

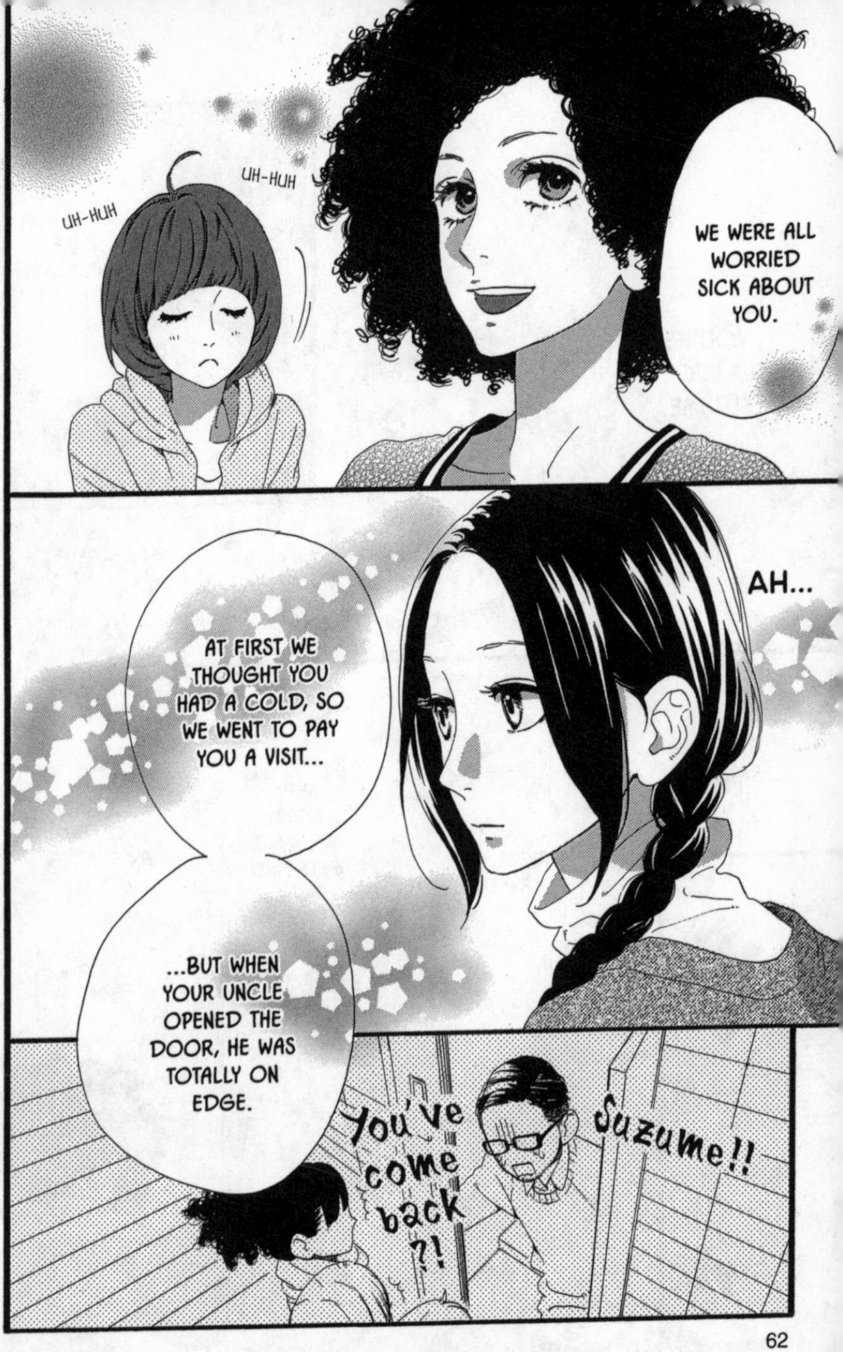
WE WERE ALL WORRIED SICK ABOUT YOU.
UH-HUH
UH-HUH
AH...
AT FIRST WE THOUGHT YOU HAD A COLD, SO WE WENT TO PAY YOU A VISIT...
...BUT WHEN YOUR UNCLE OPENED THE DOOR, HE WAS TOTALLY ON EDGE.
Suzume!!
You've come back?!

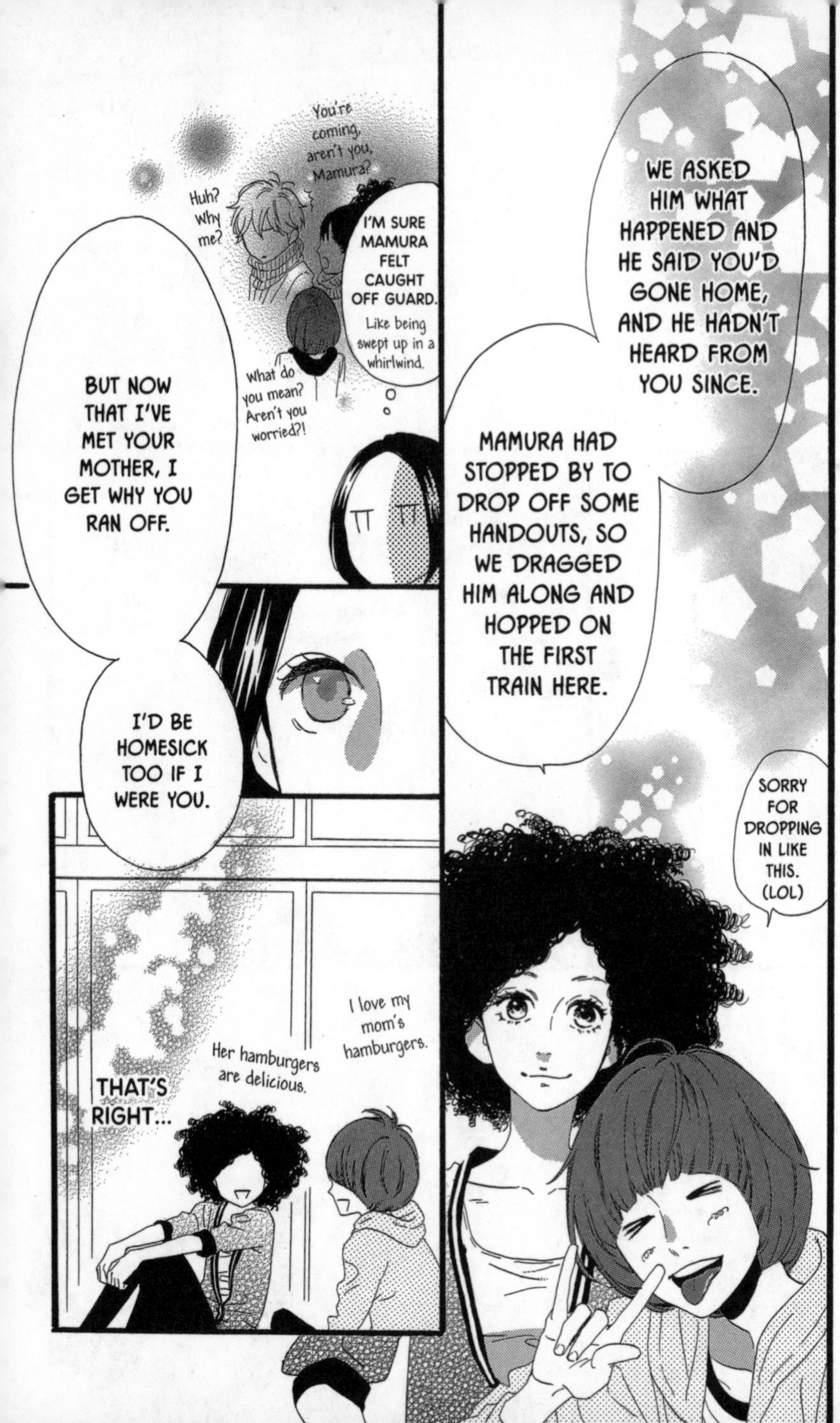
WE ASKED HIM WHAT HAPPENED AND HE SAID YOU'D GONE HOME, AND HE HADN'T HEARD FROM YOU SINCE.
MAMURA HAD STOPPED BY TO DROP OFF SOME HANDOUTS, SO WE DRAGGED HIM ALONG AND HOPPED ON THE FIRST TRAIN HERE.
SORRY FOR DROPPING IN LIKE THIS. (LOL)
I'M SURE MAMURA FELT CAUGHT OFF GUARD.
Like being swept up in a whirlwind.
You're coming, aren't you, Mamura?
Huh? Why me?
What do you mean? Aren't you worried?!
BUT NOW THAT I'VE MET YOUR MOTHER, I GET WHY YOU RAN OFF.
I'D BE HOMESICK TOO IF I WERE YOU.
I love my mom's hamburgers.
Her hamburgers are delicious.
THAT'S RIGHT...

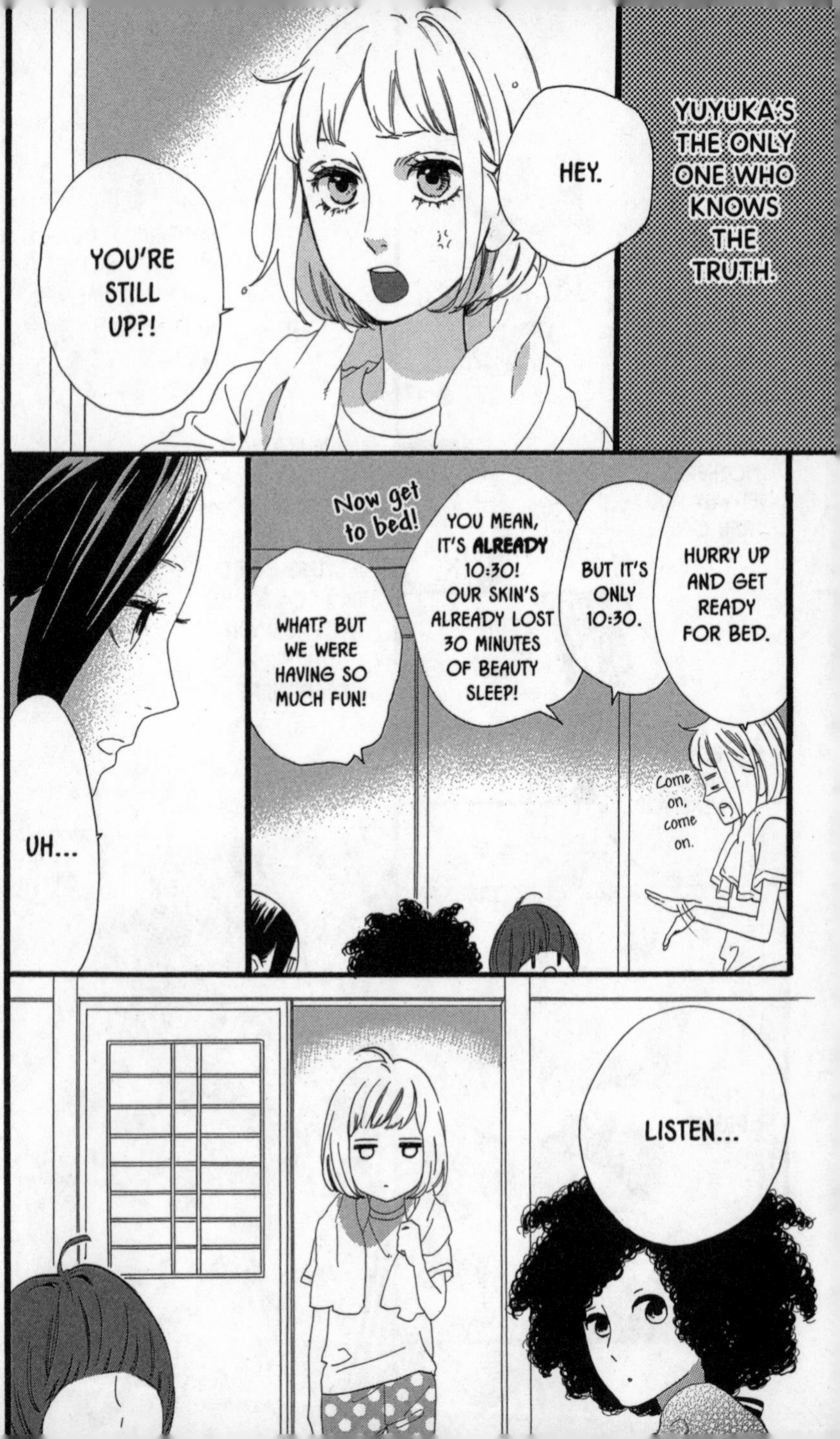
YUYUKA'S THE ONLY ONE WHO KNOWS THE TRUTH.
HEY.
YOU'RE STILL UP?!
HURRY UP AND GET READY FOR BED.
BUT IT'S ONLY 10:30.
YOU MEAN, IT'S **ALREADY** 10:30! OUR SKIN'S ALREADY LOST 30 MINUTES OF BEAUTY SLEEP!
Now get to bed!
WHAT? BUT WE WERE HAVING SO MUCH FUN!
Come on, come on.
UH...
LISTEN...

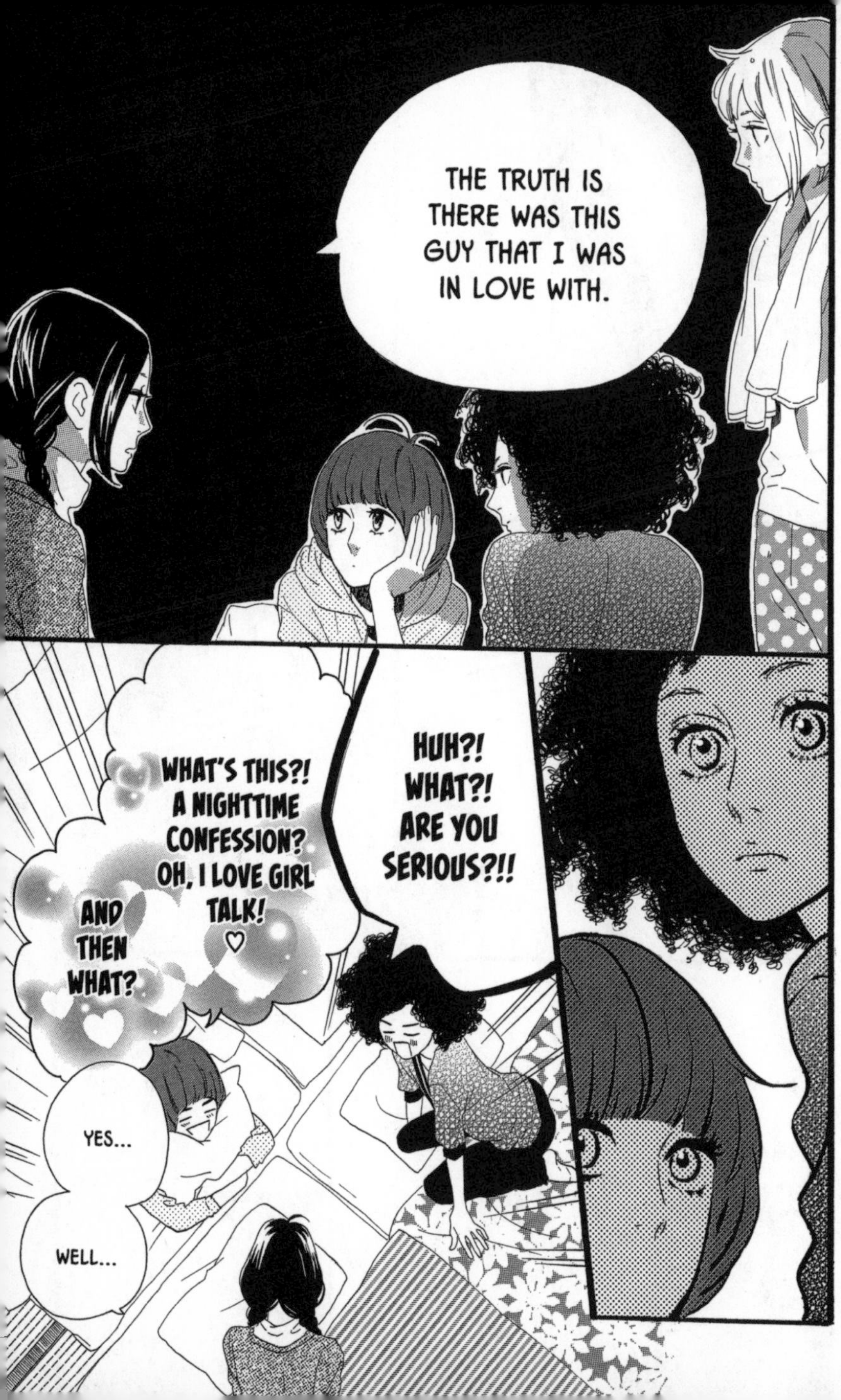
THE TRUTH IS THERE WAS THIS GUY THAT I WAS IN LOVE WITH.
HUH?! WHAT?! ARE YOU SERIOUS?!!
WHAT'S THIS?! A NIGHTTIME CONFESSION? OH, I LOVE GIRL TALK! ♡
AND THEN WHAT?
YES...
WELL...

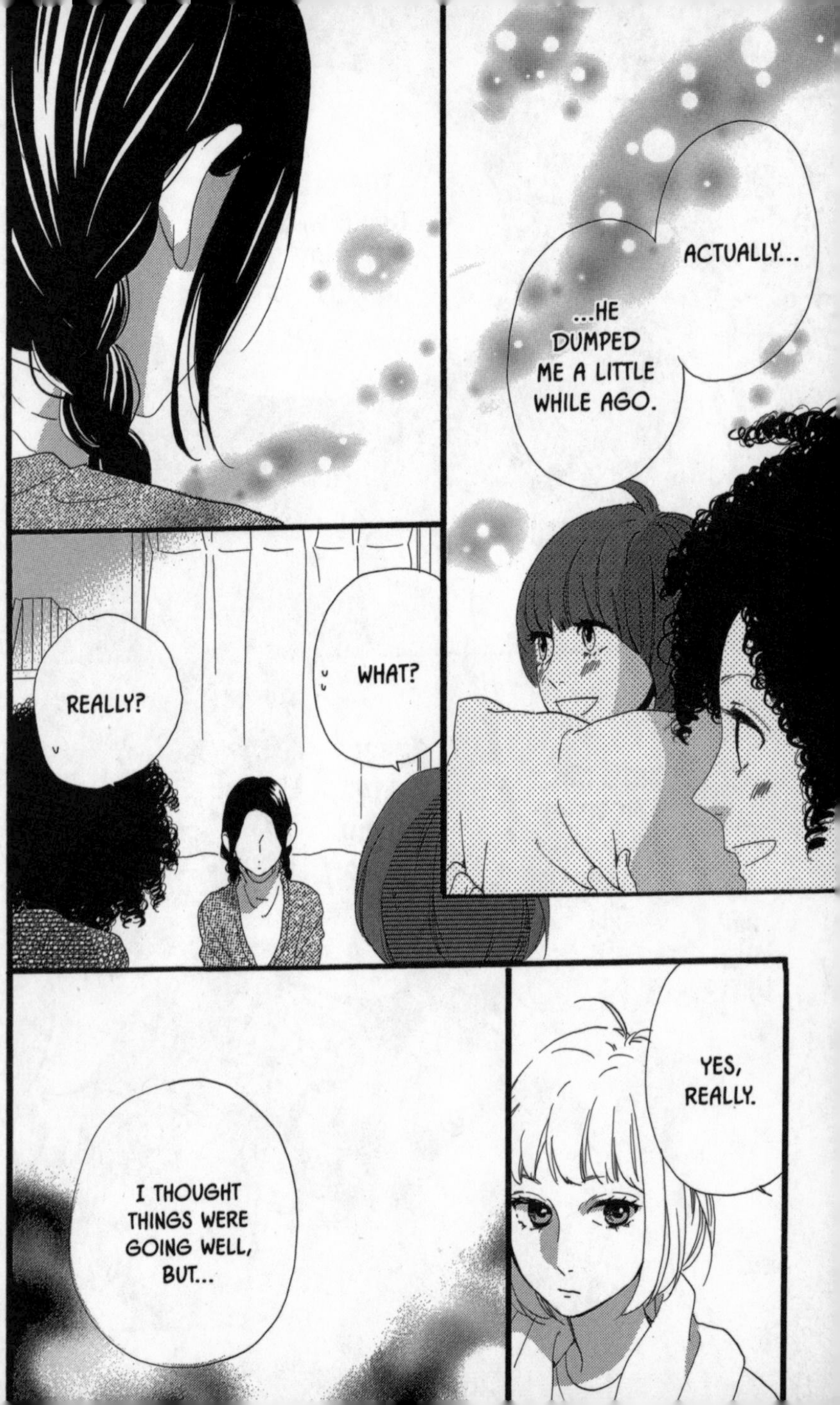
ACTUALLY...
...HE DUMPED ME A LITTLE WHILE AGO.
WHAT?
REALLY?
YES, REALLY.
I THOUGHT THINGS WERE GOING WELL, BUT...

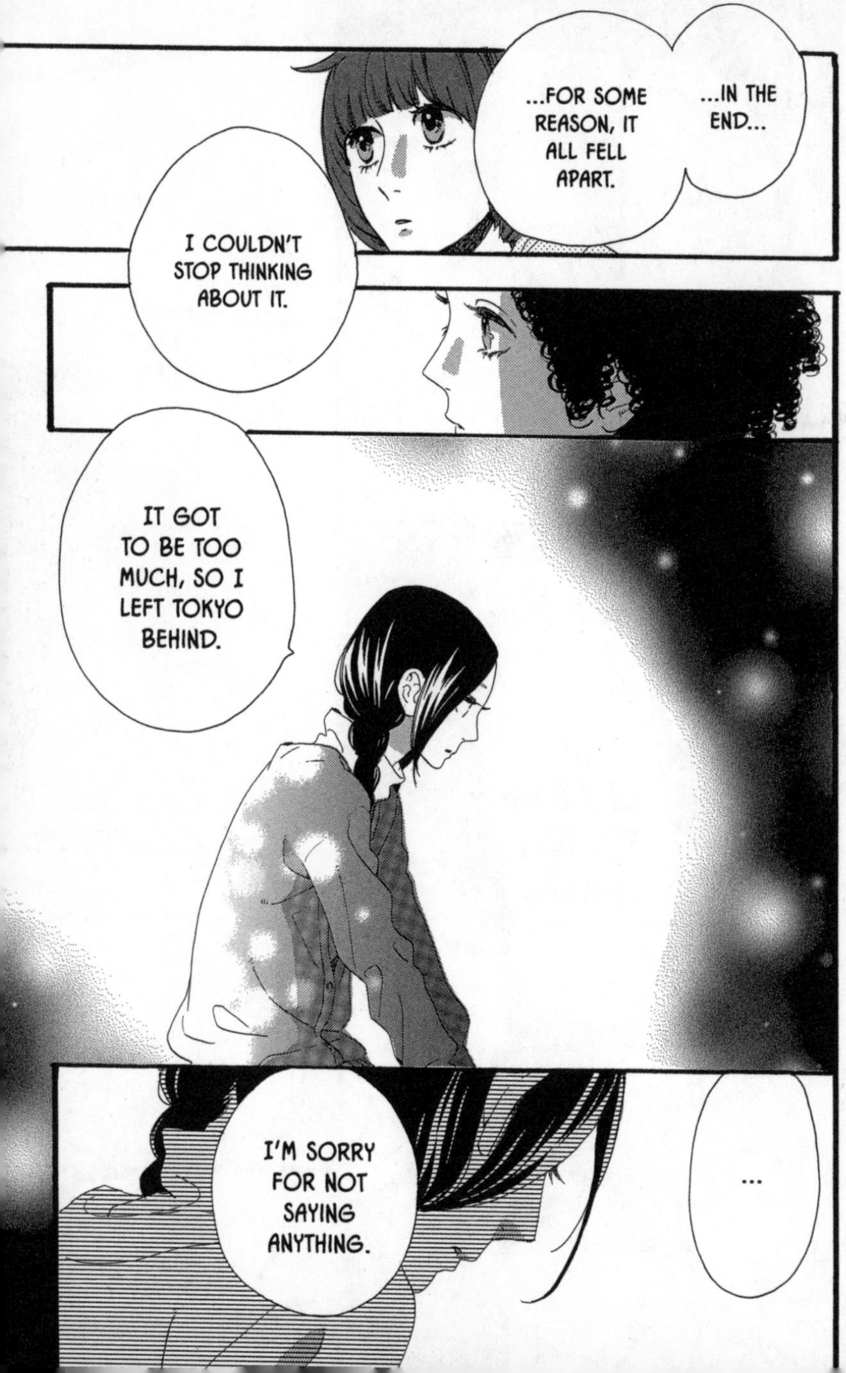
...IN THE END...
...FOR SOME REASON, IT ALL FELL APART.
I COULDN'T STOP THINKING ABOUT IT.
IT GOT TO BE TOO MUCH, SO I LEFT TOKYO BEHIND.
...
I'M SORRY FOR NOT SAYING ANYTHING.

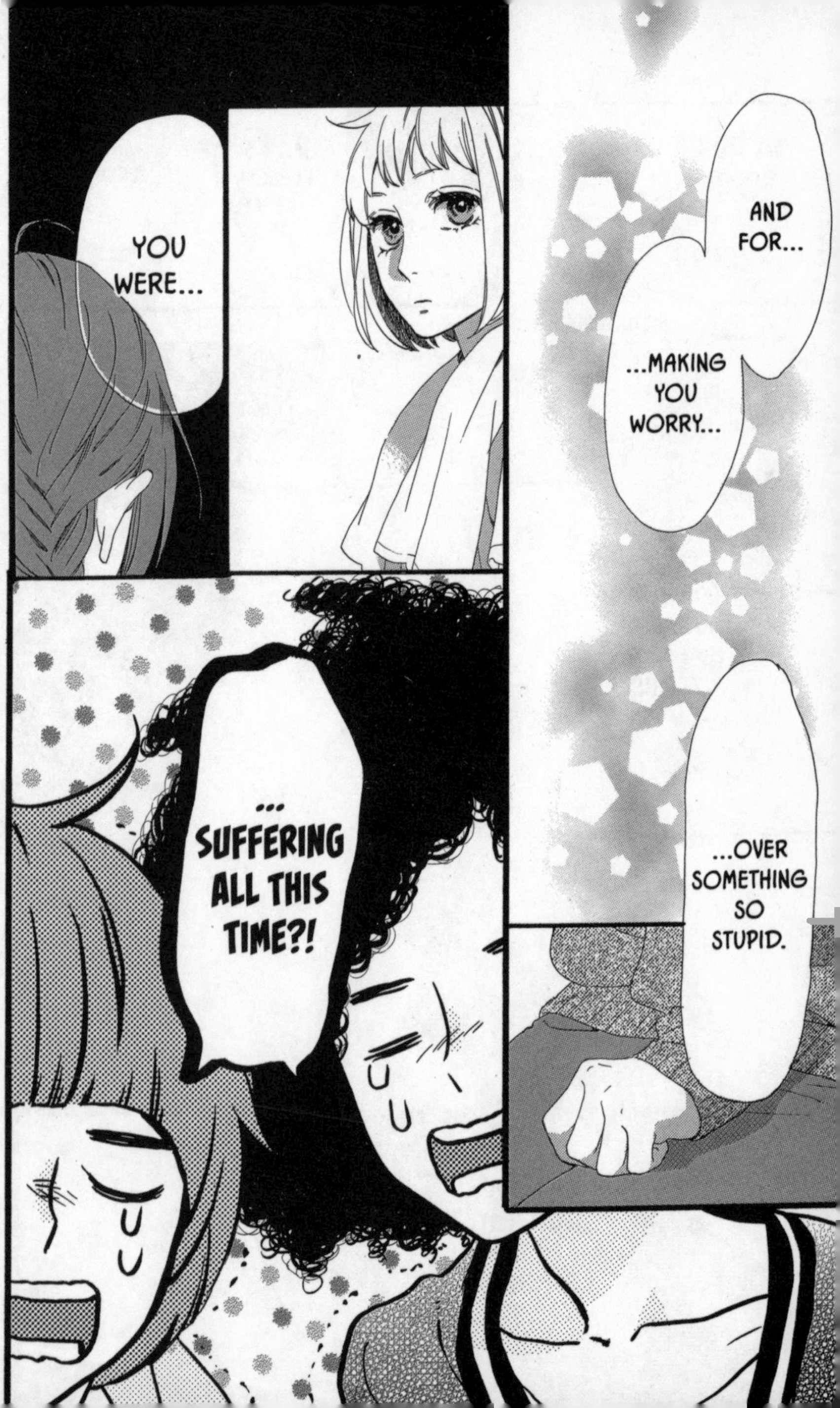
AND FOR...
...MAKING YOU WORRY...
...OVER SOMETHING SO STUPID.
YOU WERE...
...SUFFERING ALL THIS TIME?!

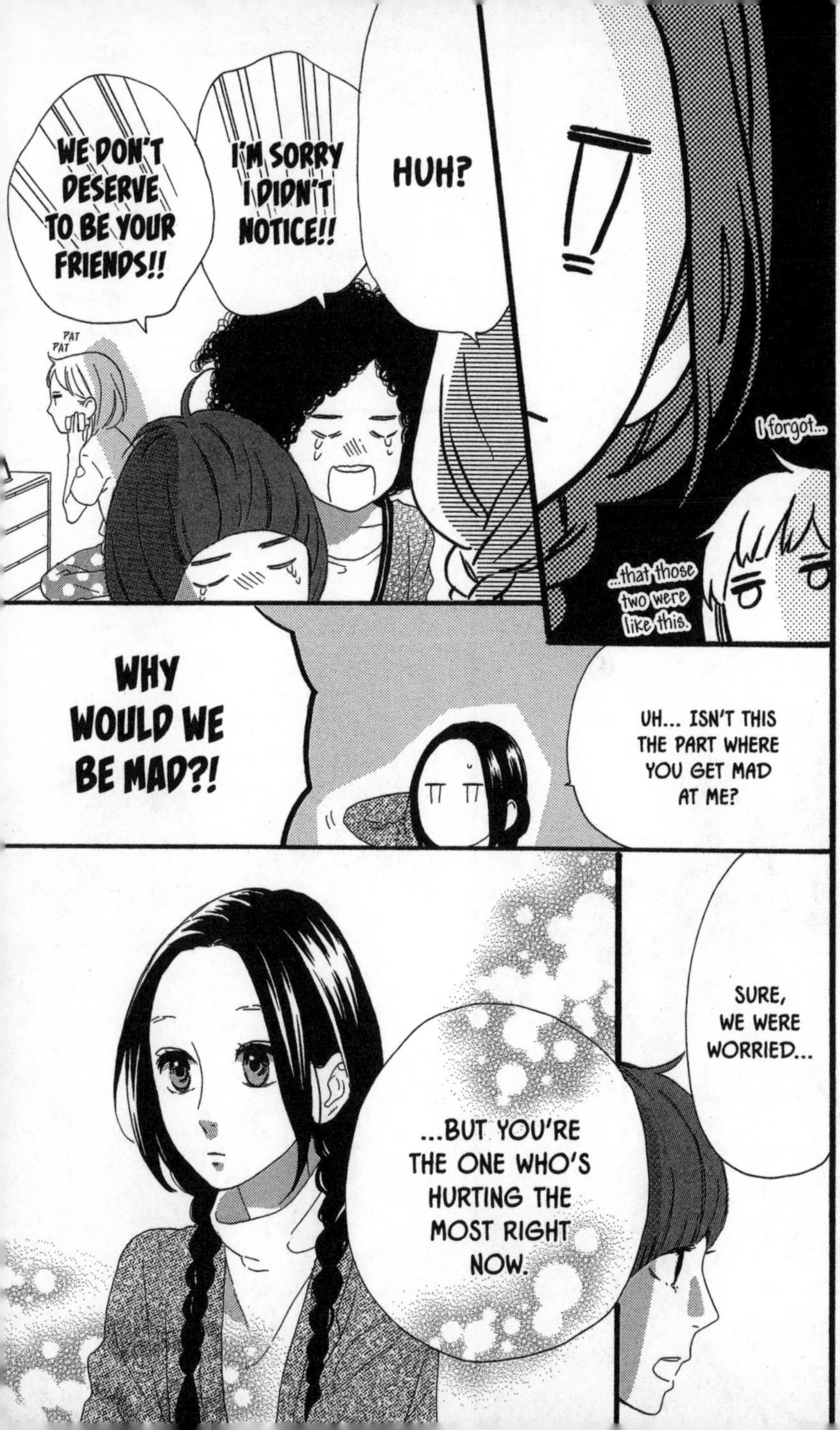
HUH?
I'M SORRY I DIDN'T NOTICE!!
WE DON'T DESERVE TO BE YOUR FRIENDS!!
PAT PAT
I forgot...
...that those two were like this.
UH... ISN'T THIS THE PART WHERE YOU GET MAD AT ME?
WHY WOULD WE BE MAD?!
SURE, WE WERE WORRIED...
...BUT YOU'RE THE ONE WHO'S HURTING THE MOST RIGHT NOW.

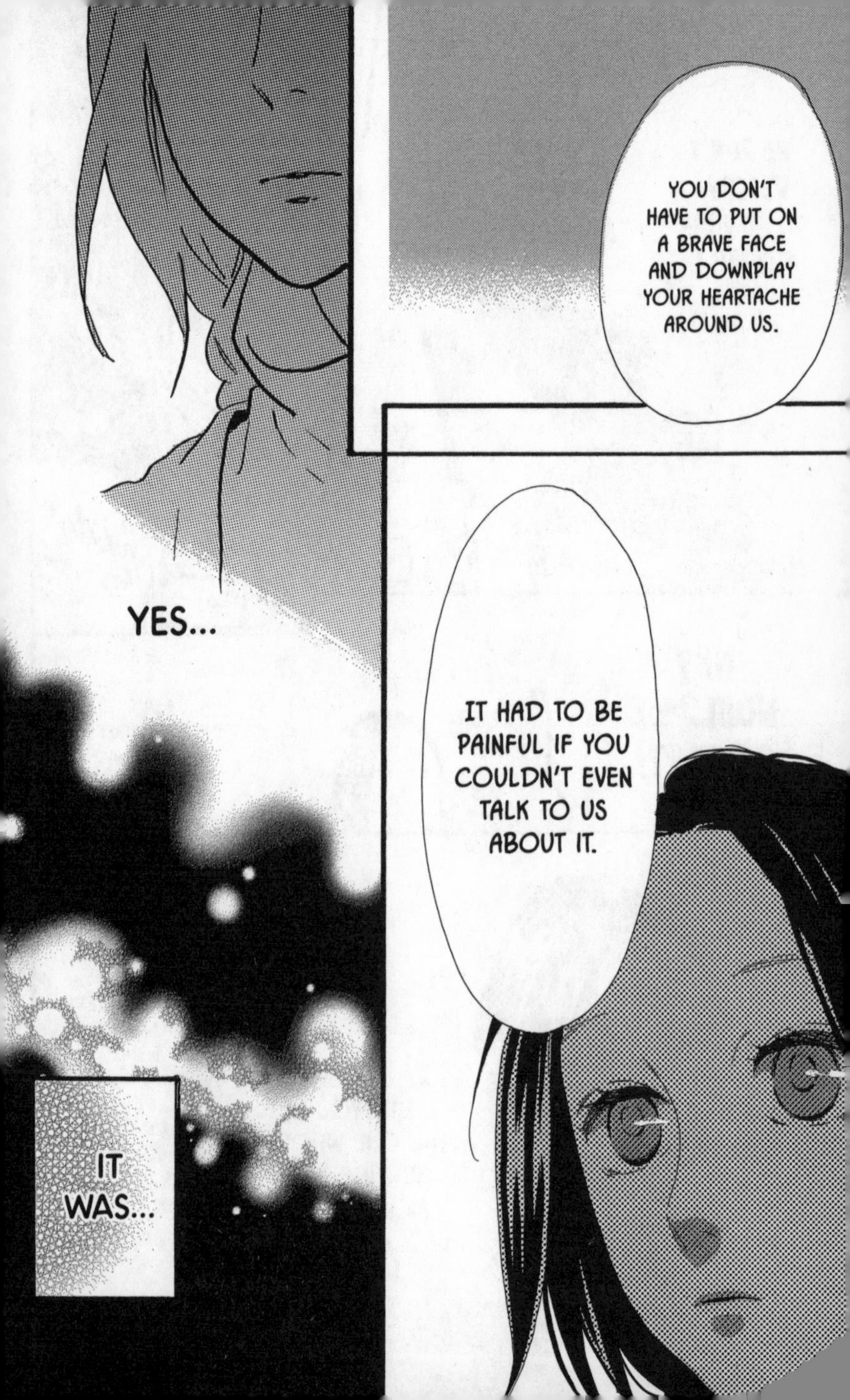
YOU DON'T HAVE TO PUT ON A BRAVE FACE AND DOWNPLAY YOUR HEARTACHE AROUND US.
IT HAD TO BE PAINFUL IF YOU COULDN'T EVEN TALK TO US ABOUT IT.
YES...
IT WAS...

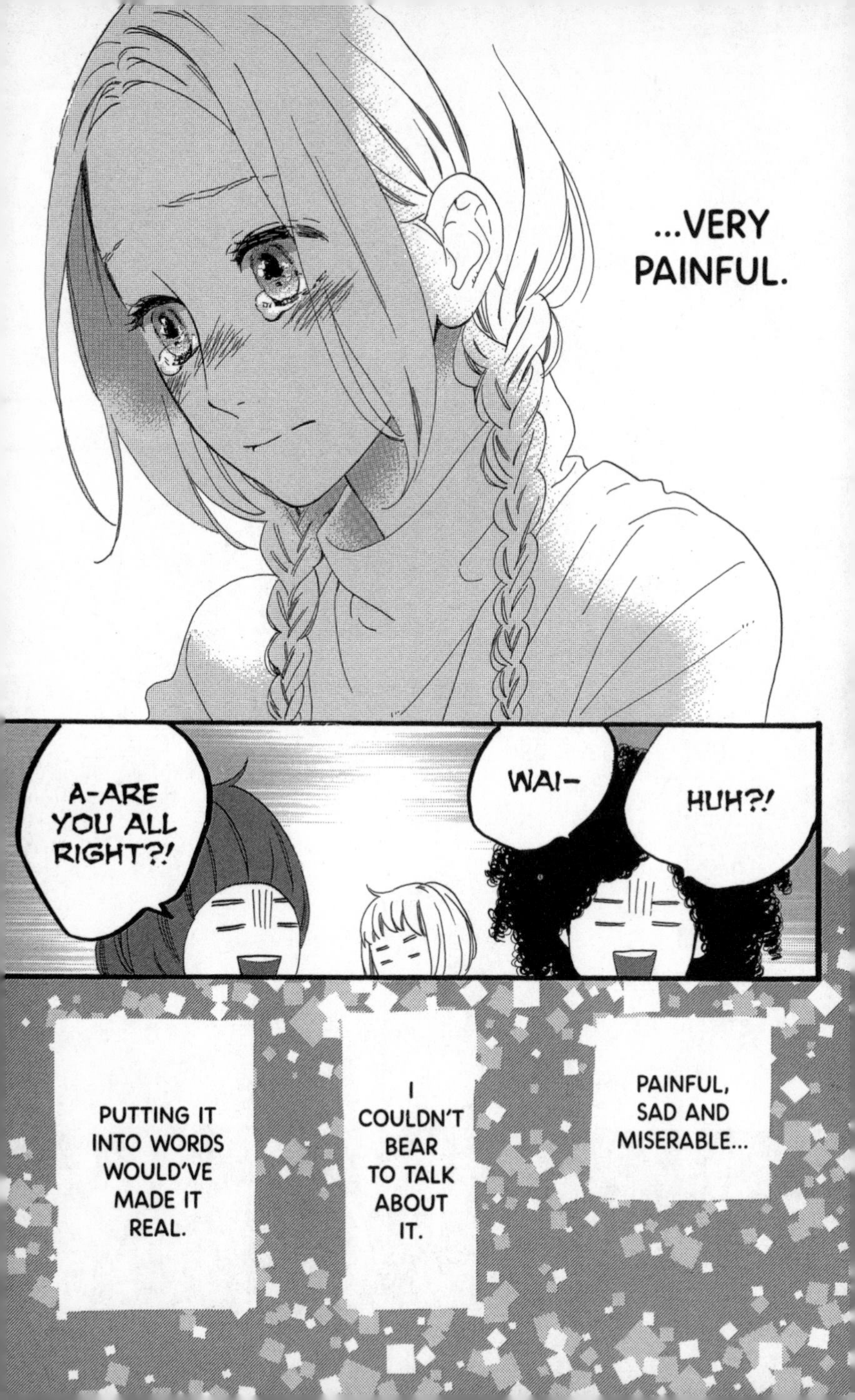
...VERY PAINFUL.
HUH?!
WAI-
A-ARE YOU ALL RIGHT?!
PAINFUL, SAD AND MISERABLE...
I COULDN'T BEAR TO TALK ABOUT IT.
PUTTING IT INTO WORDS WOULD'VE MADE IT REAL.

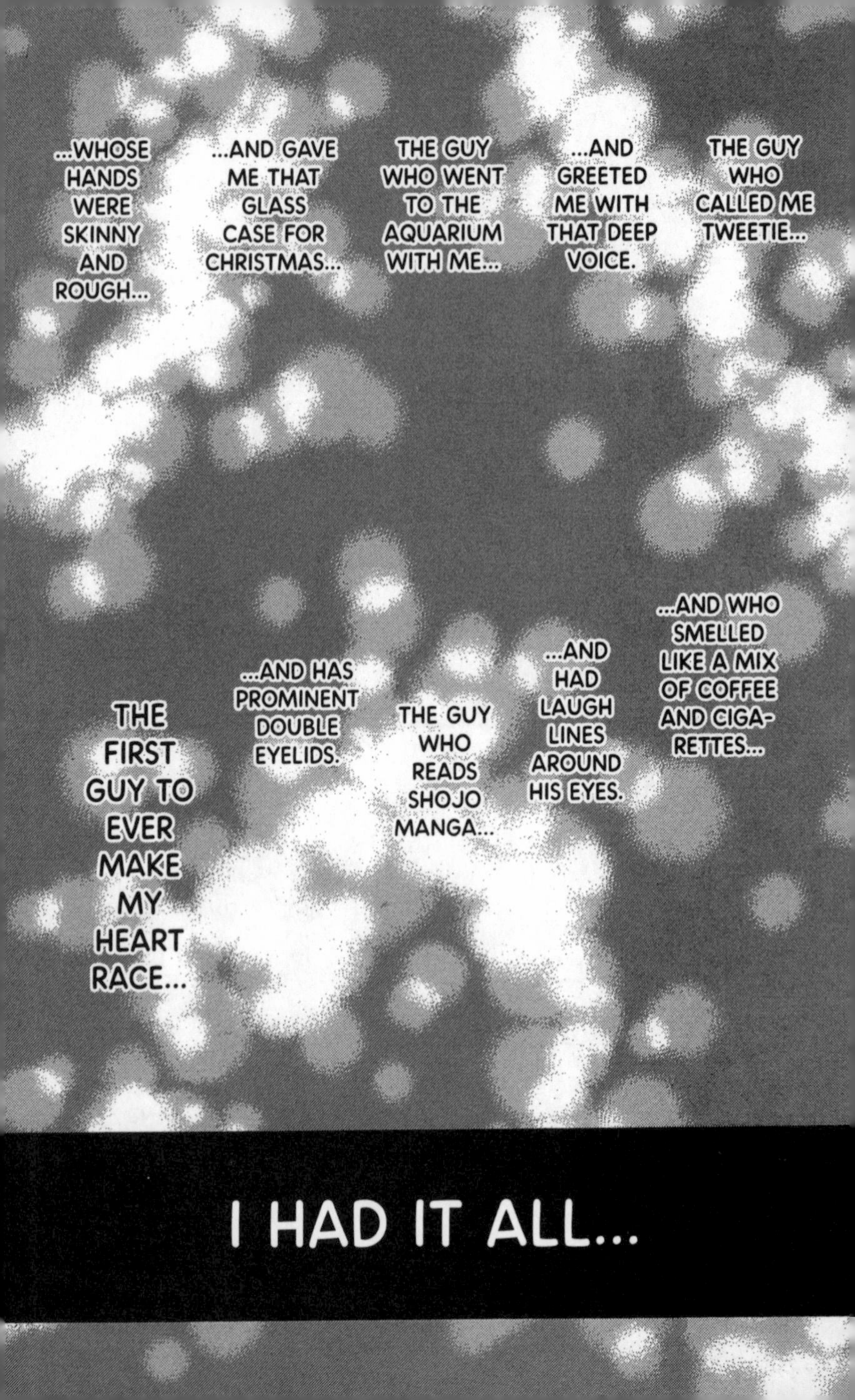
THE GUY WHO CALLED ME TWEETIE...
...AND GREETED ME WITH THAT DEEP VOICE.
THE GUY WHO WENT TO THE AQUARIUM WITH ME...
...AND GAVE ME THAT GLASS CASE FOR CHRISTMAS...
...WHOSE HANDS WERE SKINNY AND ROUGH...
...AND WHO SMELLED LIKE A MIX OF COFFEE AND CIGA-RETTES...
...AND HAD LAUGH LINES AROUND HIS EYES.
THE GUY WHO READS SHOJO MANGA...
...AND HAS PROMINENT DOUBLE EYELIDS.
THE FIRST GUY TO EVER MAKE MY HEART RACE...
I HAD IT ALL...

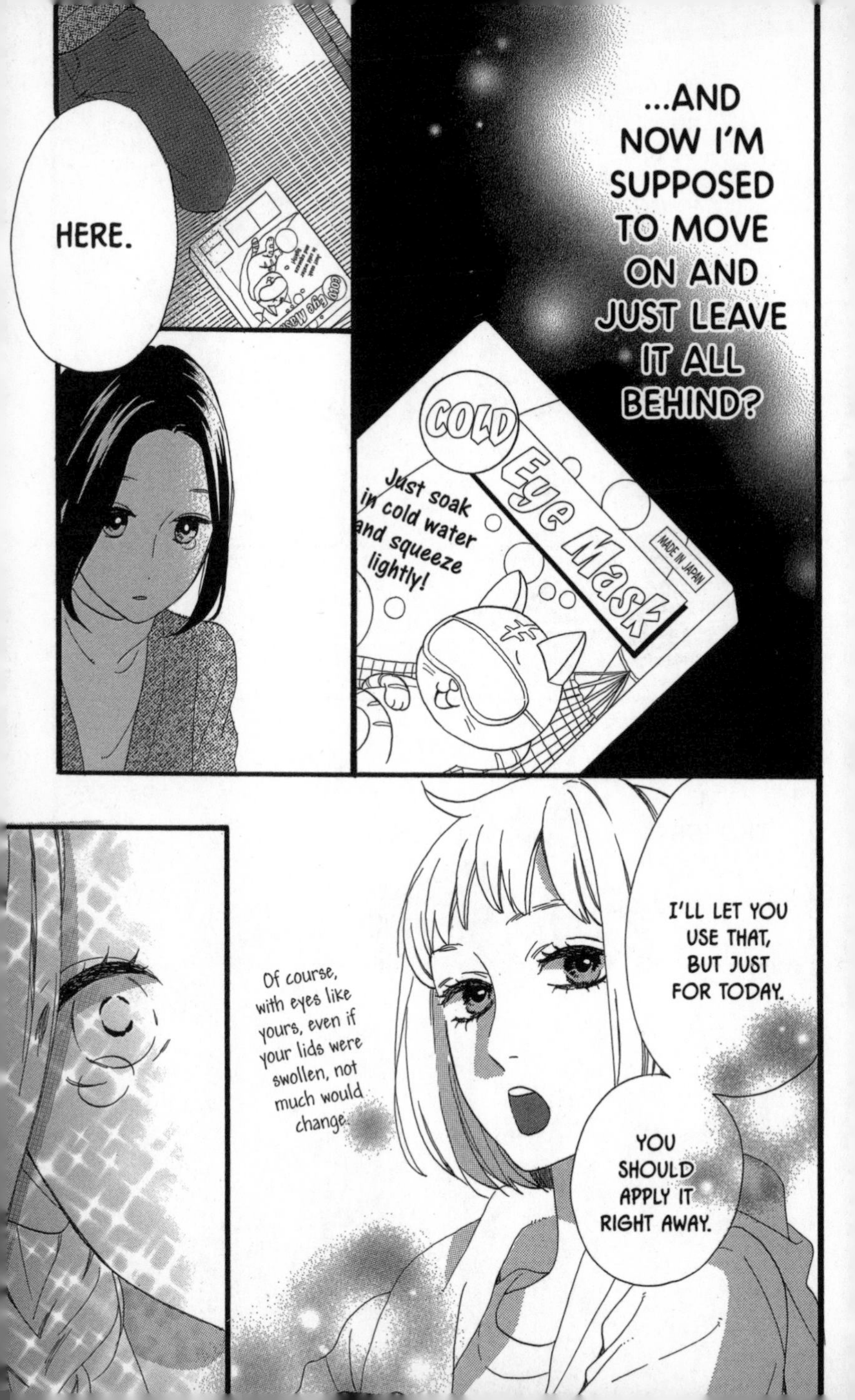
...AND NOW I'M SUPPOSED TO MOVE ON AND JUST LEAVE IT ALL BEHIND?
COLD
Eye Mask
Just soak in cold water and squeeze lightly!
MADE IN JAPAN
HERE.
I'LL LET YOU USE THAT, BUT JUST FOR TODAY.
YOU SHOULD APPLY IT RIGHT AWAY.
Of course, with eyes like yours, even if your lids were swollen, not much would change.

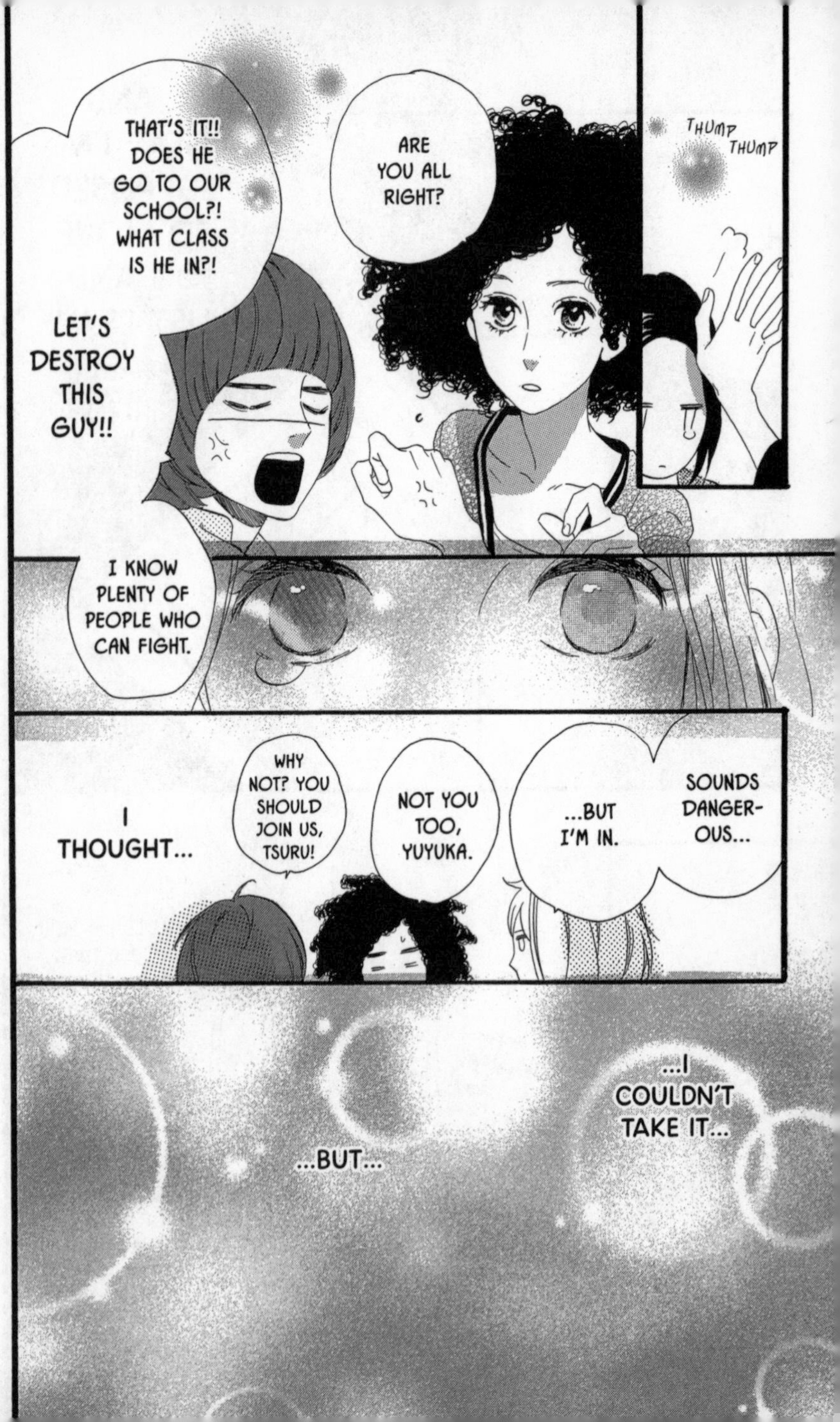
THUMP THUMP
ARE YOU ALL RIGHT?
THAT'S IT!! DOES HE GO TO OUR SCHOOL?! WHAT CLASS IS HE IN?!
LET'S DESTROY THIS GUY!!
I KNOW PLENTY OF PEOPLE WHO CAN FIGHT.
SOUNDS DANGER-OUS...
...BUT I'M IN.
NOT YOU TOO, YUYUKA.
WHY NOT? YOU SHOULD JOIN US, TSURU!
I THOUGHT...
...I COULDN'T TAKE IT...
...BUT...

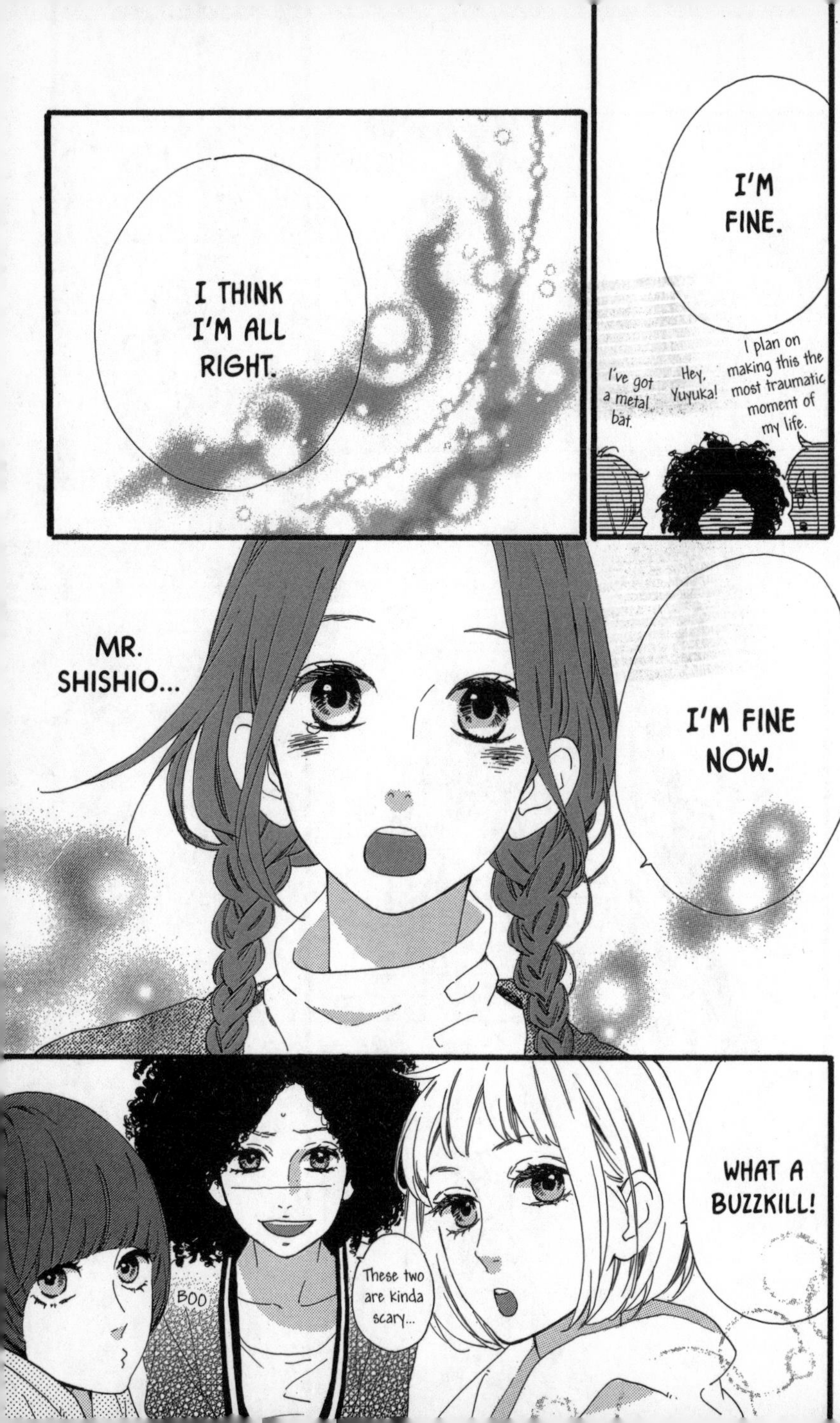
I'M FINE.
I plan on making this the most traumatic moment of my life.
Hey, Yuyuka!
I've got a metal bat.
I THINK I'M ALL RIGHT.
I'M FINE NOW.
MR. SHISHIO...
WHAT A BUZZKILL!
These two are kinda scary...
BOO

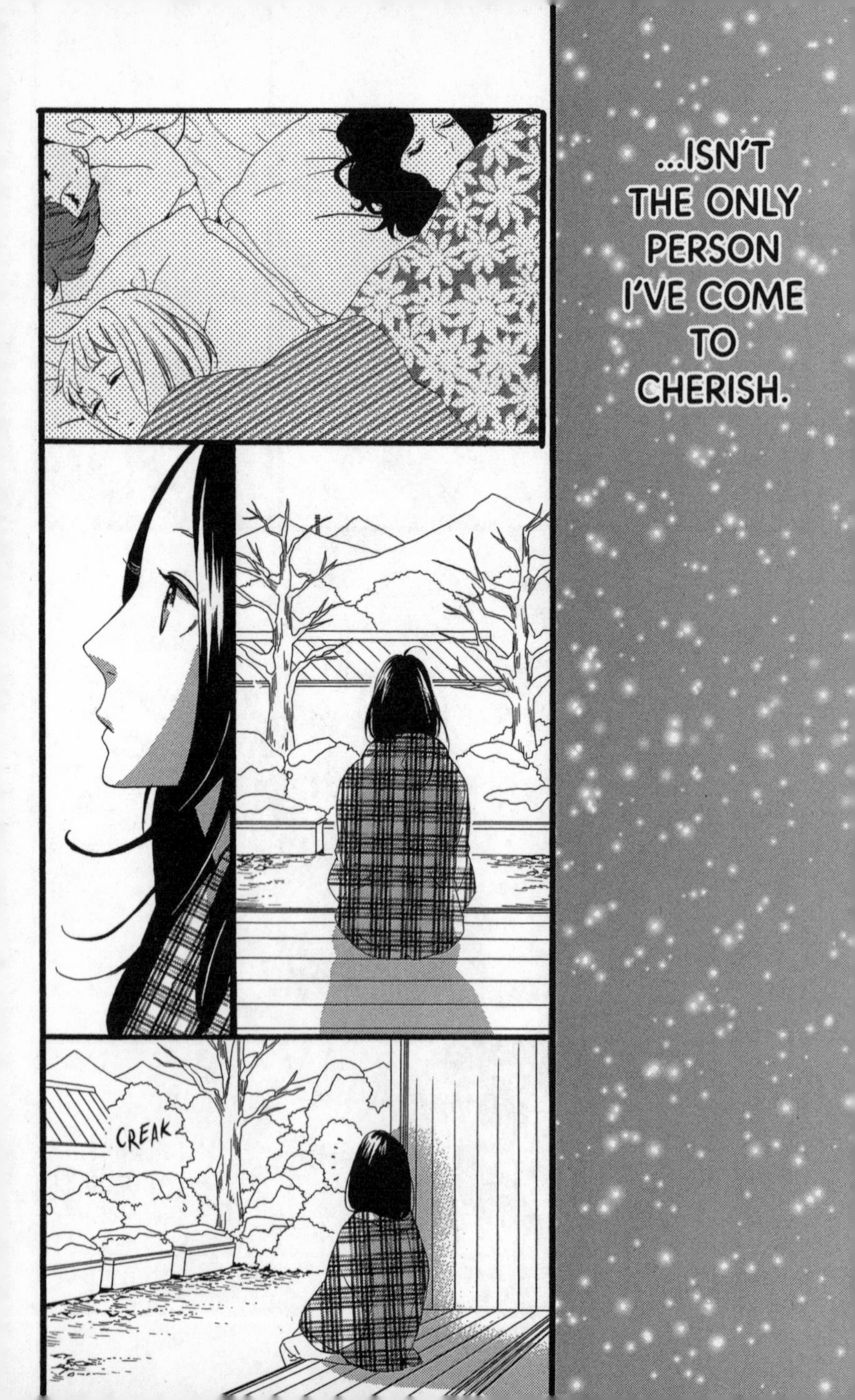
...ISN'T THE ONLY PERSON I'VE COME TO CHERISH.
CREAK
...

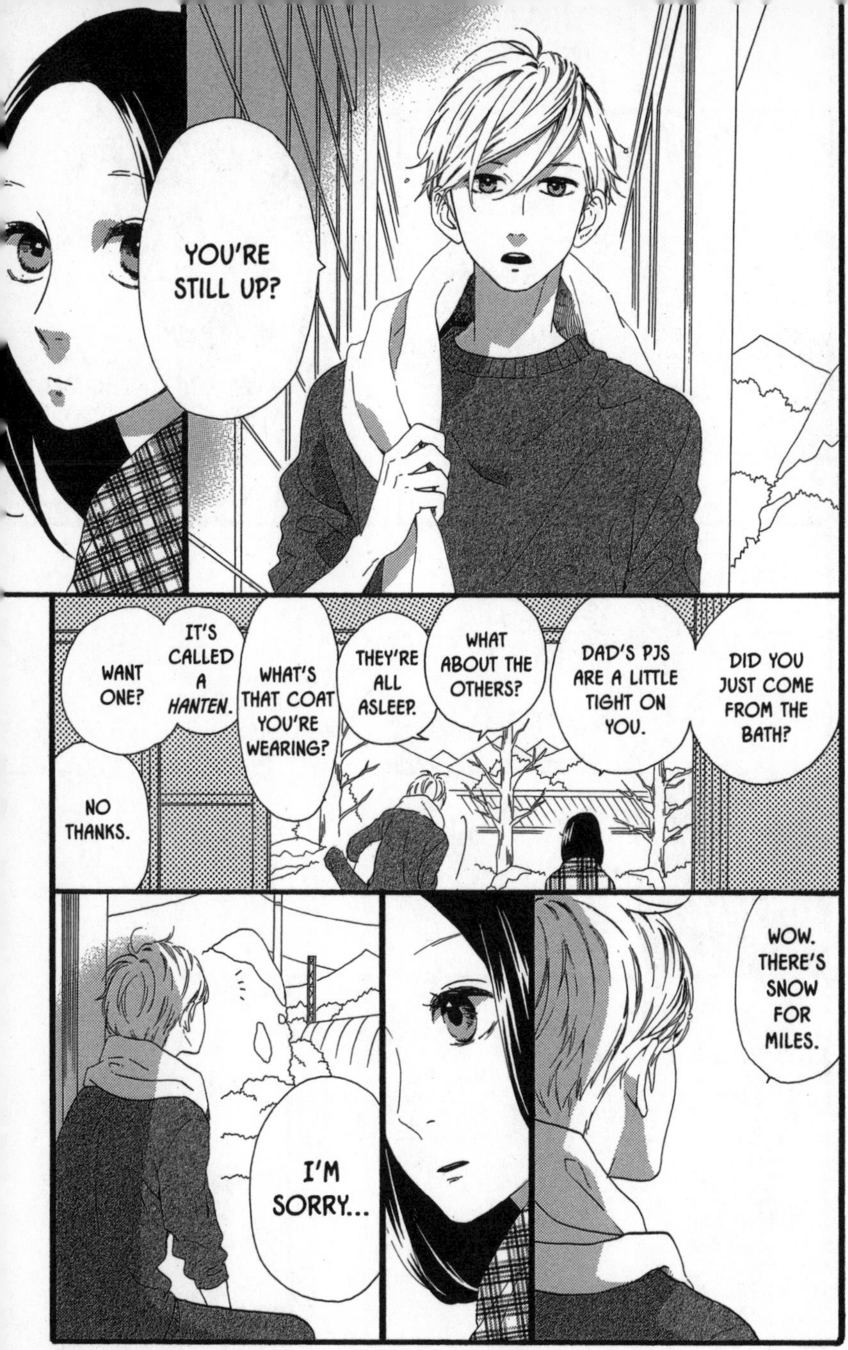
YOU'RE STILL UP?
DID YOU JUST COME FROM THE BATH?
DAD'S PJS ARE A LITTLE TIGHT ON YOU.
WHAT ABOUT THE OTHERS?
THEY'RE ALL ASLEEP.
WHAT'S THAT COAT YOU'RE WEARING?
IT'S CALLED A *HANTEN*.
WANT ONE?
NO THANKS.
WOW. THERE'S SNOW FOR MILES.
I'M SORRY...

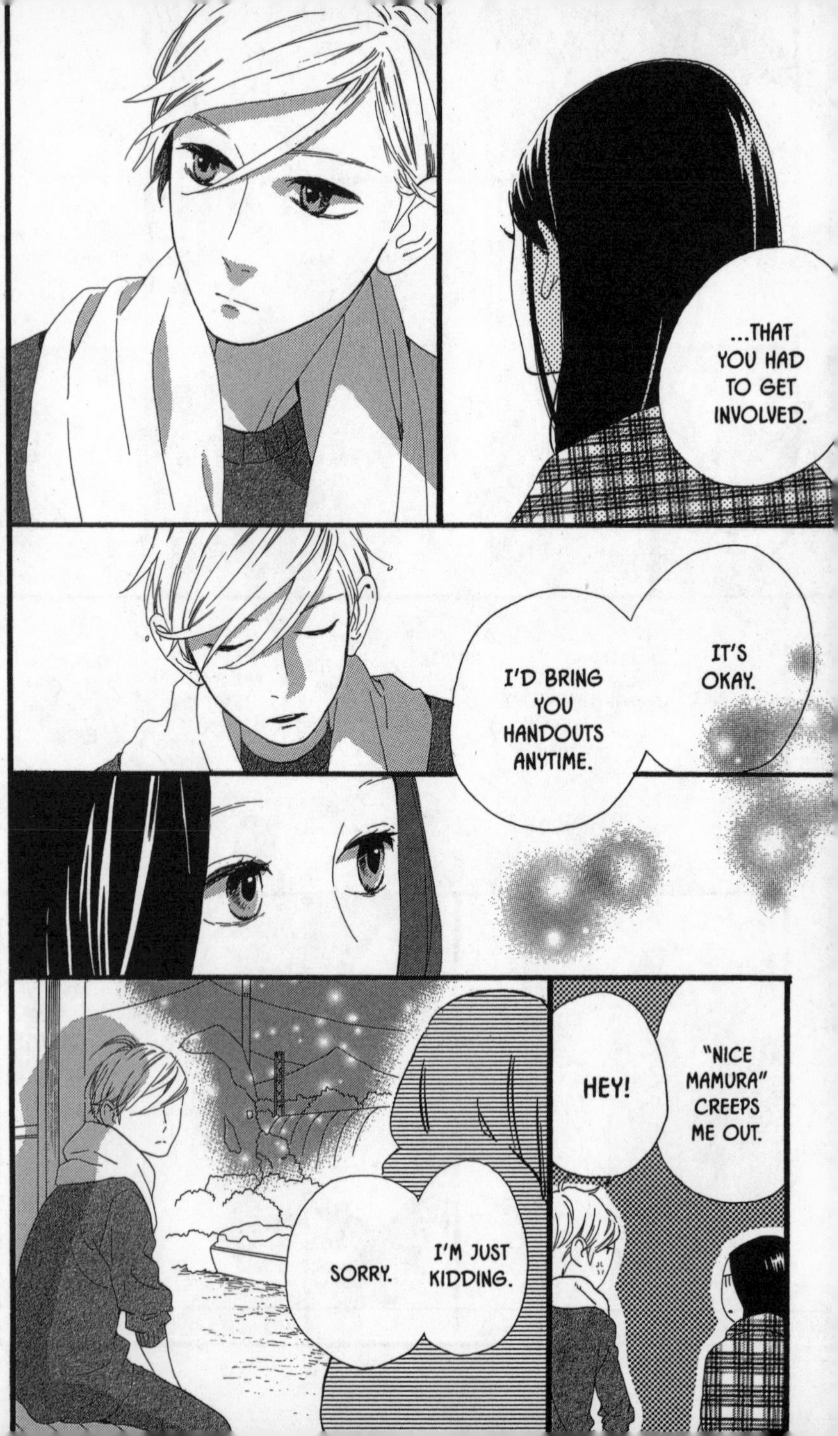
...THAT YOU HAD TO GET INVOLVED.
IT'S OKAY.
I'D BRING YOU HANDOUTS ANYTIME.
"NICE MAMURA" CREEPS ME OUT.
HEY!
I'M JUST KIDDING.
SORRY.

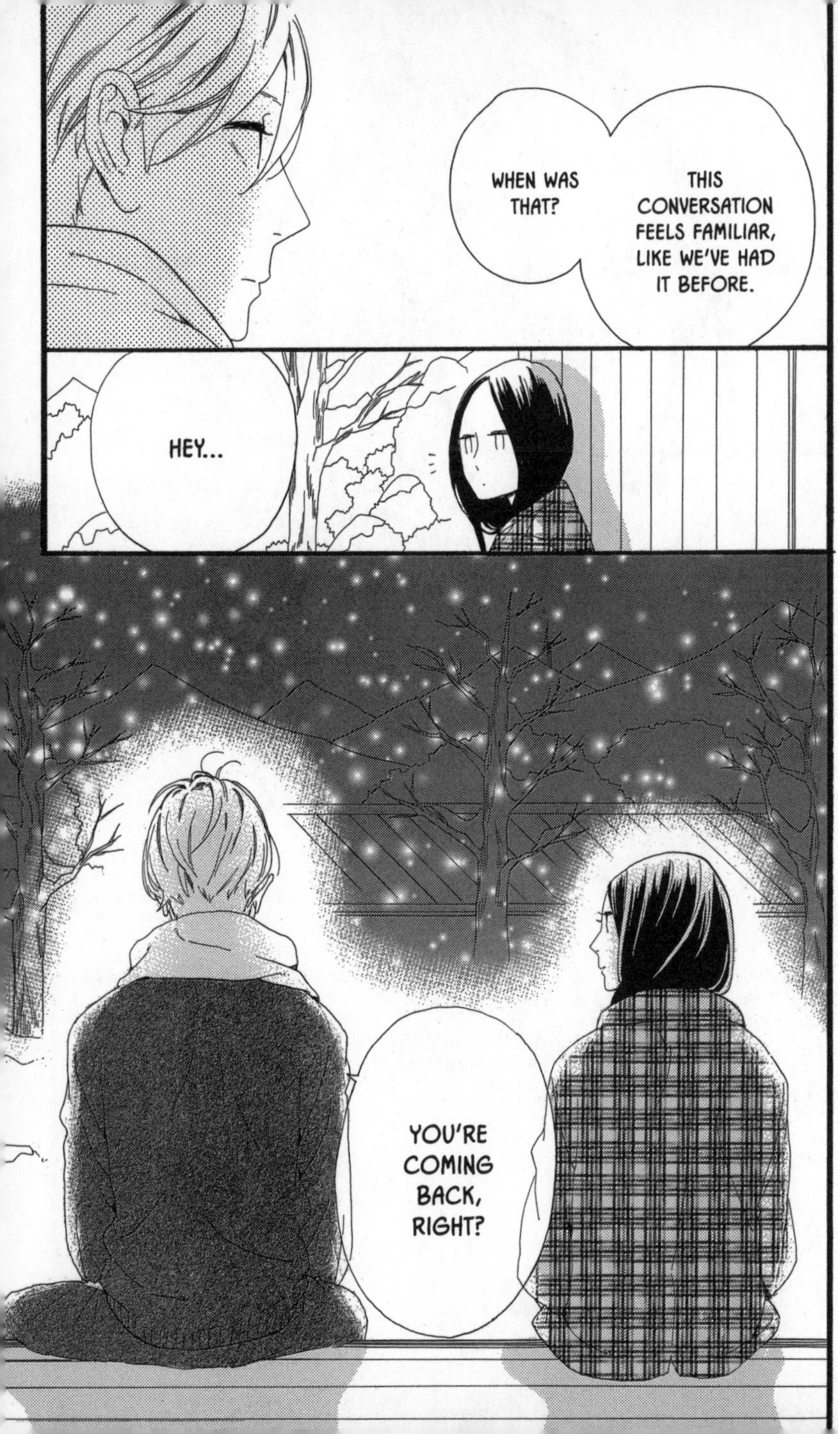
THIS CONVERSATION FEELS FAMILIAR, LIKE WE'VE HAD IT BEFORE.
WHEN WAS THAT?
HEY...
YOU'RE COMING BACK, RIGHT?

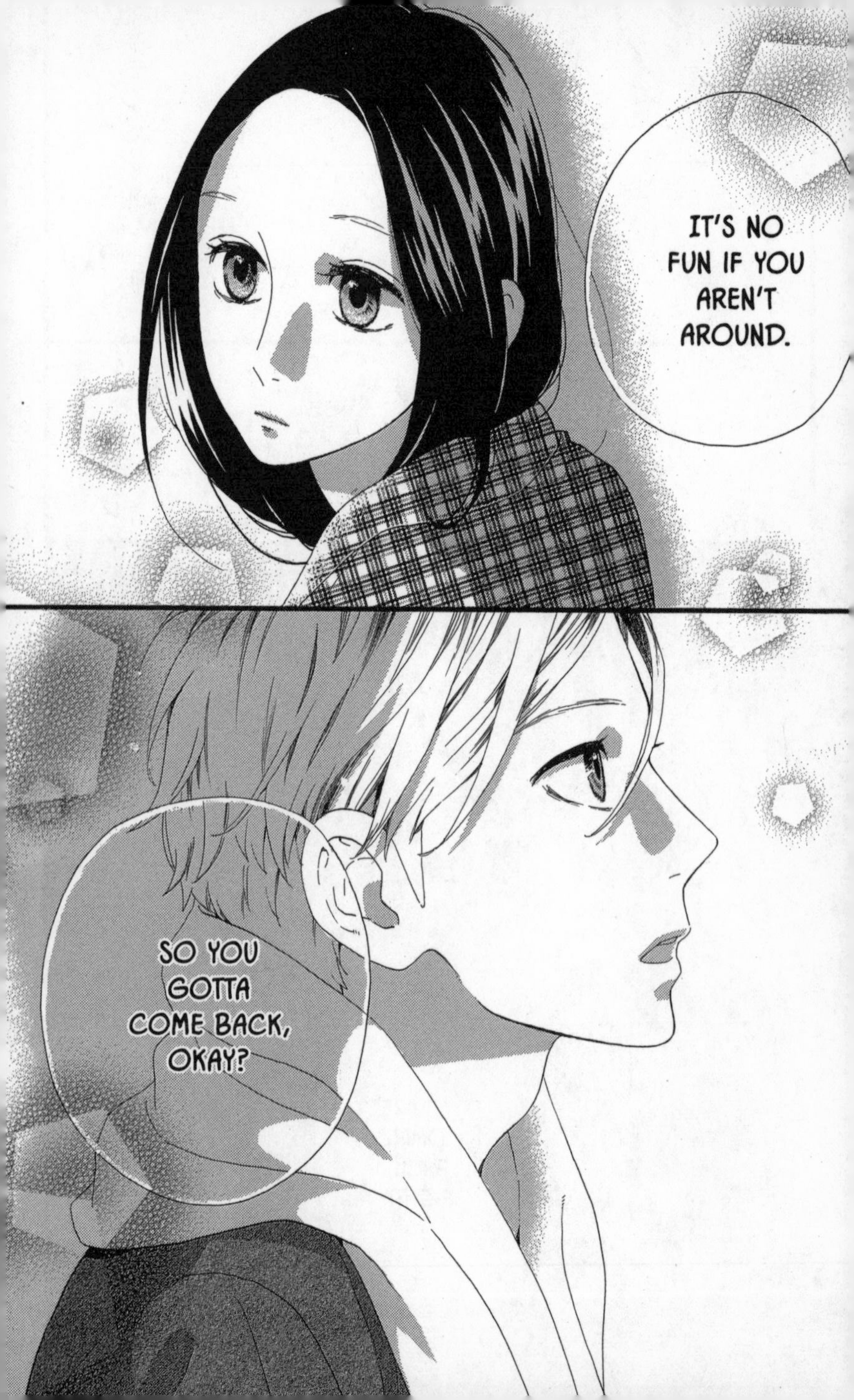
IT'S NO FUN IF YOU AREN'T AROUND.
SO YOU GOTTA COME BACK, OKAY?

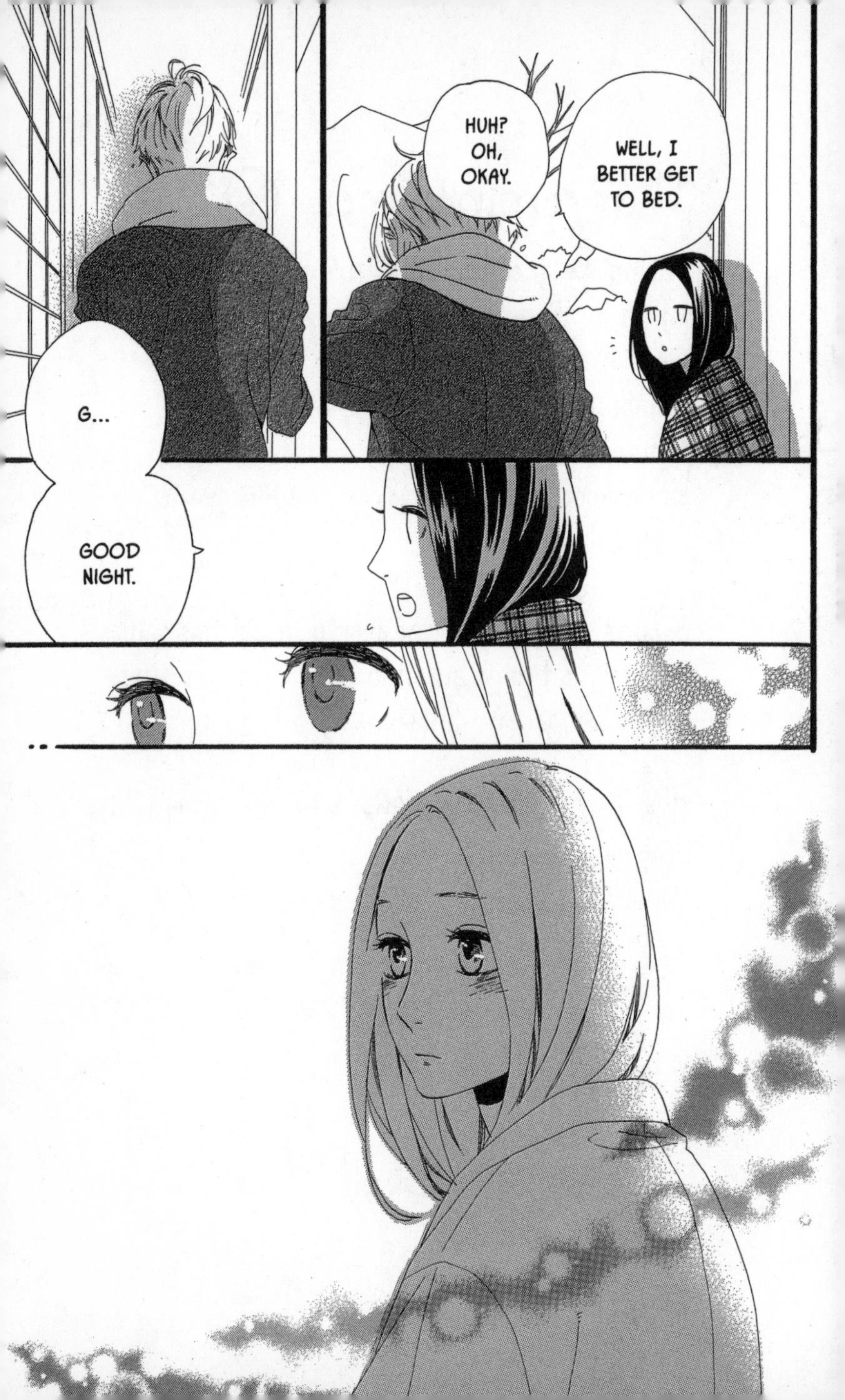
WELL, I BETTER GET TO BED.
HUH? OH, OKAY.
G... GOOD NIGHT.

That reminds me... ①

During the second half of this year, I dealt with a lot of health issues.
First of all, I'm anemic, so this summer I collapsed in the ladies room at the train station, which resulted in my first ever ambulance ride. (Thank you very much to those of you who helped me.)

Secondly, I had my first ever physical this fall!
(Next time I have an endoscopy, I'll make sure to ask for general anesthesia.)

This is just a reminder that a healthy body is the best kind of body!!
The exam I liked the most was the CT scan!

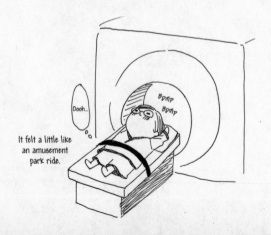

Oooh...

Bpmp
Bpmp

It felt a little like an amusement park ride.

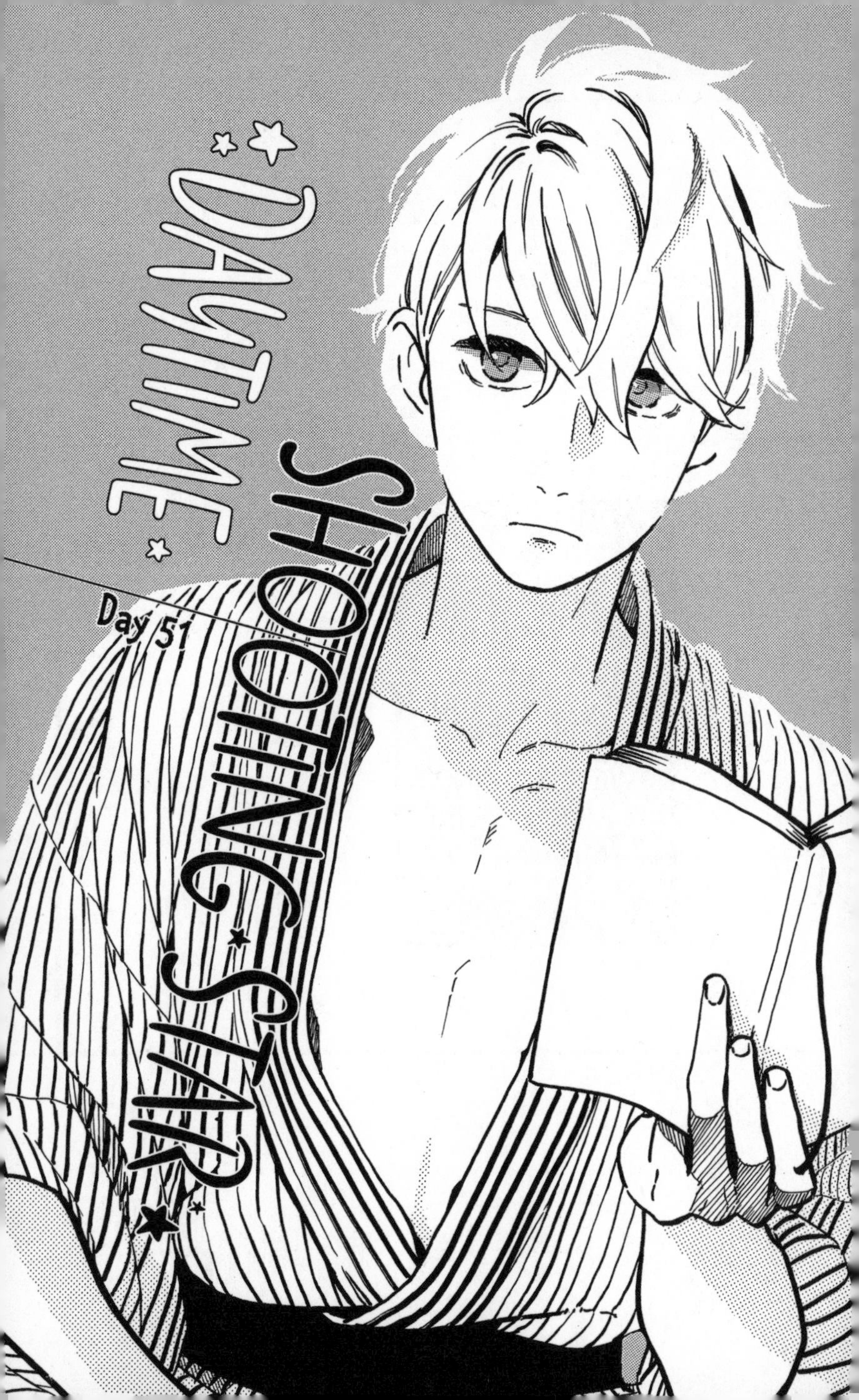
DAYTIME SHOOTING STAR
Day 51

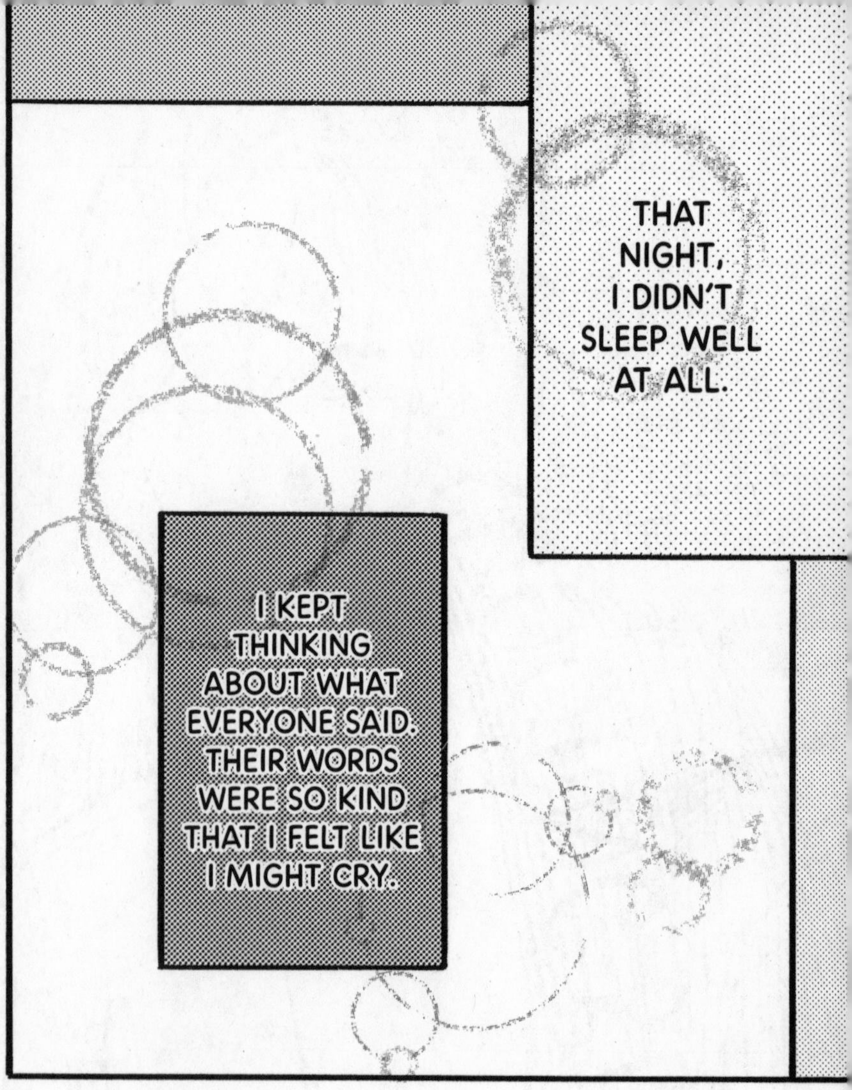
THAT NIGHT, I DIDN'T SLEEP WELL AT ALL.
I KEPT THINKING ABOUT WHAT EVERYONE SAID. THEIR WORDS WERE SO KIND THAT I FELT LIKE I MIGHT CRY.

DAYTIME SHOOTING STAR

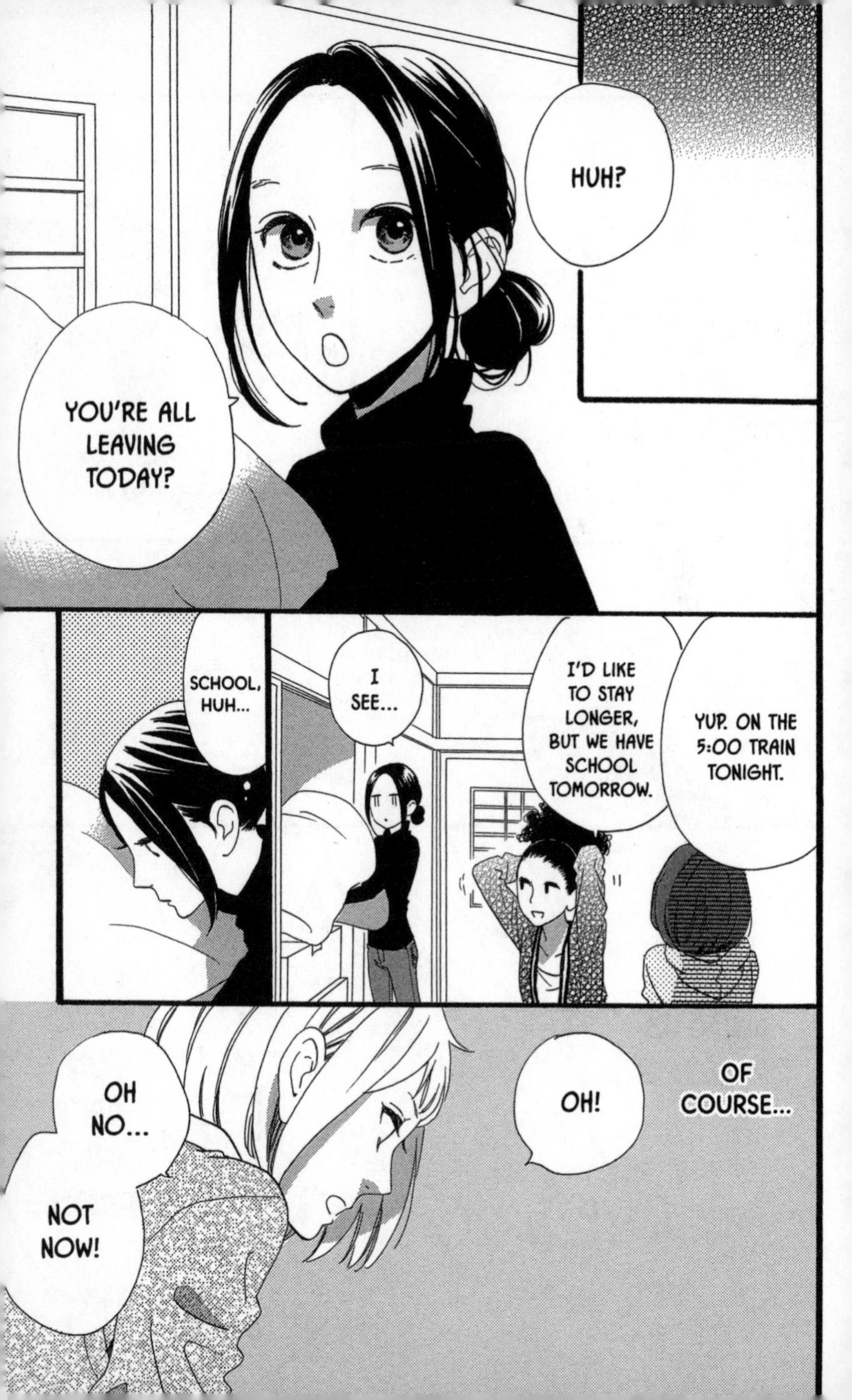
HUH?
YOU'RE ALL LEAVING TODAY?
YUP. ON THE 5:00 TRAIN TONIGHT.
I'D LIKE TO STAY LONGER, BUT WE HAVE SCHOOL TOMORROW.
I SEE...
SCHOOL, HUH...
OF COURSE...
OH!
OH NO...
NOT NOW!

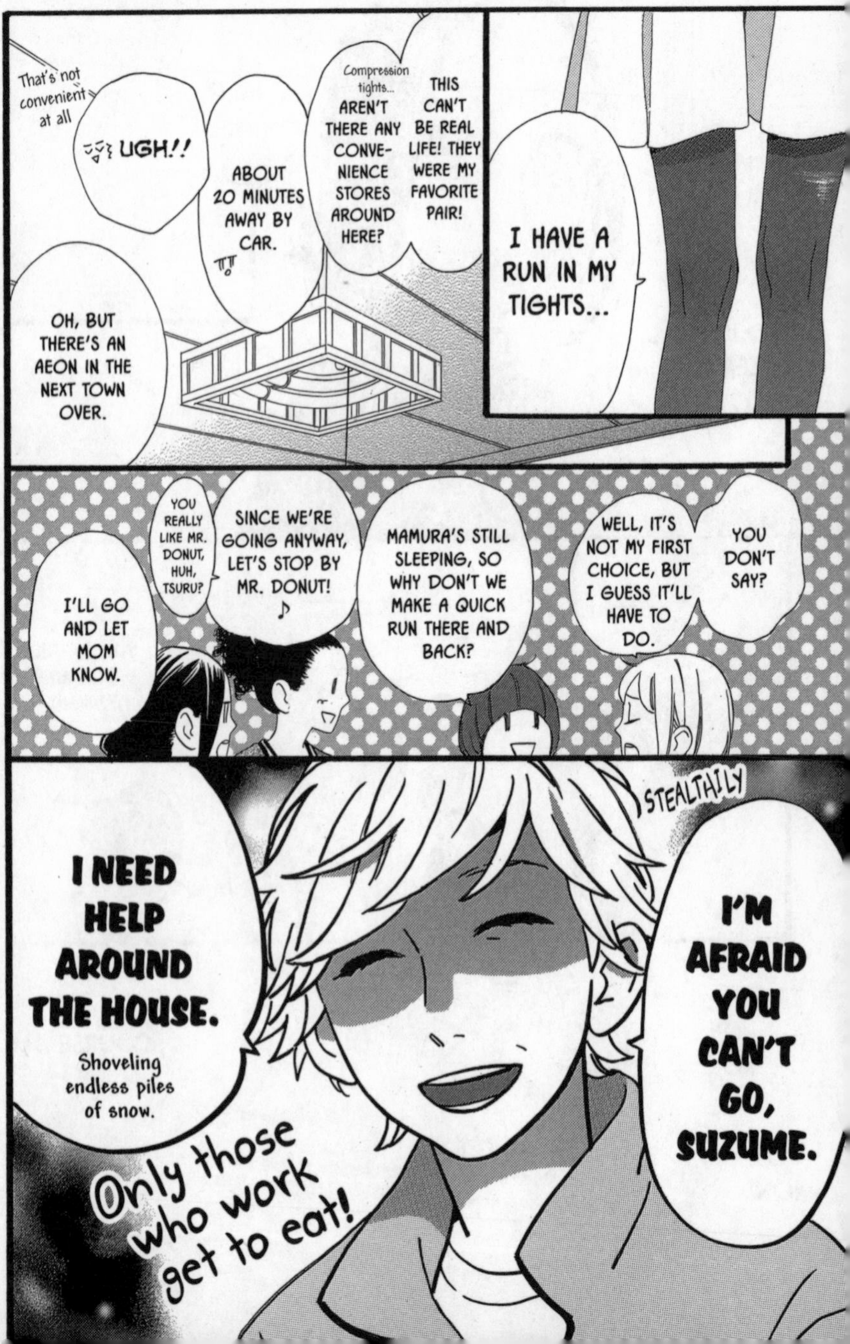
I HAVE A RUN IN MY TIGHTS...
THIS CAN'T BE REAL LIFE! THEY WERE MY FAVORITE PAIR!
Compression tights...
AREN'T THERE ANY CONVENIENCE STORES AROUND HERE?
ABOUT 20 MINUTES AWAY BY CAR.
UGH!!
That's not convenient at all
OH, BUT THERE'S AN AEON IN THE NEXT TOWN OVER.
YOU DON'T SAY?
WELL, IT'S NOT MY FIRST CHOICE, BUT I GUESS IT'LL HAVE TO DO.
MAMURA'S STILL SLEEPING, SO WHY DON'T WE MAKE A QUICK RUN THERE AND BACK?
SINCE WE'RE GOING ANYWAY, LET'S STOP BY MR. DONUT! ♪
YOU REALLY LIKE MR. DONUT, HUH, TSURU?
I'LL GO AND LET MOM KNOW.
STEALTHILY
I'M AFRAID YOU CAN'T GO, SUZUME.
I NEED HELP AROUND THE HOUSE.
Shoveling endless piles of snow.
Only those who work get to eat!

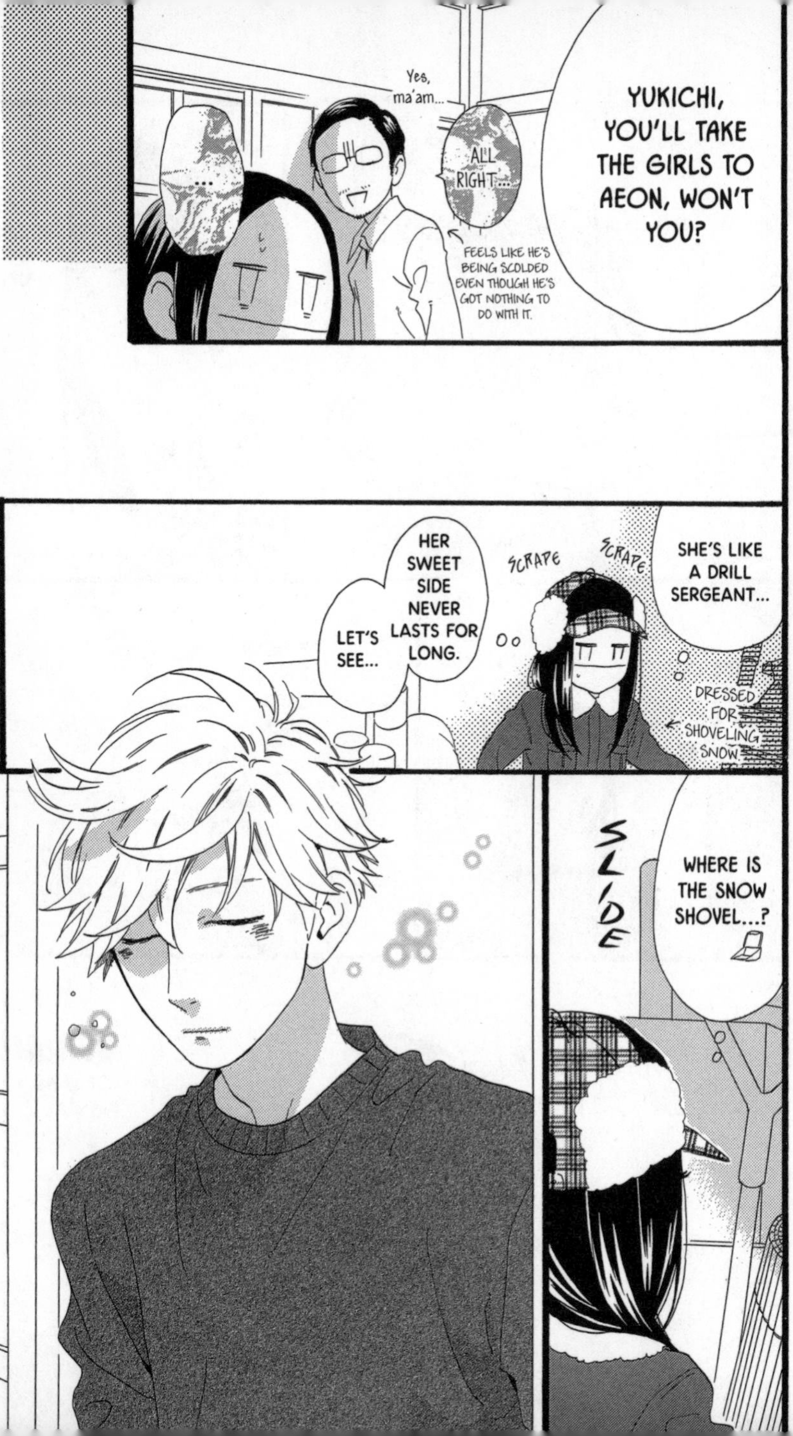
YUKICHI, YOU'LL TAKE THE GIRLS TO AEON, WON'T YOU?
ALL RIGHT...
Yes, ma'am...
FEELS LIKE HE'S BEING SCOLDED EVEN THOUGH HE'S GOT NOTHING TO DO WITH IT.
...
SHE'S LIKE A DRILL SERGEANT...
DRESSED FOR SHOVELING SNOW
SCRAPE
SCRAPE
HER SWEET SIDE NEVER LASTS FOR LONG.
LET'S SEE...
WHERE IS THE SNOW SHOVEL...?
SLIDE

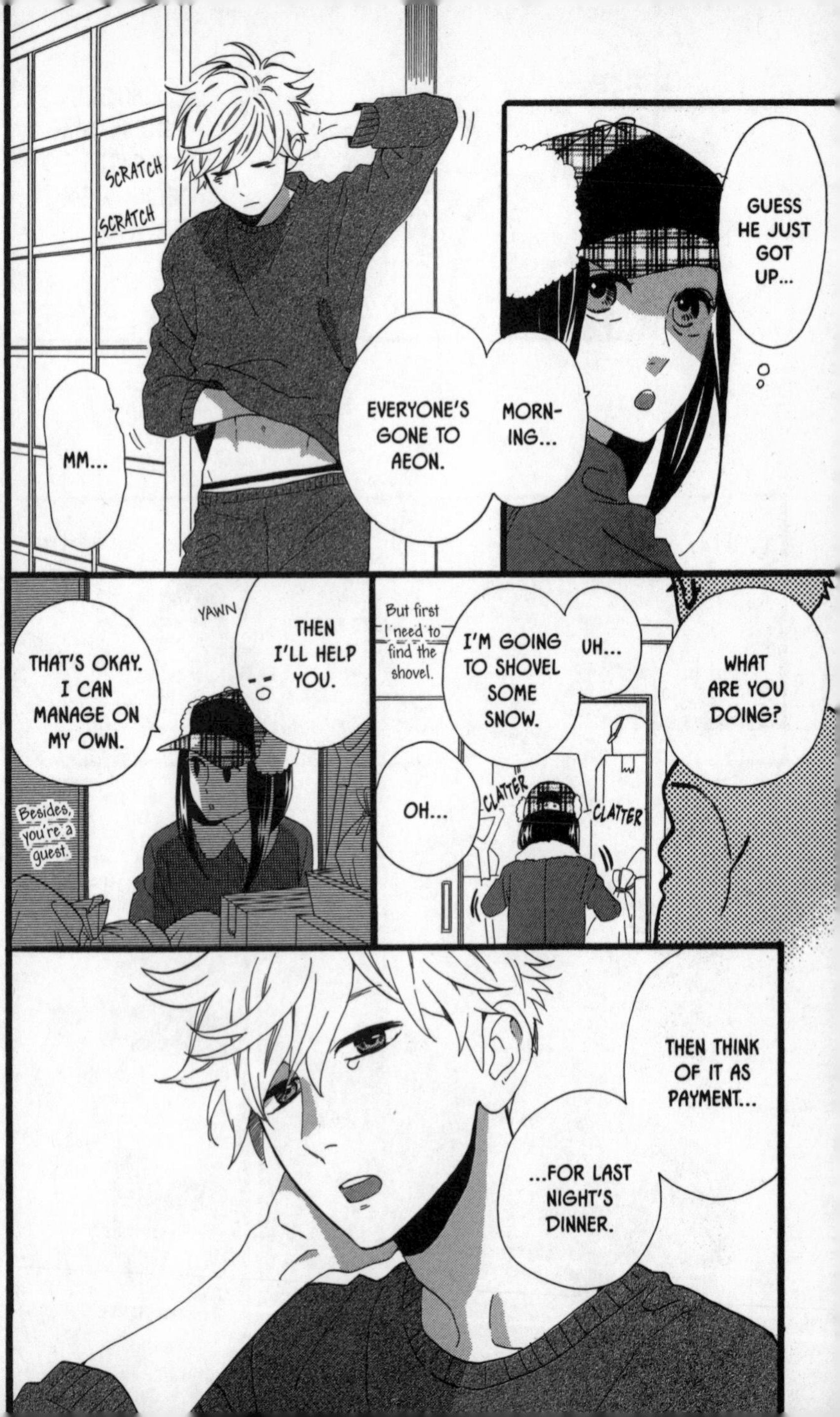
GUESS HE JUST GOT UP...
SCRATCH
SCRATCH
MORN-ING...
EVERYONE'S GONE TO AEON.
MM...
WHAT ARE YOU DOING?
UH...
I'M GOING TO SHOVEL SOME SNOW.
But first I need to find the shovel.
CLATTER
CLATTER
OH...
YAWN
THEN I'LL HELP YOU.
THAT'S OKAY. I CAN MANAGE ON MY OWN.
Besides, you're a guest.
THEN THINK OF IT AS PAYMENT...
...FOR LAST NIGHT'S DINNER.

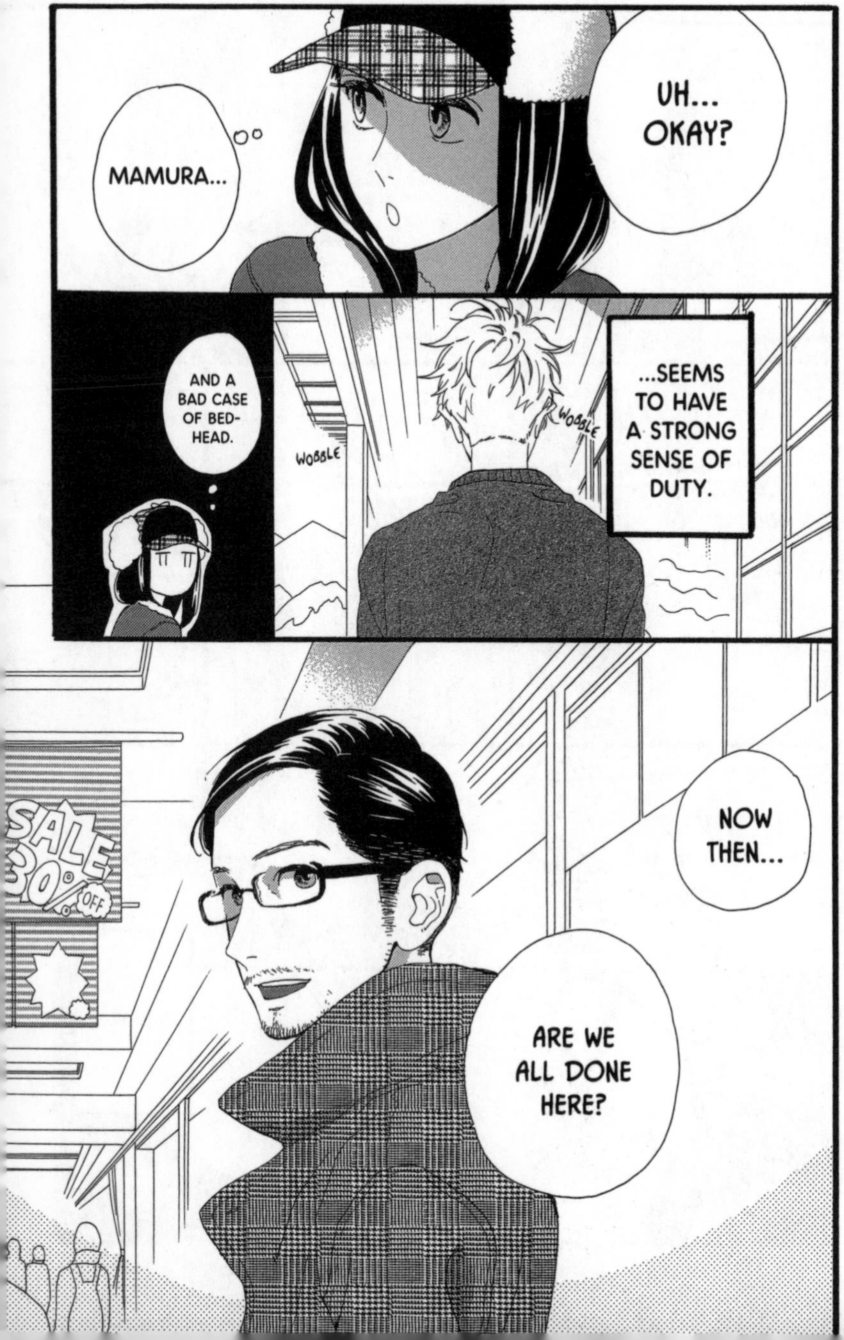
UH... OKAY?
MAMURA...
...SEEMS TO HAVE A STRONG SENSE OF DUTY.
WOBBLE
WOBBLE
AND A BAD CASE OF BED-HEAD.
NOW THEN...
ARE WE ALL DONE HERE?
SALE 30% OFF

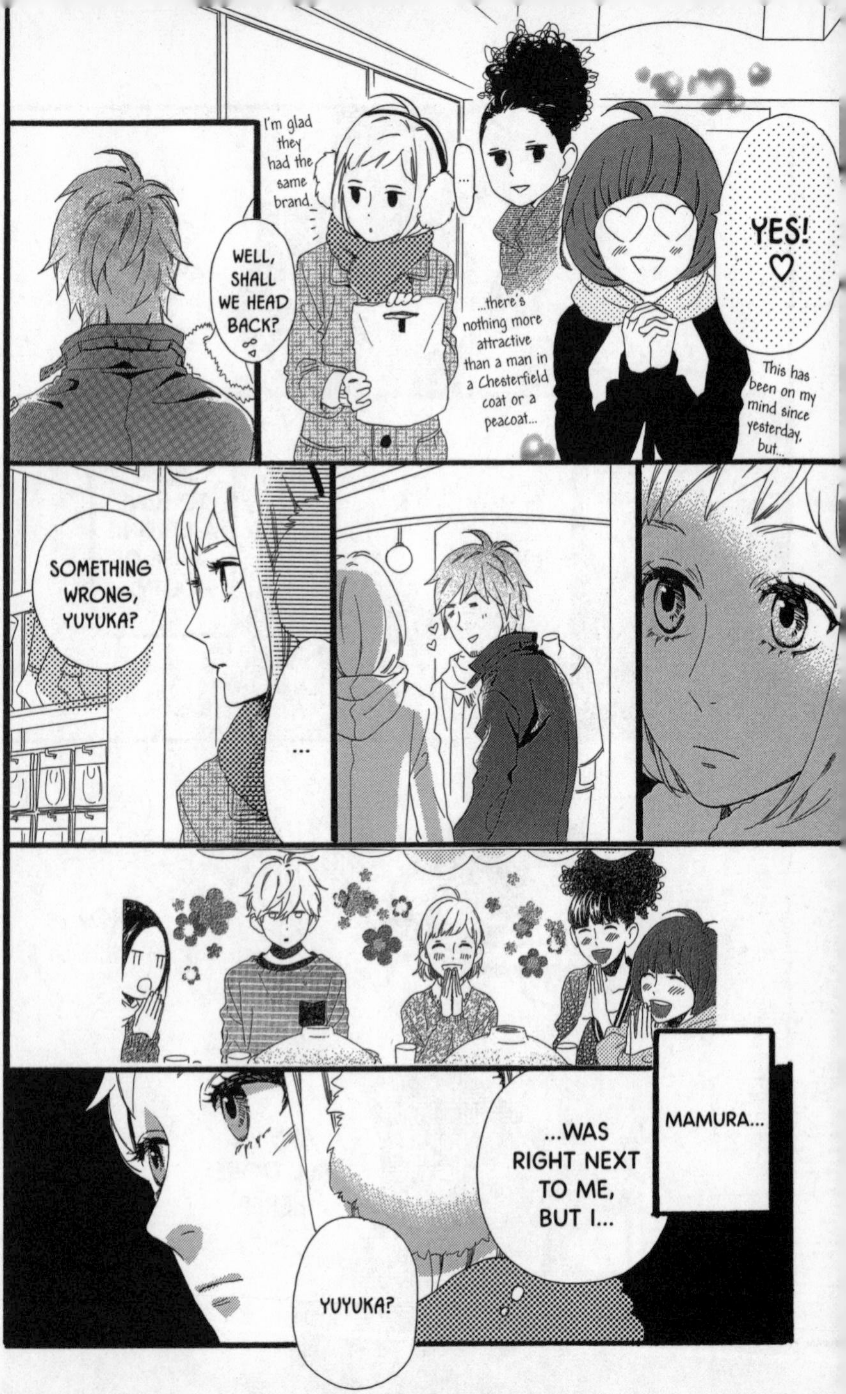
YES! ♡
This has been on my mind since yesterday, but...
...
...there's nothing more attractive than a man in a Chesterfield coat or a peacoat...
I'm glad they had the same brand.
WELL, SHALL WE HEAD BACK?
...
SOMETHING WRONG, YUYUKA?
MAMURA...
...WAS RIGHT NEXT TO ME, BUT I...
YUYUKA?

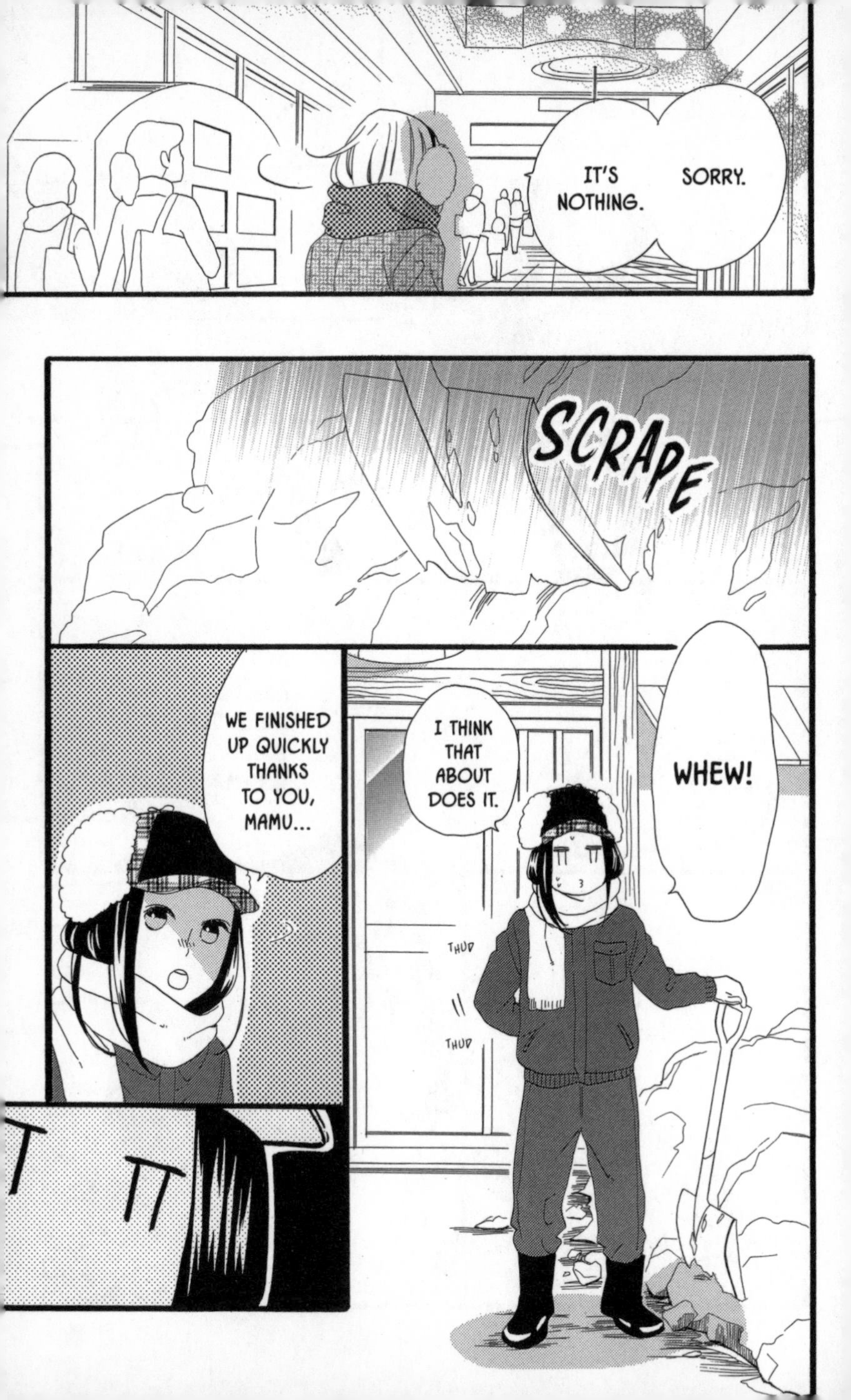
SORRY.
IT'S NOTHING.
SCRAPE
WHEW!
I THINK THAT ABOUT DOES IT.
THUD
THUD
WE FINISHED UP QUICKLY THANKS TO YOU, MAMU...

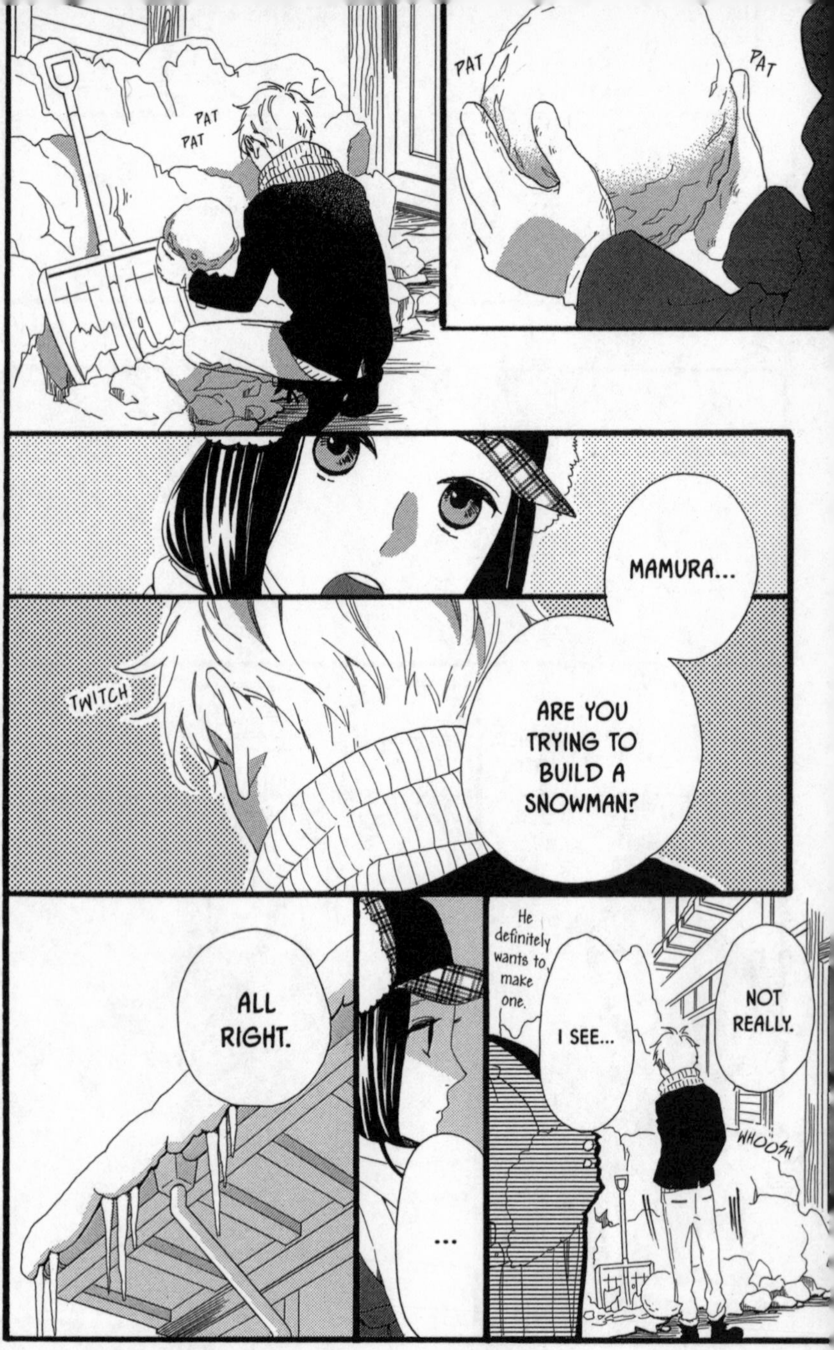
PAT
PAT
PAT
PAT
MAMURA...
ARE YOU TRYING TO BUILD A SNOWMAN?
TWITCH
NOT REALLY.
WHOOSH
I SEE...
He definitely wants to make one.
...
ALL RIGHT.

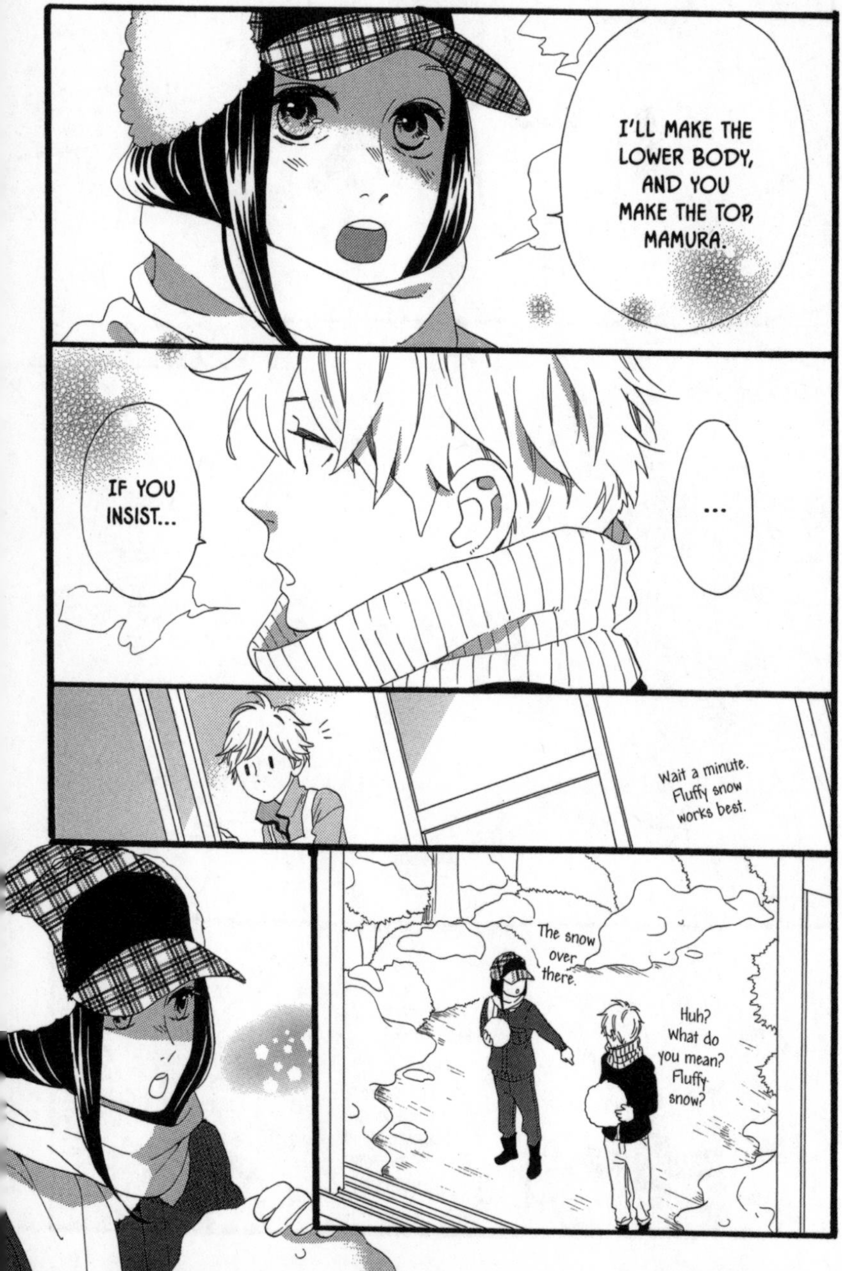
I'LL MAKE THE LOWER BODY, AND YOU MAKE THE TOP, MAMURA.
...
IF YOU INSIST...
Wait a minute. Fluffy snow works best.
The snow over there.
Huh? What do you mean? Fluffy snow?

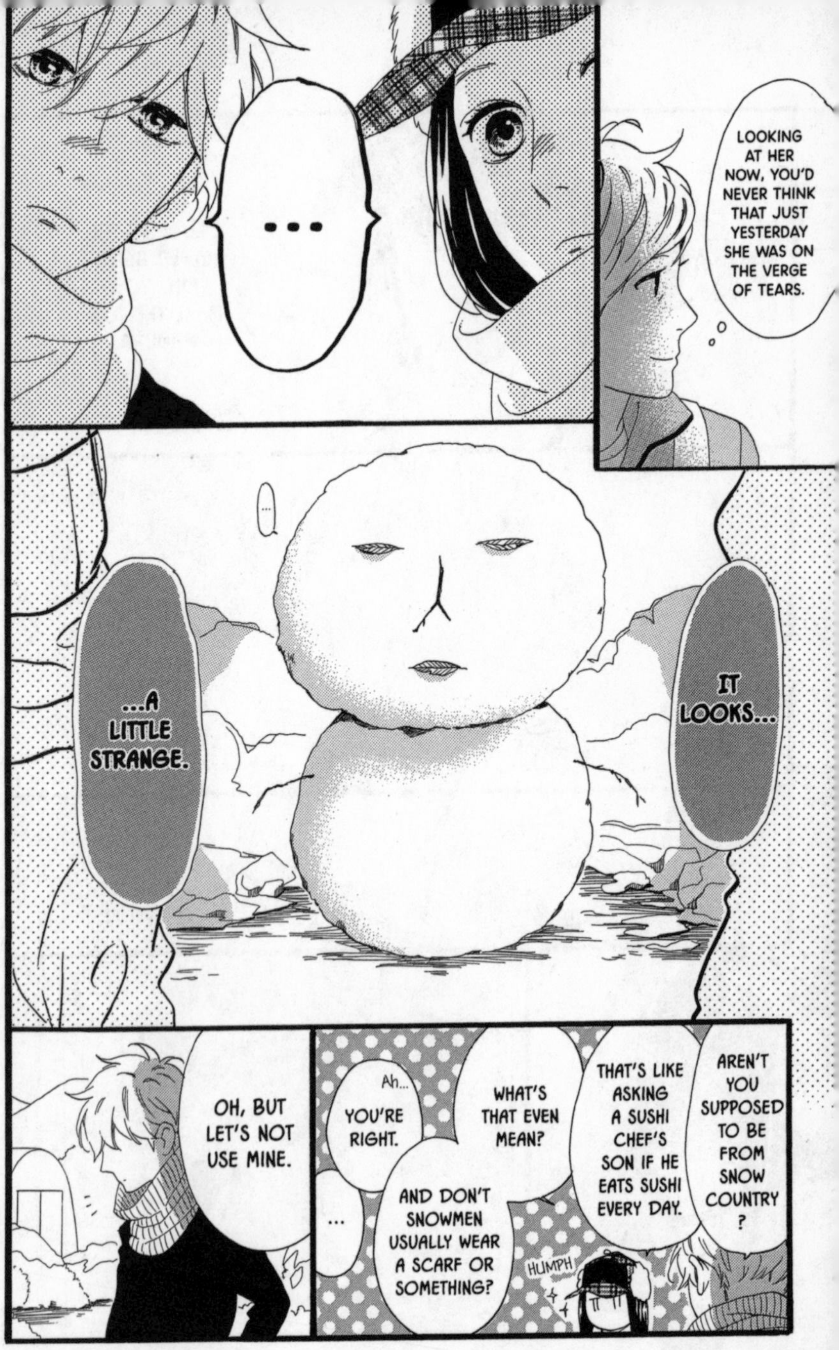

LOOKING AT HER NOW, YOU'D NEVER THINK THAT JUST YESTERDAY SHE WAS ON THE VERGE OF TEARS.
...
IT LOOKS...
...A LITTLE STRANGE.
...
AREN'T YOU SUPPOSED TO BE FROM SNOW COUNTRY?
THAT'S LIKE ASKING A SUSHI CHEF'S SON IF HE EATS SUSHI EVERY DAY.
WHAT'S THAT EVEN MEAN?
Ah... YOU'RE RIGHT.
AND DON'T SNOWMEN USUALLY WEAR A SCARF OR SOMETHING?
...
HUMPH
OH, BUT LET'S NOT USE MINE.

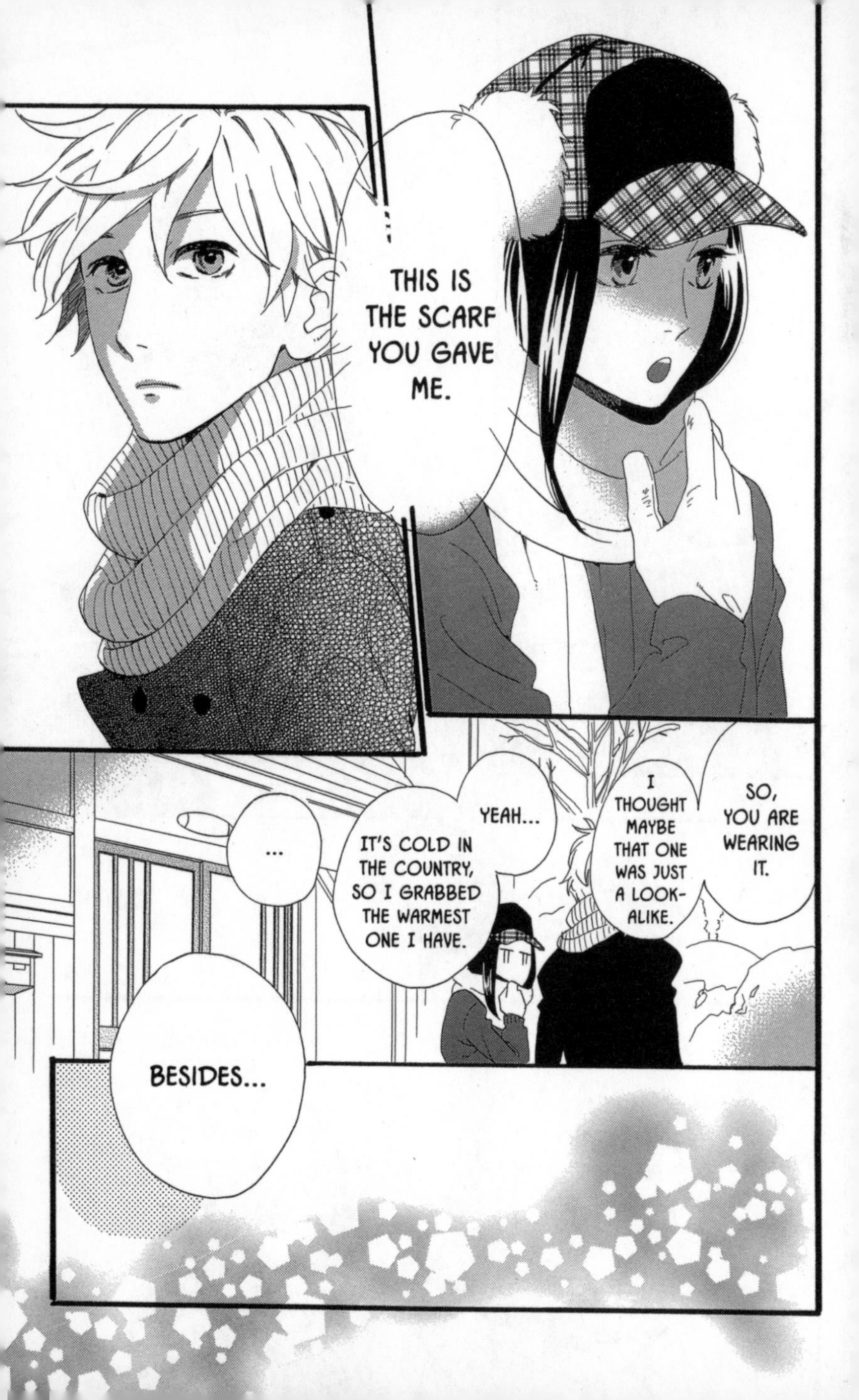
THIS IS THE SCARF YOU GAVE ME.
SO, YOU ARE WEARING IT.
I THOUGHT MAYBE THAT ONE WAS JUST A LOOK-ALIKE.
YEAH...
IT'S COLD IN THE COUNTRY, SO I GRABBED THE WARMEST ONE I HAVE.
...
BESIDES...

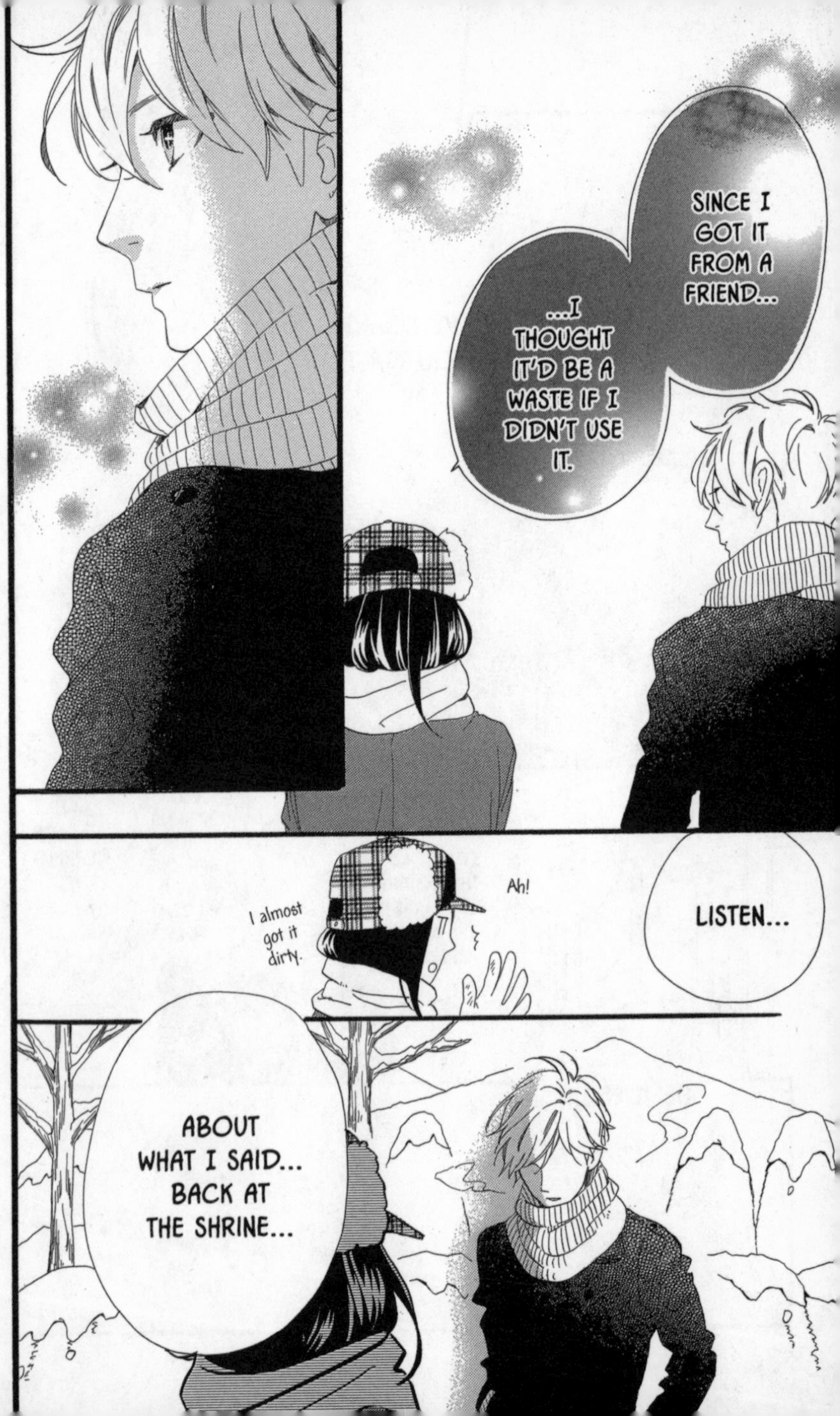
SINCE I GOT IT FROM A FRIEND...
...I THOUGHT IT'D BE A WASTE IF I DIDN'T USE IT.
LISTEN...
Ah!
I almost got it dirty.
ABOUT WHAT I SAID... BACK AT THE SHRINE...

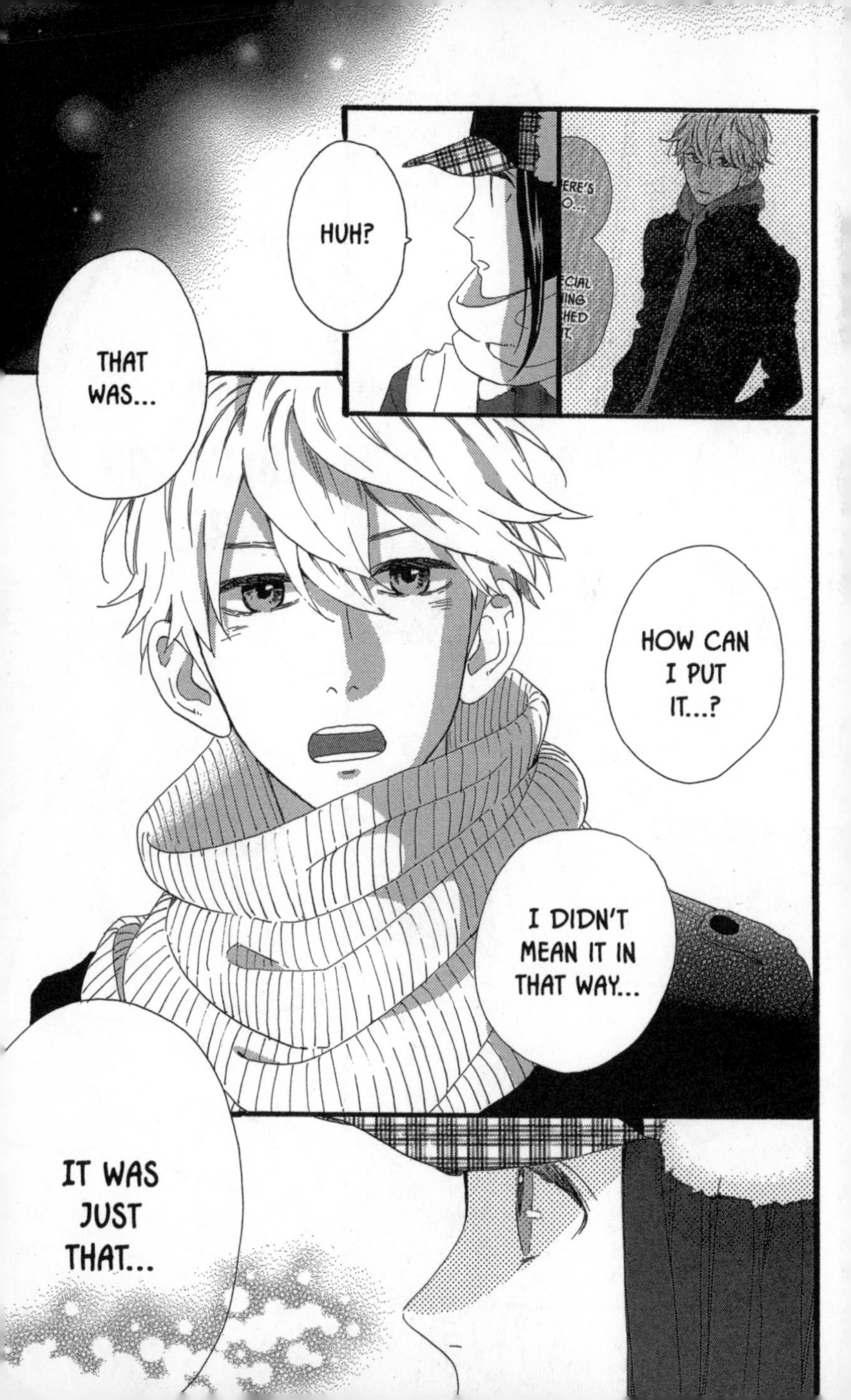
HUH?
THAT WAS...
HOW CAN I PUT IT...?
I DIDN'T MEAN IT IN THAT WAY...
IT WAS JUST THAT...

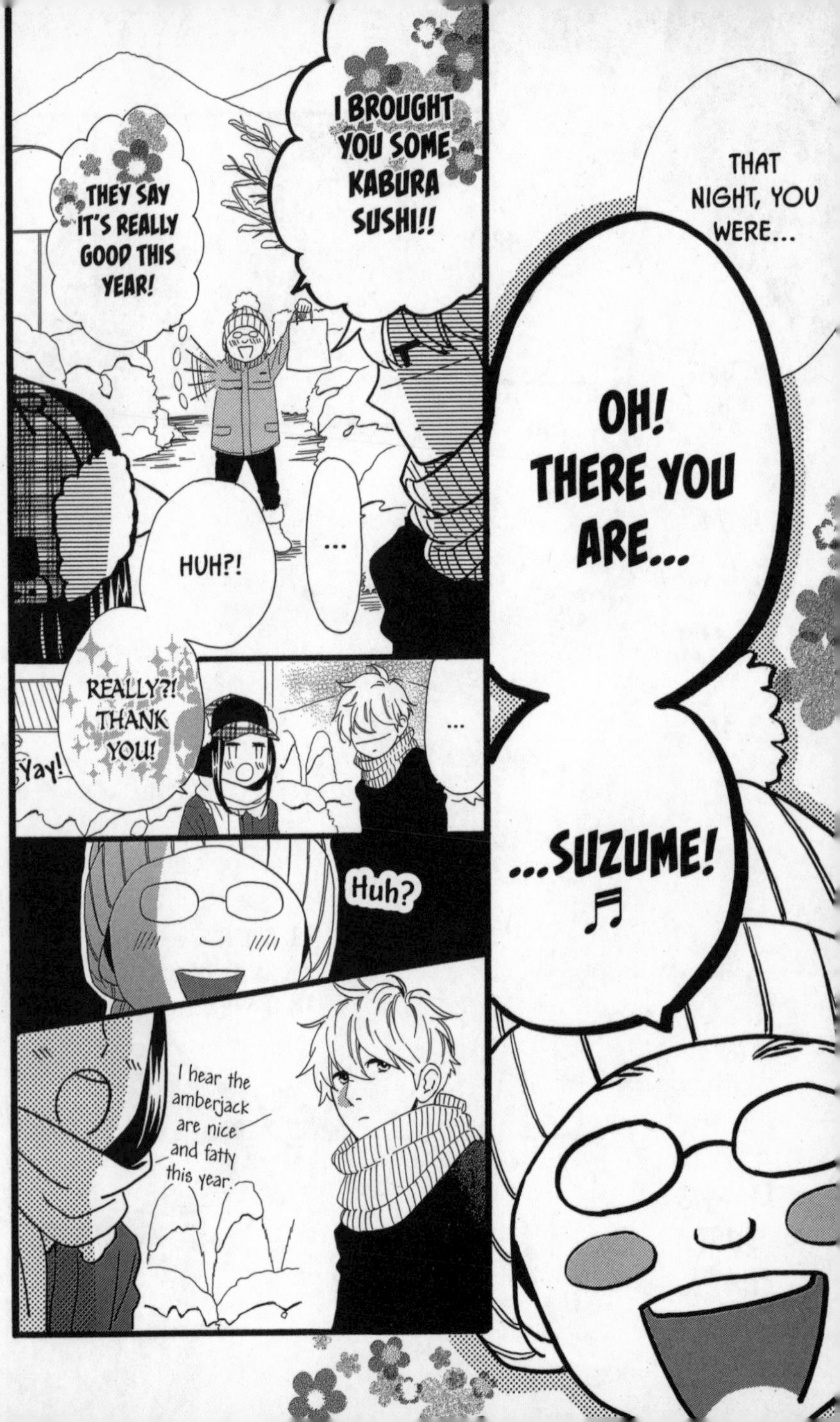
THAT NIGHT, YOU WERE...
OH! THERE YOU ARE...
...SUZUME! ♬
I BROUGHT YOU SOME KABURA SUSHI!!
THEY SAY IT'S REALLY GOOD THIS YEAR!
...
HUH?!
...
REALLY?! THANK YOU!
Yay!
Huh?
I hear the amberjack are nice and fatty this year.

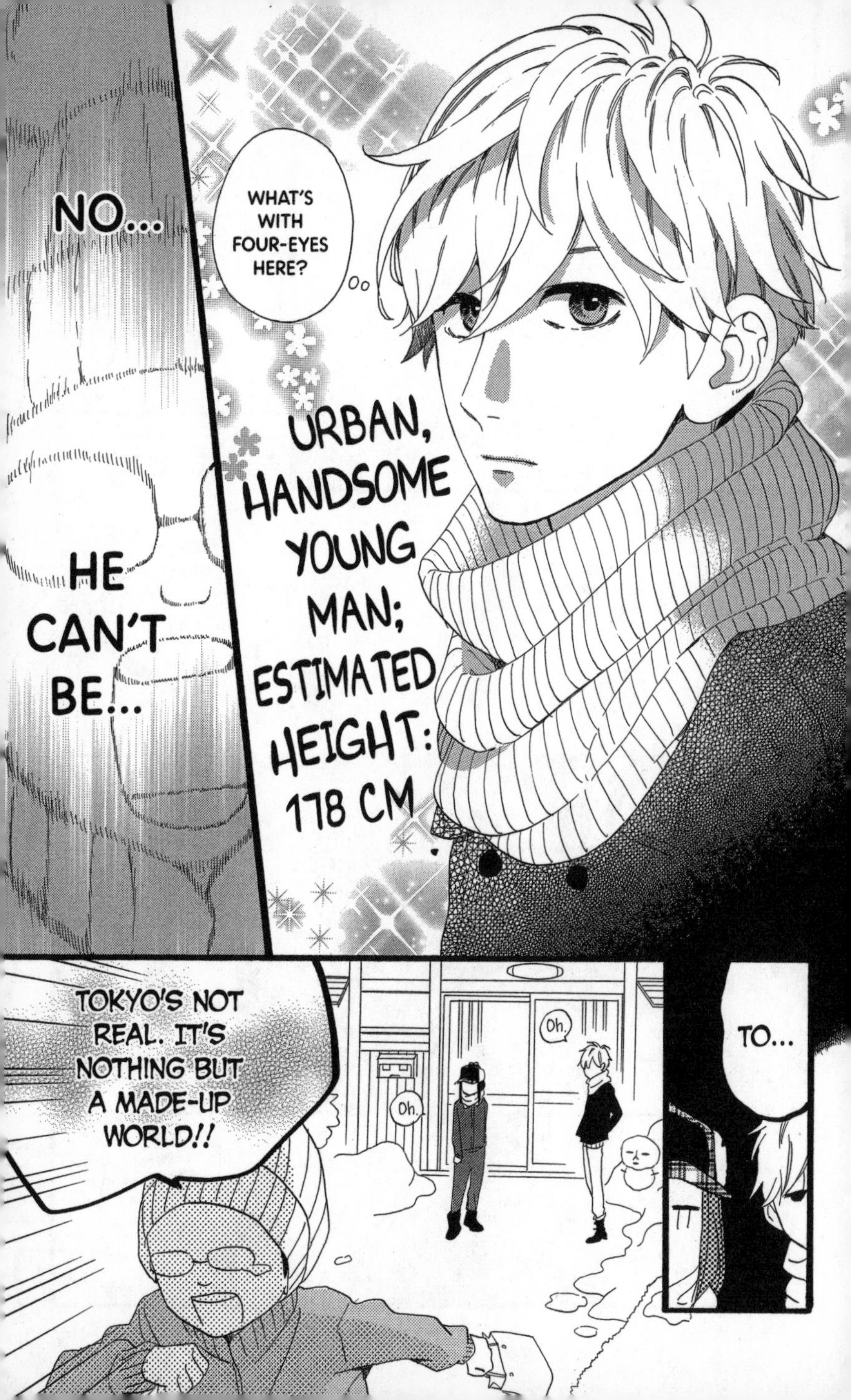
WHAT'S WITH FOUR-EYES HERE?
URBAN, HANDSOME YOUNG MAN; ESTIMATED HEIGHT: 178 CM
NO...
HE CAN'T BE...
TO...
Oh.
Oh.
TOKYO'S NOT REAL. IT'S NOTHING BUT A MADE-UP WORLD!!

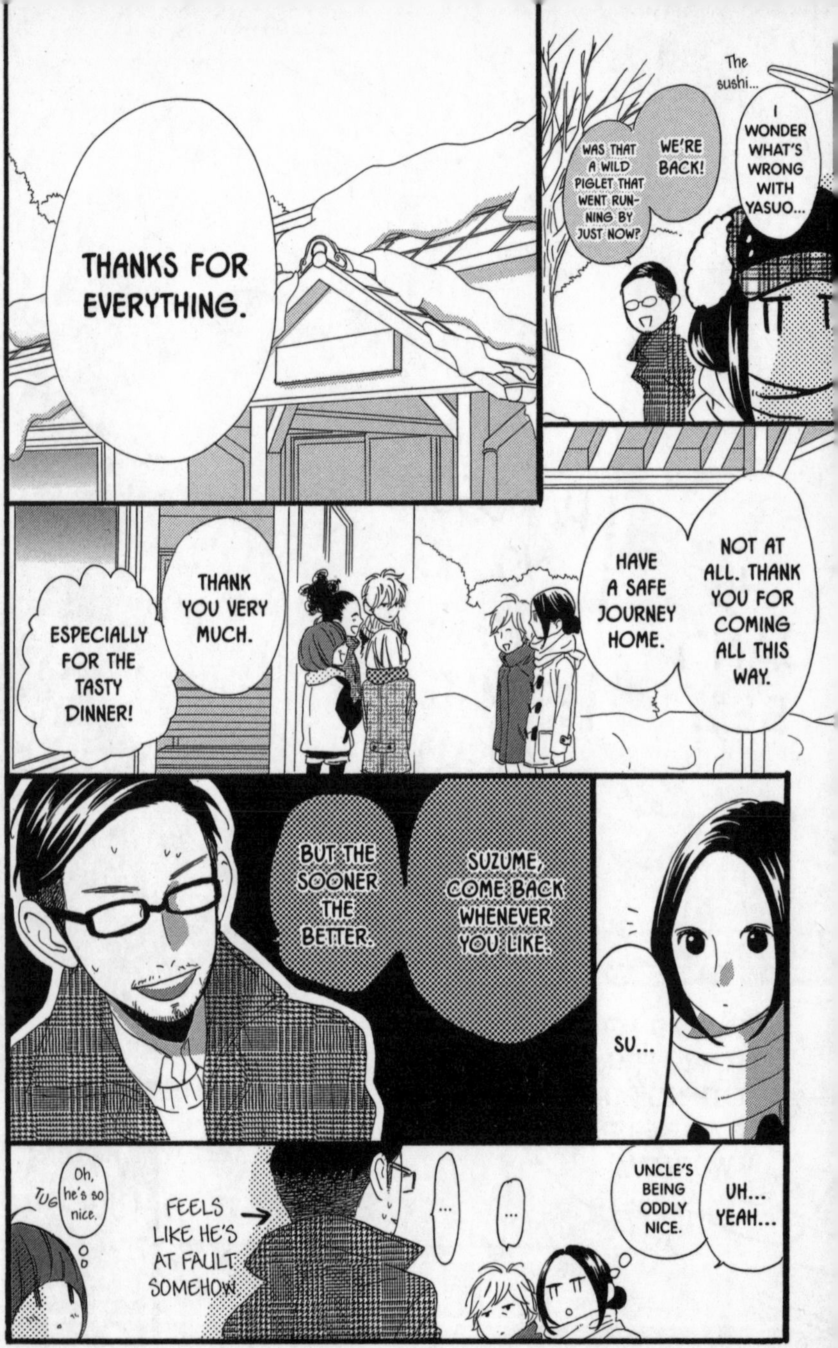
The sushi...
I WONDER WHAT'S WRONG WITH YASUO...
WE'RE BACK!
WAS THAT A WILD PIGLET THAT WENT RUN-NING BY JUST NOW?
THANKS FOR EVERYTHING.
NOT AT ALL. THANK YOU FOR COMING ALL THIS WAY.
HAVE A SAFE JOURNEY HOME.
THANK YOU VERY MUCH.
ESPECIALLY FOR THE TASTY DINNER!
SU...
SUZUME, COME BACK WHENEVER YOU LIKE.
BUT THE SOONER THE BETTER.
UH... YEAH...
UNCLE'S BEING ODDLY NICE.
...
...
FEELS LIKE HE'S AT FAULT SOMEHOW
TUG
Oh, he's so nice.

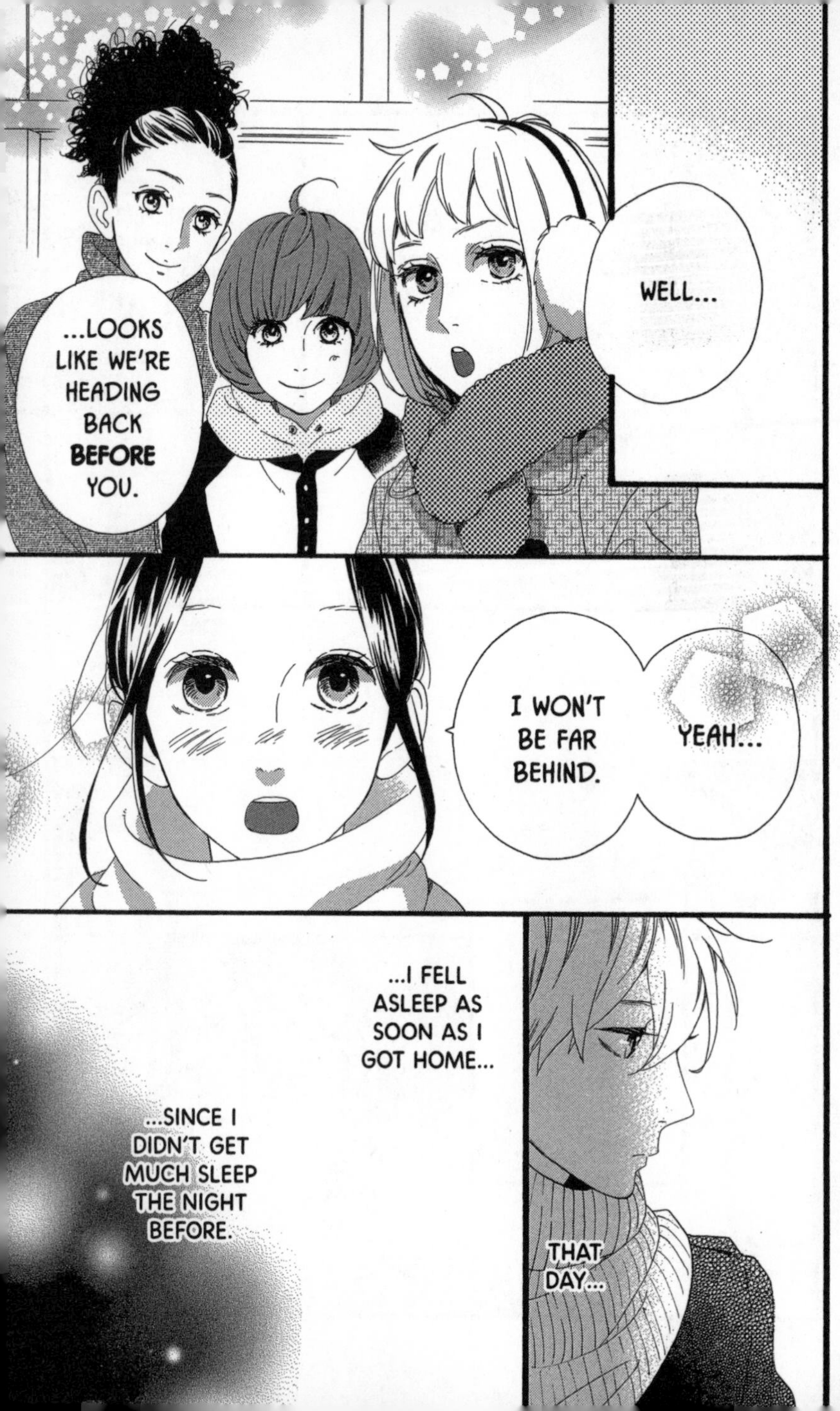
WELL...
...LOOKS LIKE WE'RE HEADING BACK BEFORE YOU.
YEAH...
I WON'T BE FAR BEHIND.
THAT DAY...
...I FELL ASLEEP AS SOON AS I GOT HOME...
...SINCE I DIDN'T GET MUCH SLEEP THE NIGHT BEFORE.

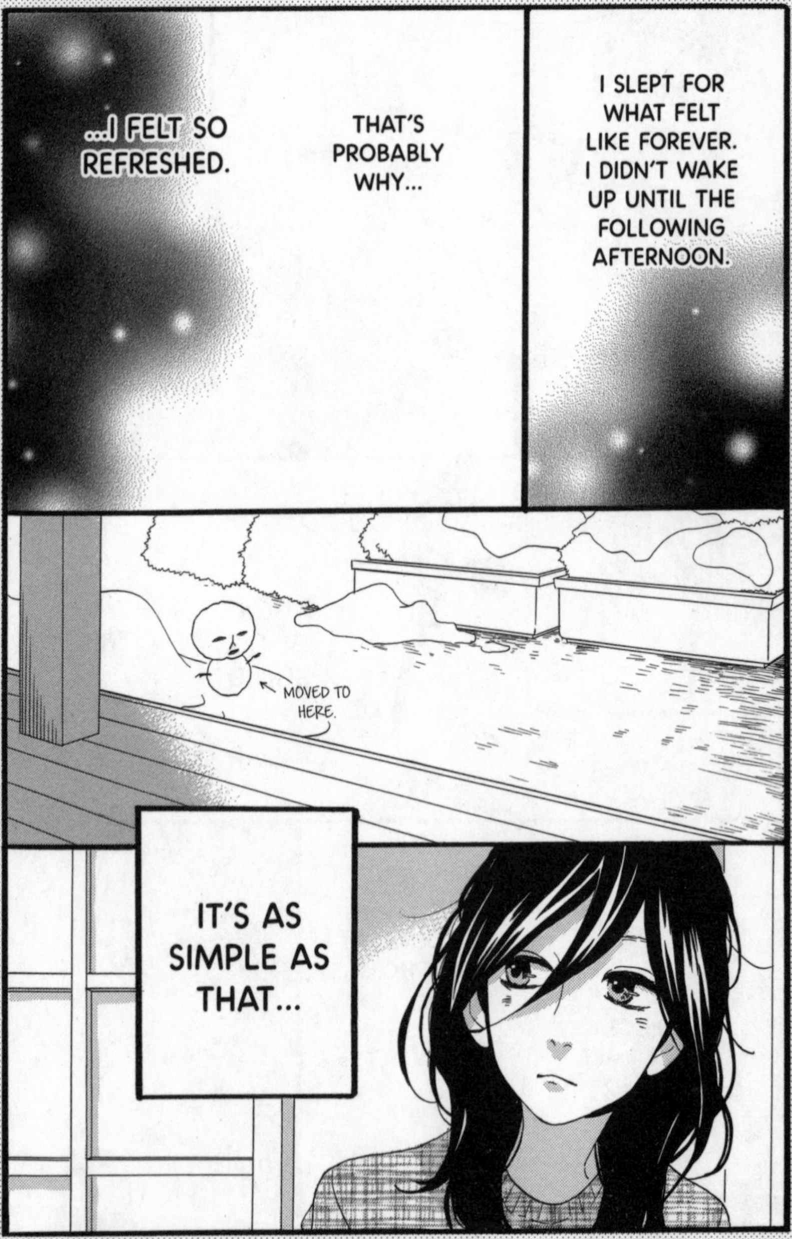
I SLEPT FOR WHAT FELT LIKE FOREVER. I DIDN'T WAKE UP UNTIL THE FOLLOWING AFTERNOON.
THAT'S PROBABLY WHY...
...I FELT SO REFRESHED.
MOVED TO HERE.
IT'S AS SIMPLE AS THAT...

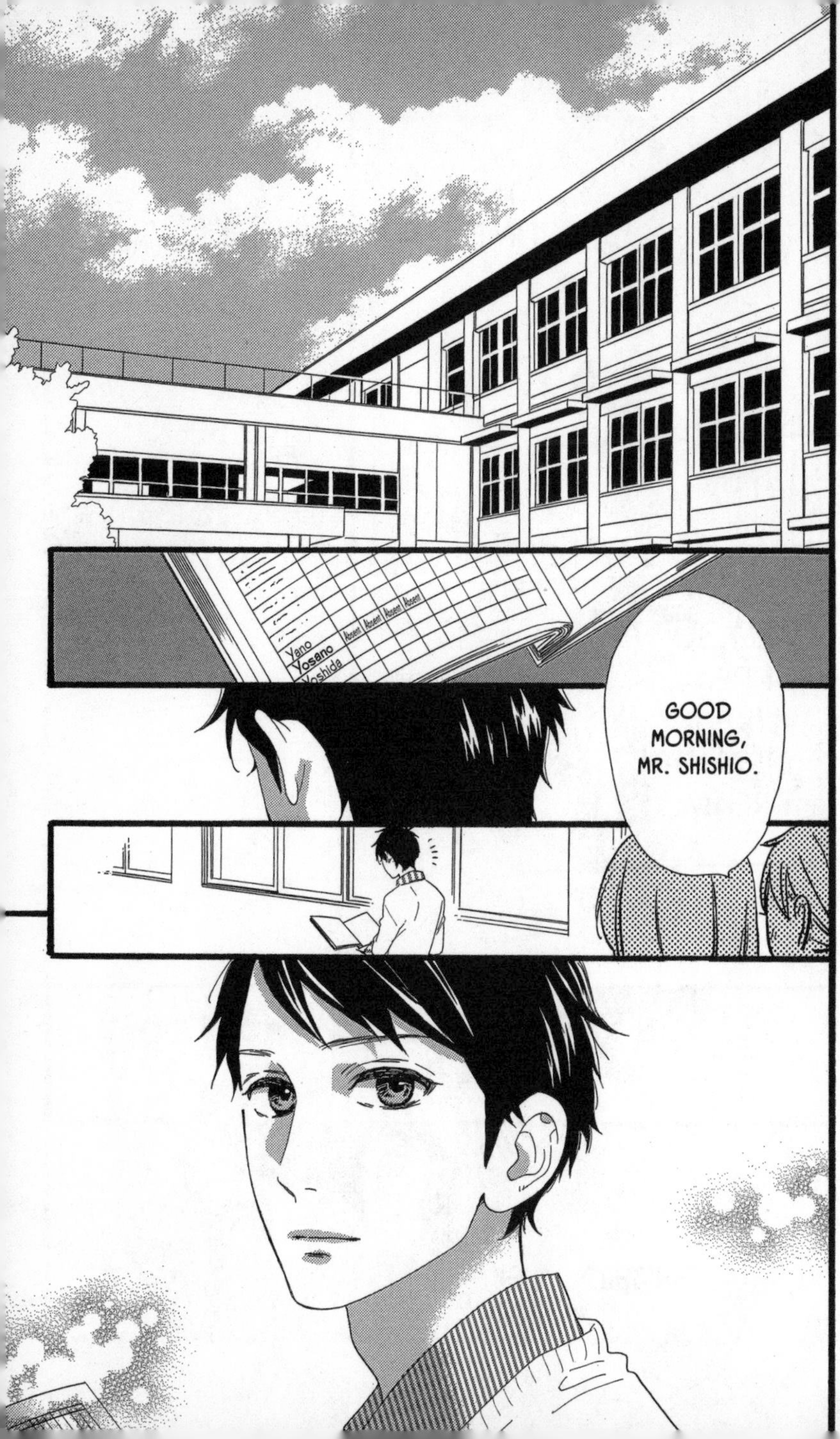

Yano
Yosano
Yoshida
Absent
Absent
Absent
Absent
GOOD MORNING, MR. SHISHIO.

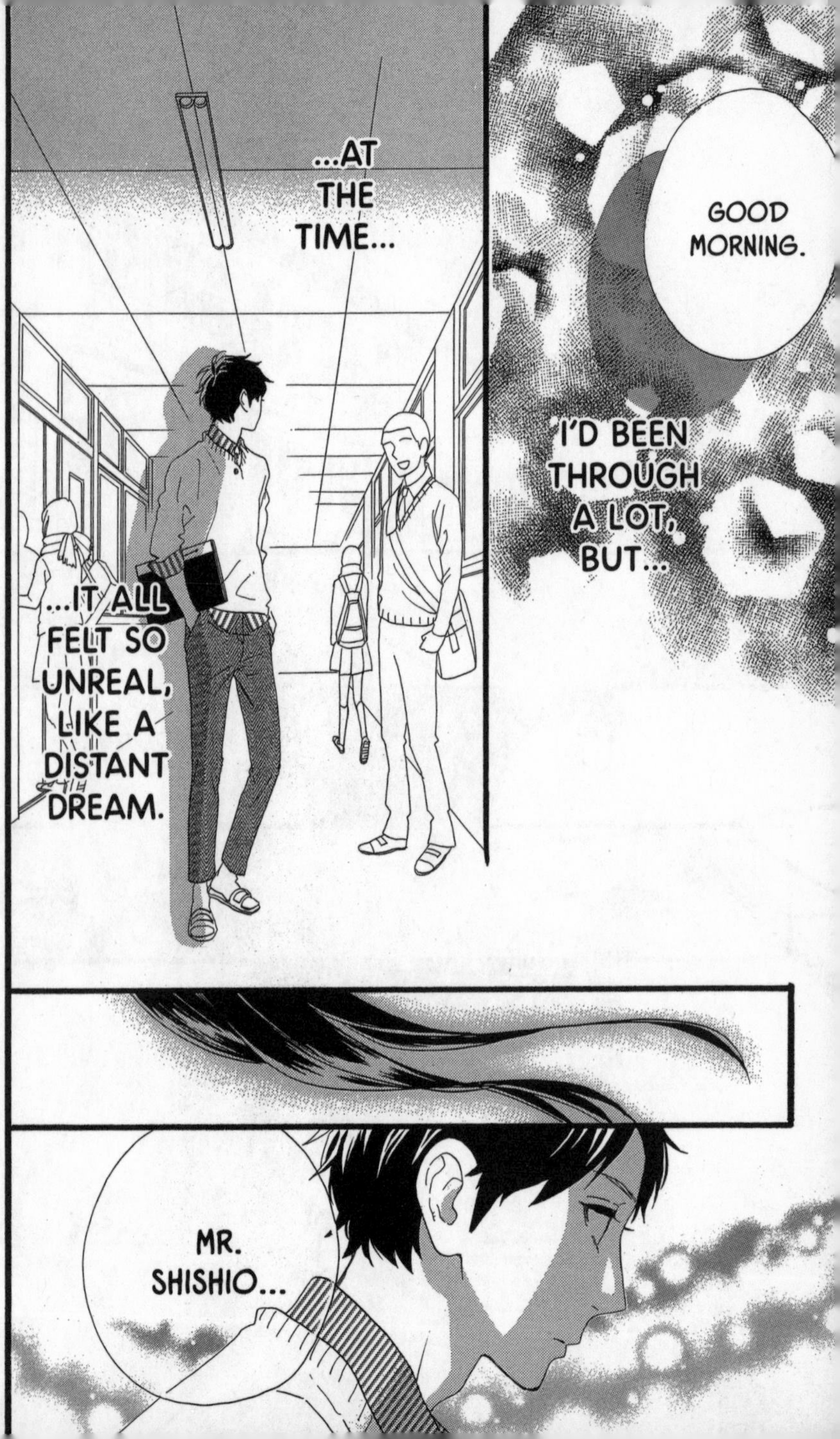
GOOD MORNING.
I'D BEEN THROUGH A LOT, BUT...
...AT THE TIME...
...IT ALL FELT SO UNREAL, LIKE A DISTANT DREAM.
MR. SHISHIO...

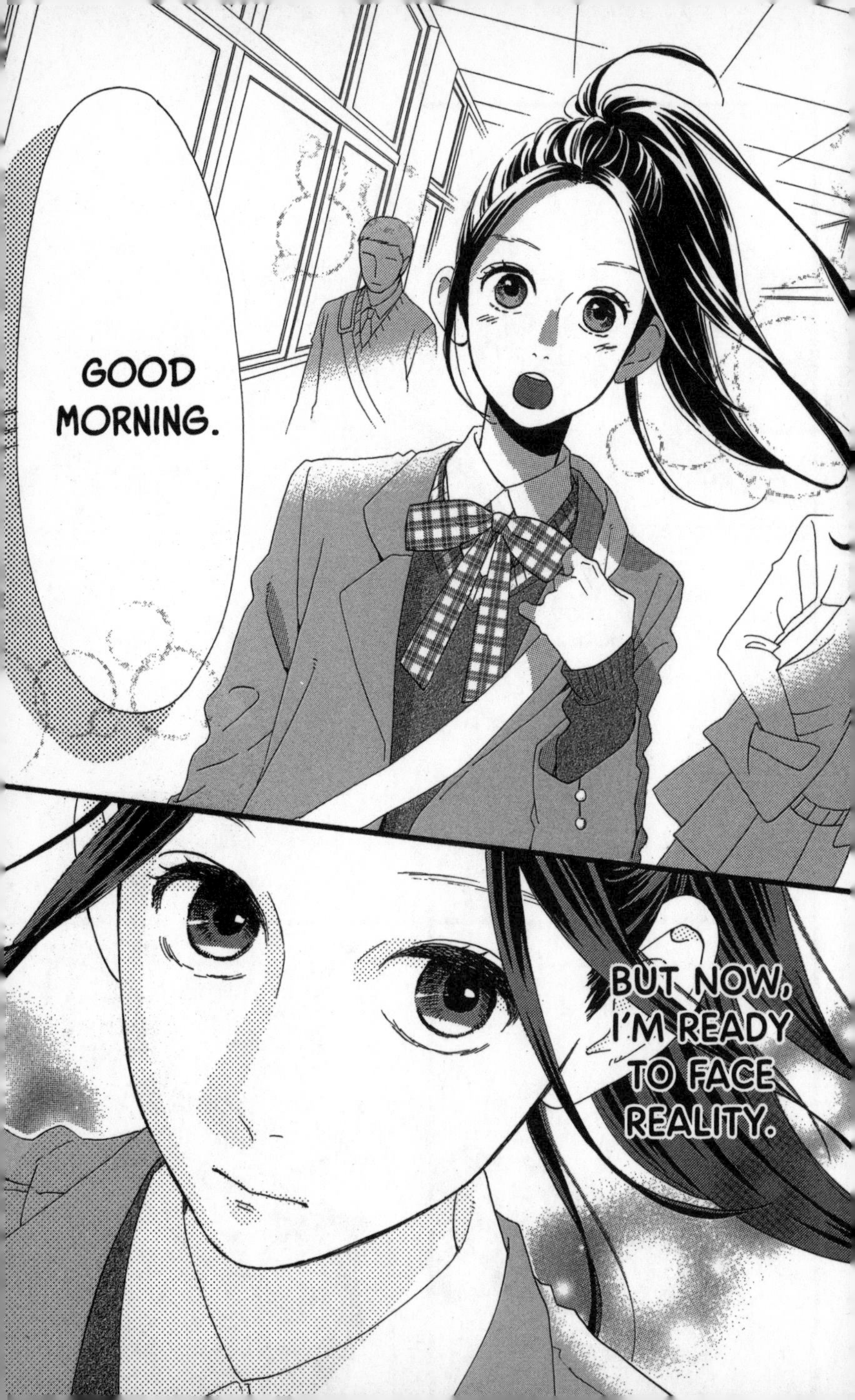
GOOD MORNING.
BUT NOW, I'M READY TO FACE REALITY.

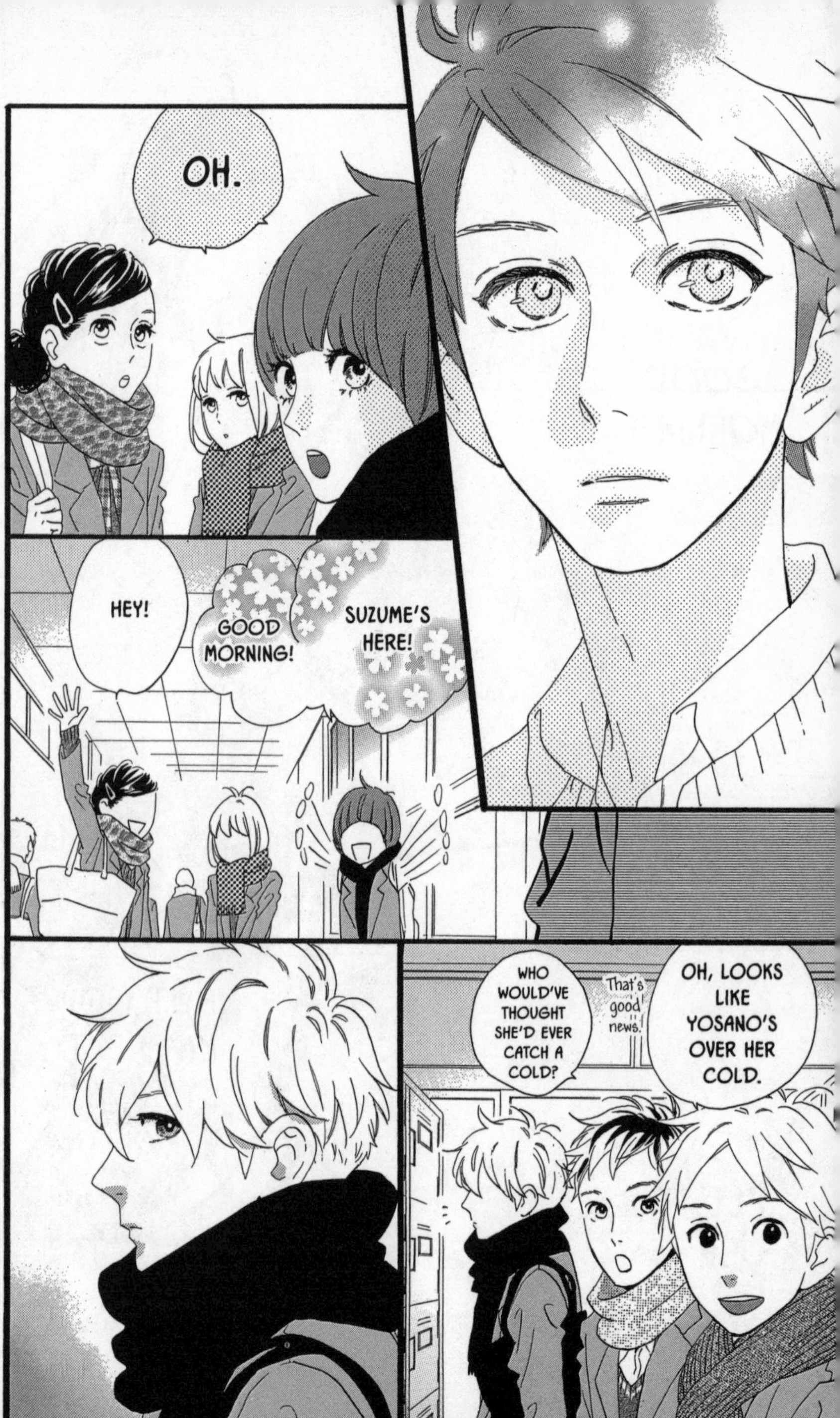
OH.
SUZUME'S HERE!
GOOD MORNING!
HEY!
OH, LOOKS LIKE YOSANO'S OVER HER COLD.
That's good news.
WHO WOULD'VE THOUGHT SHE'D EVER CATCH A COLD?

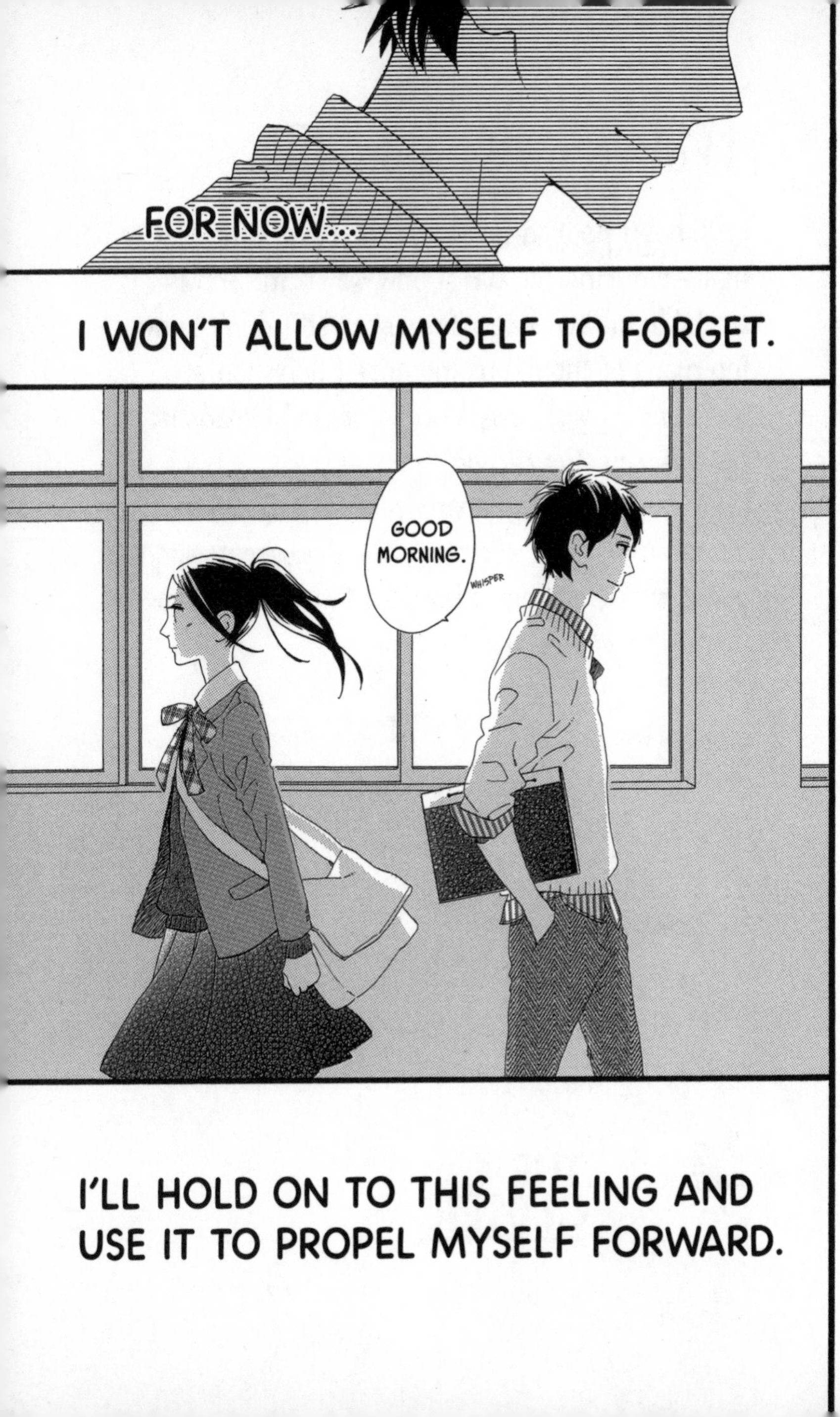
FOR NOW...
I WON'T ALLOW MYSELF TO FORGET.
GOOD MORNING.
WHISPER
I'LL HOLD ON TO THIS FEELING AND USE IT TO PROPEL MYSELF FORWARD.

That reminds me... ②

I often get hooked on those American soap operas that air during the day. I only watch the shows available on broadcast television, so I don't know too many of them, but the ones I do watch are addicting. I wish they'd hurry up and broadcast Season 3 of *The Closer*.

I don't really watch Japanese dramas (because it's too much like work for me). However, foreign police shows are great because I'm able to enjoy them with a clear mind.

glee
I like Mike on *Glee*.
Poor Finn passed away. It's so sad....
Mr. Tsundere a.k.a. Flynn.
These older detectives work really hard.
Provenza
Average age a little high.
Lt. Tao is therapeutic for me.
PC
I don't mix business with pleasure.
Young detective Gabriel, who is forced to take care of his boss's cat.
THE CLOSER

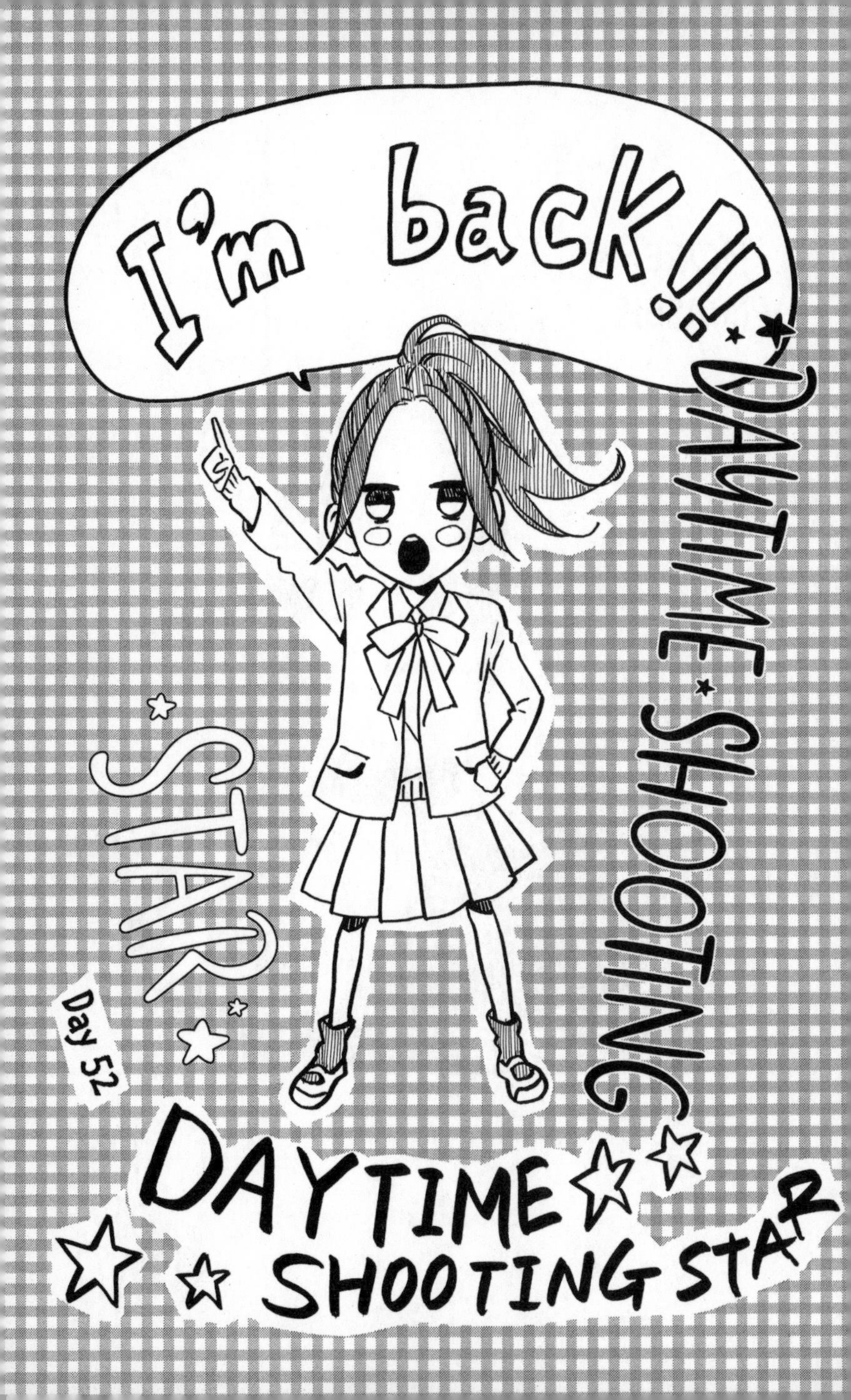
I'm back!!!
DAYTIME SHOOTING STAR
Day 52
DAYTIME SHOOTING STAR

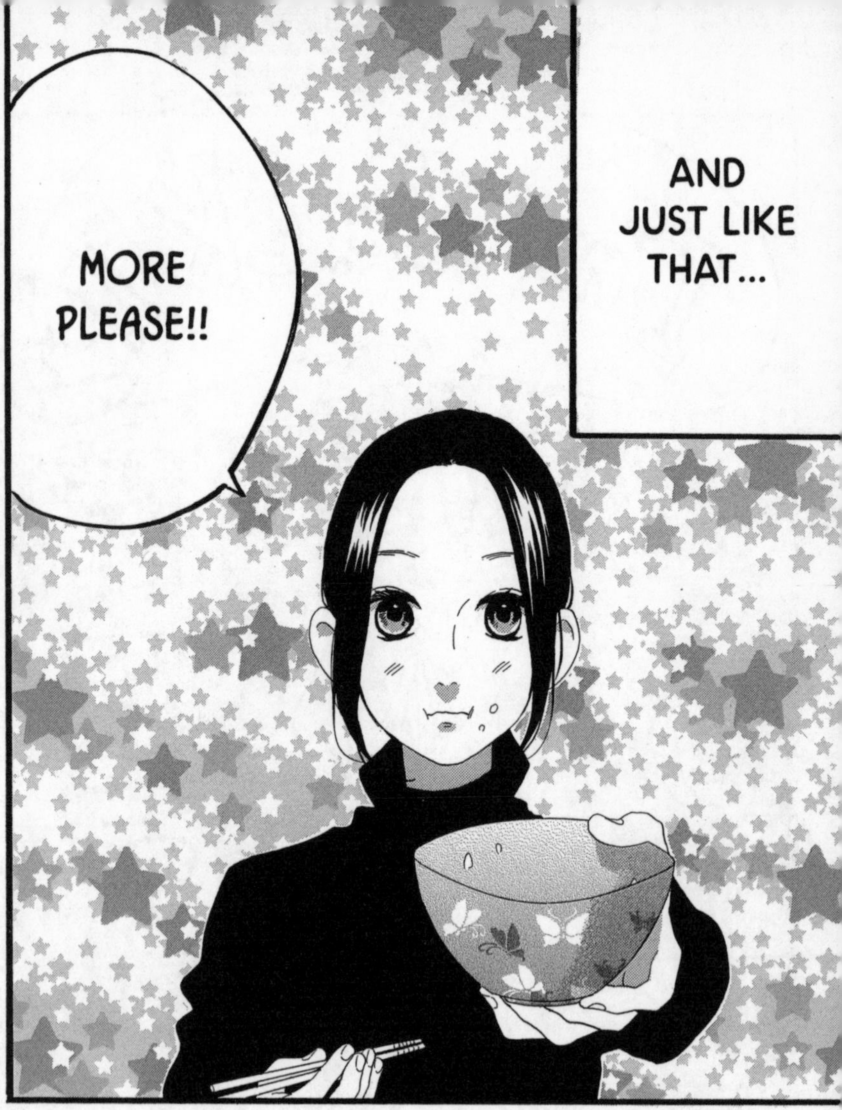
AND JUST LIKE THAT...
MORE PLEASE!!

DAYTIME SHOOTING STAR

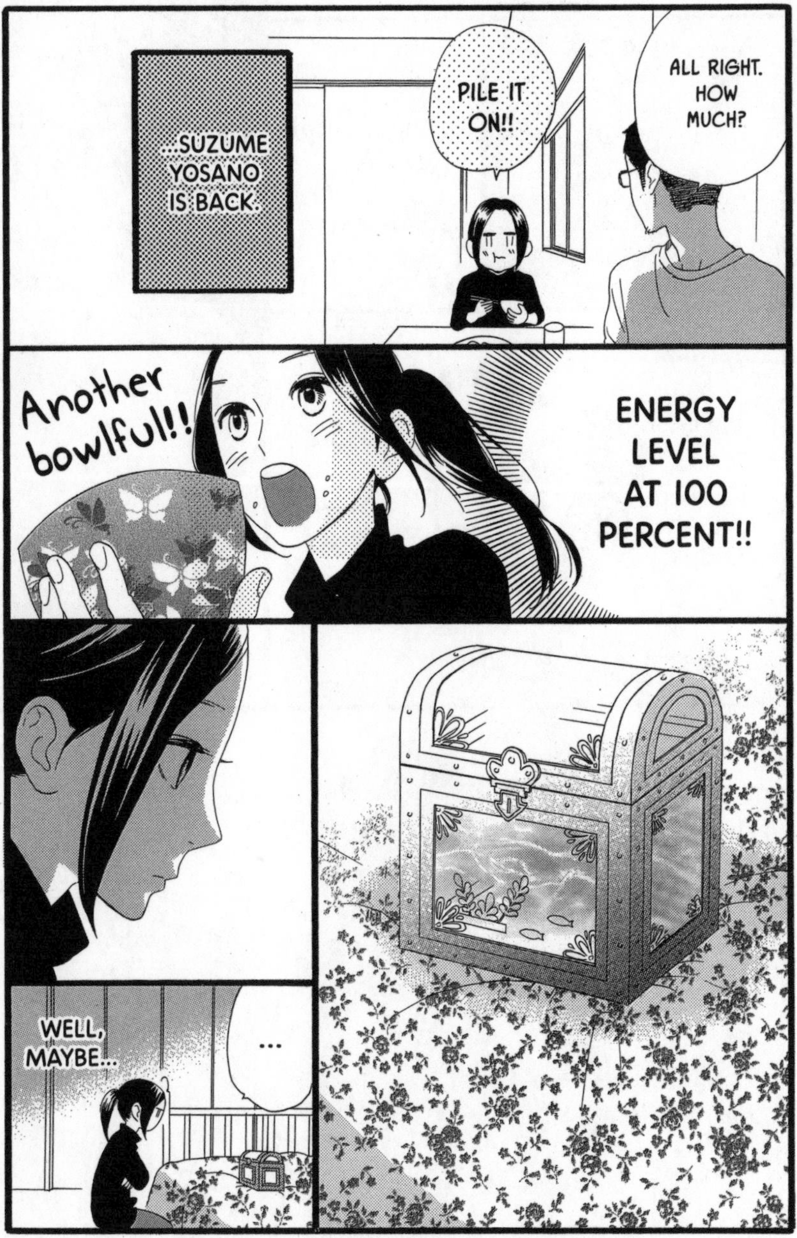
ALL RIGHT. HOW MUCH?
PILE IT ON!!
...SUZUME YOSANO IS BACK.
ENERGY LEVEL AT 100 PERCENT!!
Another bowlful!!
...
WELL, MAYBE...

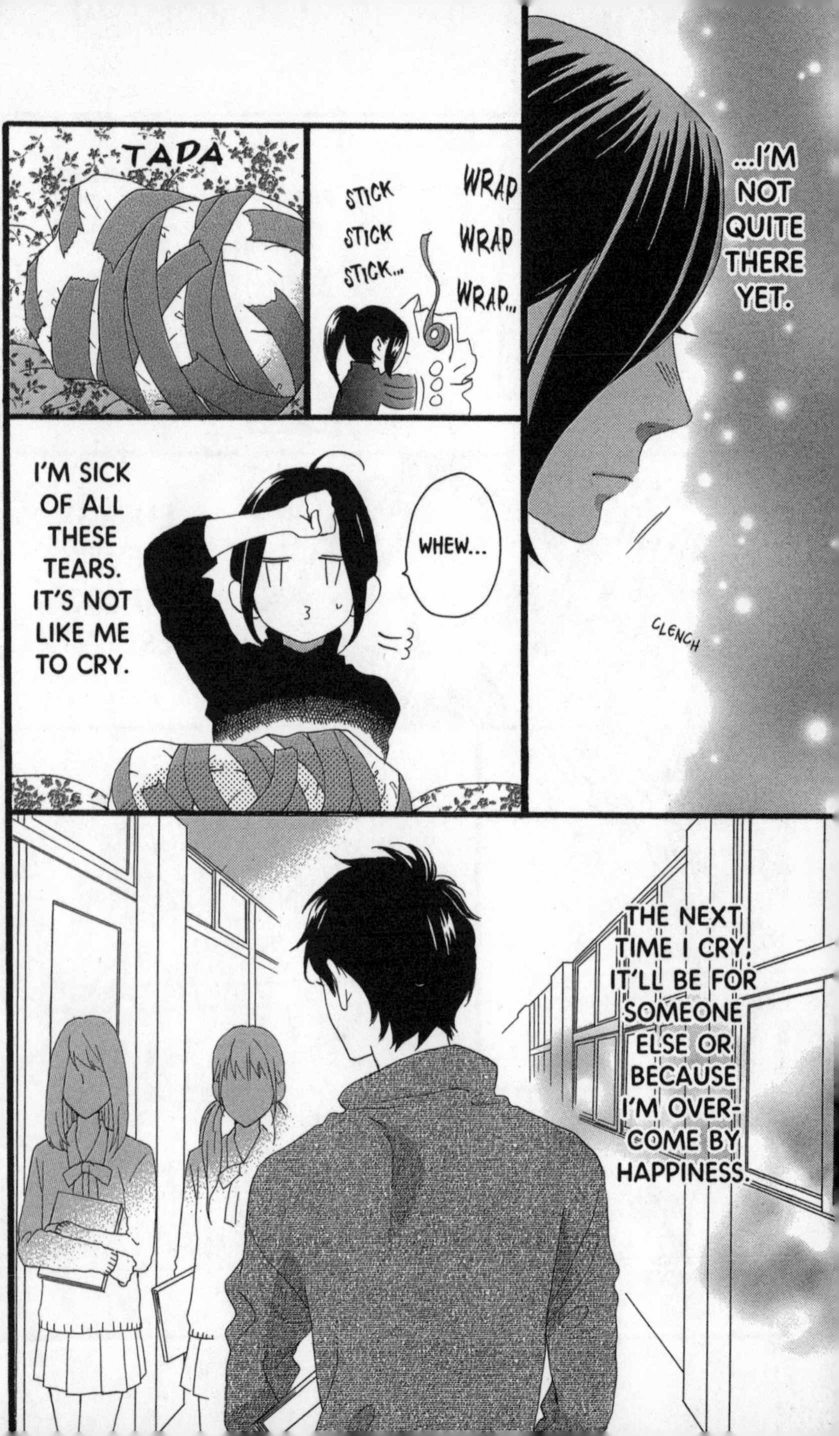
...I'M NOT QUITE THERE YET.
CLENCH
STICK STICK STICK...
WRAP WRAP WRAP...
TADA
I'M SICK OF ALL THESE TEARS. IT'S NOT LIKE ME TO CRY.
WHEW...
THE NEXT TIME I CRY, IT'LL BE FOR SOMEONE ELSE OR BECAUSE I'M OVER-COME BY HAPPINESS.

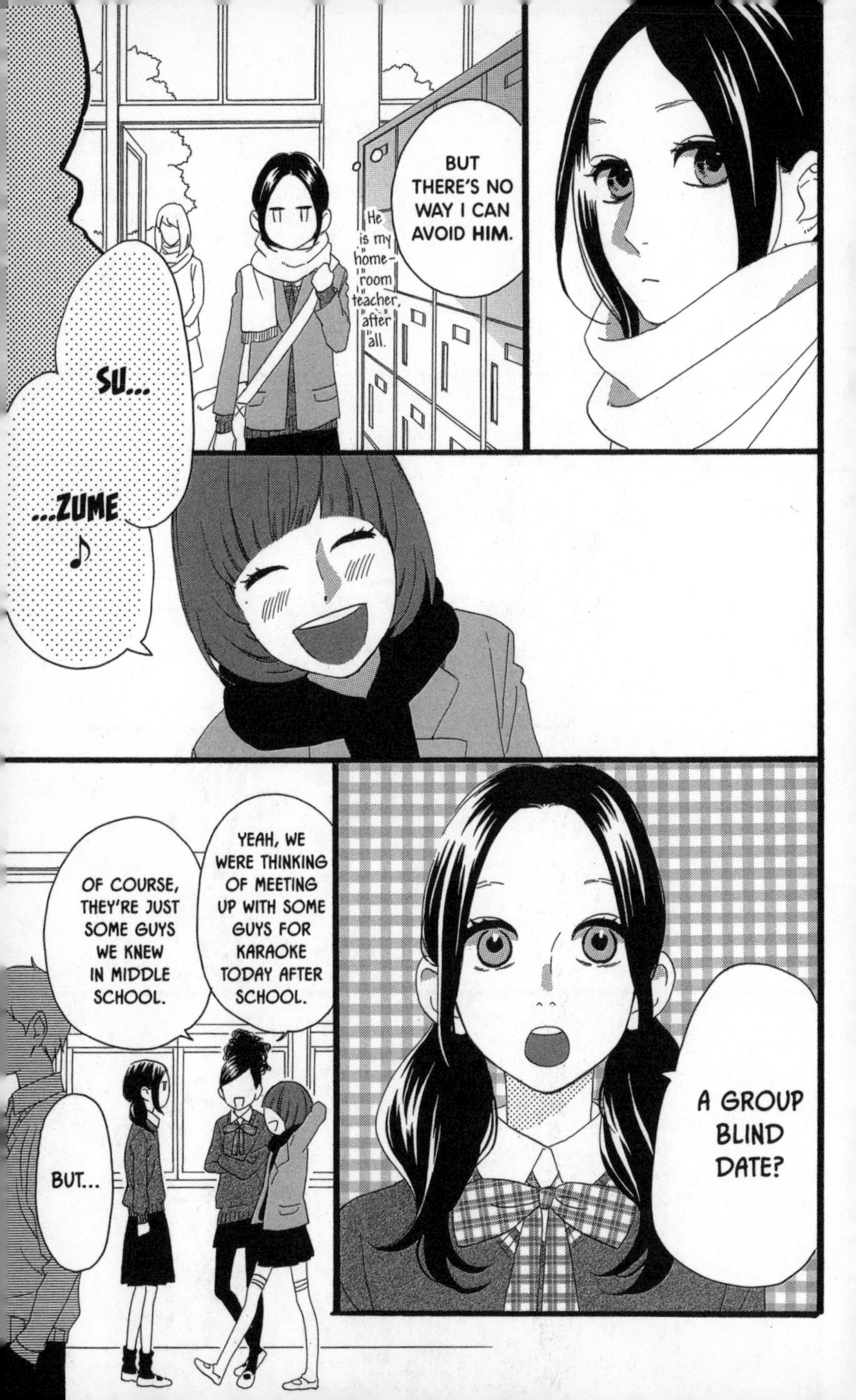
BUT THERE'S NO WAY I CAN AVOID HIM.
He is my home-room teacher, after all.
SU...
...ZUME ♪
A GROUP BLIND DATE?
YEAH, WE WERE THINKING OF MEETING UP WITH SOME GUYS FOR KARAOKE TODAY AFTER SCHOOL.
OF COURSE, THEY'RE JUST SOME GUYS WE KNEW IN MIDDLE SCHOOL.
BUT...

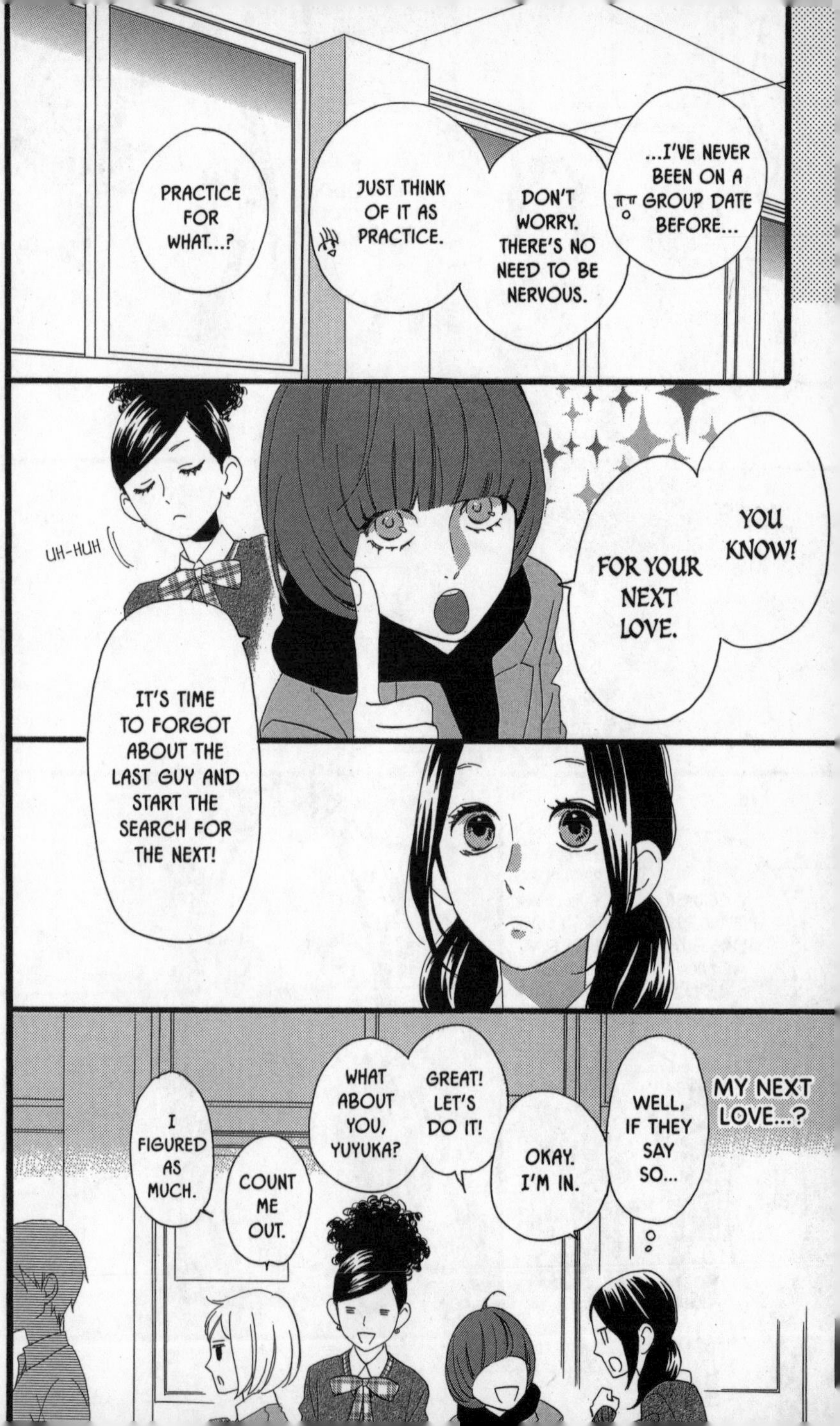
...I'VE NEVER BEEN ON A GROUP DATE BEFORE...
DON'T WORRY. THERE'S NO NEED TO BE NERVOUS.
JUST THINK OF IT AS PRACTICE.
PRACTICE FOR WHAT...?
YOU KNOW!
FOR YOUR NEXT LOVE.
UH-HUH
IT'S TIME TO FORGOT ABOUT THE LAST GUY AND START THE SEARCH FOR THE NEXT!
MY NEXT LOVE...?
WELL, IF THEY SAY SO...
OKAY. I'M IN.
GREAT! LET'S DO IT!
WHAT ABOUT YOU, YUYUKA?
COUNT ME OUT.
I FIGURED AS MUCH.

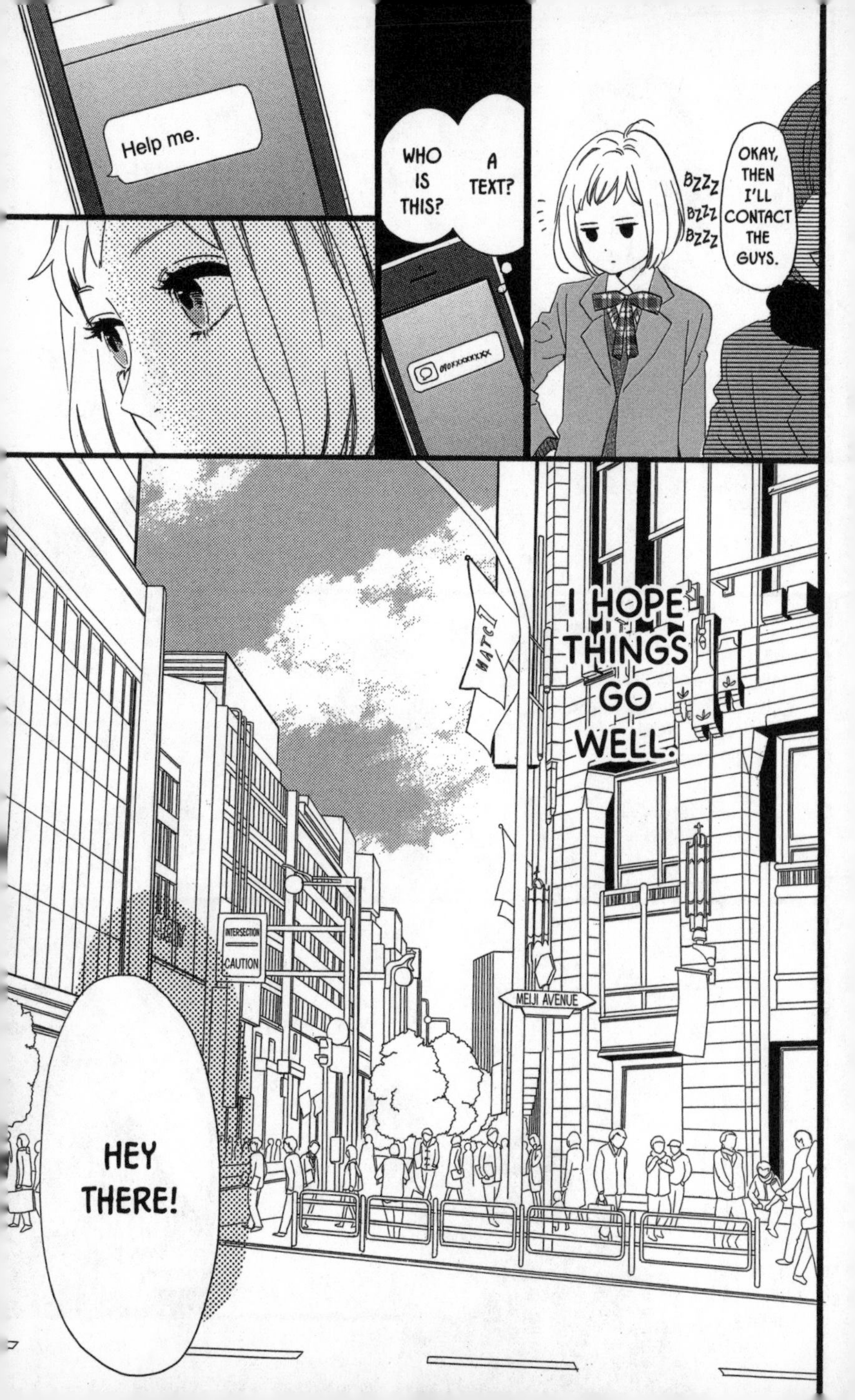
OKAY, THEN I'LL CONTACT THE GUYS.
BZZZ BZZZ BZZZ
A TEXT?
WHO IS THIS?
Help me.
I HOPE THINGS GO WELL.
INTERSECTION CAUTION
MEIJI AVENUE
HEY THERE!

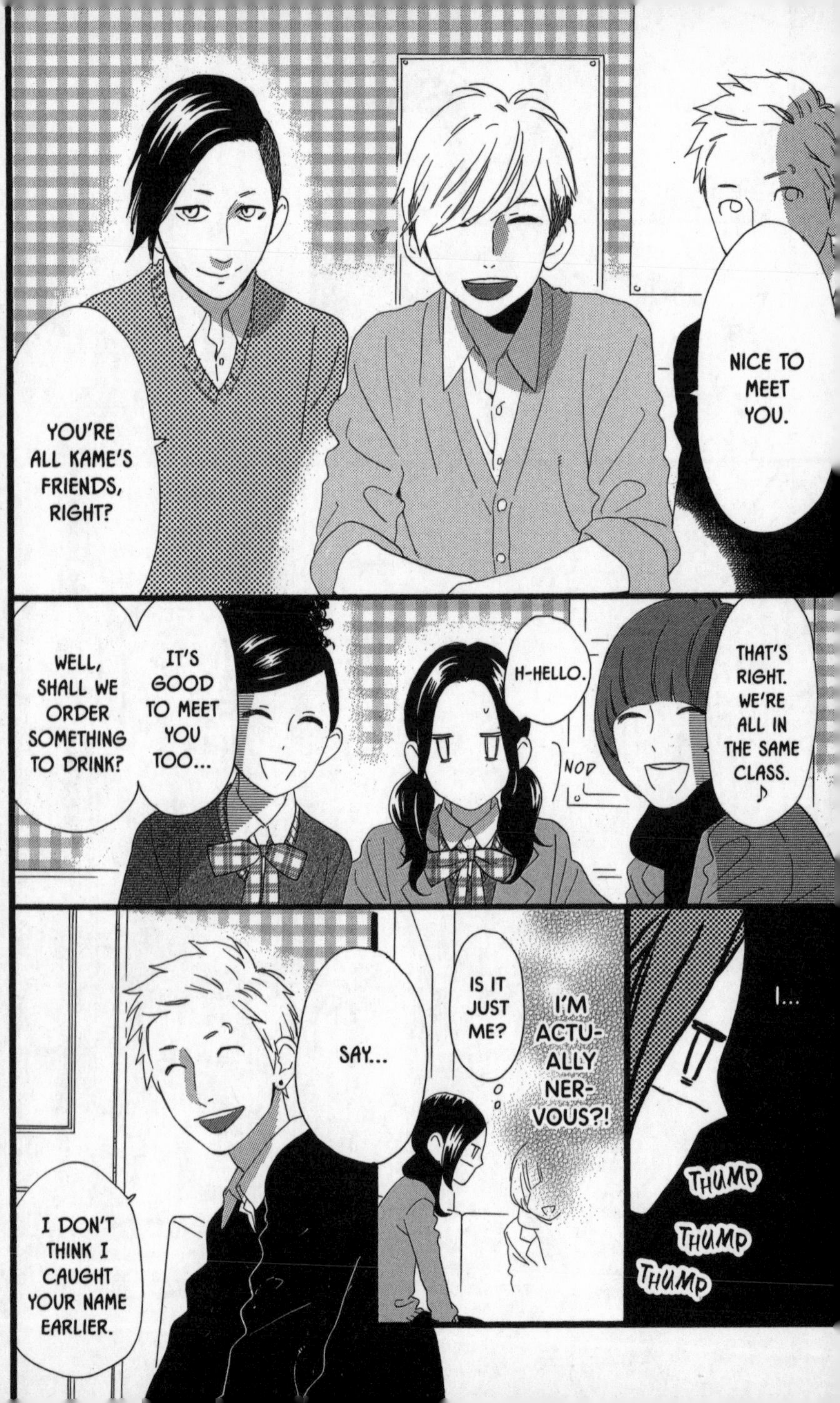
NICE TO MEET YOU.
YOU'RE ALL KAME'S FRIENDS, RIGHT?
THAT'S RIGHT. WE'RE ALL IN THE SAME CLASS. ♪
H-HELLO.
NOD
IT'S GOOD TO MEET YOU TOO...
WELL, SHALL WE ORDER SOMETHING TO DRINK?
I...
THUMP
THUMP
THUMP
I'M ACTU-ALLY NER-VOUS?!
IS IT JUST ME?
SAY...
I DON'T THINK I CAUGHT YOUR NAME EARLIER.

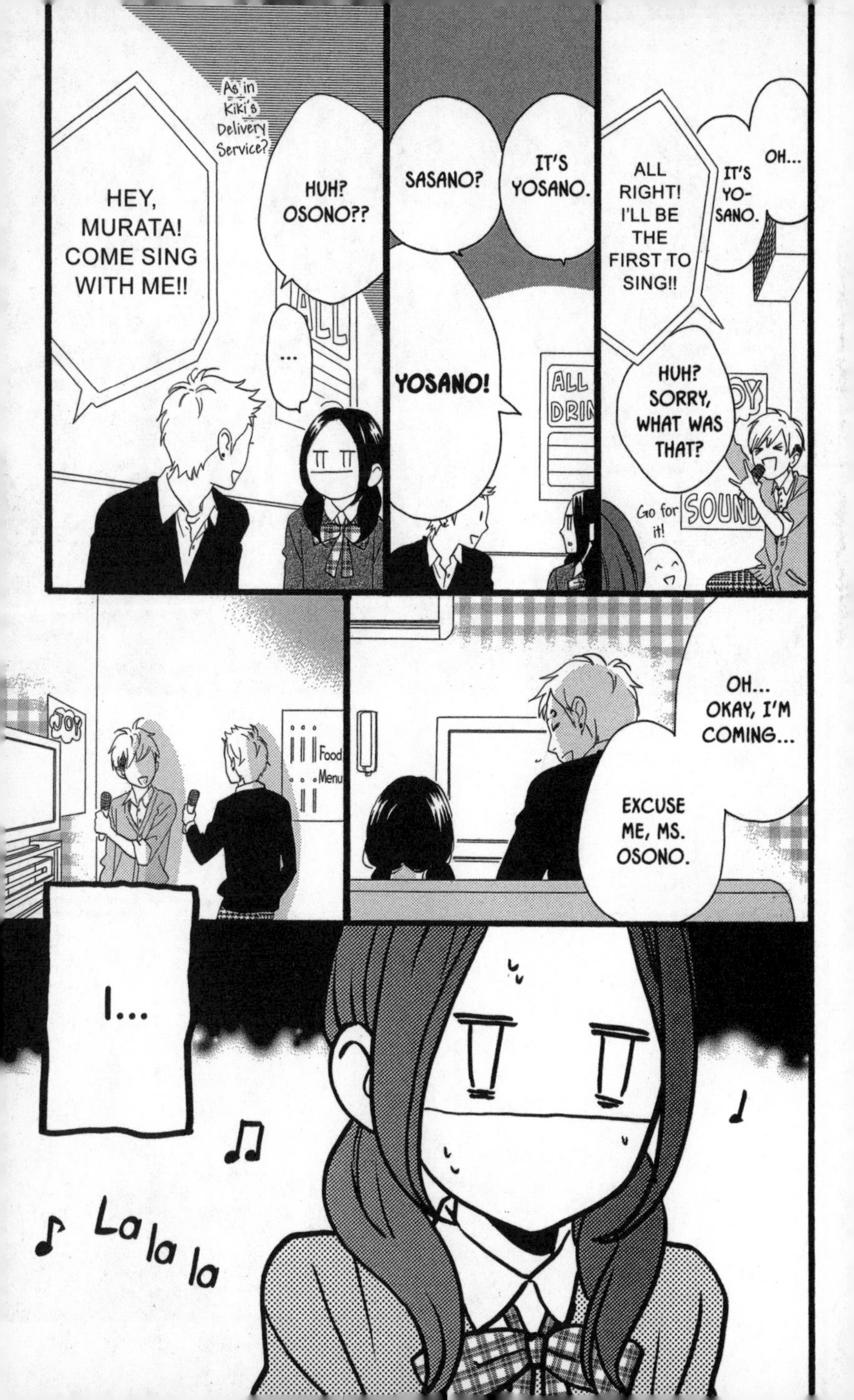
OH... IT'S YO-SANO.
ALL RIGHT! I'LL BE THE FIRST TO SING!!
HUH? SORRY, WHAT WAS THAT?
SOUND
Go for it!
IT'S YOSANO.
SASANO?
YOSANO!
ALL DRIN
HUH? OSONO??
As in Kiki's Delivery Service?
HEY, MURATA! COME SING WITH ME!!
...
OH... OKAY, I'M COMING...
EXCUSE ME, MS. OSONO.
JOY
Food Menu
I...
La la la

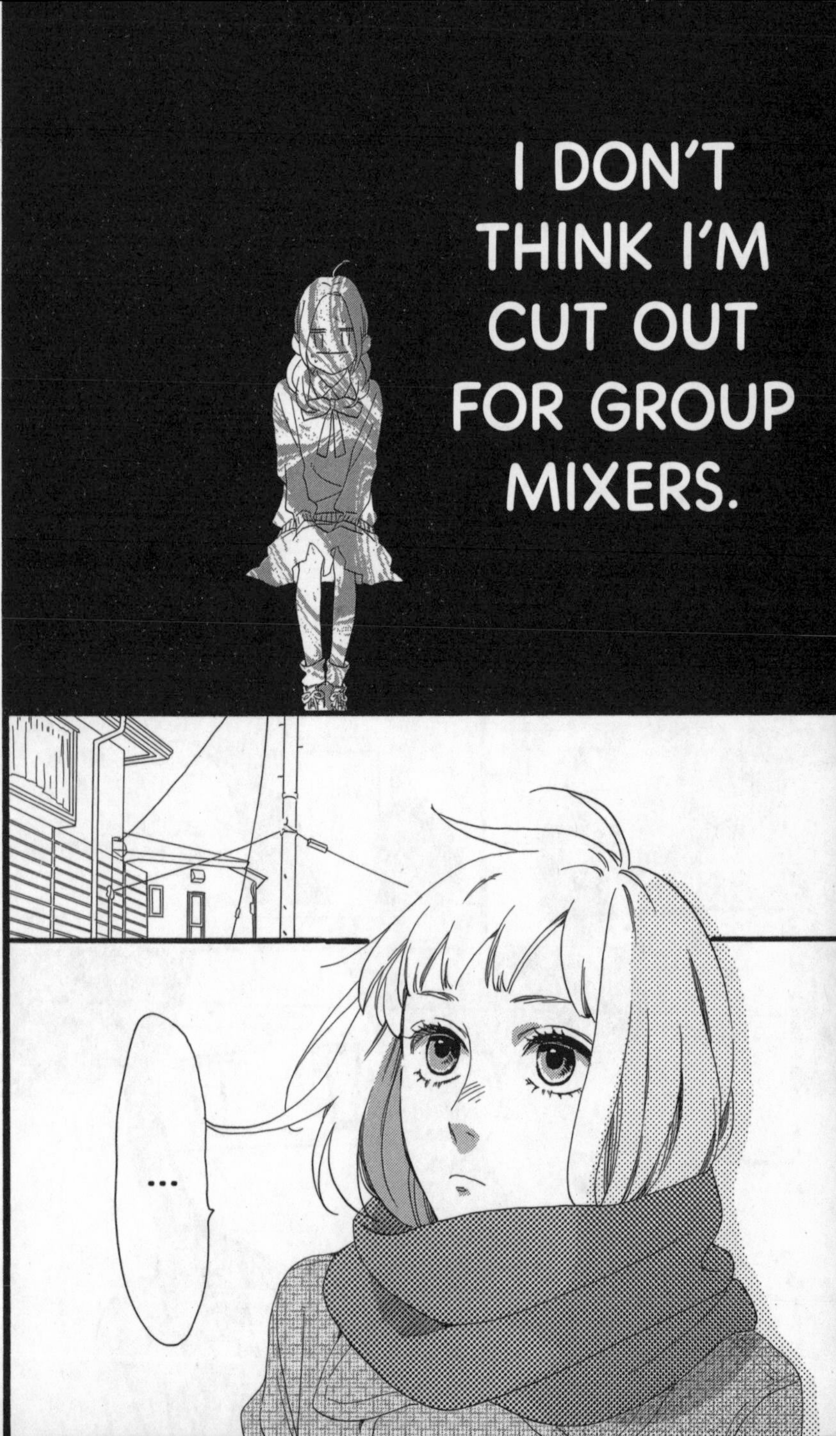
I DON'T THINK I'M CUT OUT FOR GROUP MIXERS.
...

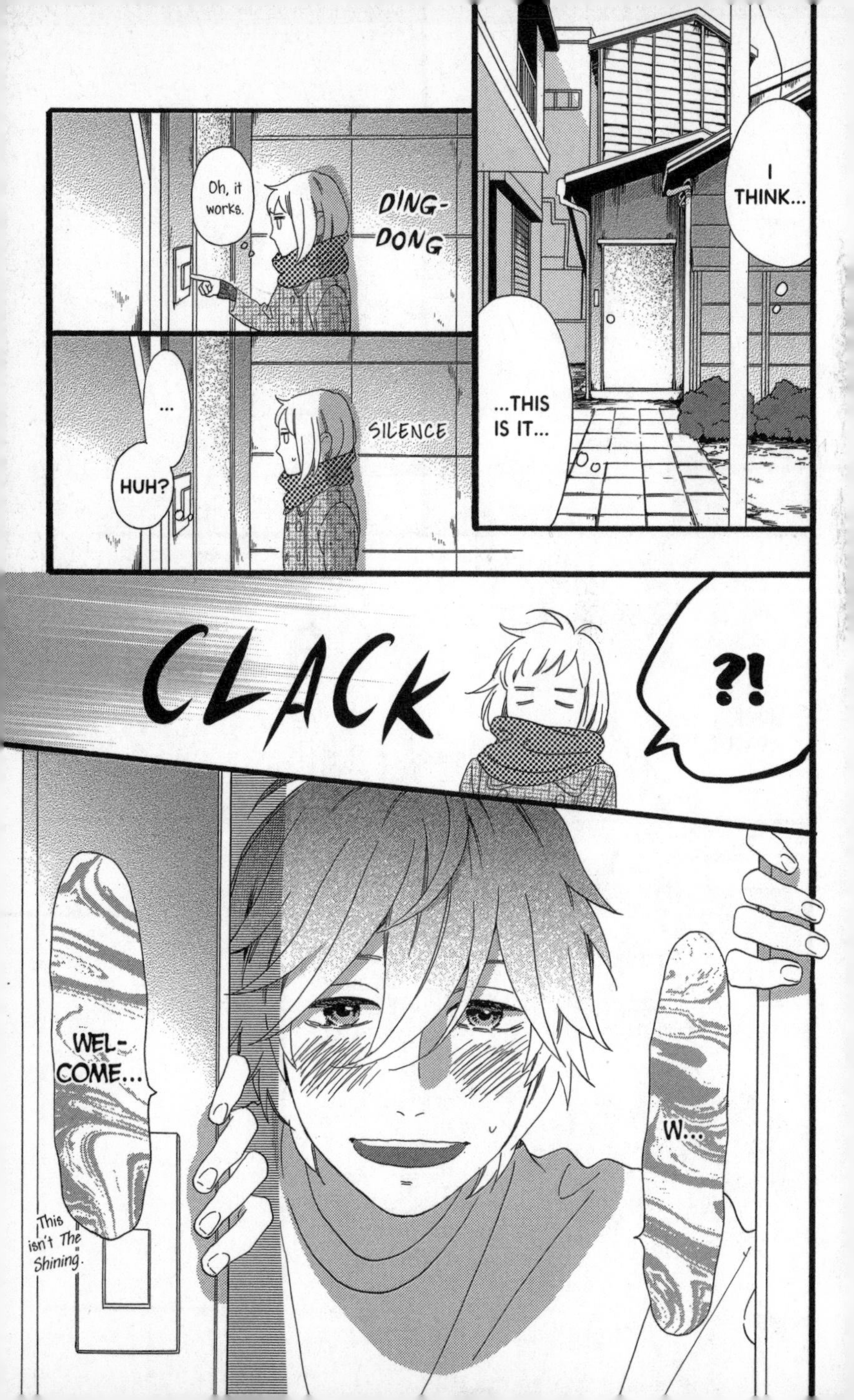
I THINK...
...THIS IS IT...
DING-DONG
Oh, it works.
SILENCE
...
HUH?
?!
CLACK
W...
...WEL-COME...
This isn't The Shining.

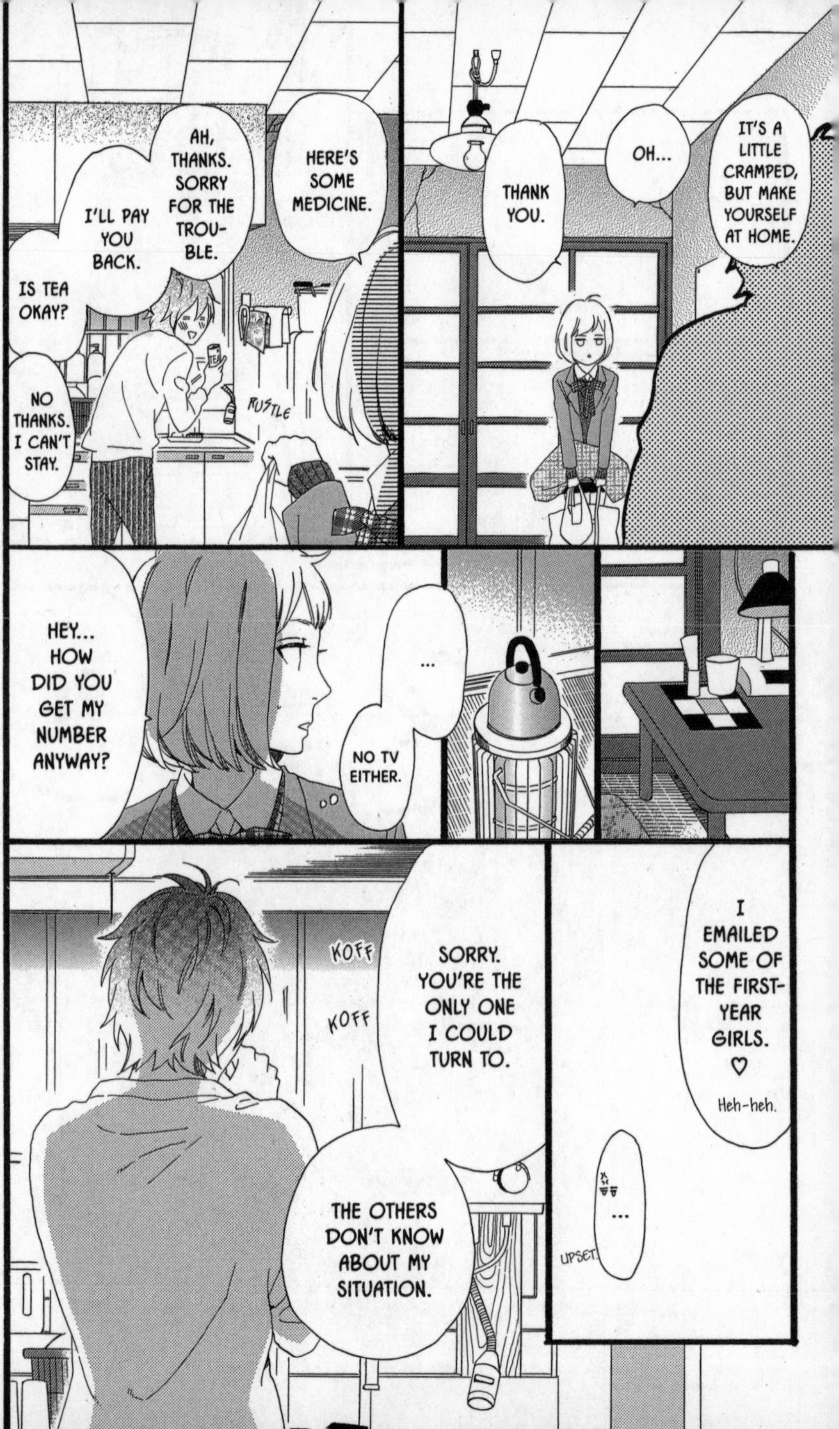
IT'S A LITTLE CRAMPED, BUT MAKE YOURSELF AT HOME.
OH...
THANK YOU.
HERE'S SOME MEDICINE.
AH, THANKS. SORRY FOR THE TROUBLE.
I'LL PAY YOU BACK.
IS TEA OKAY?
RUSTLE
NO THANKS. I CAN'T STAY.
...
NO TV EITHER.
HEY... HOW DID YOU GET MY NUMBER ANYWAY?
I EMAILED SOME OF THE FIRST-YEAR GIRLS. ♡
Heh-heh.
...
UPSET
SORRY. YOU'RE THE ONLY ONE I COULD TURN TO.
KOFF
KOFF
THE OTHERS DON'T KNOW ABOUT MY SITUATION.

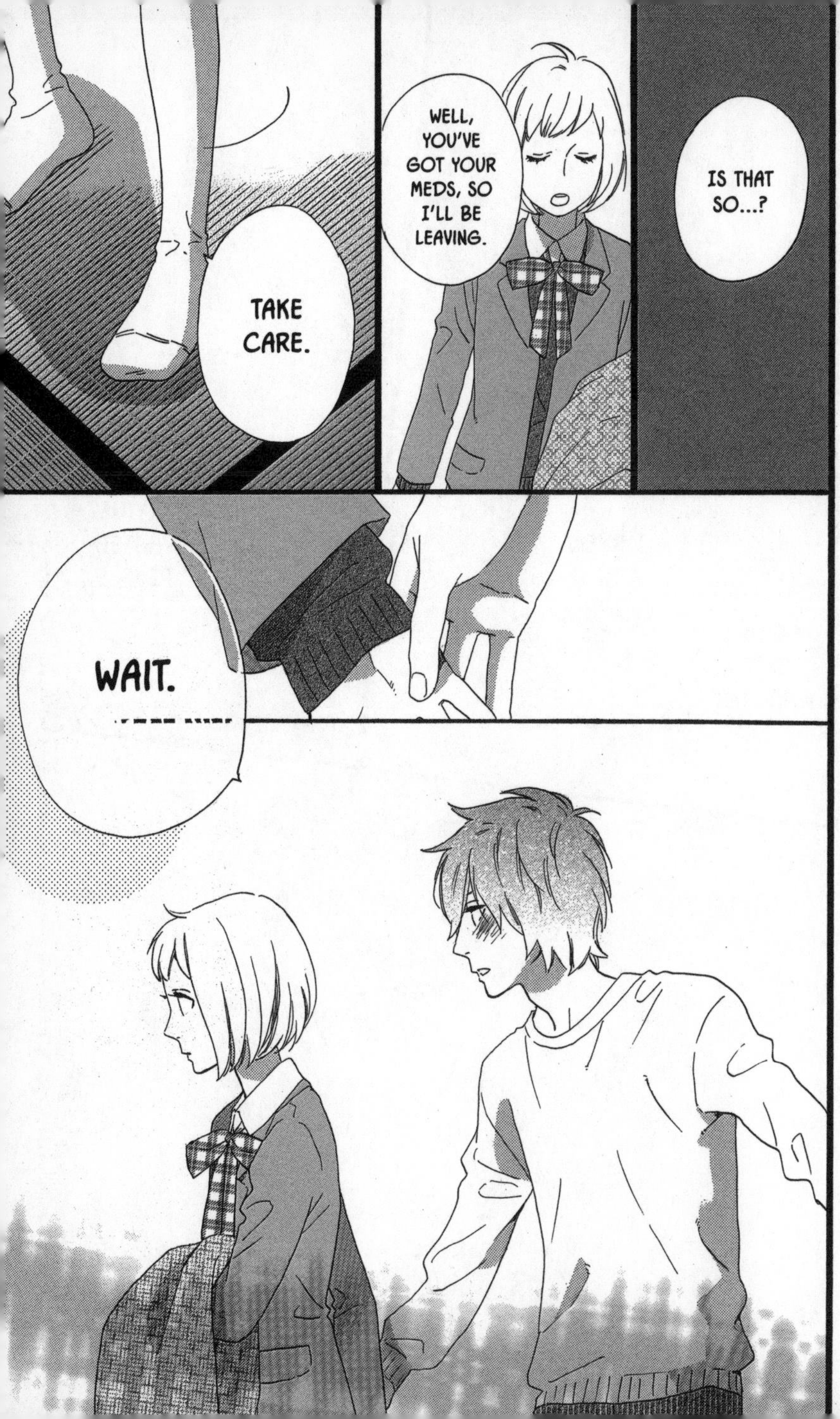
IS THAT SO...?
WELL, YOU'VE GOT YOUR MEDS, SO I'LL BE LEAVING.
TAKE CARE.
WAIT.

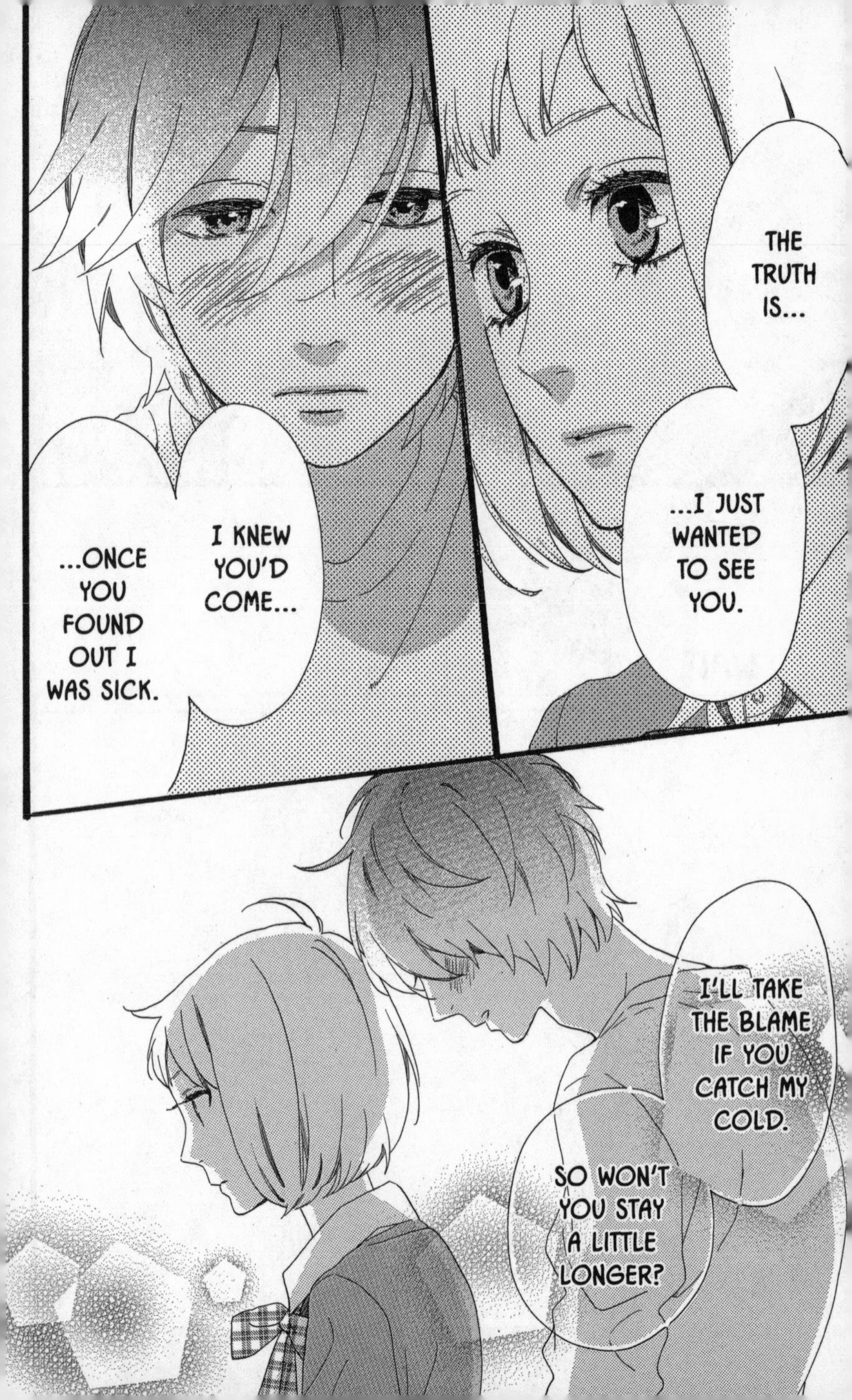
THE TRUTH IS...
...I JUST WANTED TO SEE YOU.
I KNEW YOU'D COME...
...ONCE YOU FOUND OUT I WAS SICK.
I'LL TAKE THE BLAME IF YOU CATCH MY COLD.
SO WON'T YOU STAY A LITTLE LONGER?

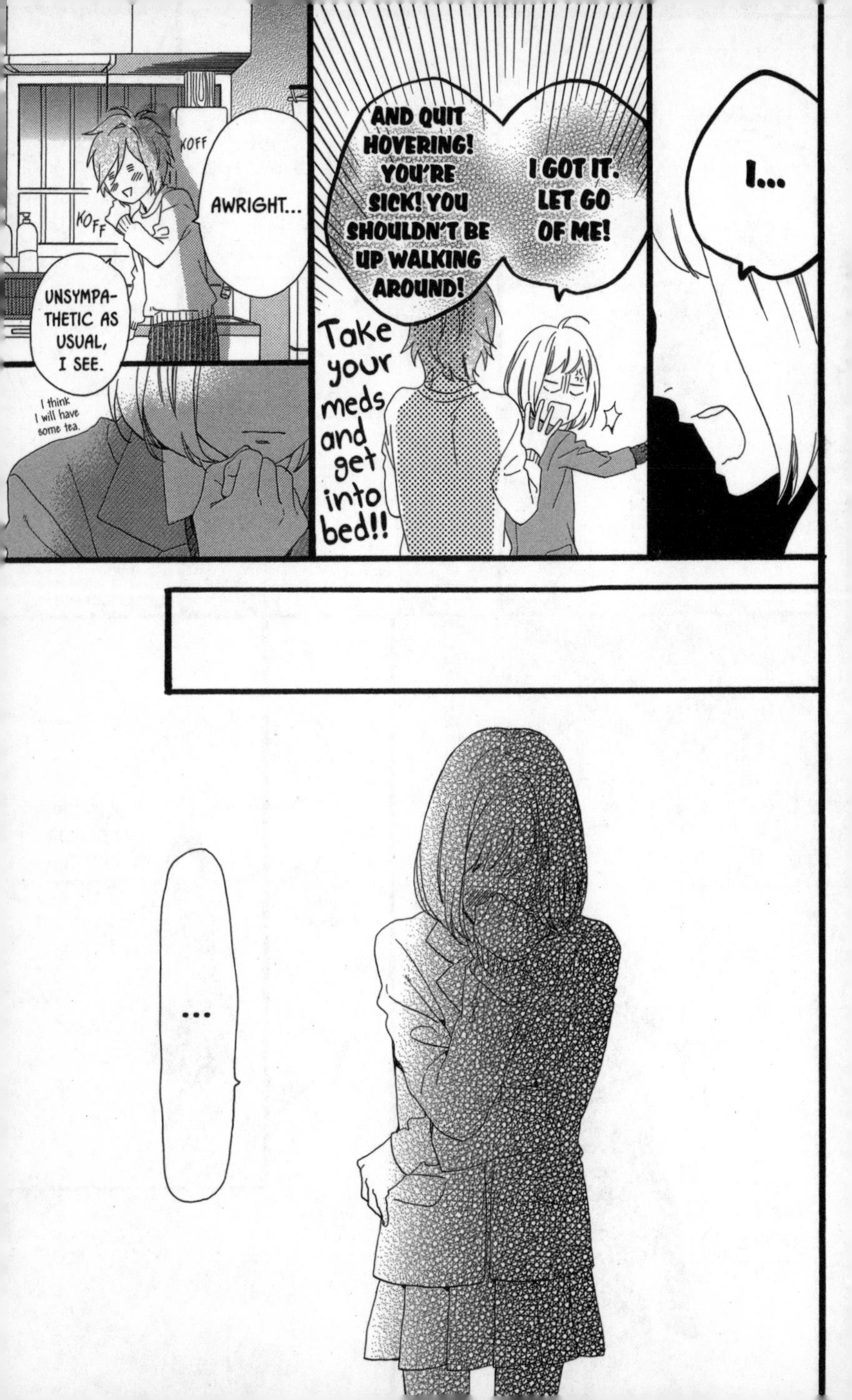
I...
Take your meds and get into bed!!
AND QUIT HOVERING! YOU'RE SICK! YOU SHOULDN'T BE UP WALKING AROUND!
I GOT IT. LET GO OF ME!
KOFF
KOFF
AWRIGHT...
UNSYMPA-THETIC AS USUAL, I SEE.
I think I will have some tea.
...

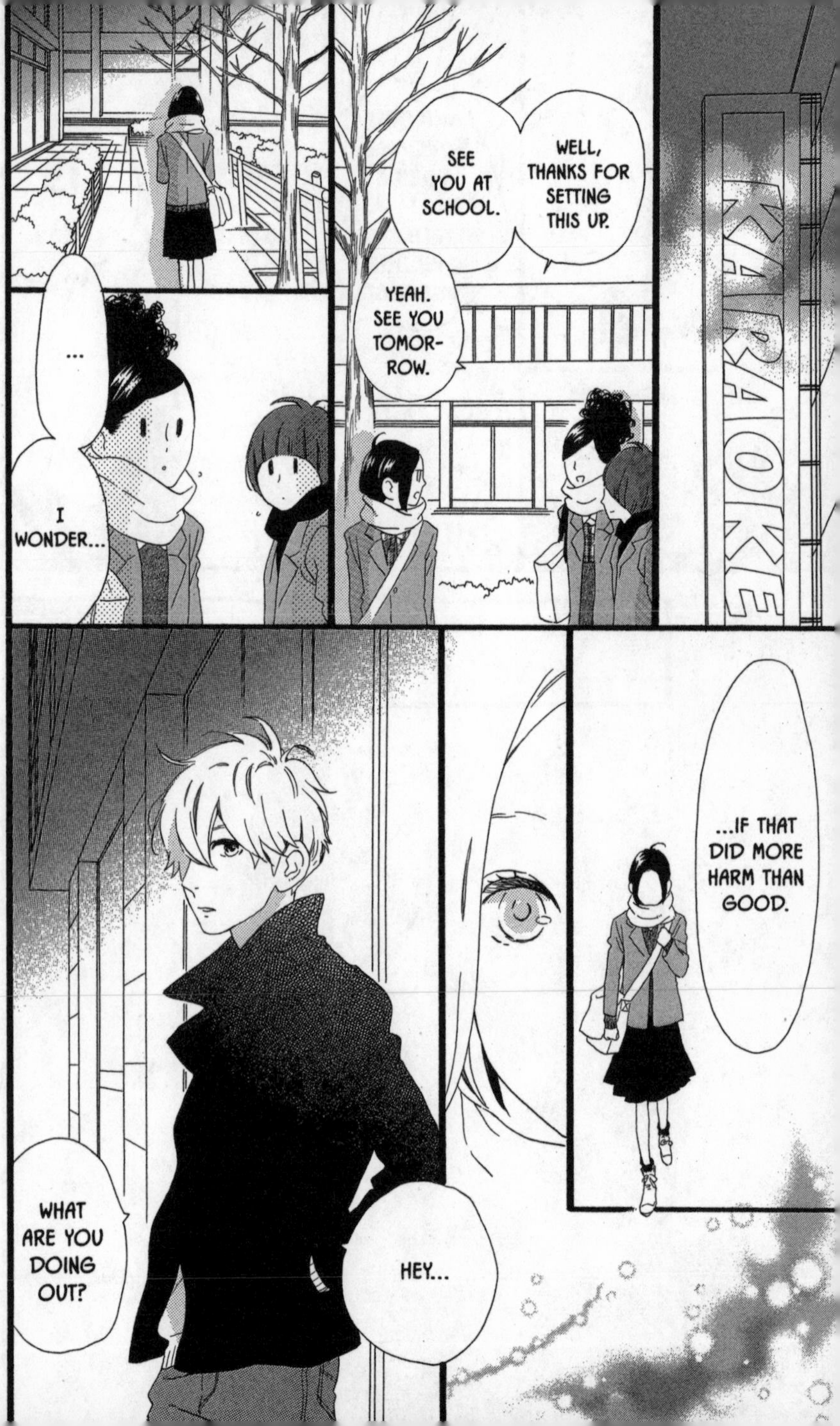
KARAOKE
WELL, THANKS FOR SETTING THIS UP.
SEE YOU AT SCHOOL.
YEAH. SEE YOU TOMORROW.
...
I WONDER...
...IF THAT DID MORE HARM THAN GOOD.
HEY...
WHAT ARE YOU DOING OUT?

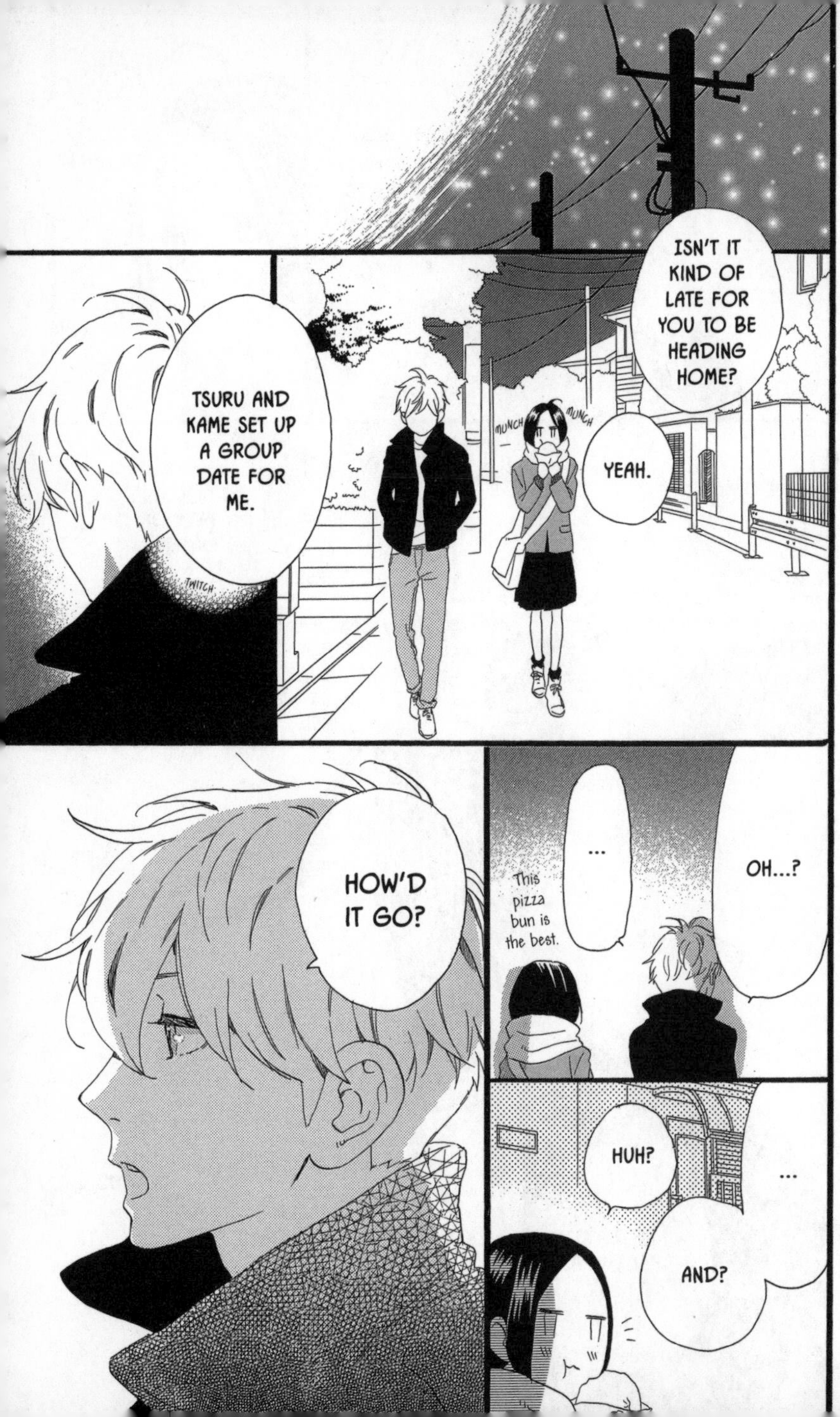
ISN'T IT KIND OF LATE FOR YOU TO BE HEADING HOME?
MUNCH
MUNCH
YEAH.
TSURU AND KAME SET UP A GROUP DATE FOR ME.
TWITCH
OH...?
...
This pizza bun is the best.
HUH?
...
AND?
HOW'D IT GO?

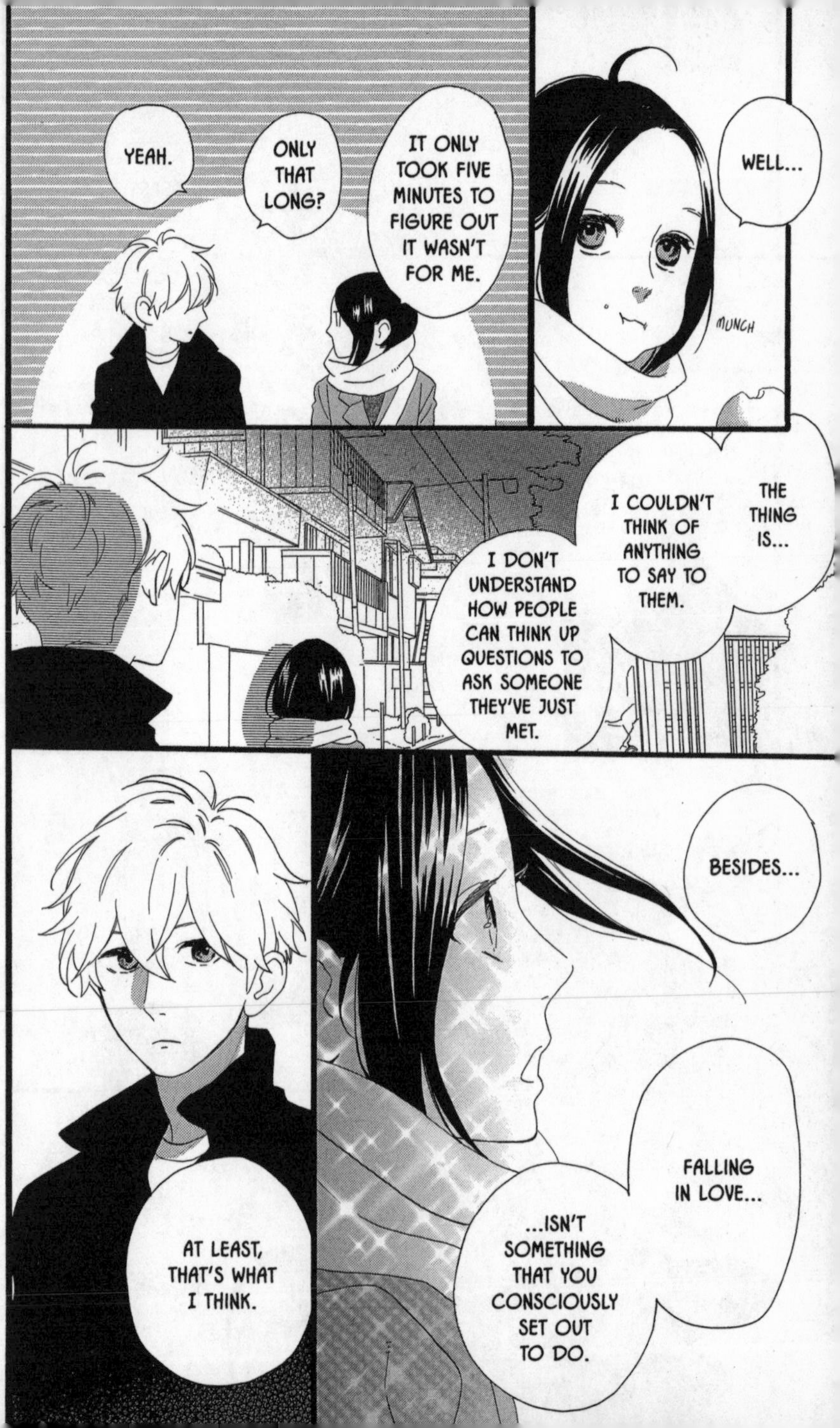
WELL...
MUNCH
IT ONLY TOOK FIVE MINUTES TO FIGURE OUT IT WASN'T FOR ME.
ONLY THAT LONG?
YEAH.
THE THING IS...
I COULDN'T THINK OF ANYTHING TO SAY TO THEM.
I DON'T UNDERSTAND HOW PEOPLE CAN THINK UP QUESTIONS TO ASK SOMEONE THEY'VE JUST MET.
BESIDES...
FALLING IN LOVE...
...ISN'T SOMETHING THAT YOU CONSCIOUSLY SET OUT TO DO.
AT LEAST, THAT'S WHAT I THINK.

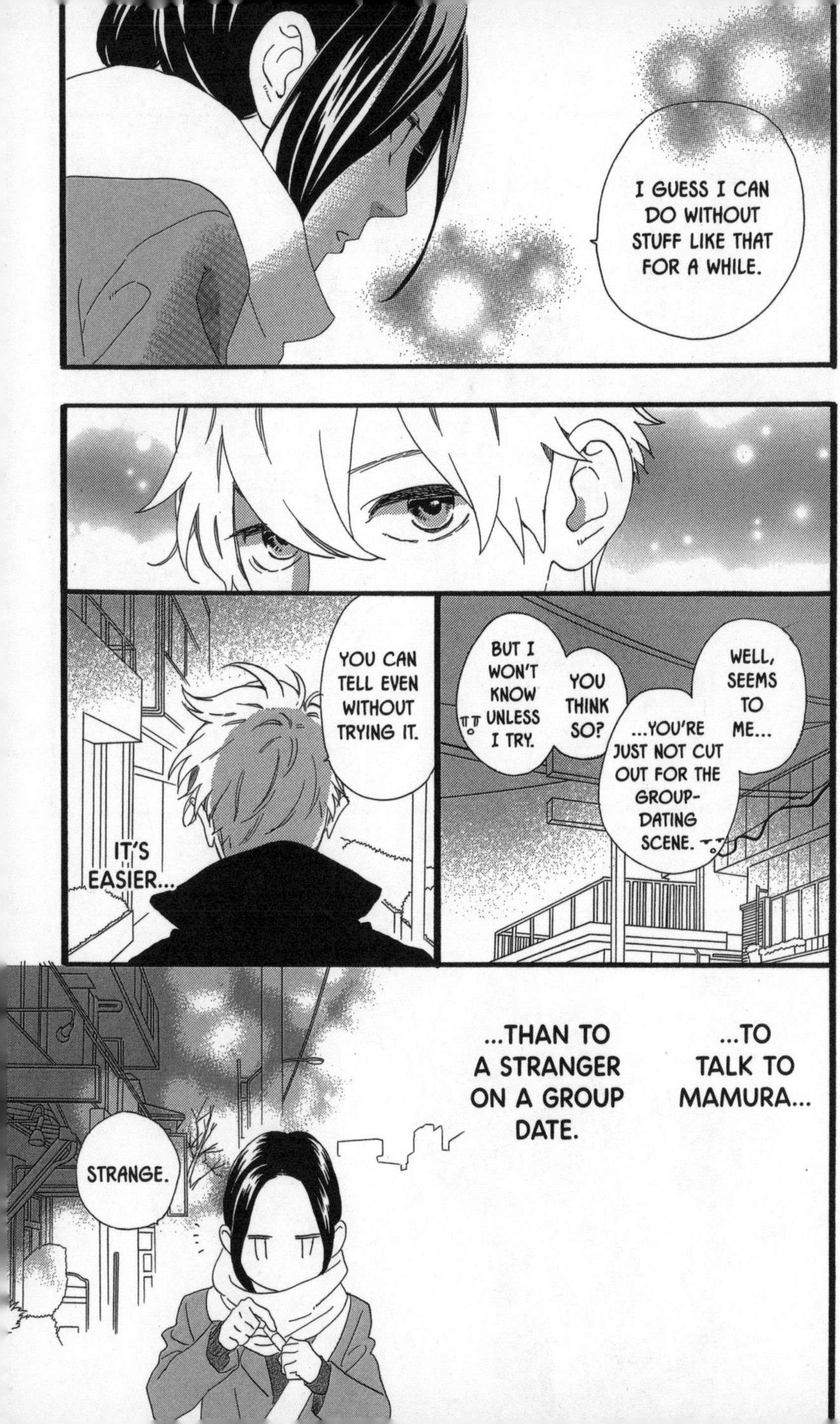
I GUESS I CAN DO WITHOUT STUFF LIKE THAT FOR A WHILE.
WELL, SEEMS TO ME...
...YOU'RE JUST NOT CUT OUT FOR THE GROUP-DATING SCENE.
YOU THINK SO?
BUT I WON'T KNOW UNLESS I TRY.
YOU CAN TELL EVEN WITHOUT TRYING IT.
IT'S EASIER...
...TO TALK TO MAMURA...
...THAN TO A STRANGER ON A GROUP DATE.
STRANGE.

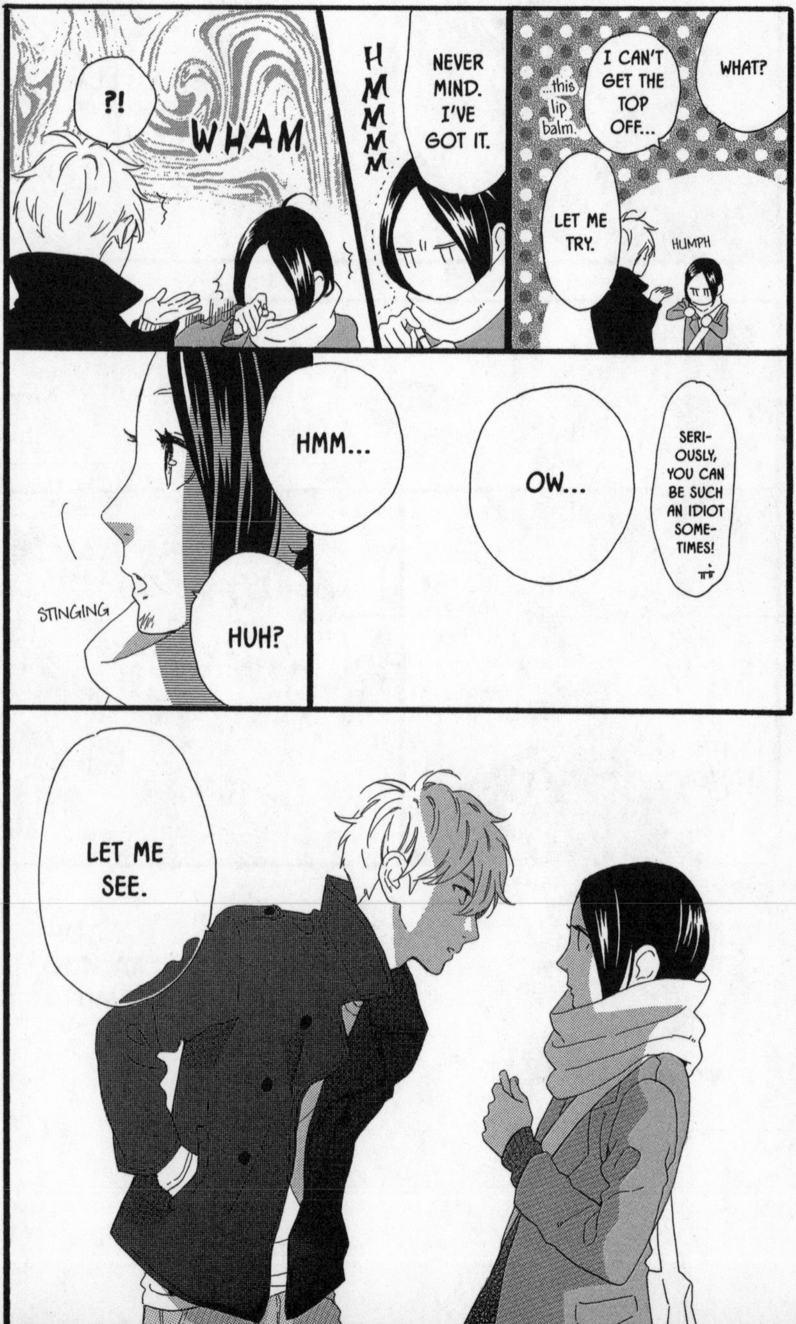

WHAT?
I CAN'T GET THE TOP OFF...
...this lip balm.
LET ME TRY.
HUMPH
NEVER MIND. I'VE GOT IT.
HMMMM
?!
WHAM
SERI-OUSLY, YOU CAN BE SUCH AN IDIOT SOME-TIMES!
OW...
HMM...
HUH?
STINGING
LET ME SEE.

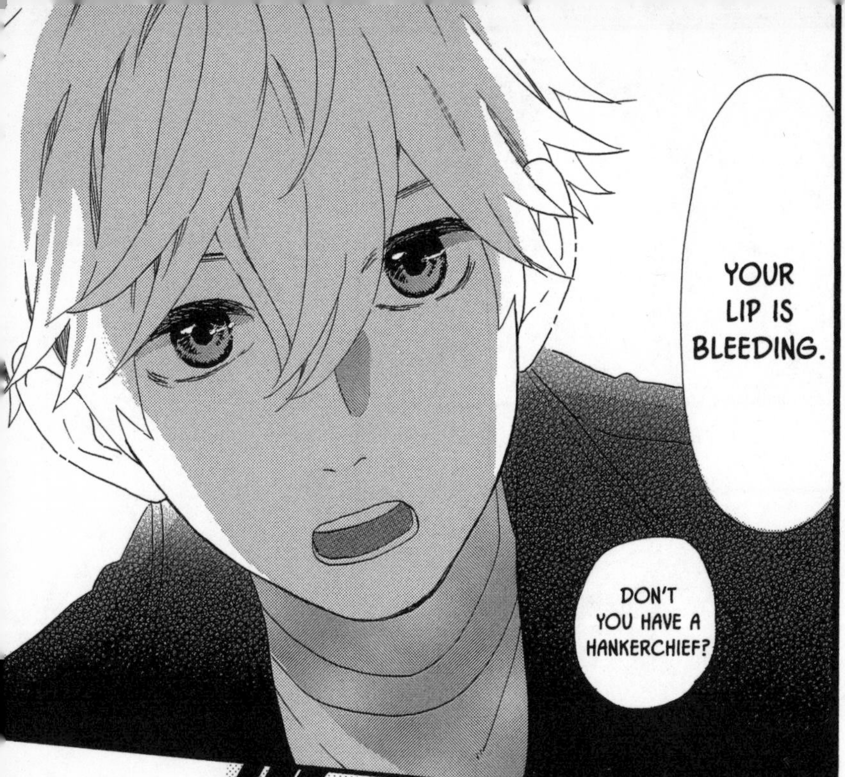
YOUR LIP IS BLEEDING.
DON'T YOU HAVE A HANKERCHIEF?
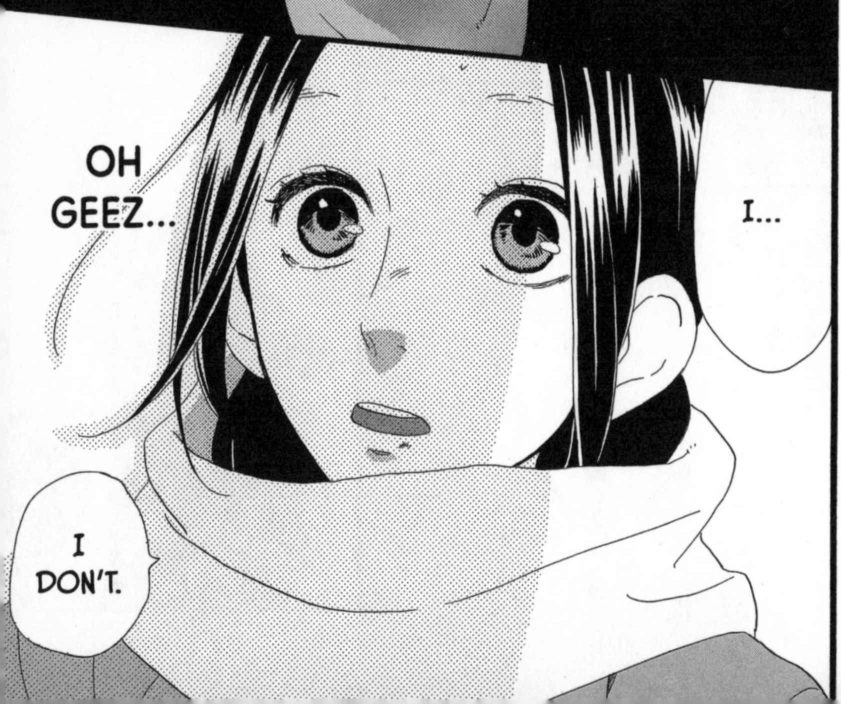
I...
OH GEEZ...
I DON'T.

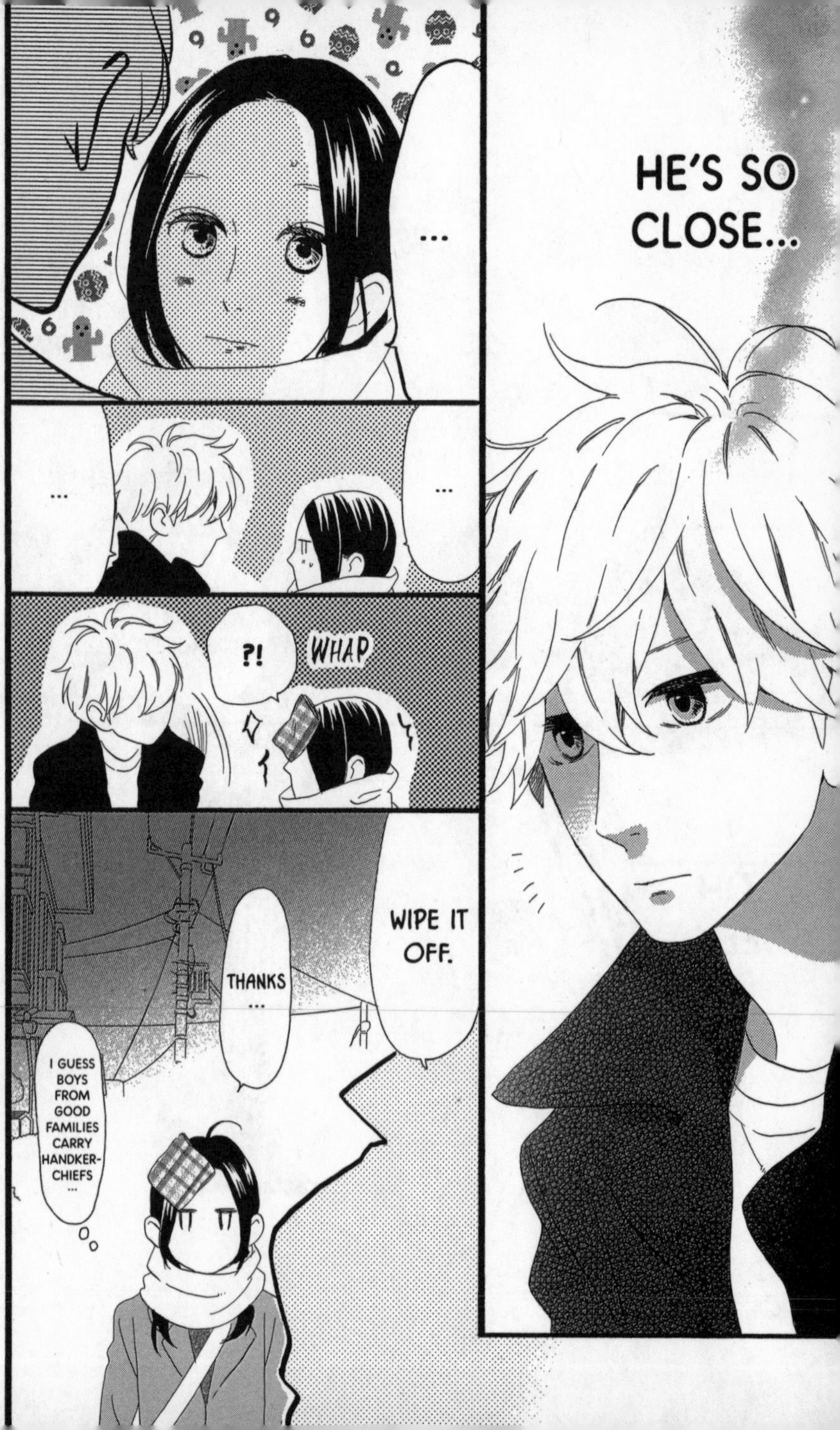
HE'S SO CLOSE...
...
...
...
WHAP
?!
WIPE IT OFF.
THANKS ...
I GUESS BOYS FROM GOOD FAMILIES CARRY HANDKER-CHIEFS ...

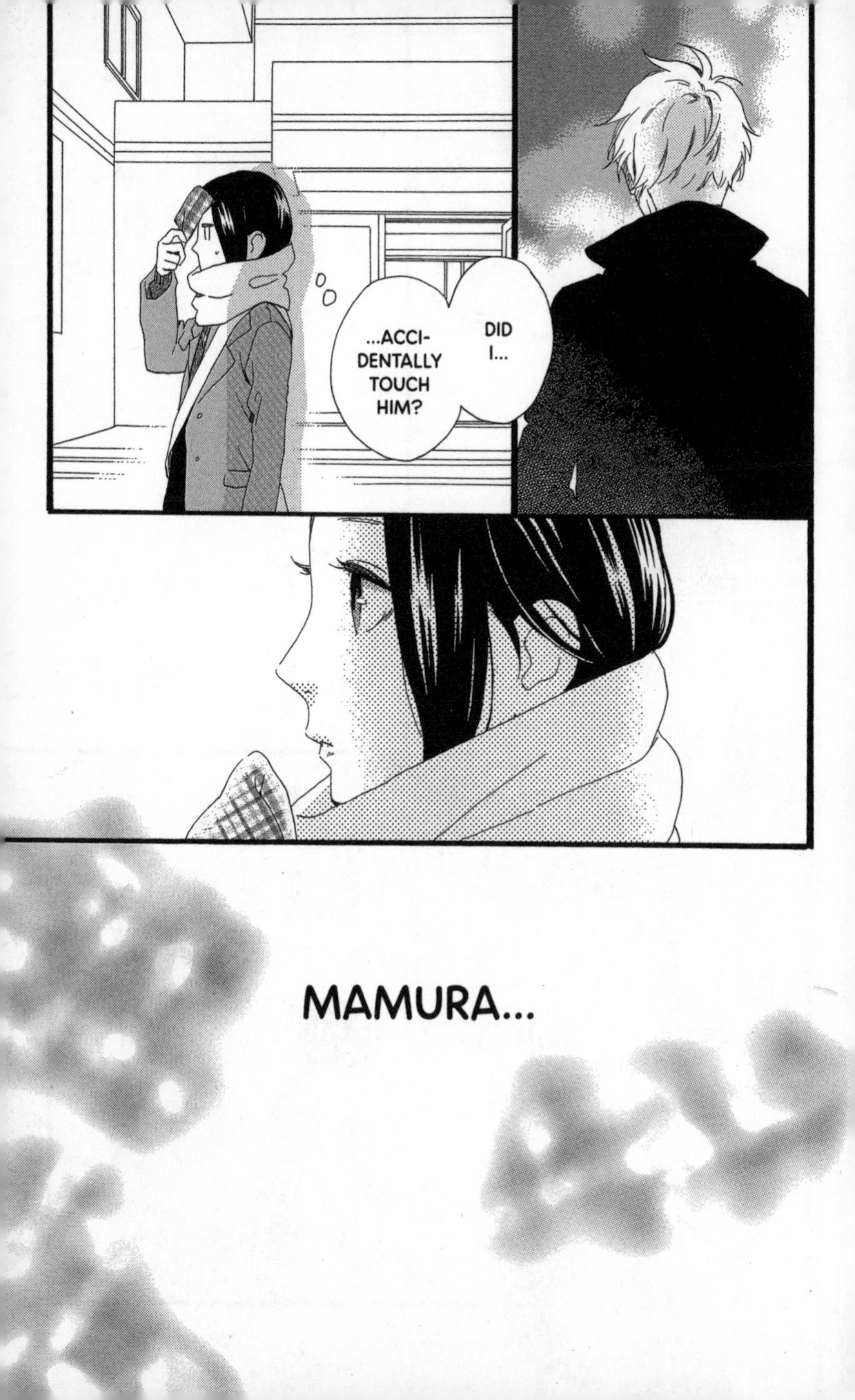
DID I...
...ACCI-DENTALLY TOUCH HIM?
MAMURA...

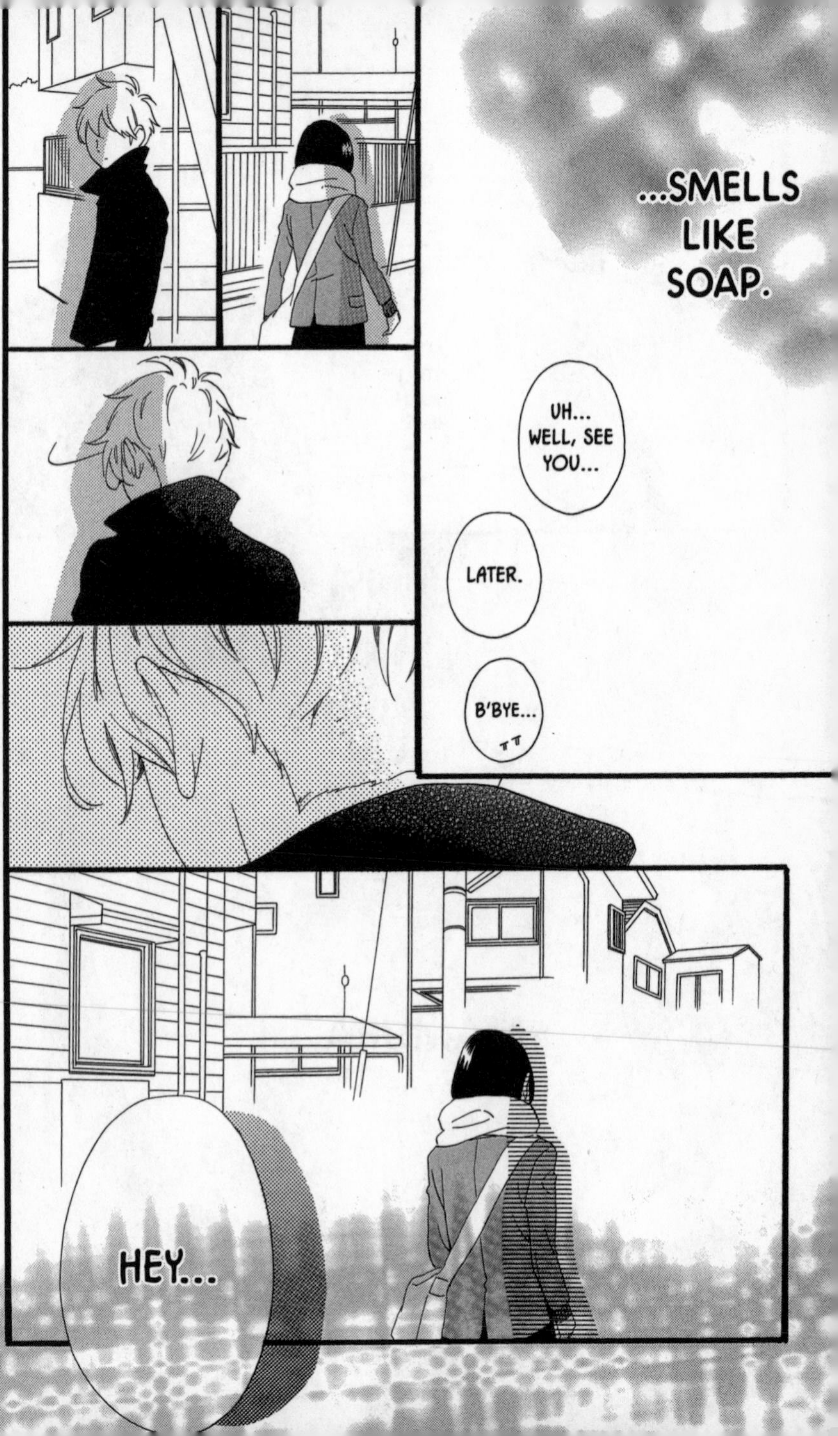
...SMELLS LIKE SOAP.
UH... WELL, SEE YOU...
LATER.
B'BYE...
HEY...

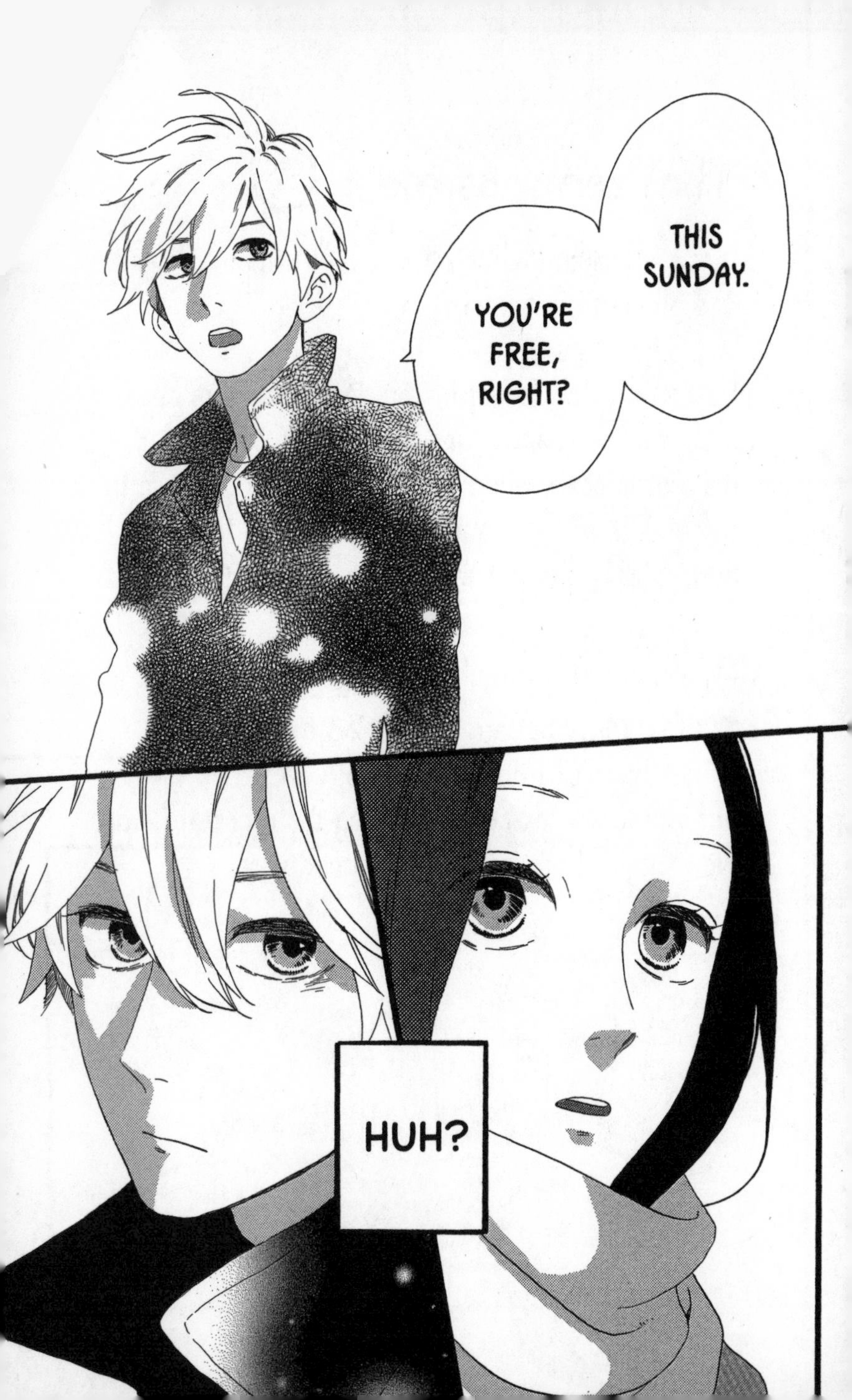
THIS SUNDAY. YOU'RE FREE, RIGHT?
HUH?

That reminds me... ③

It was my birthday the other day. My mom, sister and dad all sent me presents.

I asked my dad to get me an iRobot vacuum cleaner, and wow, is it handy! Seriously, it's really good. But it's a little scary when it suddenly starts cleaning in the middle of the night. I wonder why it does that. Huh? Surely, I'm not the only one this happens to.

My sister and my mother both got me **coffee makers.** What am I supposed to do with two coffee makers? I don't need two! I ended up taking one to my workplace and leaving the other at home. Now they're both being put to good use.

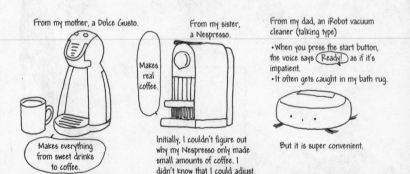

From my mother, a Dolce Gusto.

Makes everything from sweet drinks to coffee.

From my sister, a Nespresso.

Makes real coffee.

Initially, I couldn't figure out why my Nespresso only made small amounts of coffee. I didn't know that I could adjust the amount!

From my dad, an iRobot vacuum cleaner (talking type)

- When you press the start button, the voice says (Ready!) as if it's impatient.
- It often gets caught in my bath rug.

But it is super convenient.

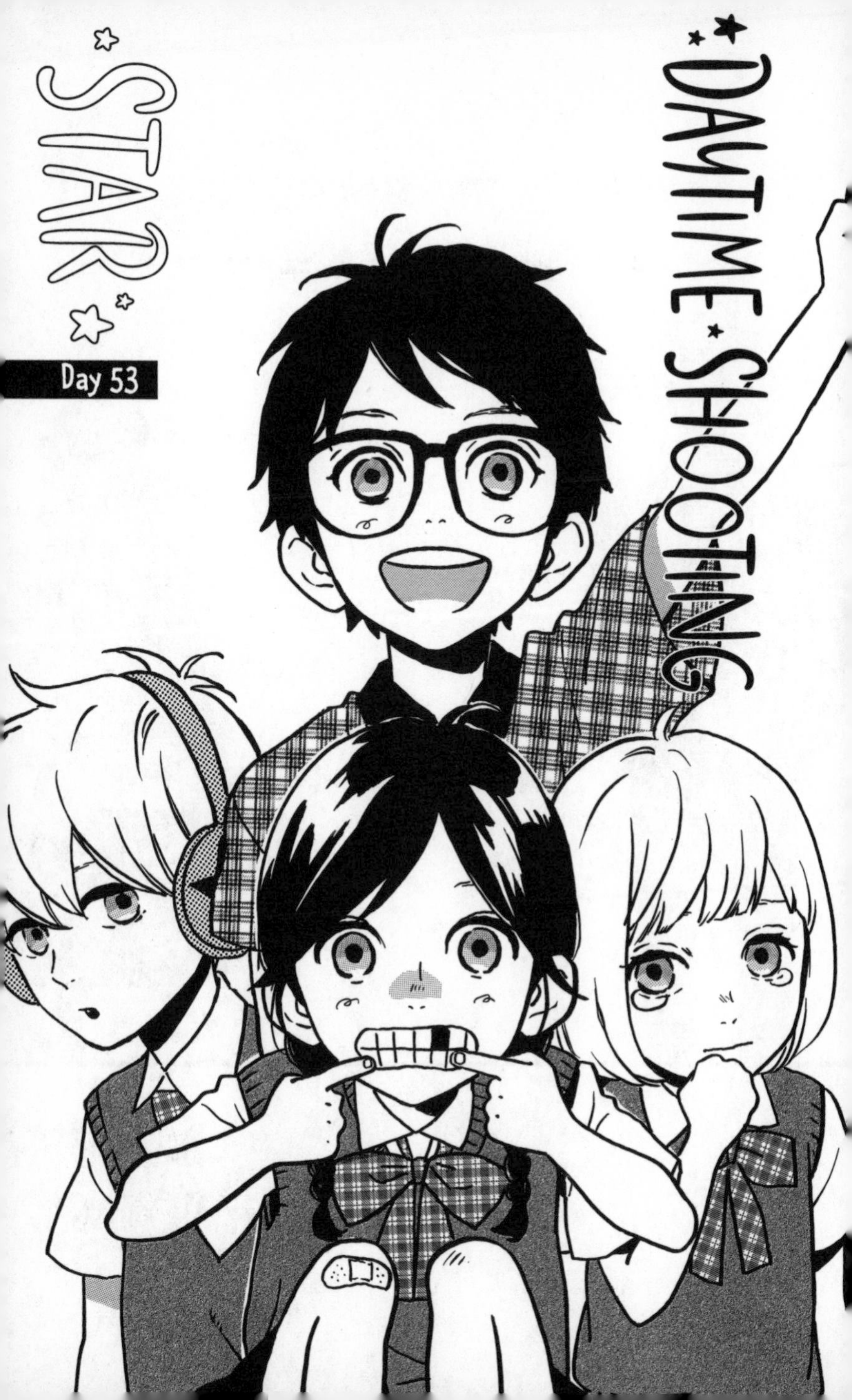
DAYTIME SHOOTING STAR
Day 53

"THIS SUNDAY.

YOU'RE FREE, RIGHT?"

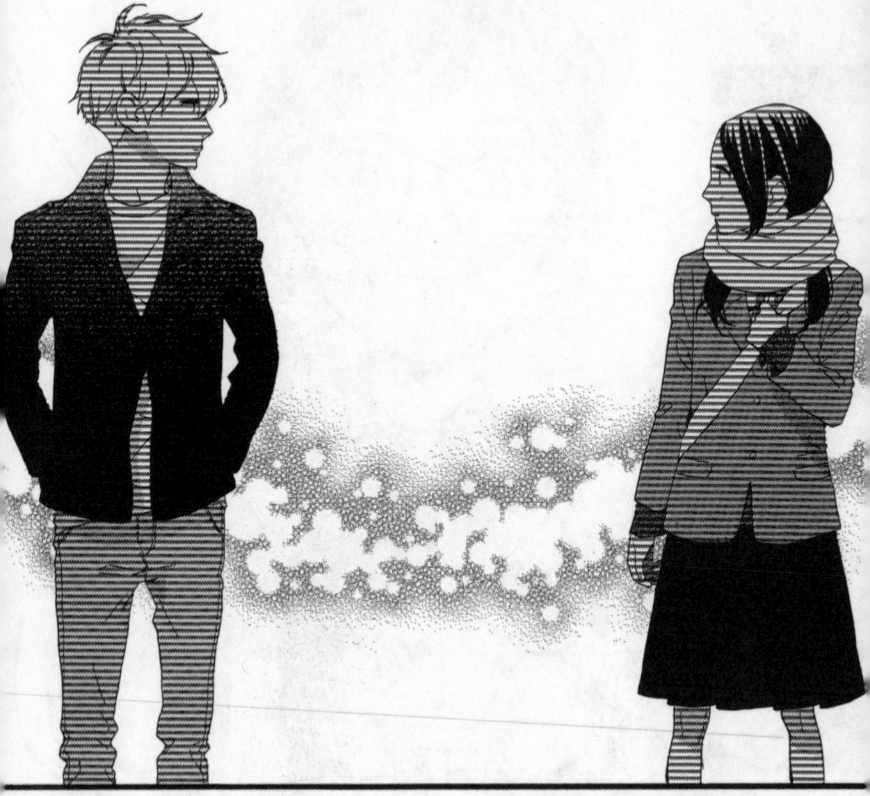

DAYTIME SHOOTING STAR

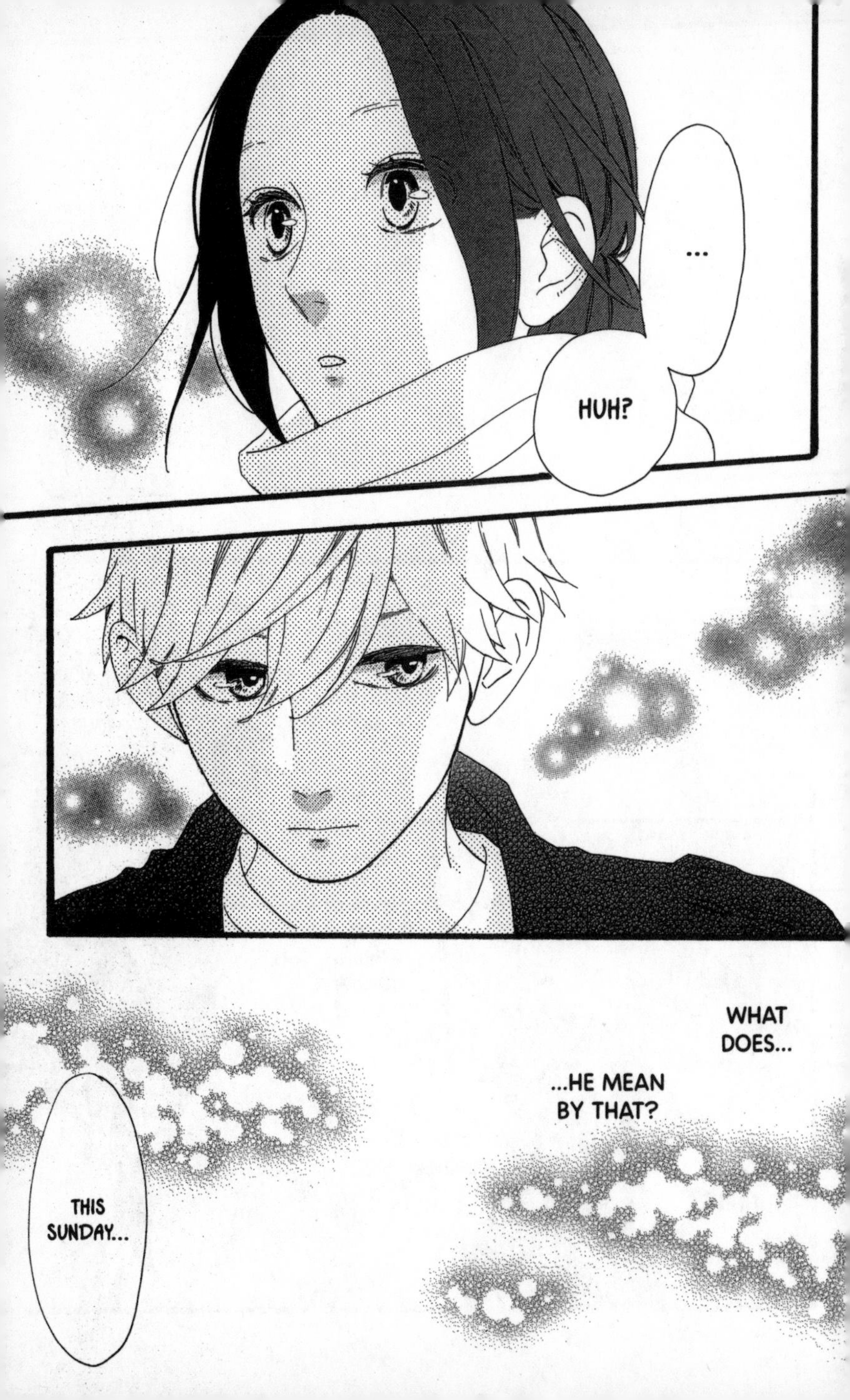
...
HUH?
WHAT DOES...
...HE MEAN BY THAT?
THIS SUNDAY...

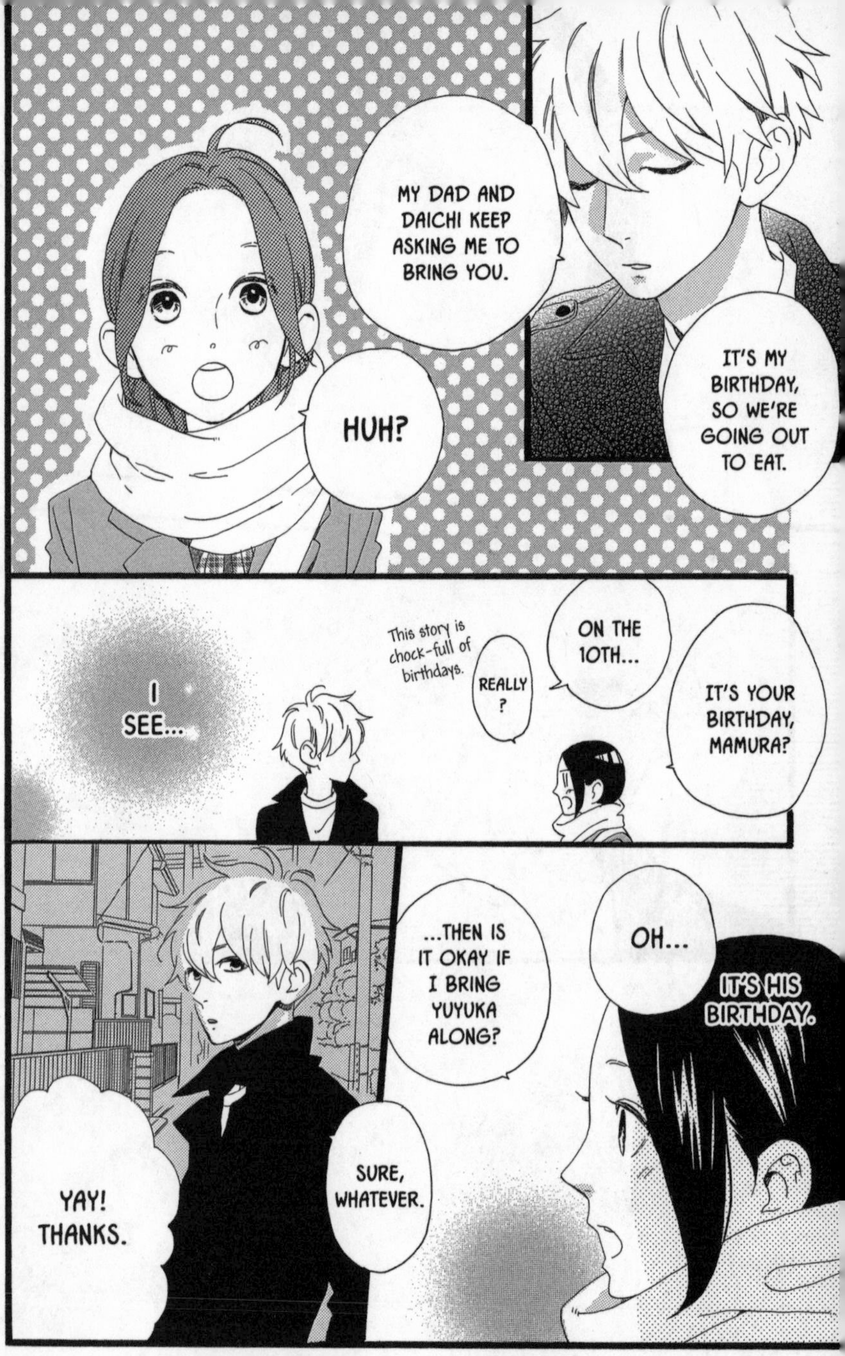
IT'S MY BIRTHDAY, SO WE'RE GOING OUT TO EAT.
MY DAD AND DAICHI KEEP ASKING ME TO BRING YOU.
HUH?
IT'S YOUR BIRTHDAY, MAMURA?
ON THE 10TH...
REALLY?
This story is chock-full of birthdays.
I SEE...
OH...
IT'S HIS BIRTHDAY.
...THEN IS IT OKAY IF I BRING YUYUKA ALONG?
SURE, WHATEVER.
YAY! THANKS.

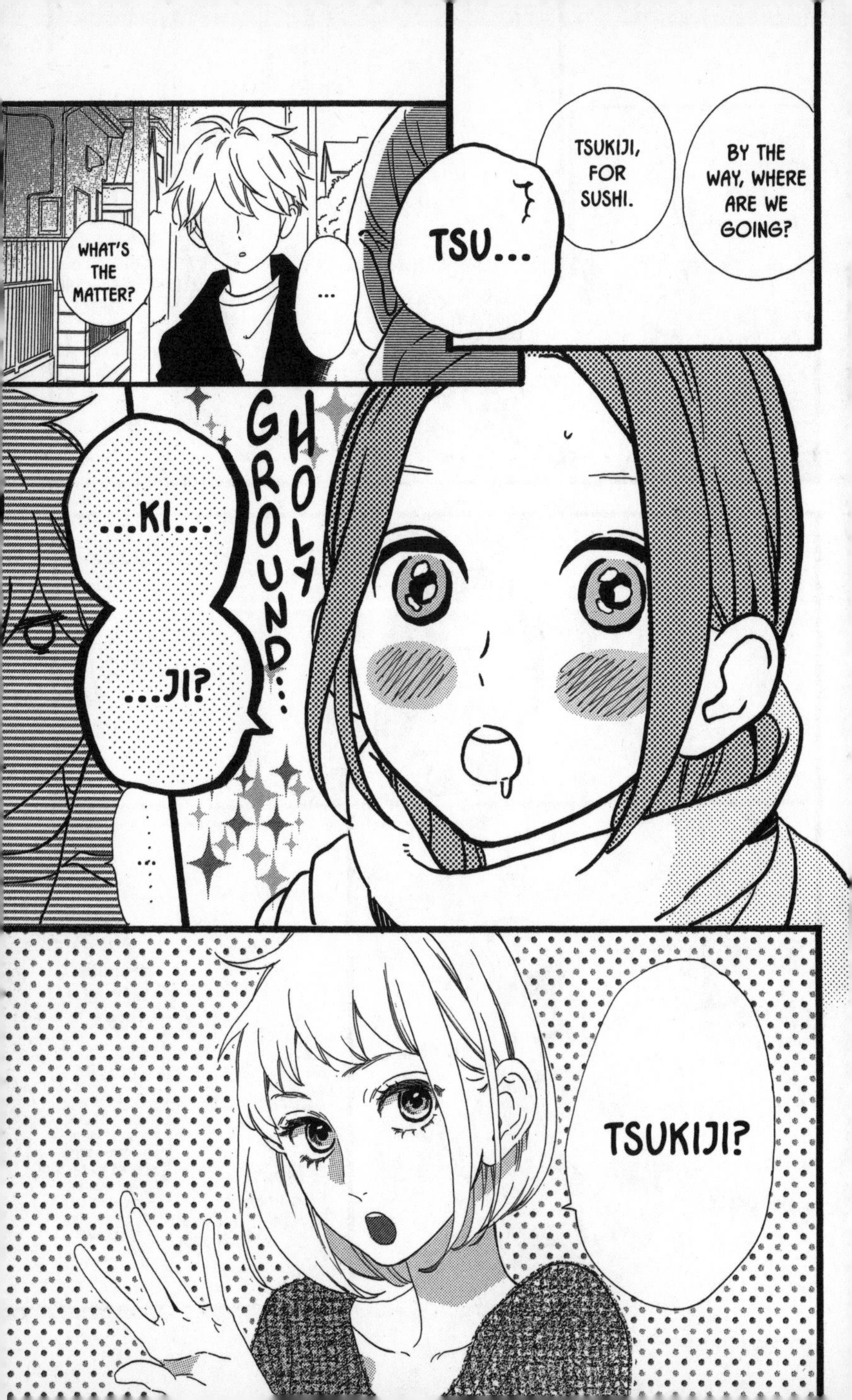
BY THE WAY, WHERE ARE WE GOING?
TSUKIJI, FOR SUSHI.
TSU...
...
WHAT'S THE MATTER?
HOLY GROUND...
...KI... ...JI?
TSUKIJI?

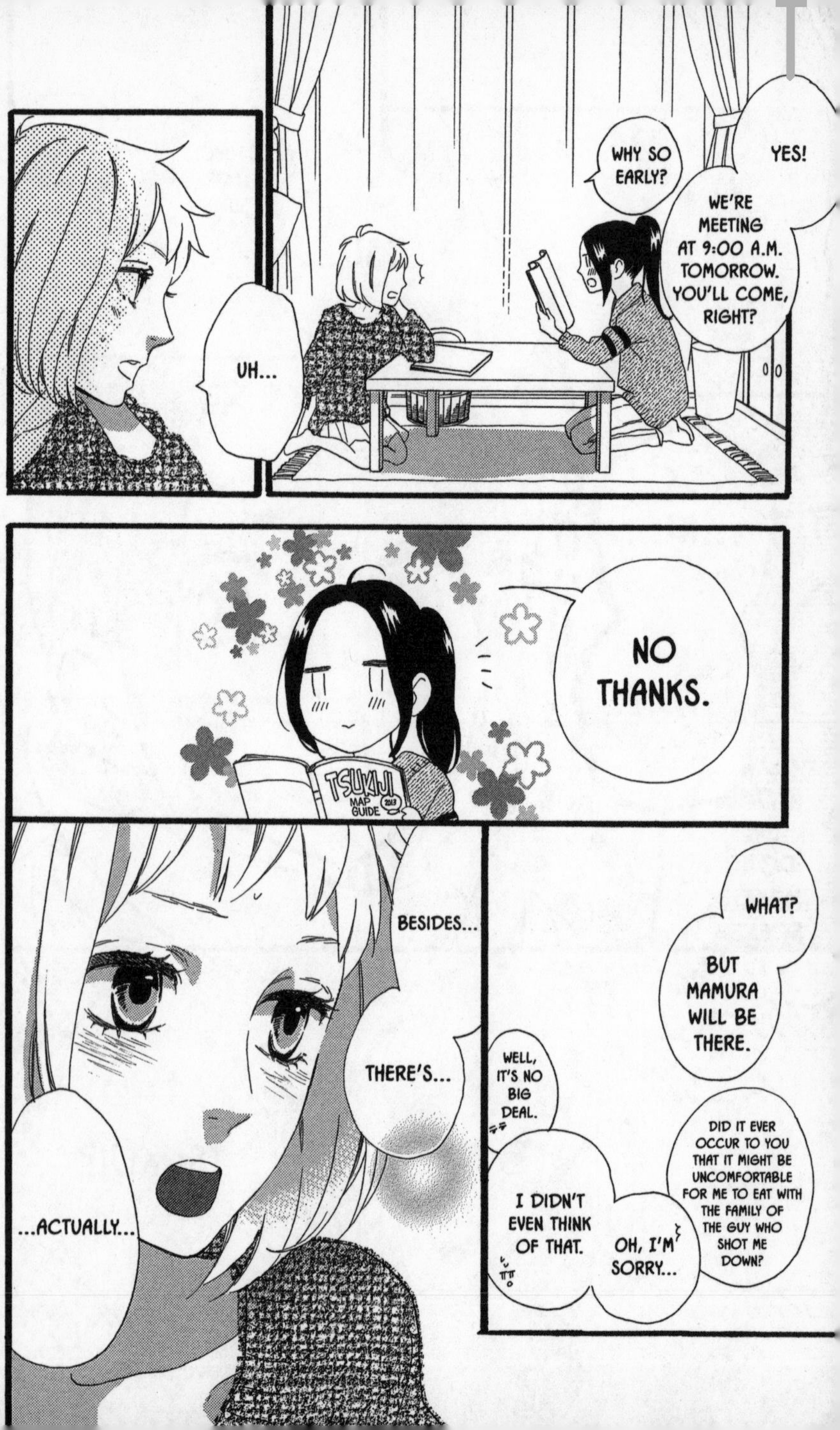
YES!
WE'RE MEETING AT 9:00 A.M. TOMORROW. YOU'LL COME, RIGHT?
WHY SO EARLY?
UH...
NO THANKS.
TSUKIJI MAP GUIDE 2013
WHAT?
BUT MAMURA WILL BE THERE.
DID IT EVER OCCUR TO YOU THAT IT MIGHT BE UNCOMFORTABLE FOR ME TO EAT WITH THE FAMILY OF THE GUY WHO SHOT ME DOWN?
OH, I'M SORRY...
I DIDN'T EVEN THINK OF THAT.
WELL, IT'S NO BIG DEAL.
BESIDES...
THERE'S...
...ACTUALLY...

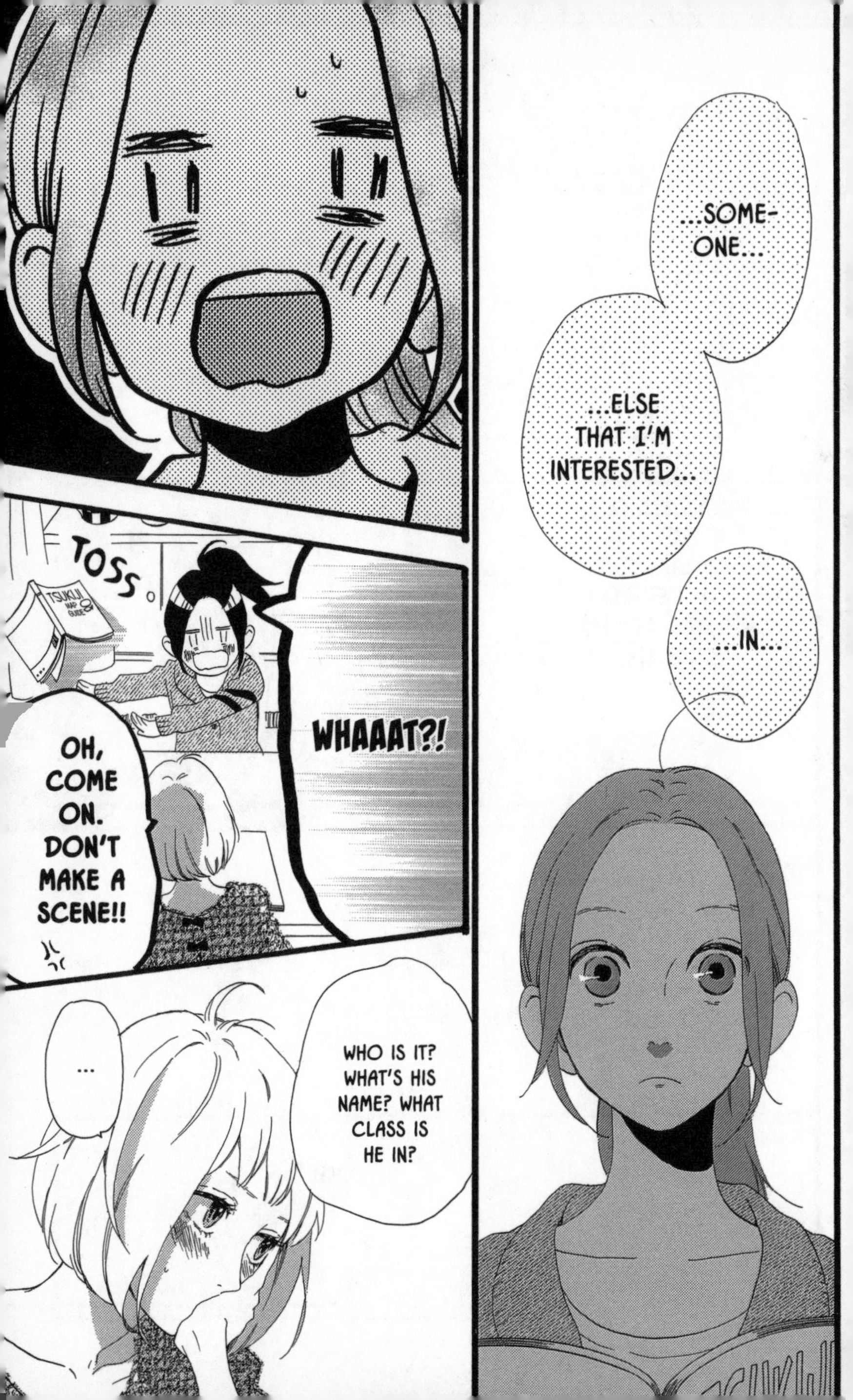
...SOME-ONE...
...ELSE THAT I'M INTERESTED...
...IN...
WHAAAT?!
TOSS
TSUKIJI MAP GUIDE
OH, COME ON. DON'T MAKE A SCENE!!
WHO IS IT? WHAT'S HIS NAME? WHAT CLASS IS HE IN?
...

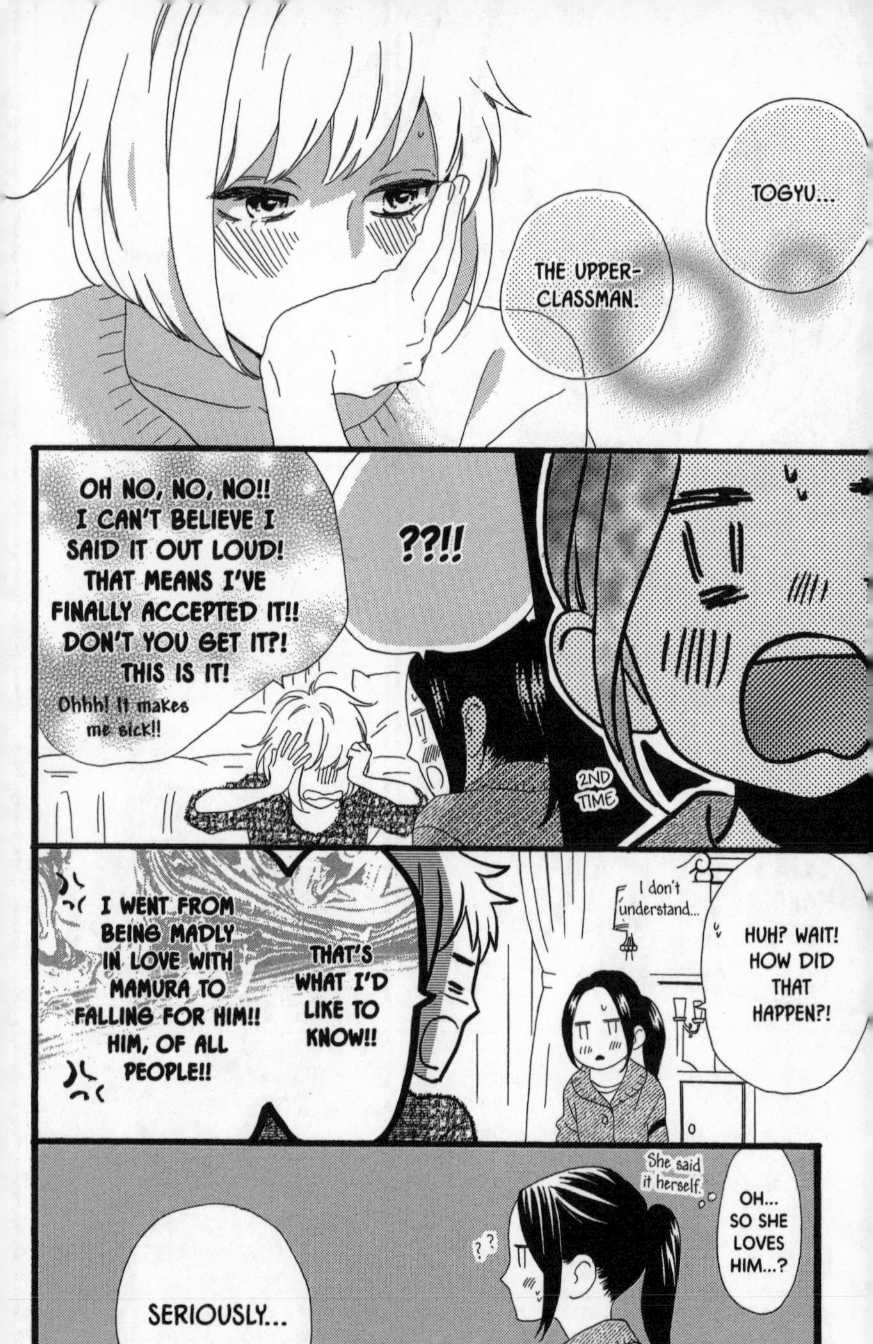
TOGYU...
THE UPPER-CLASSMAN.
??!!
2ND TIME
OH NO, NO, NO!! I CAN'T BELIEVE I SAID IT OUT LOUD! THAT MEANS I'VE FINALLY ACCEPTED IT!! DON'T YOU GET IT?! THIS IS IT!
Ohhh! It makes me sick!!
HUH? WAIT! HOW DID THAT HAPPEN?!
I don't understand...
THAT'S WHAT I'D LIKE TO KNOW!!
I WENT FROM BEING MADLY IN LOVE WITH MAMURA TO FALLING FOR HIM!! HIM, OF ALL PEOPLE!!
OH... SO SHE LOVES HIM...?
She said it herself.
SERIOUSLY...

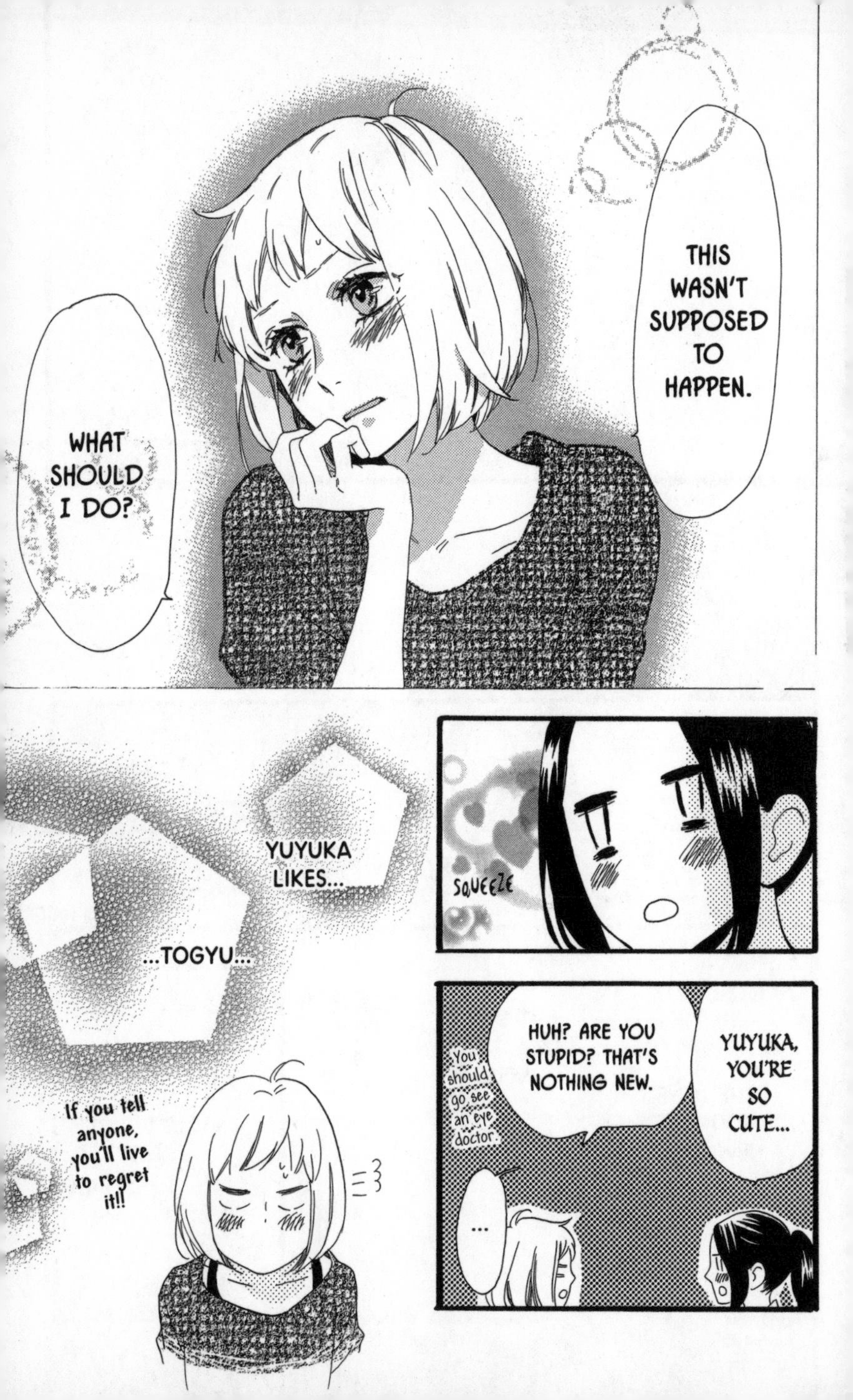
THIS WASN'T SUPPOSED TO HAPPEN.
WHAT SHOULD I DO?
SQUEEZE
YUYUKA, YOU'RE SO CUTE...
HUH? ARE YOU STUPID? THAT'S NOTHING NEW.
You should go see an eye doctor.
...
YUYUKA LIKES...
...TOGYU...
If you tell anyone, you'll live to regret it!!

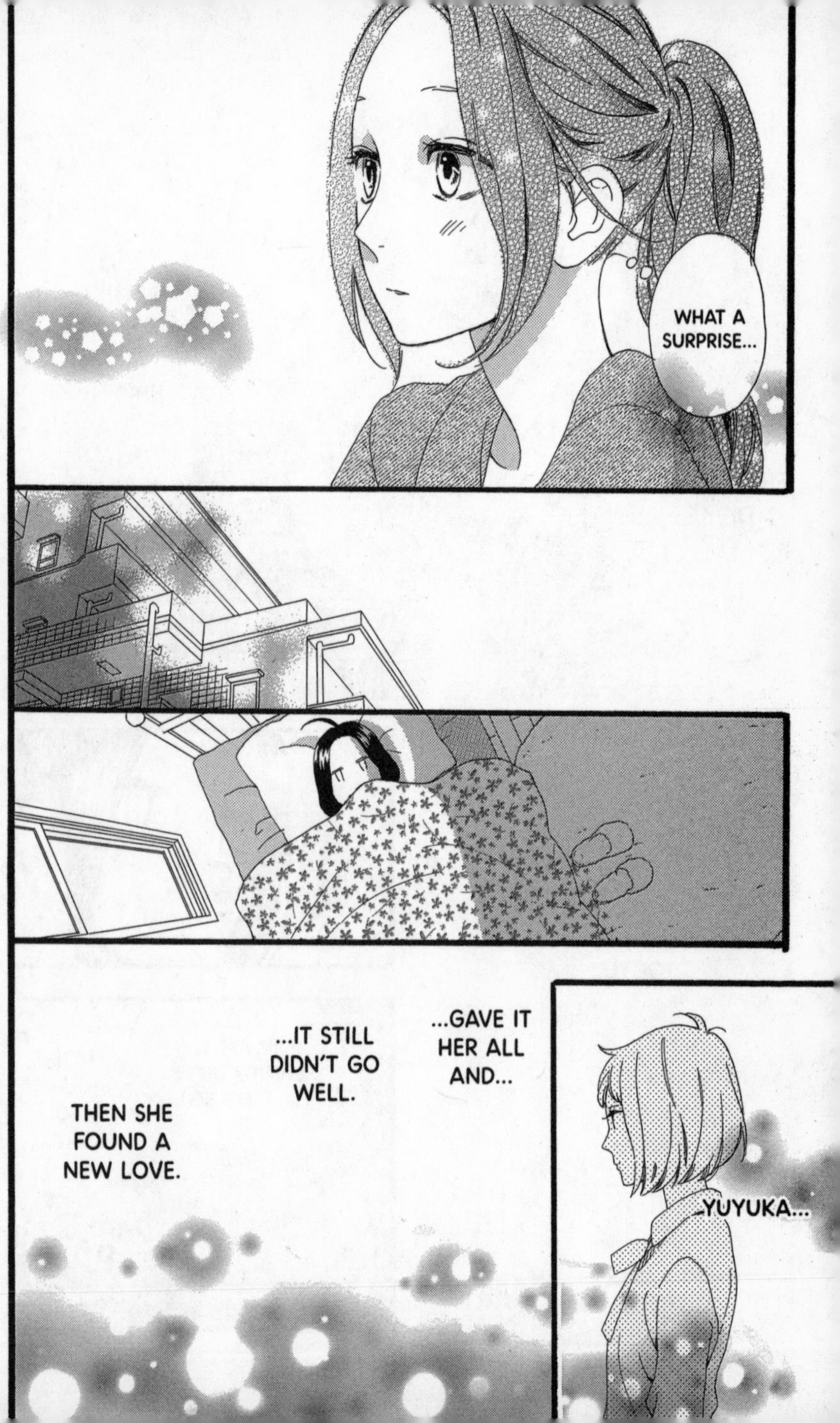
WHAT A SURPRISE...
YUYUKA...
...GAVE IT HER ALL AND...
...IT STILL DIDN'T GO WELL.
THEN SHE FOUND A NEW LOVE.

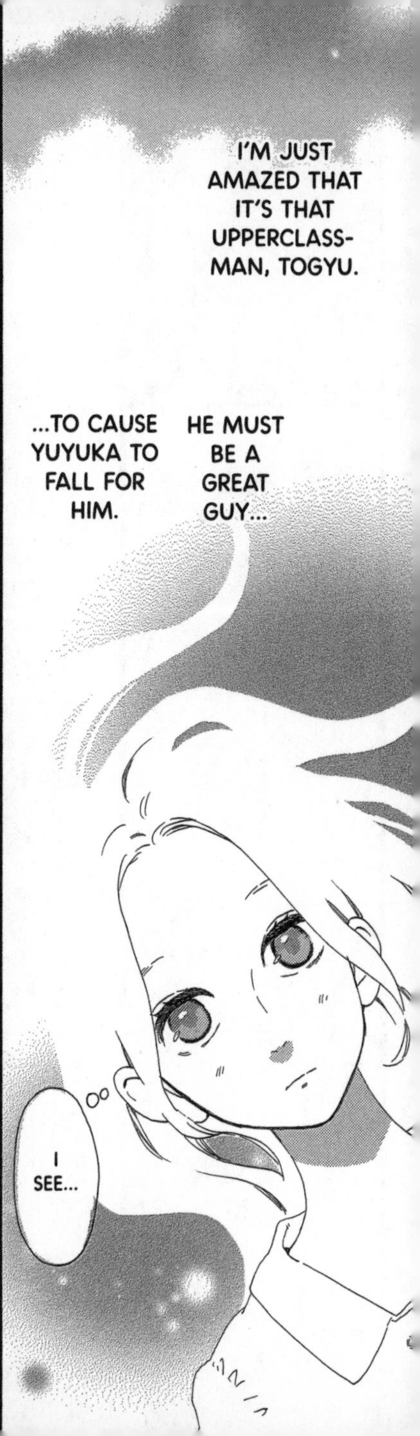
I'M JUST AMAZED THAT IT'S THAT UPPERCLASS-MAN, TOGYU.
HE MUST BE A GREAT GUY...
...TO CAUSE YUYUKA TO FALL FOR HIM.
I SEE...

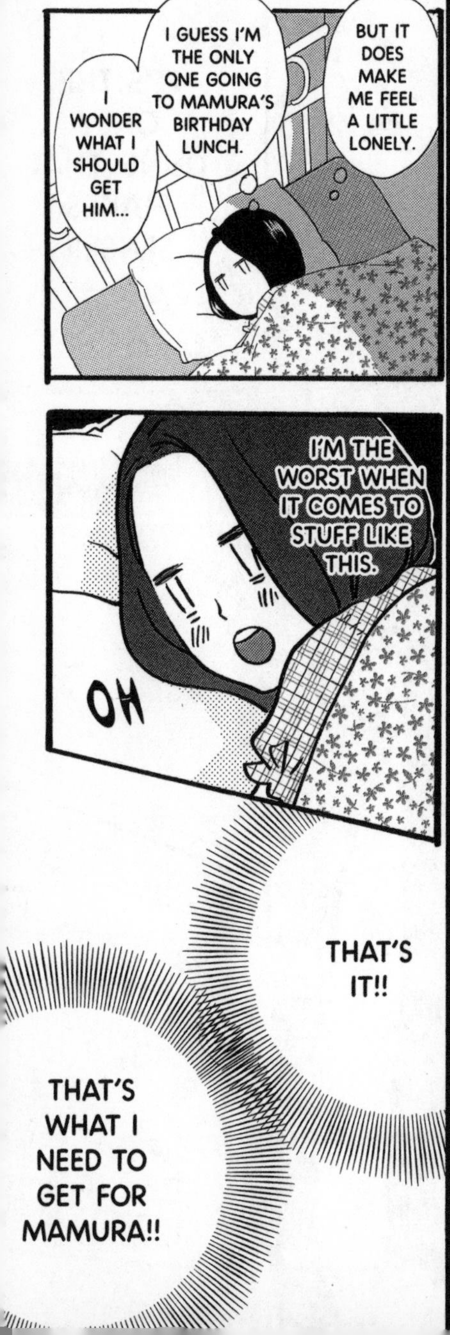
BUT IT DOES MAKE ME FEEL A LITTLE LONELY.
I GUESS I'M THE ONLY ONE GOING TO MAMURA'S BIRTHDAY LUNCH.
I WONDER WHAT I SHOULD GET HIM...
I'M THE WORST WHEN IT COMES TO STUFF LIKE THIS.
OH
THAT'S IT!!
THAT'S WHAT I NEED TO GET FOR MAMURA!!

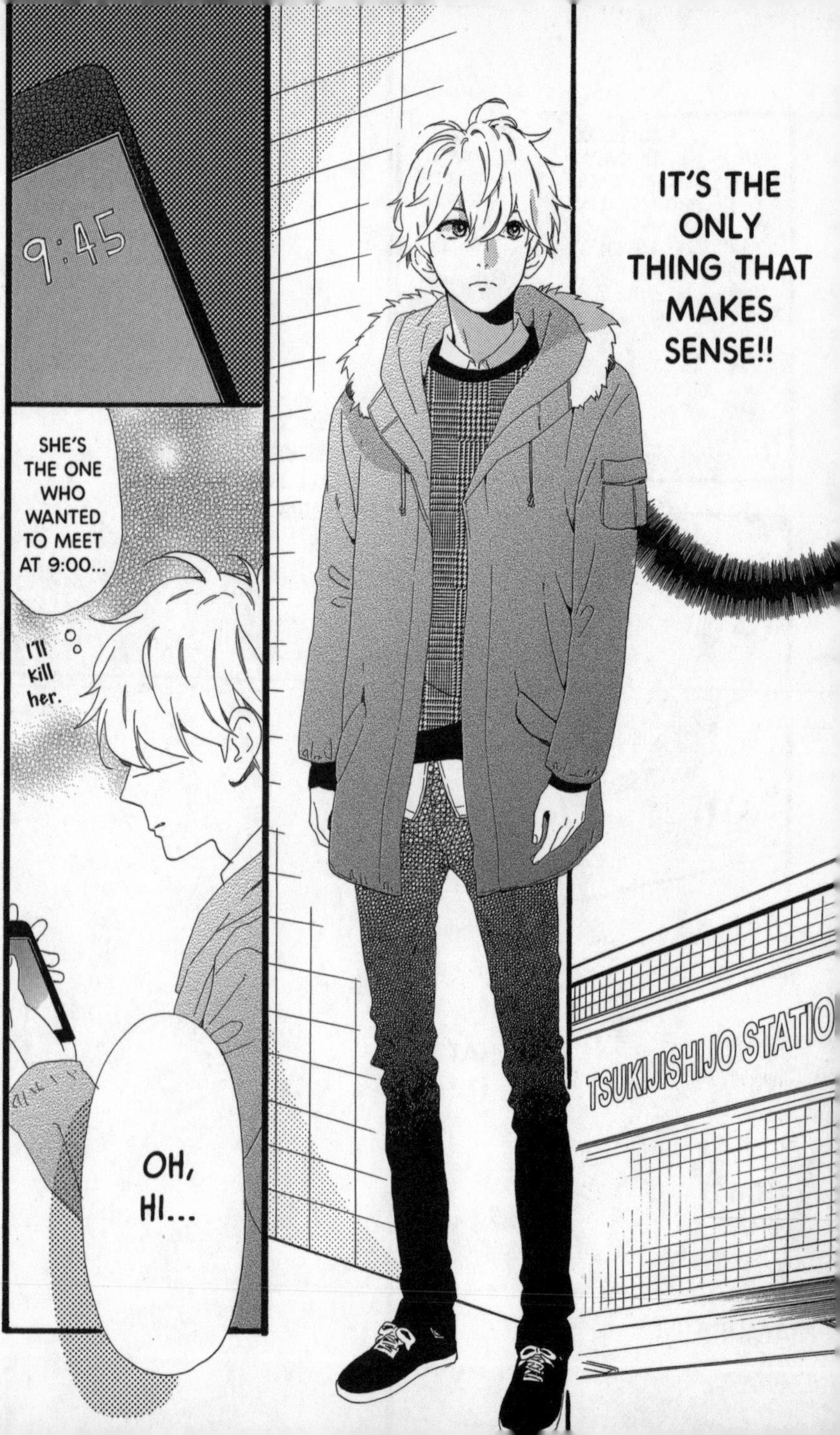
IT'S THE ONLY THING THAT MAKES SENSE!!
TSUKIJISHIJO STATIO
9:45
SHE'S THE ONE WHO WANTED TO MEET AT 9:00...
I'll kill her.
OH, HI...

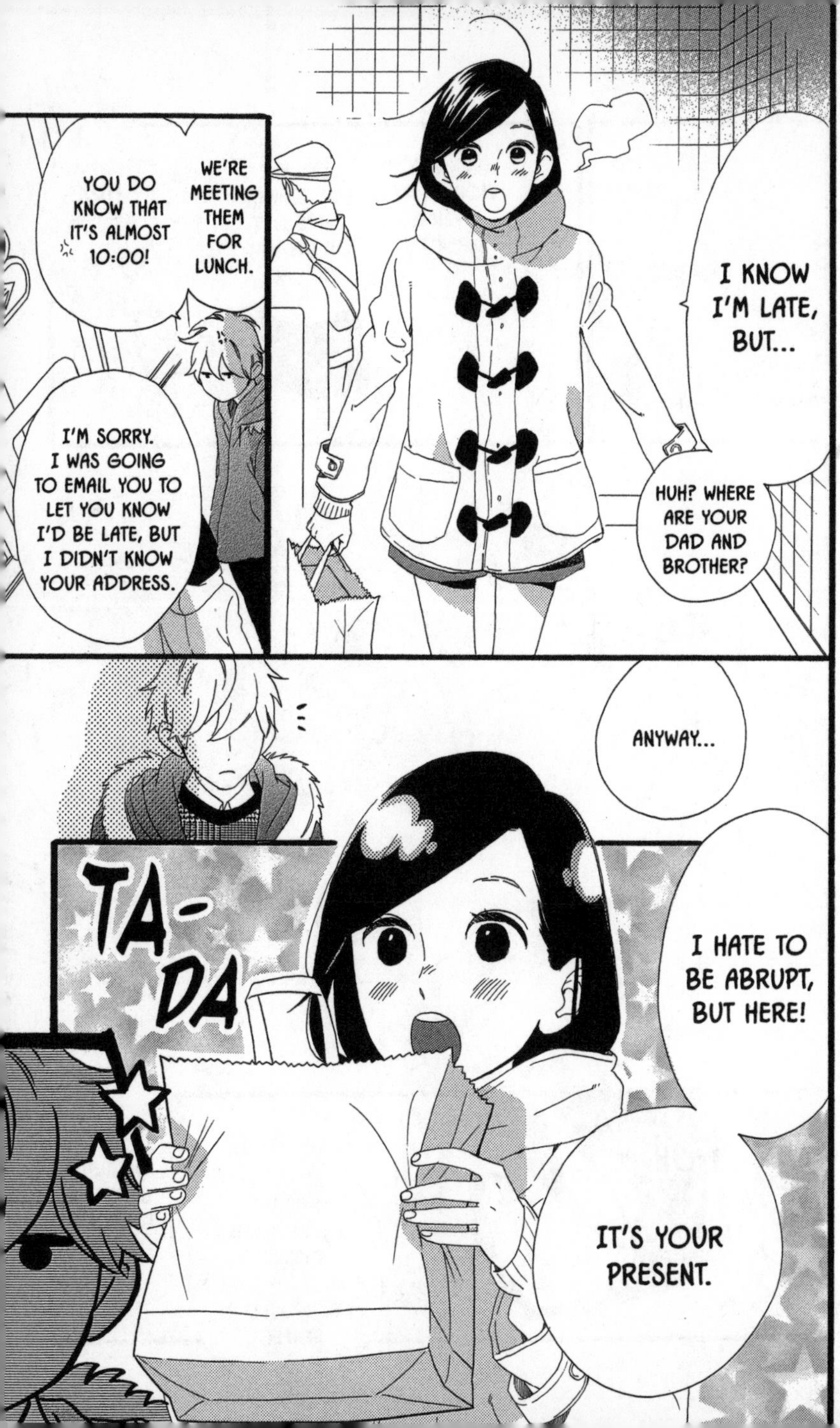
I KNOW I'M LATE, BUT...
HUH? WHERE ARE YOUR DAD AND BROTHER?
WE'RE MEETING THEM FOR LUNCH.
YOU DO KNOW THAT IT'S ALMOST 10:00!
I'M SORRY. I WAS GOING TO EMAIL YOU TO LET YOU KNOW I'D BE LATE, BUT I DIDN'T KNOW YOUR ADDRESS.
ANYWAY...
I HATE TO BE ABRUPT, BUT HERE!
TA-DA
IT'S YOUR PRESENT.

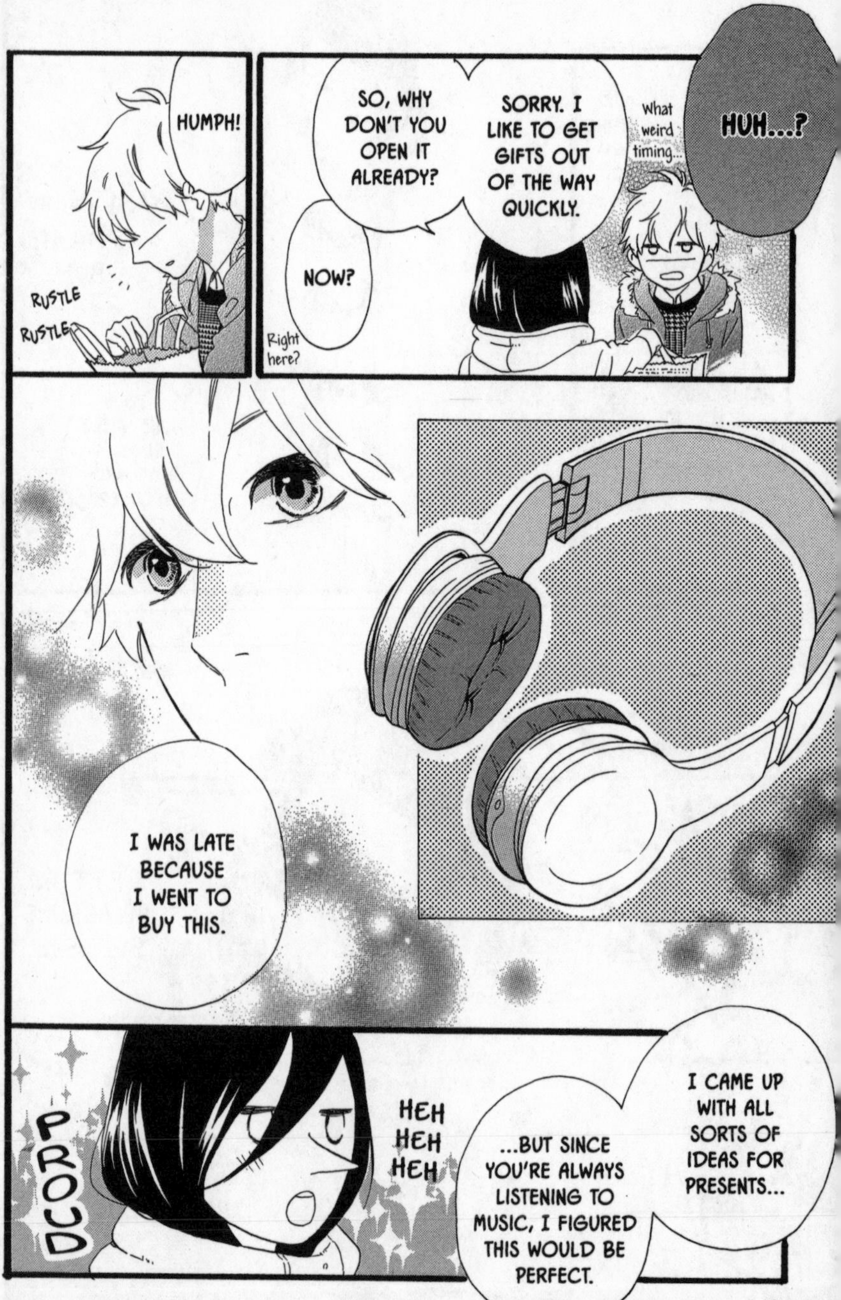
HUH...?
What weird timing...
SORRY. I LIKE TO GET GIFTS OUT OF THE WAY QUICKLY.
SO, WHY DON'T YOU OPEN IT ALREADY?
NOW?
Right here?
HUMPH!
RUSTLE
RUSTLE
I WAS LATE BECAUSE I WENT TO BUY THIS.
I CAME UP WITH ALL SORTS OF IDEAS FOR PRESENTS...
...BUT SINCE YOU'RE ALWAYS LISTENING TO MUSIC, I FIGURED THIS WOULD BE PERFECT.
HEH HEH HEH
PROUD

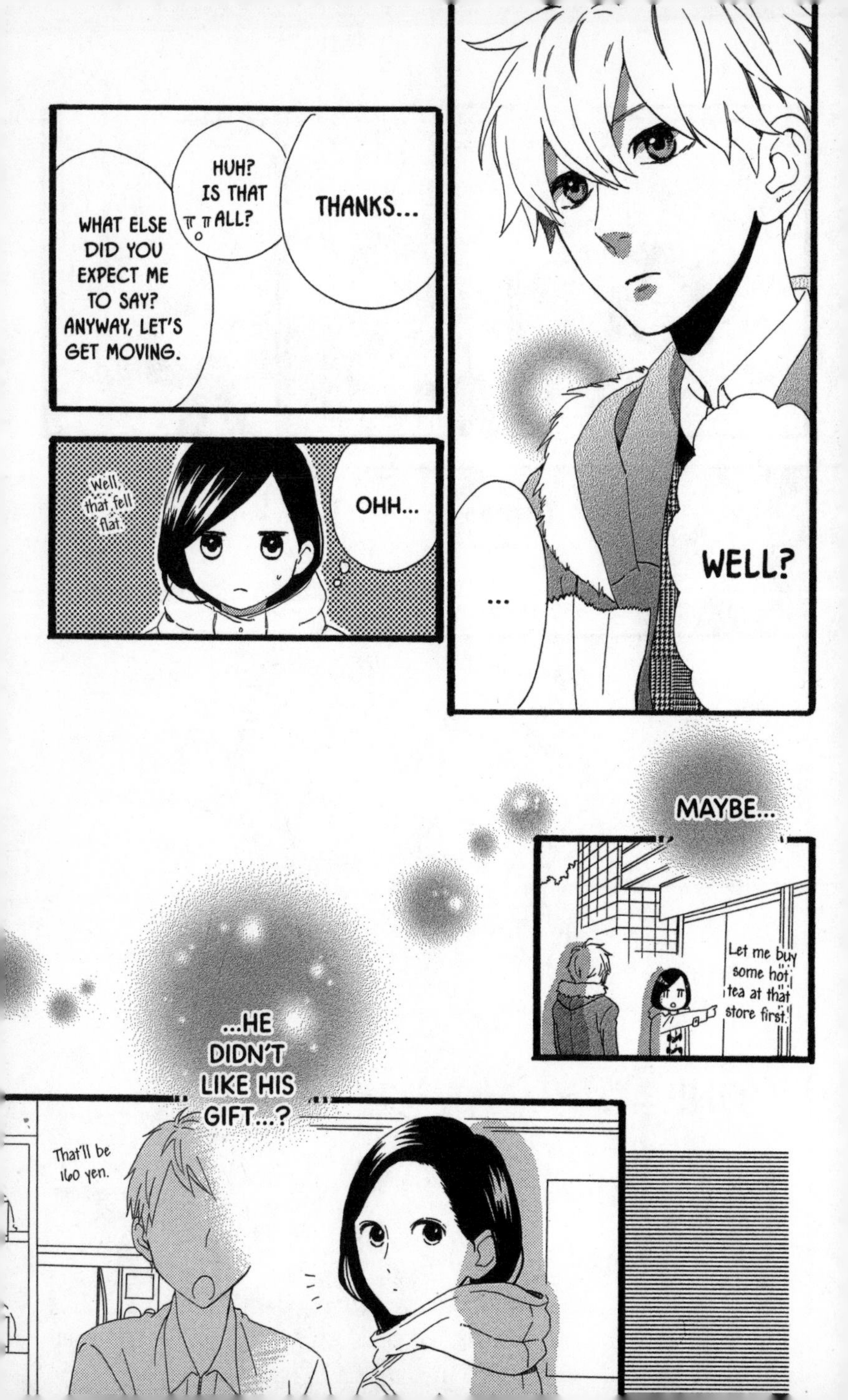
WELL?
...
THANKS...
HUH? IS THAT ALL?
WHAT ELSE DID YOU EXPECT ME TO SAY? ANYWAY, LET'S GET MOVING.
OHH...
Well, that fell flat.
MAYBE...
Let me buy some hot tea at that store first.
...HE DIDN'T LIKE HIS GIFT...?
That'll be 160 yen.

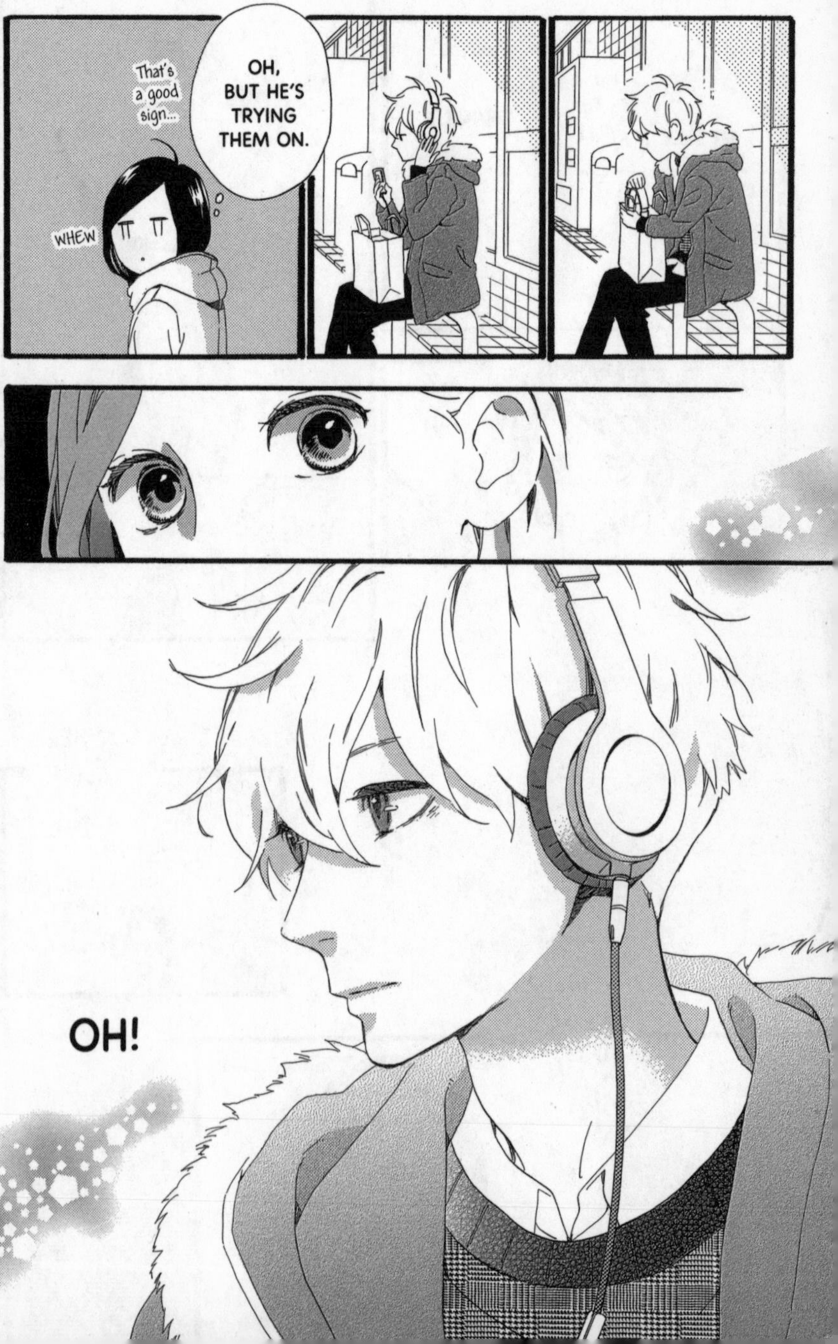
OH, BUT HE'S TRYING THEM ON.
That's a good sign...
WHEW
OH!

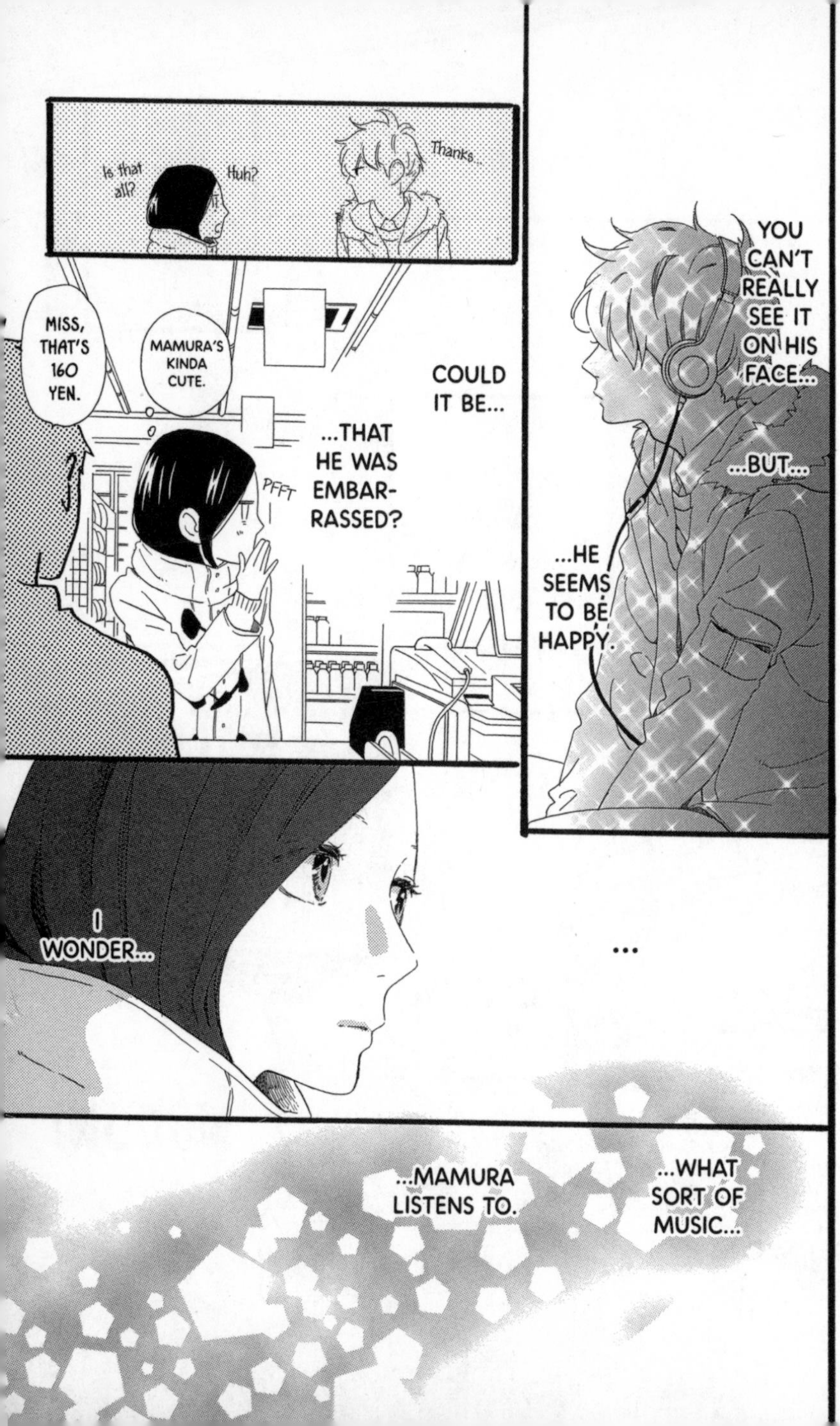
YOU CAN'T REALLY SEE IT ON HIS FACE...
...BUT...
...HE SEEMS TO BE HAPPY.
Thanks...
Huh?
Is that all?
COULD IT BE...
...THAT HE WAS EMBARRASSED?
PFFT
MAMURA'S KINDA CUTE.
MISS, THAT'S 160 YEN.
...
I WONDER...
...WHAT SORT OF MUSIC...
...MAMURA LISTENS TO.

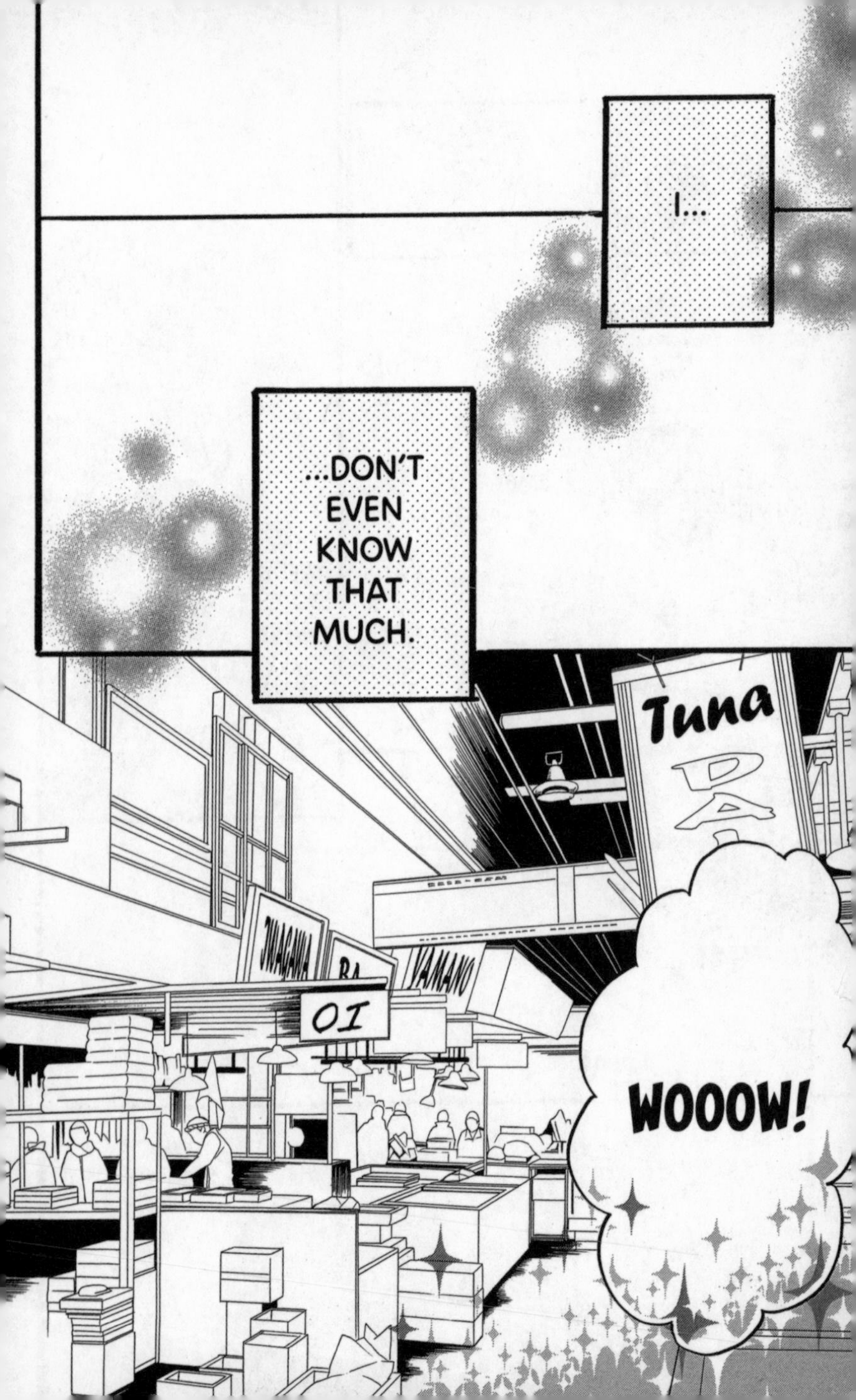
I...
...DON'T EVEN KNOW THAT MUCH.
Tuna
WOOOW!
YAMANO
OI

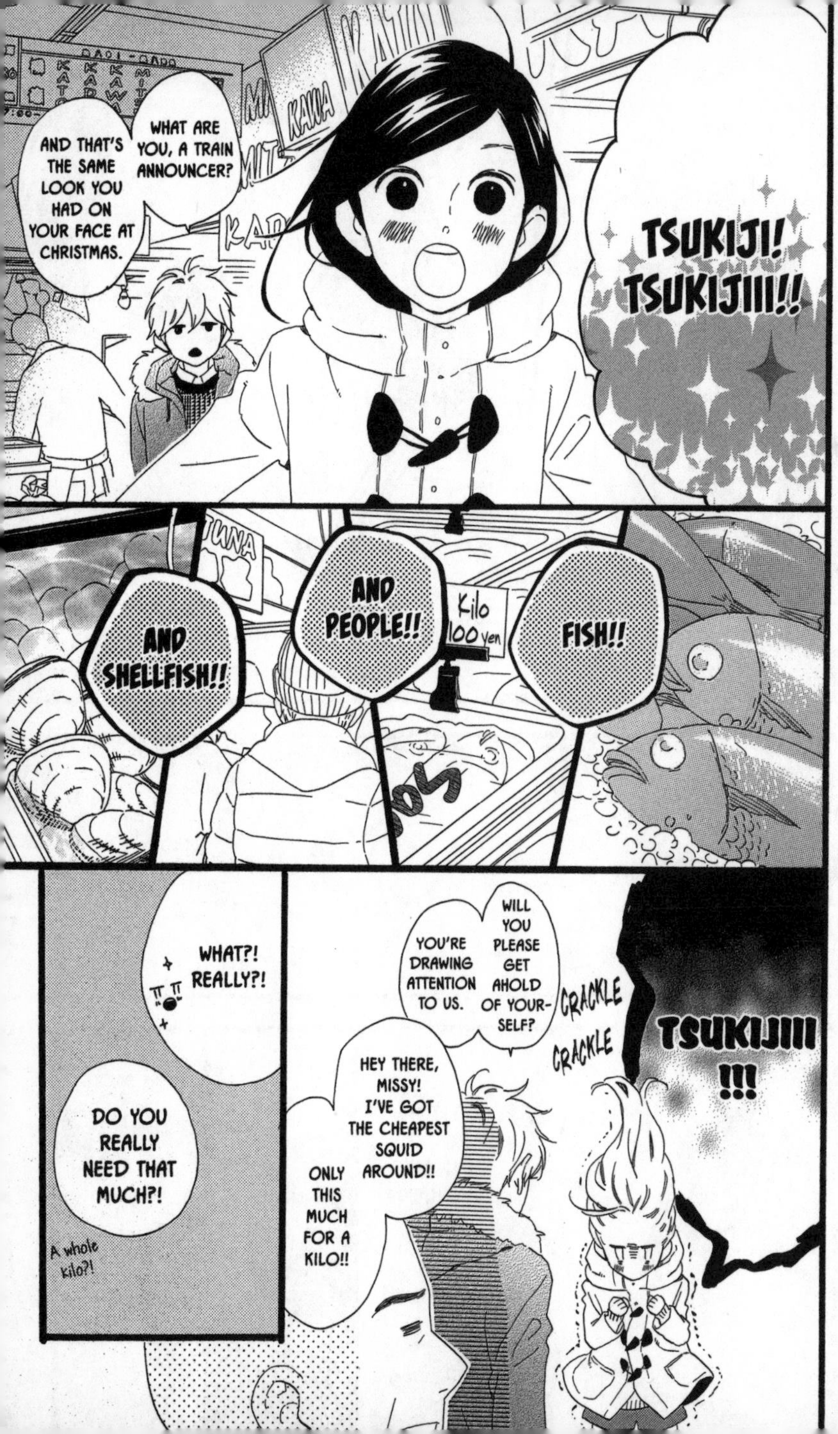
TSUKIJI! TSUKIJIII!!
WHAT ARE YOU, A TRAIN ANNOUNCER?
AND THAT'S THE SAME LOOK YOU HAD ON YOUR FACE AT CHRISTMAS.
KAWA
FISH!!
Kilo 100 yen
AND PEOPLE!!
TUNA
AND SHELLFISH!!
TSUKIJIII!!!
CRACKLE CRACKLE
WILL YOU PLEASE GET AHOLD OF YOURSELF?
YOU'RE DRAWING ATTENTION TO US.
HEY THERE, MISSY! I'VE GOT THE CHEAPEST SQUID AROUND!!
ONLY THIS MUCH FOR A KILO!!
WHAT?! REALLY?!
DO YOU REALLY NEED THAT MUCH?!
A whole kilo?!

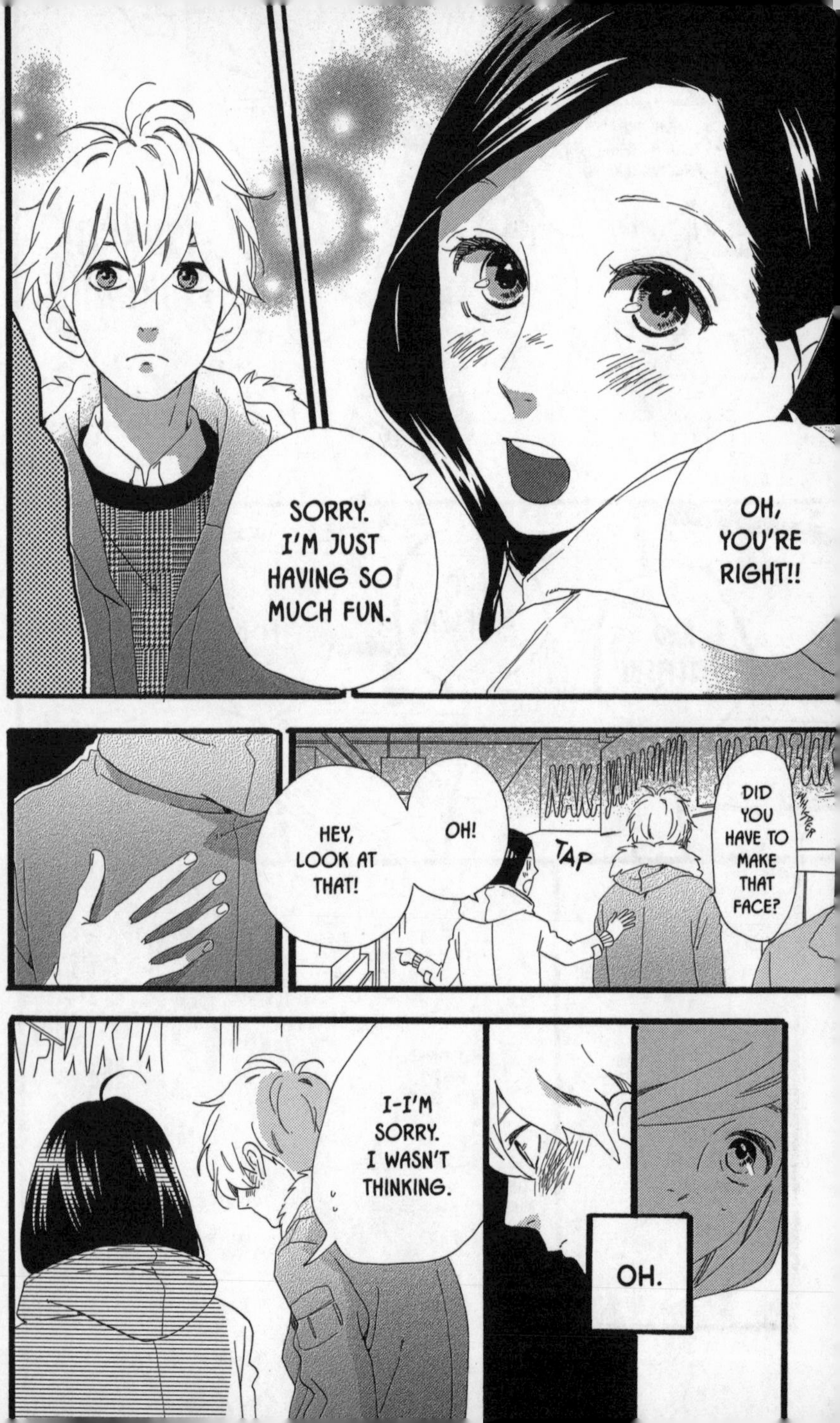
OH, YOU'RE RIGHT!!
SORRY. I'M JUST HAVING SO MUCH FUN.
DID YOU HAVE TO MAKE THAT FACE?
WHISPER
OH!
HEY, LOOK AT THAT!
TAP
OH.
I-I'M SORRY. I WASN'T THINKING.

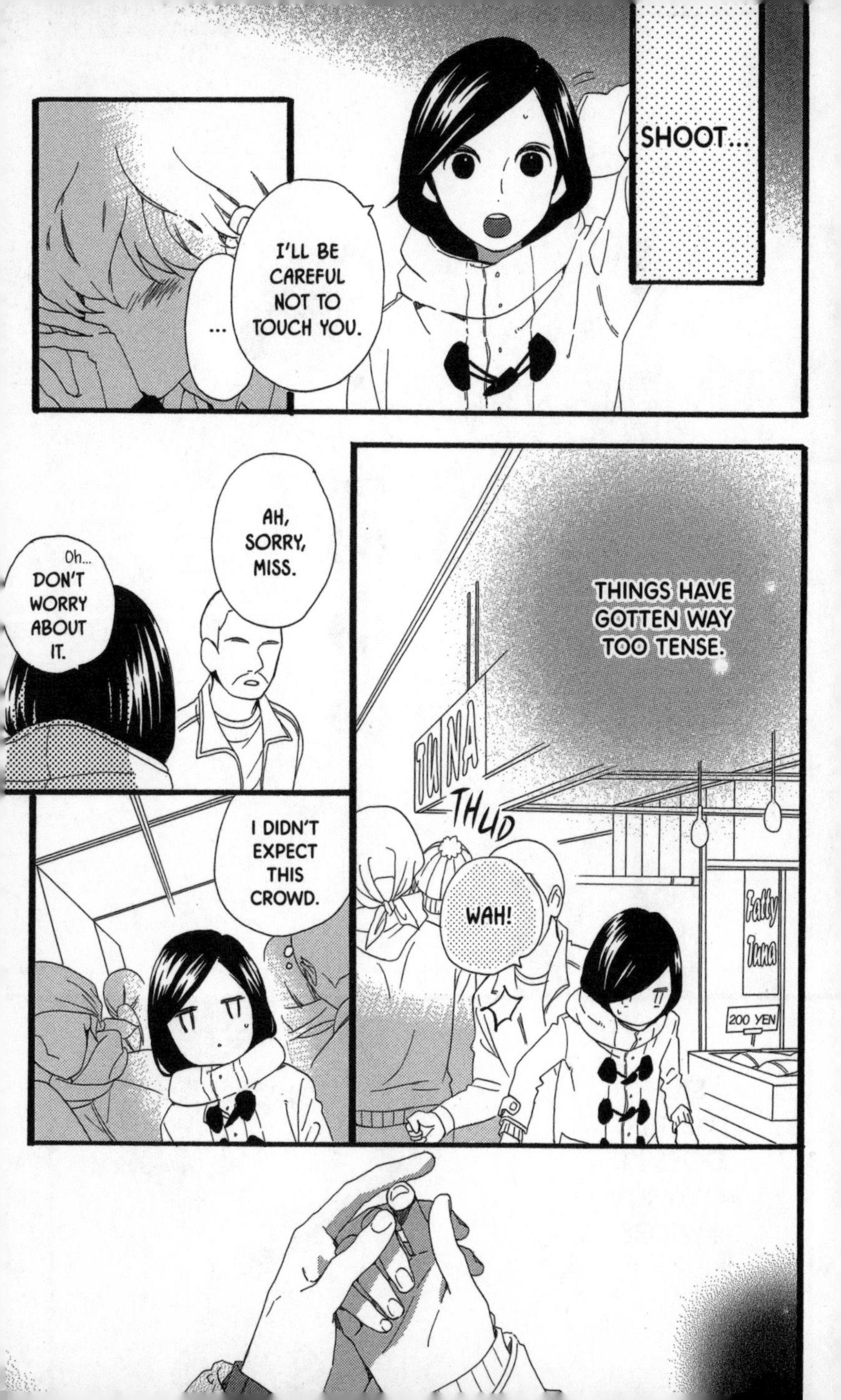
SHOOT...
I'LL BE CAREFUL NOT TO TOUCH YOU.
...
THINGS HAVE GOTTEN WAY TOO TENSE.
TUNA
THUD
WAH!
Fatty Tuna
200 YEN
AH, SORRY, MISS.
Oh... DON'T WORRY ABOUT IT.
I DIDN'T EXPECT THIS CROWD.

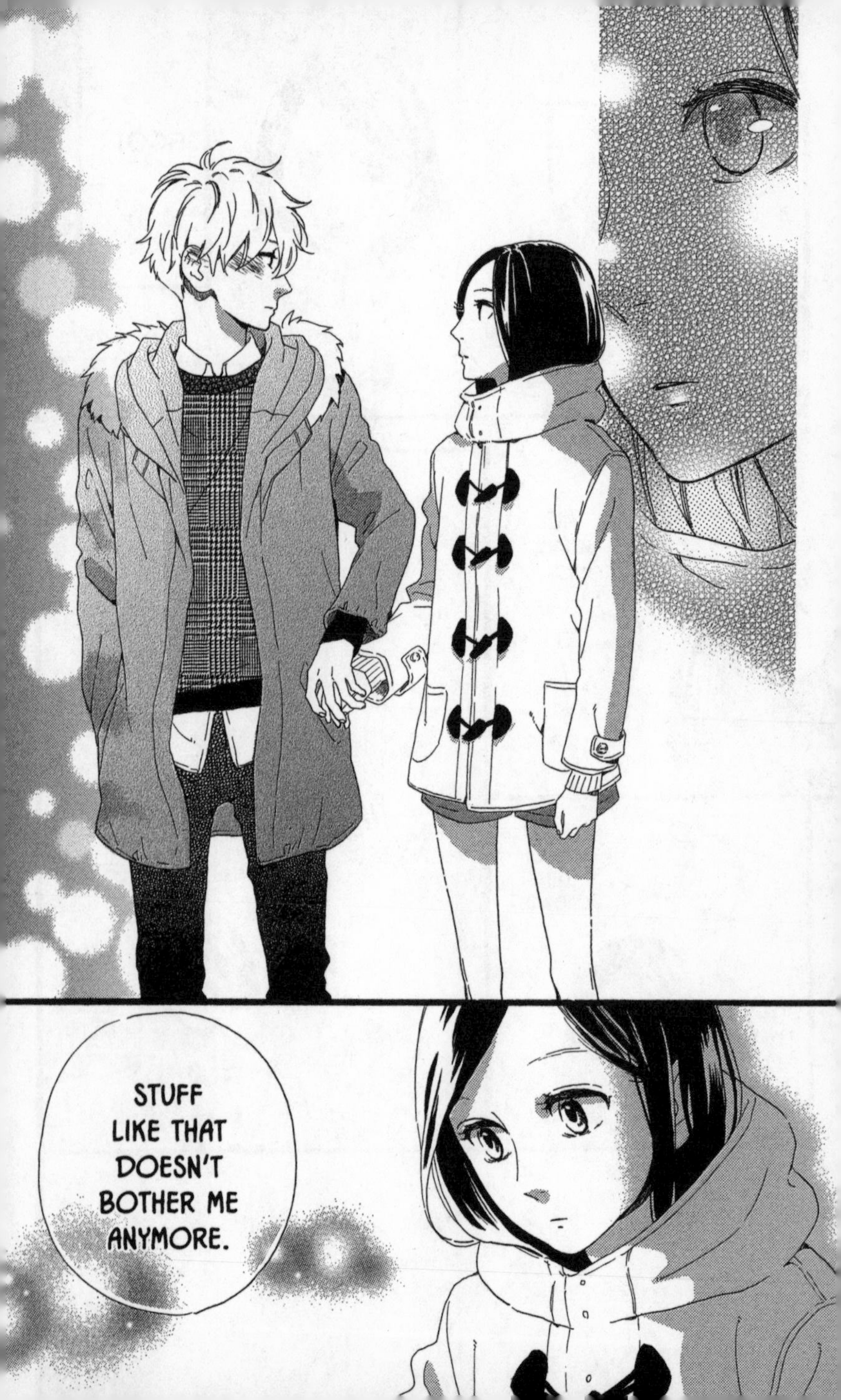
STUFF LIKE THAT DOESN'T BOTHER ME ANYMORE.

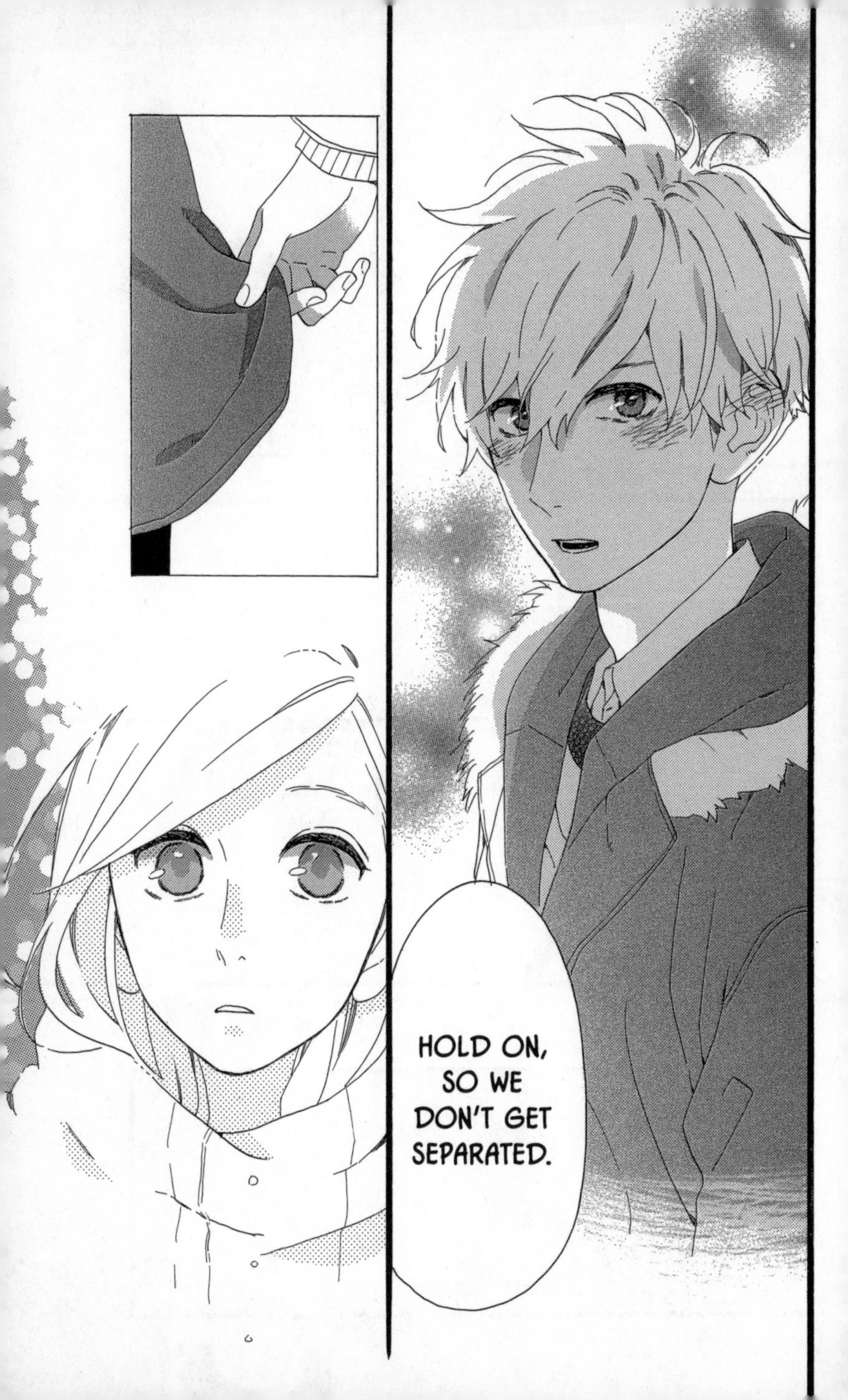
HOLD ON, SO WE DON'T GET SEPARATED.

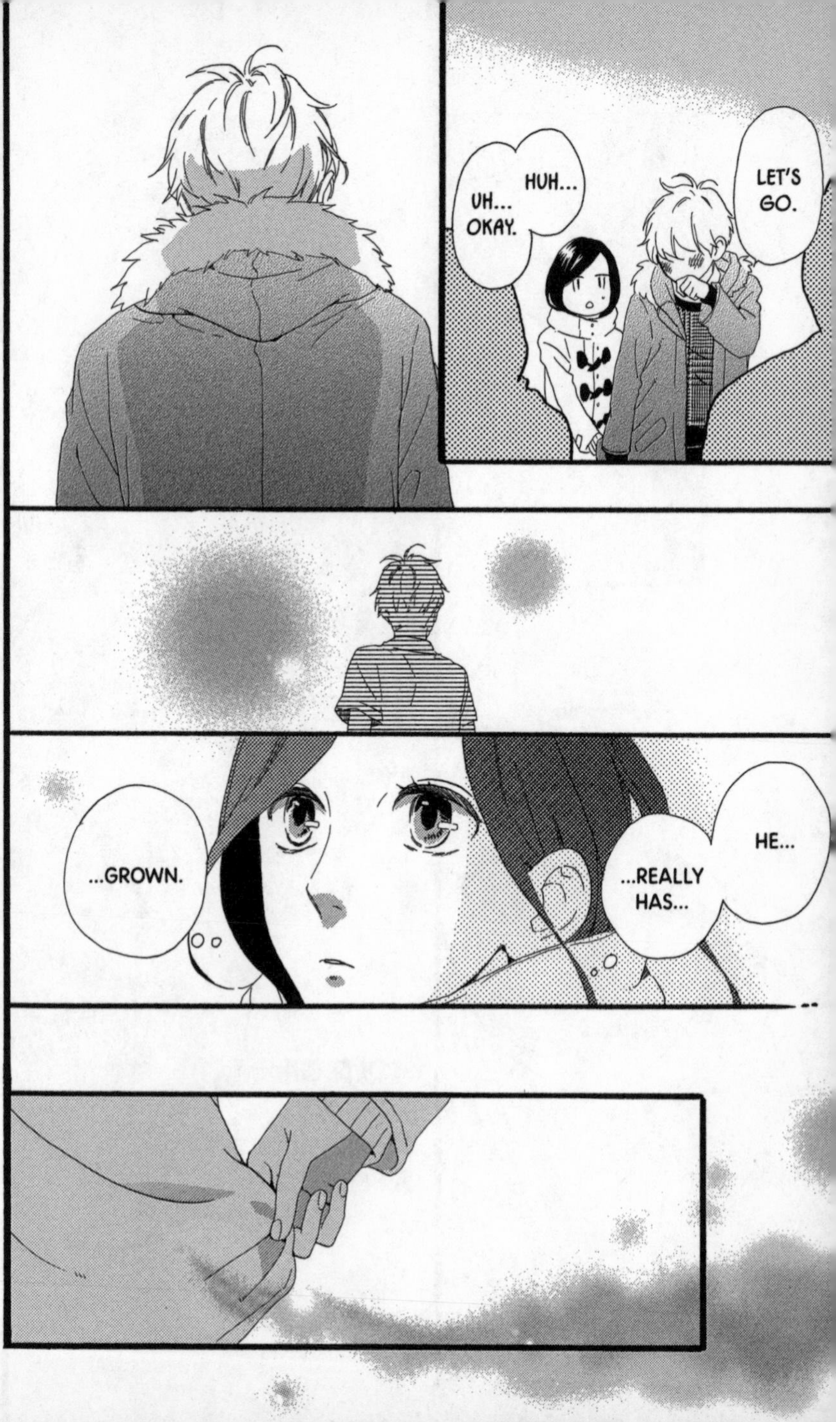
LET'S GO.
HUH... UH... OKAY.
HE...
...REALLY HAS...
...GROWN.

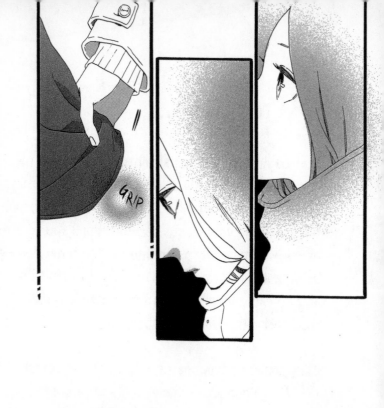

GRIP

Afterword...

And so due to time constraints, I am ending my commentary here. My afterword is short, but not because I have nothing to say... *koff koff.* Although, I am awaiting your requests. And thank you to all of you who have been sending me fan letters! They bring a smile to my face! I'm sorry I haven't been able to reply to you all. But rest assured that I do read each and every one of them!!

Also, someone has been sending me the cutest *WALL-E* postcards. Where can I get some? Thank you for all your letters! I will try my best to continue to create interesting manga! Let's meet again in volume 9!

Special Thanx

My editor, my assistants, designers, the printer staff, everyone in the editorial department, my family, friends and all of my readers.

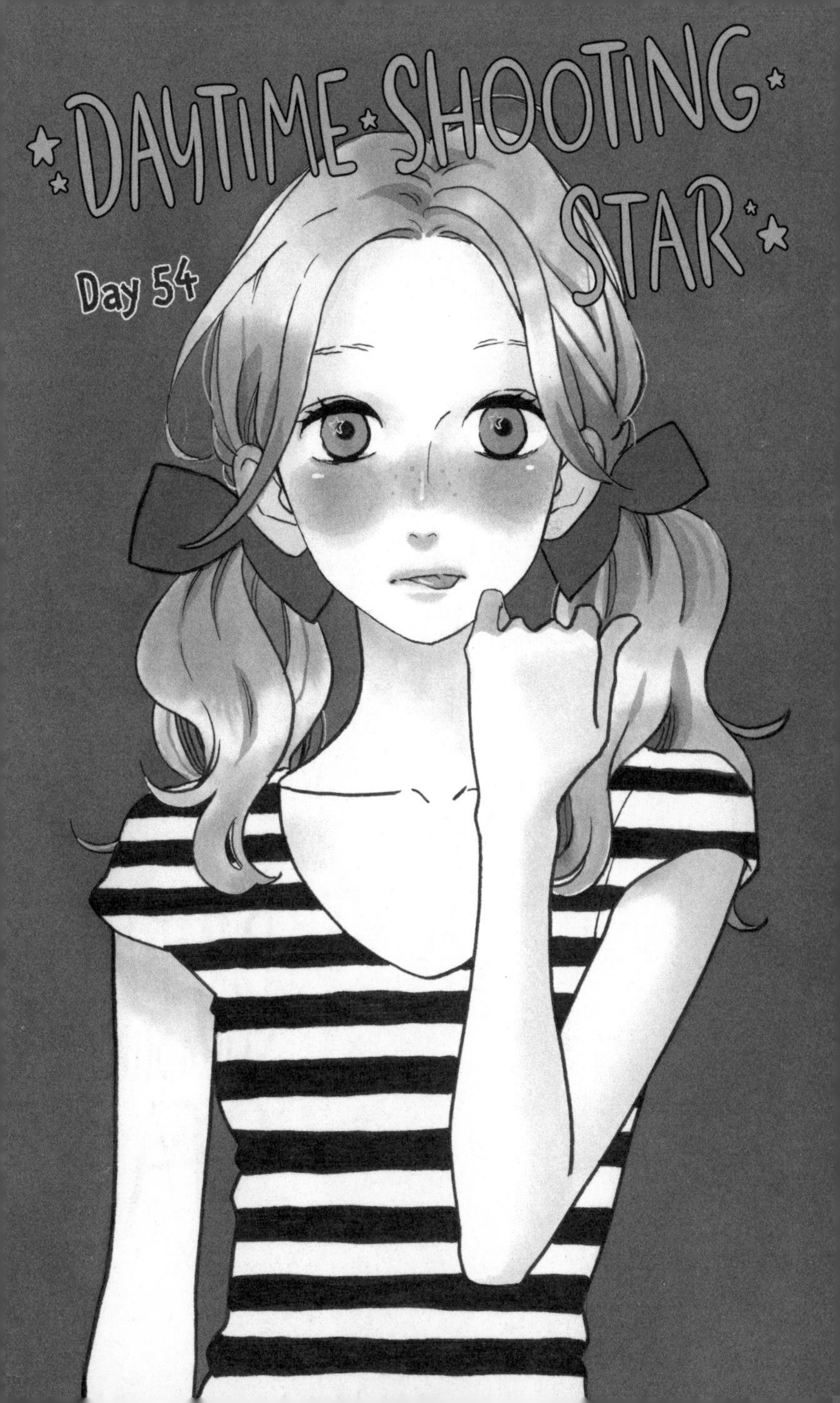

DAYTIME SHOOTING STAR
Day 54

DAYTIME
SHOOTING
STAR

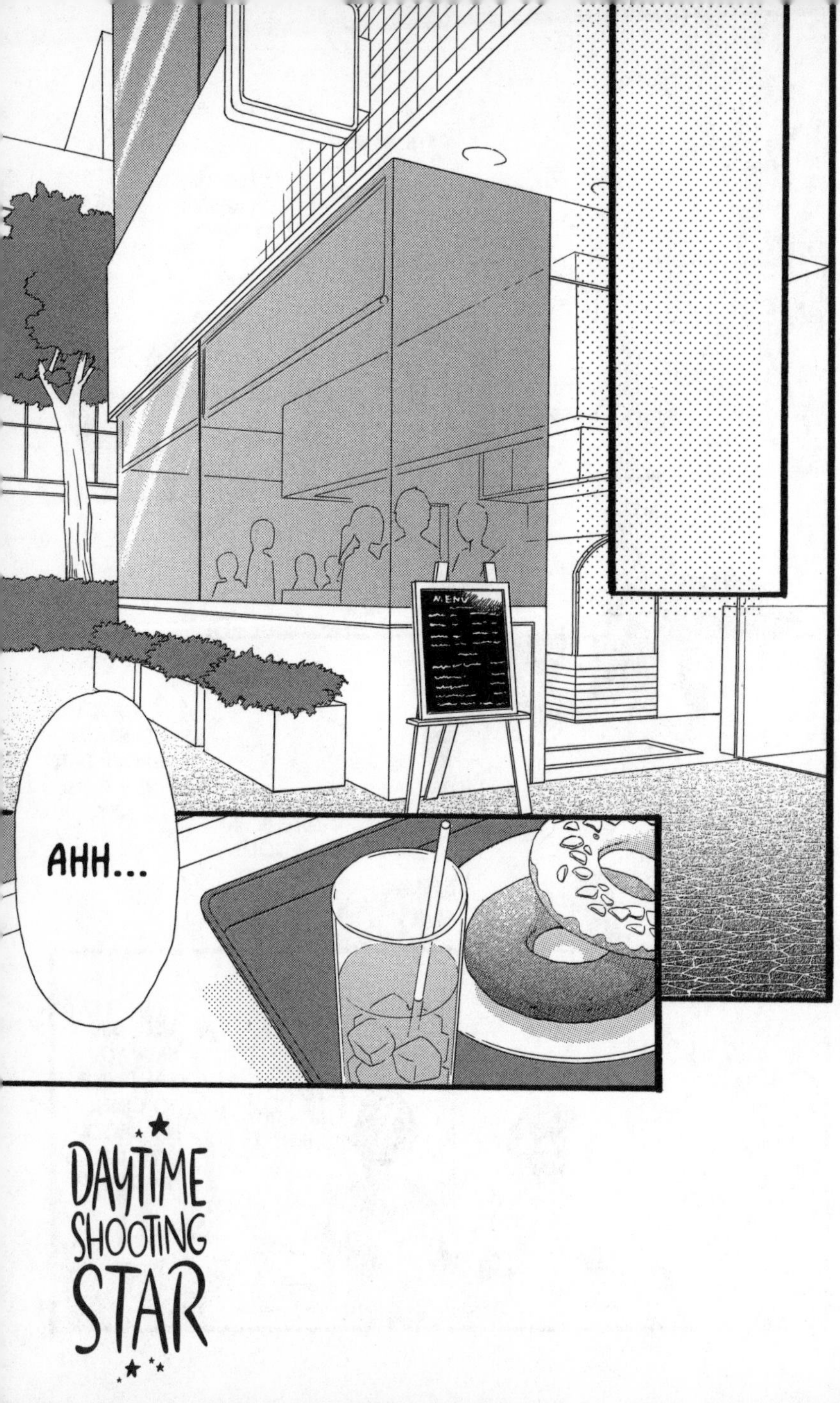
AHH...
DAYTIME SHOOTING STAR

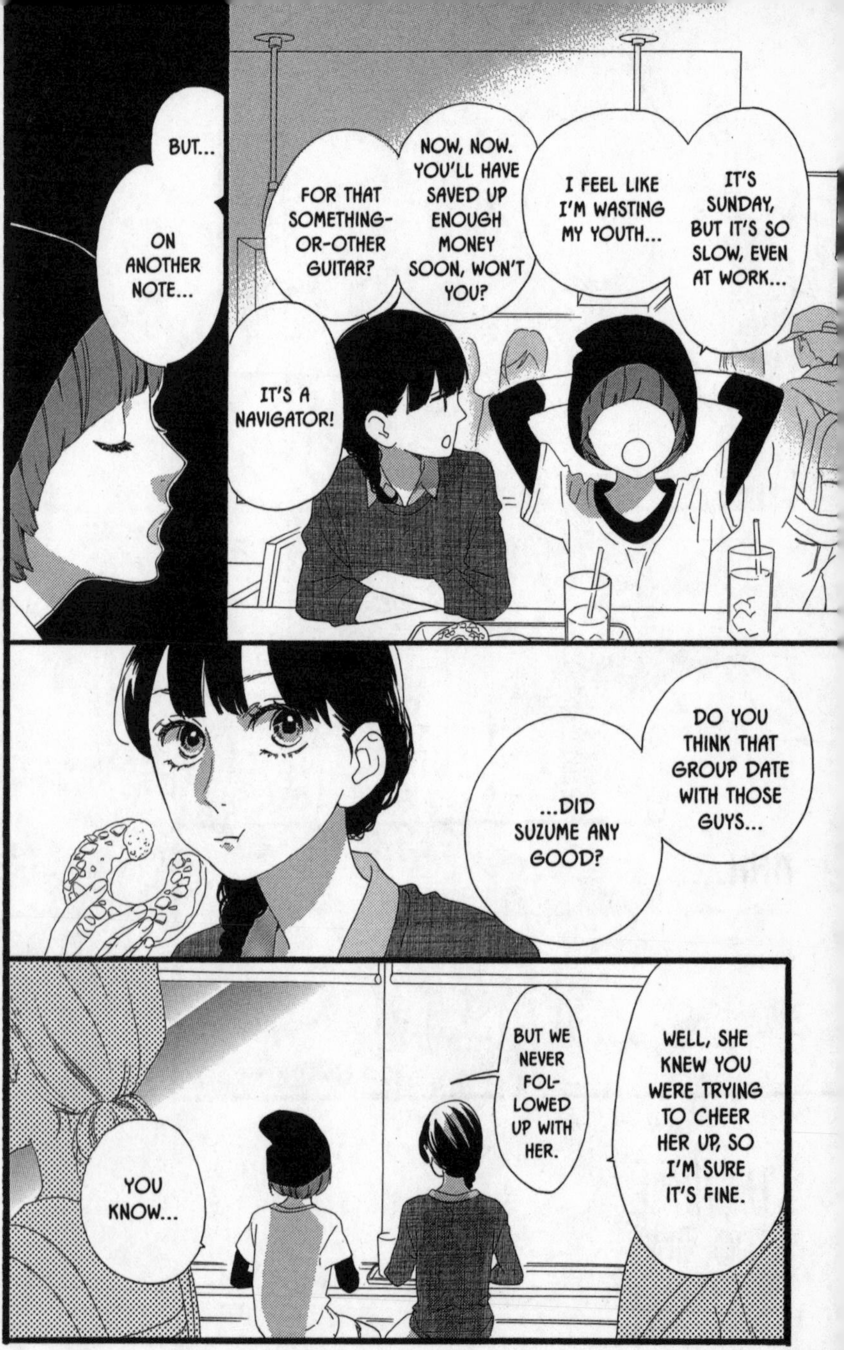
IT'S SUNDAY, BUT IT'S SO SLOW, EVEN AT WORK...
I FEEL LIKE I'M WASTING MY YOUTH...
NOW, NOW. YOU'LL HAVE SAVED UP ENOUGH MONEY SOON, WON'T YOU?
FOR THAT SOMETHING-OR-OTHER GUITAR?
IT'S A NAVIGATOR!
BUT...
ON ANOTHER NOTE...
DO YOU THINK THAT GROUP DATE WITH THOSE GUYS...
...DID SUZUME ANY GOOD?
WELL, SHE KNEW YOU WERE TRYING TO CHEER HER UP, SO I'M SURE IT'S FINE.
BUT WE NEVER FOL-LOWED UP WITH HER.
YOU KNOW...

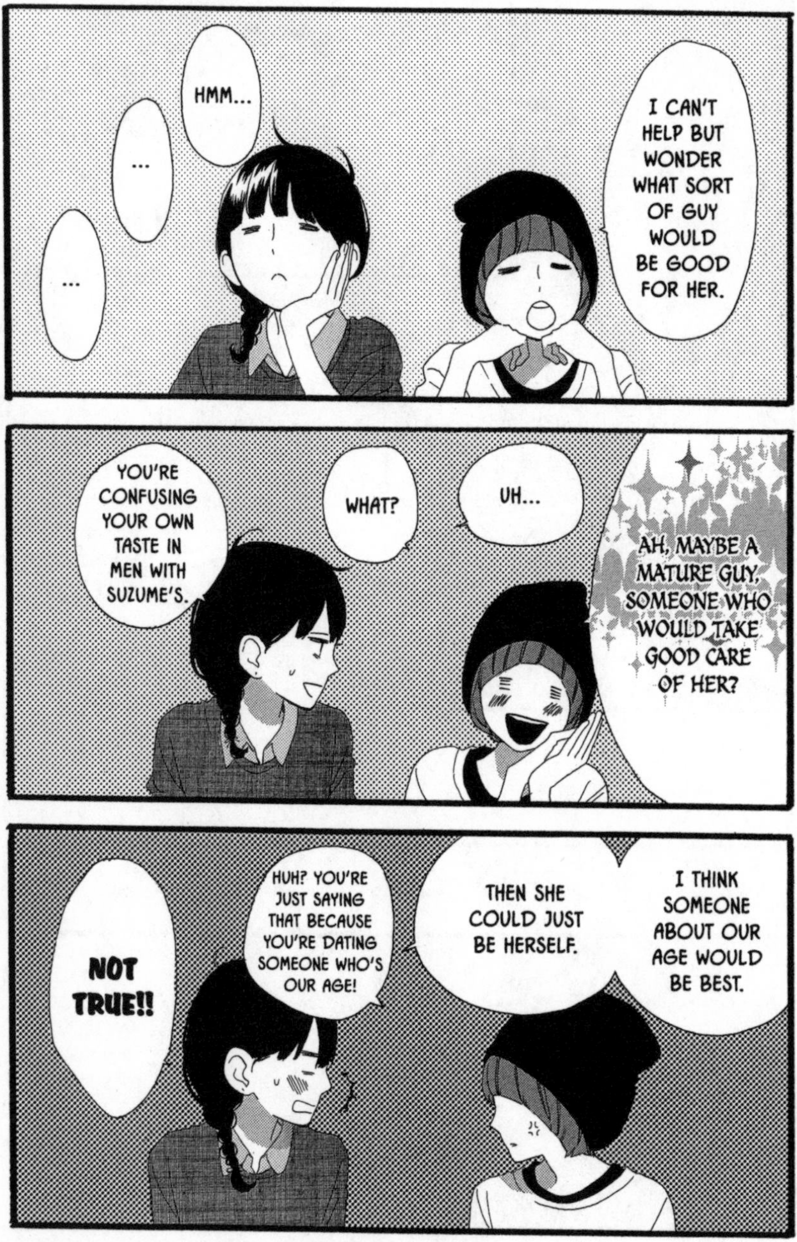
I CAN'T HELP BUT WONDER WHAT SORT OF GUY WOULD BE GOOD FOR HER.
HMM...
...
...
AH, MAYBE A MATURE GUY, SOMEONE WHO WOULD TAKE GOOD CARE OF HER?
UH...
WHAT?
YOU'RE CONFUSING YOUR OWN TASTE IN MEN WITH SUZUME'S.
I THINK SOMEONE ABOUT OUR AGE WOULD BE BEST.
THEN SHE COULD JUST BE HERSELF.
HUH? YOU'RE JUST SAYING THAT BECAUSE YOU'RE DATING SOMEONE WHO'S OUR AGE!
NOT TRUE!!

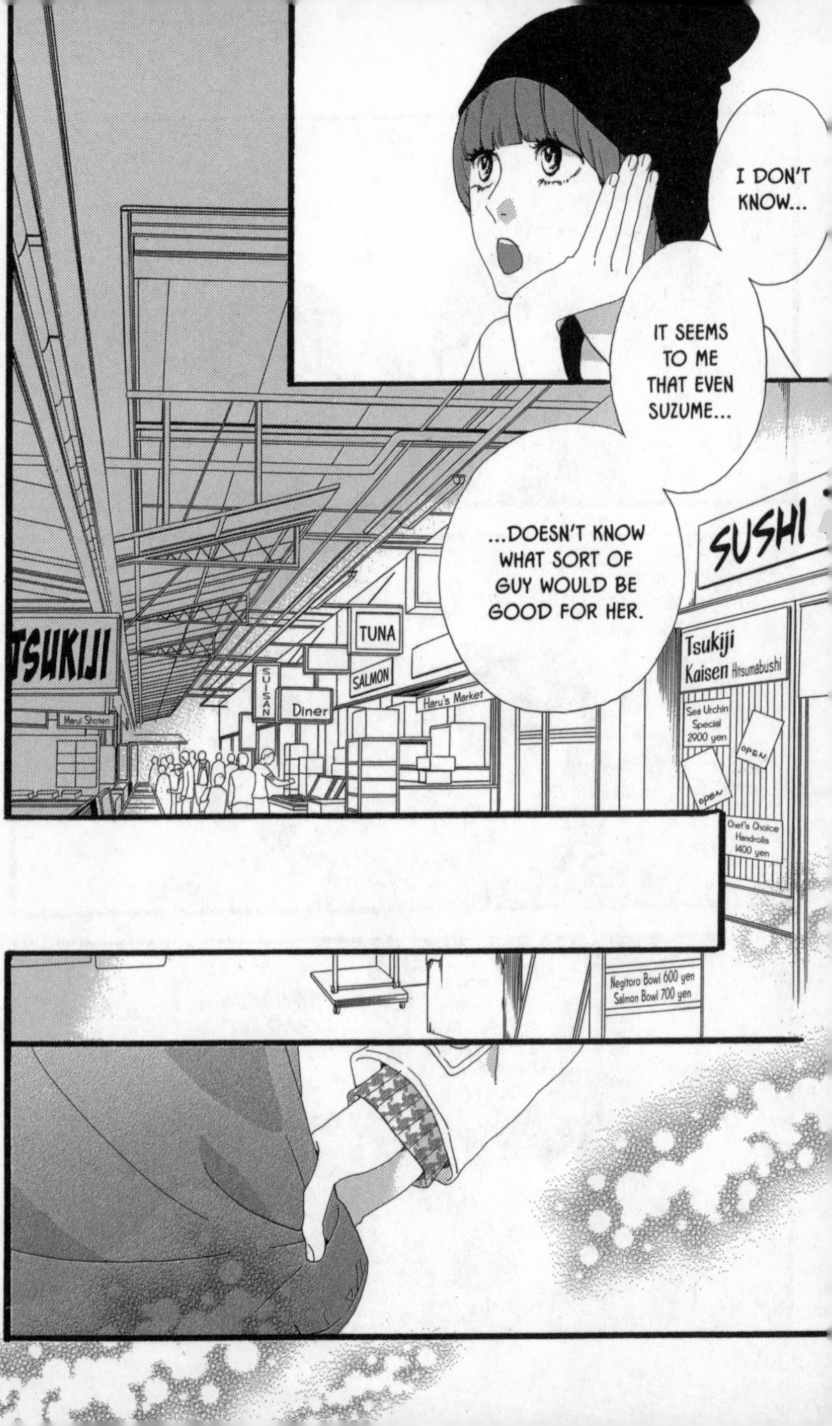
I DON'T KNOW...
IT SEEMS TO ME THAT EVEN SUZUME...
...DOESN'T KNOW WHAT SORT OF GUY WOULD BE GOOD FOR HER.
SUSHI
Tsukiji Kaisen Hitsumabushi
Sea Urchin Special 2900 yen
OPEN
OPEN
Chef's Choice Handrolls 1400 yen
Negitoro Bowl 600 yen
Salmon Bowl 700 yen
Haru's Market
TUNA
SALMON
Diner
SUISAN
TSUKIJI
Maruji Shoten

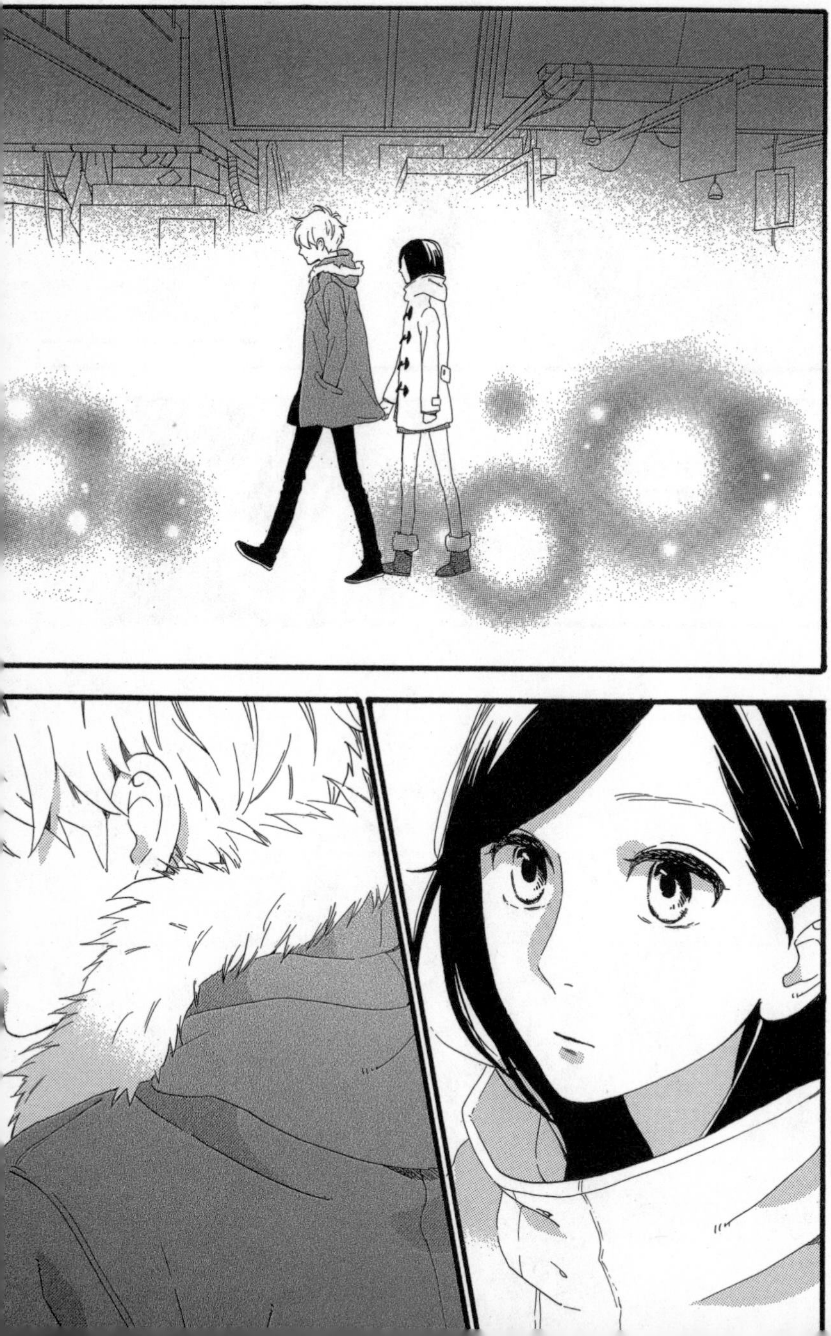

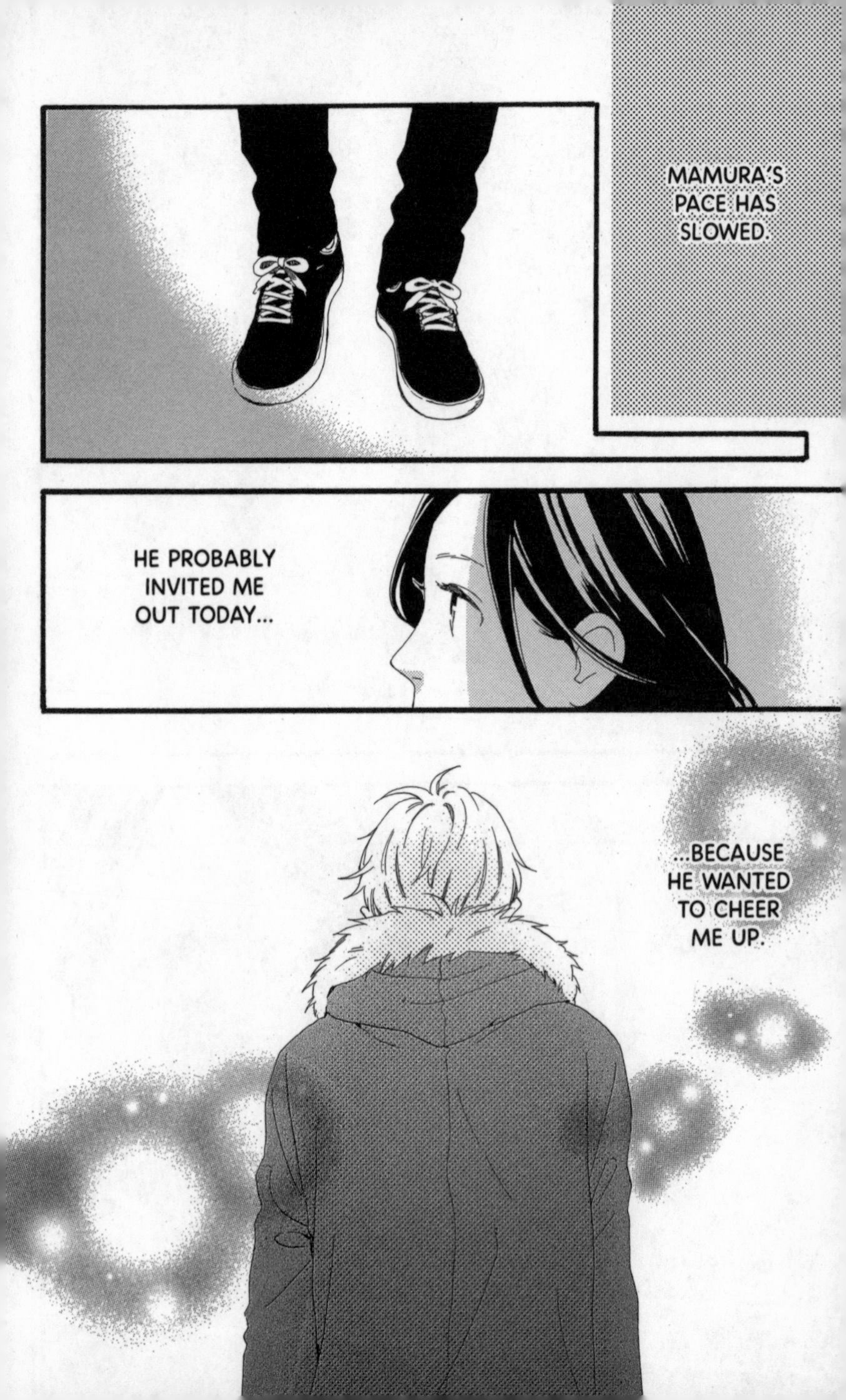
MAMURA'S PACE HAS SLOWED.
HE PROBABLY INVITED ME OUT TODAY...
...BECAUSE HE WANTED TO CHEER ME UP.

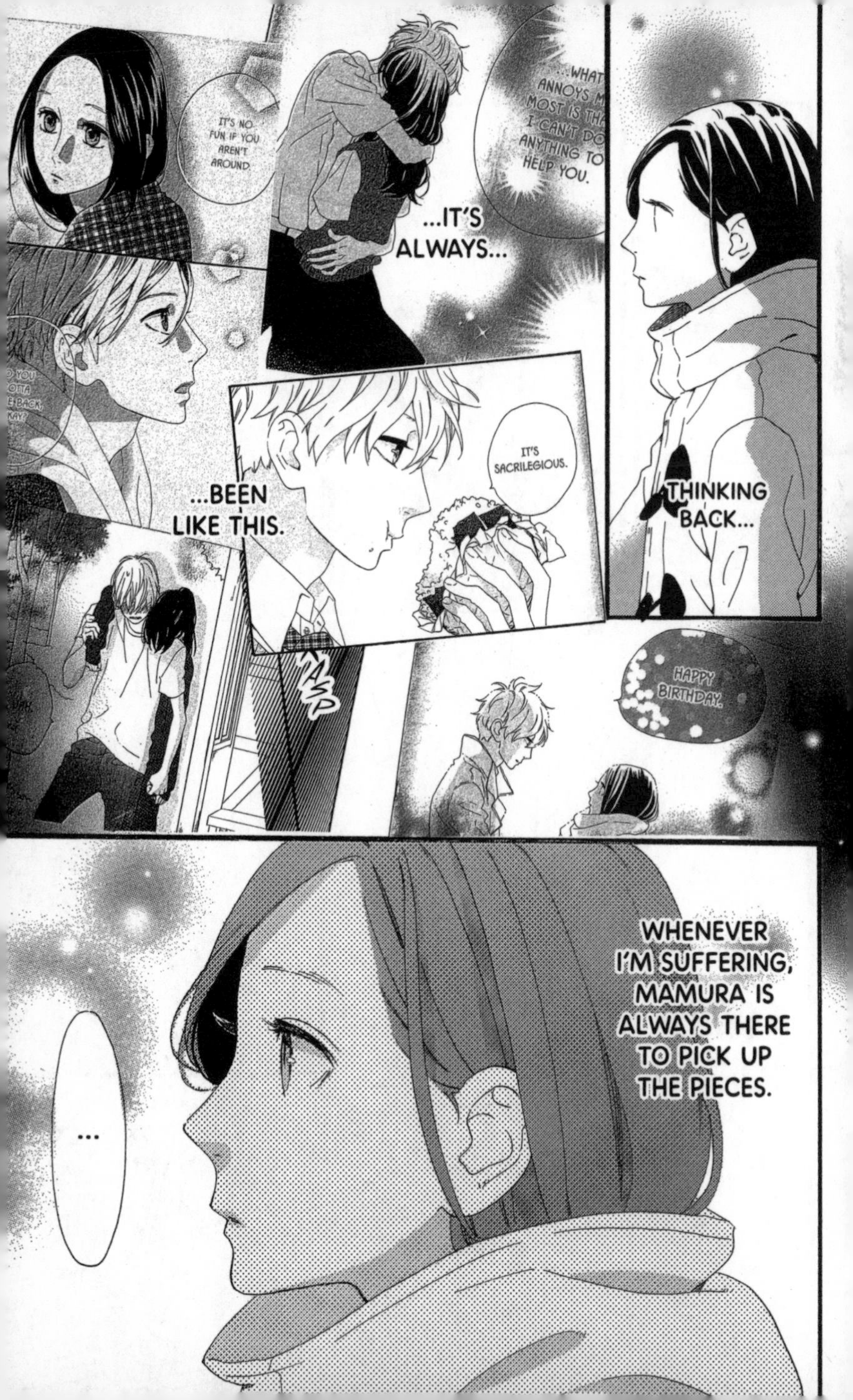

THINKING BACK...
...WHAT ANNOYS M MOST IS THA I CAN'T DO ANYTHING TO HELP YOU.
...IT'S ALWAYS...
IT'S NO FUN IF YOU AREN'T AROUND.
IT'S SACRILEGIOUS.
...BEEN LIKE THIS.
HAPPY BIRTHDAY.
WHENEVER I'M SUFFERING, MAMURA IS ALWAYS THERE TO PICK UP THE PIECES.
...

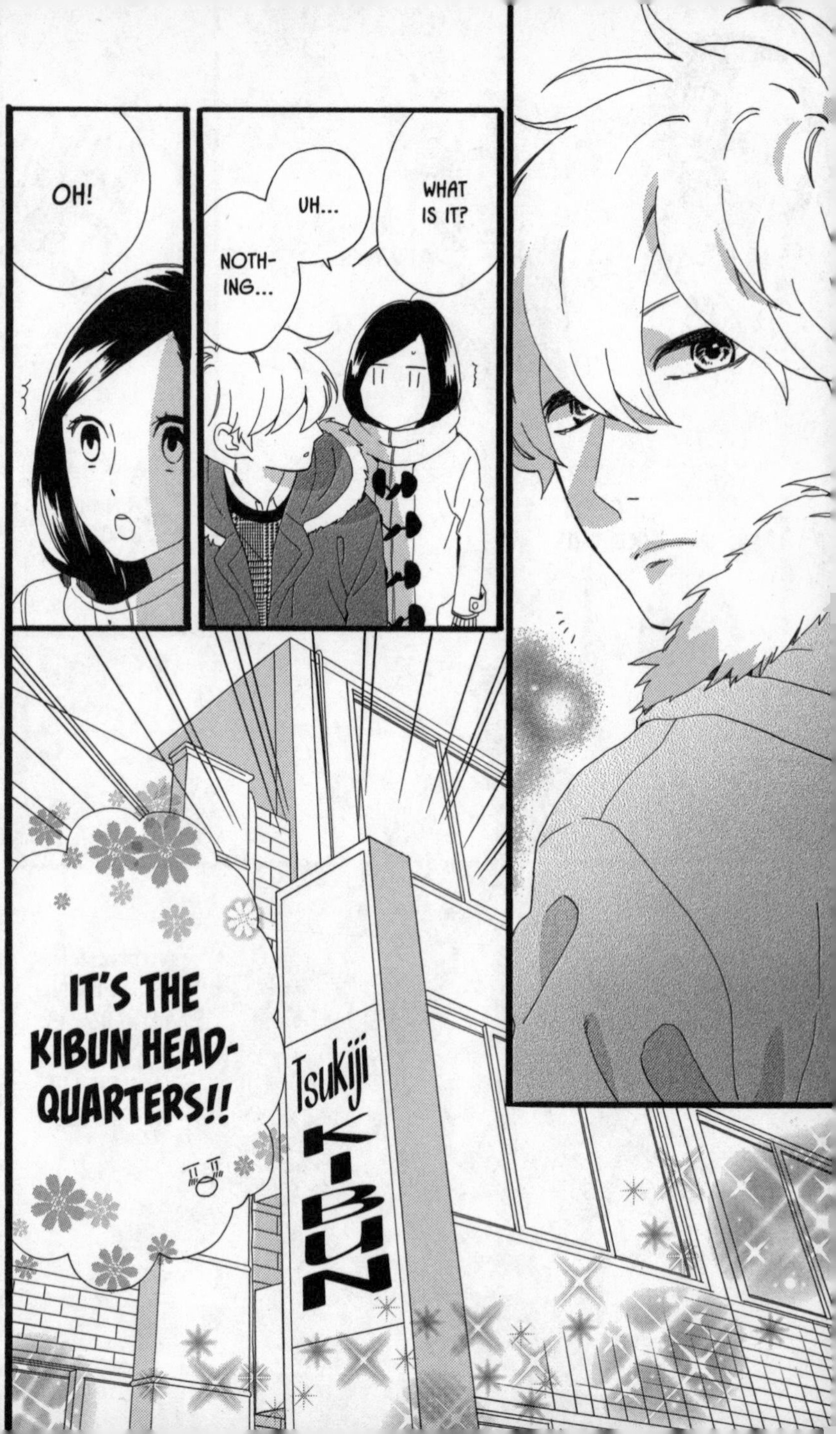
WHAT IS IT?
UH...
NOTHING...
OH!
Tsukiji KIBUN
IT'S THE KIBUN HEADQUARTERS!!

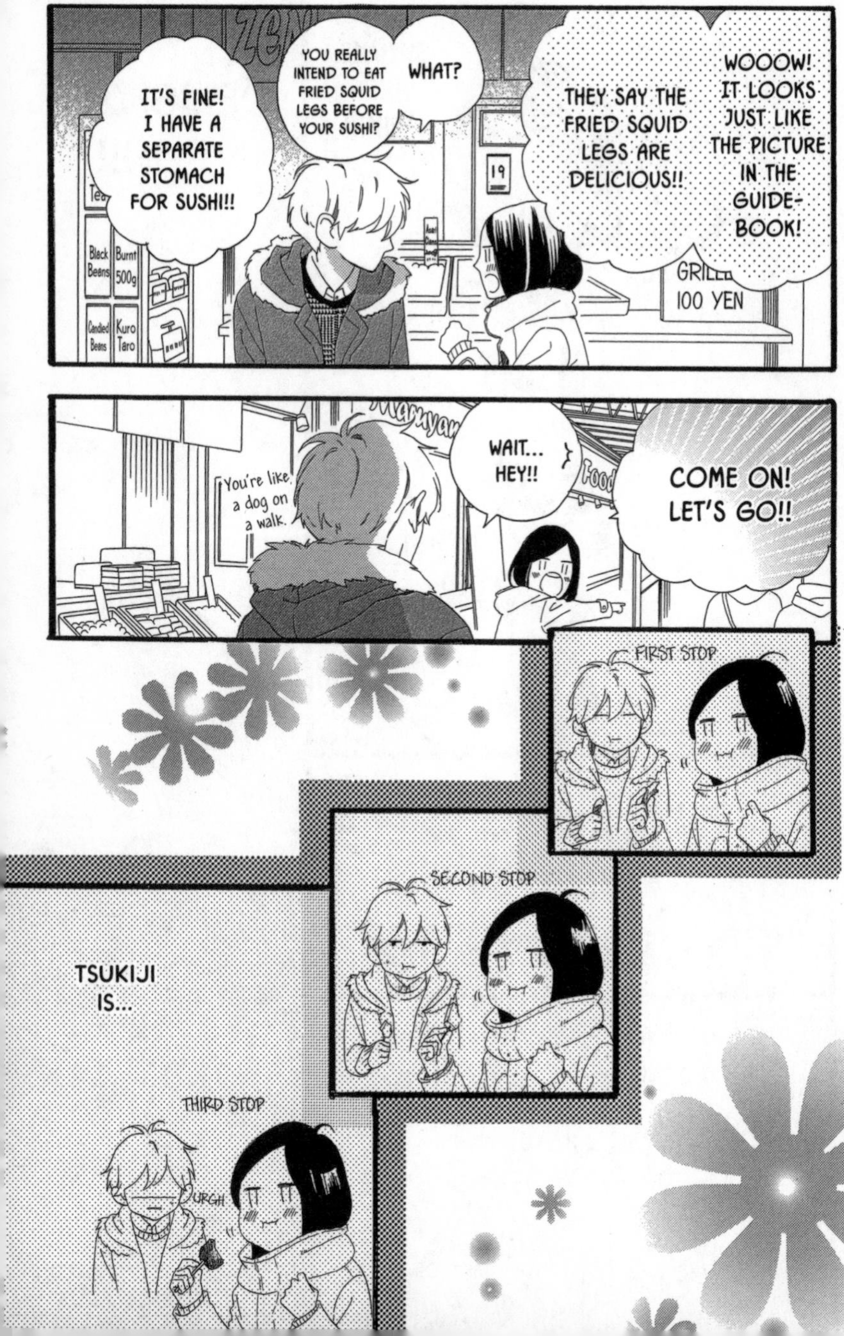
WOOOW! IT LOOKS JUST LIKE THE PICTURE IN THE GUIDE-BOOK!
THEY SAY THE FRIED SQUID LEGS ARE DELICIOUS!!
GRILLE
100 YEN
WHAT?
YOU REALLY INTEND TO EAT FRIED SQUID LEGS BEFORE YOUR SUSHI?
IT'S FINE! I HAVE A SEPARATE STOMACH FOR SUSHI!!
Burnt 500g
Black Beens
Kuro Taro
Candied Beens
COME ON! LET'S GO!!
WAIT... HEY!!
You're like a dog on a walk.
FIRST STOP
SECOND STOP
TSUKIJI IS...
THIRD STOP
URGH

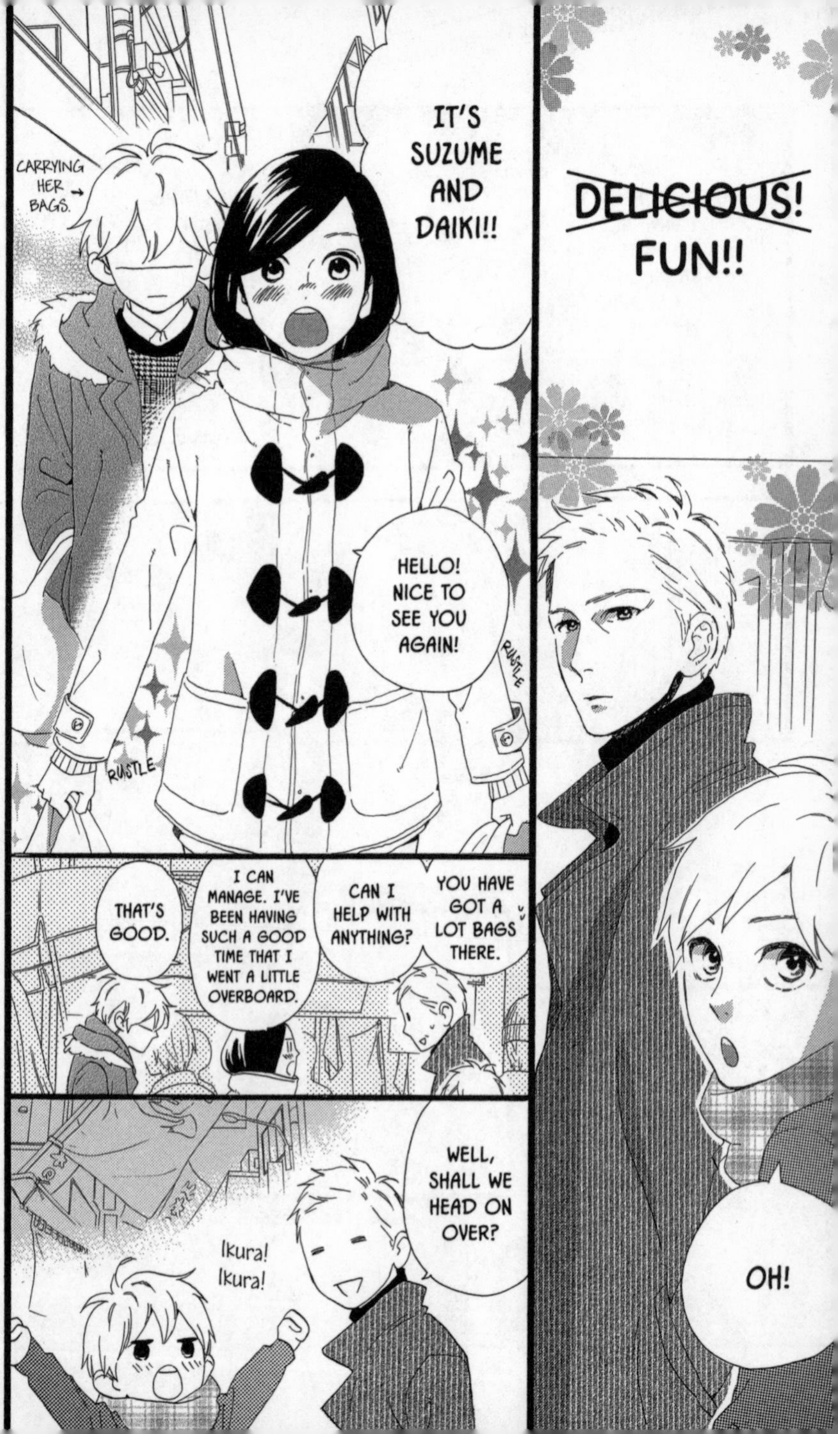
~~DELICIOUS~~! FUN!!
OH!
IT'S SUZUME AND DAIKI!!
CARRYING HER BAGS.
HELLO! NICE TO SEE YOU AGAIN!
RUSTLE
RUSTLE
YOU HAVE GOT A LOT BAGS THERE.
CAN I HELP WITH ANYTHING?
I CAN MANAGE. I'VE BEEN HAVING SUCH A GOOD TIME THAT I WENT A LITTLE OVERBOARD.
THAT'S GOOD.
WELL, SHALL WE HEAD ON OVER?
Ikura! Ikura!

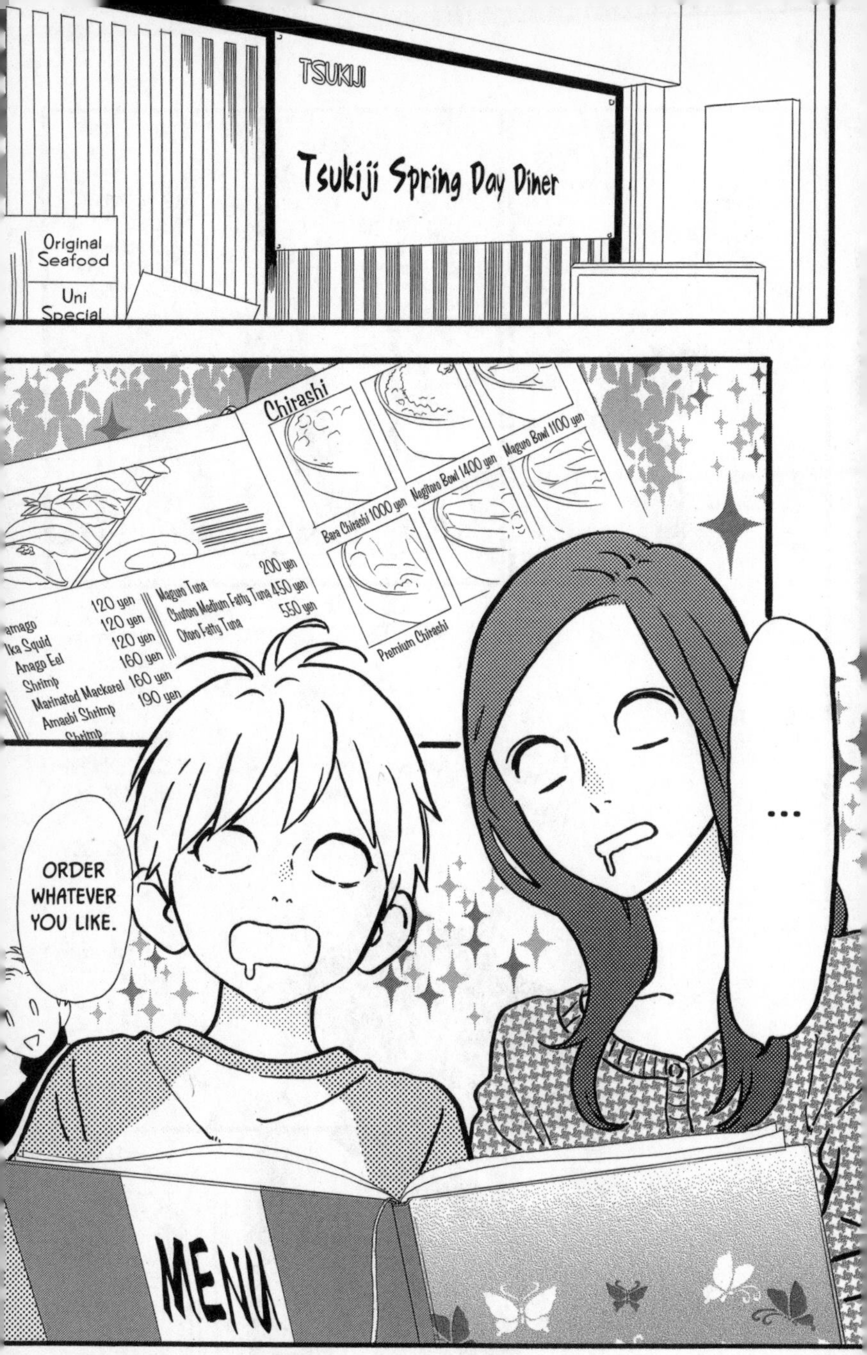
TSUKIJI
Tsukiji Spring Day Diner
Original Seafood
Uni Special
Chirashi
Maguro Bowl 1100 yen
Negitoro Bowl 1400 yen
Bara Chirashi 1000 yen
Premium Chirashi
Maguro Tuna 200 yen
Chutoro Medium Fatty Tuna 450 yen
Otoro Fatty Tuna 550 yen
120 yen
Ika Squid 120 yen
Anago Eel 120 yen
Shrimp 160 yen
Marinated Mackerel 160 yen
Amaebi Shrimp 190 yen
...
ORDER WHATEVER YOU LIKE.
MENU

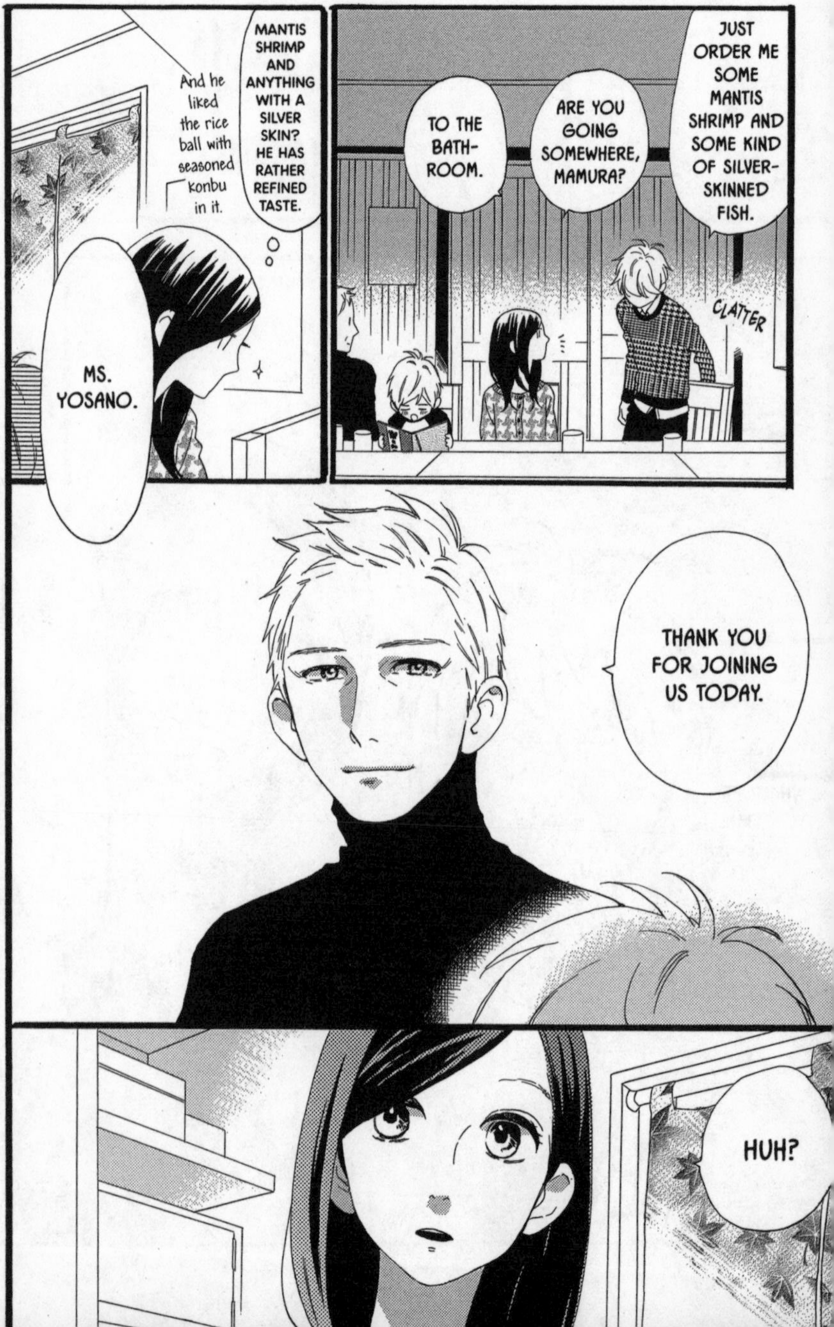
JUST ORDER ME SOME MANTIS SHRIMP AND SOME KIND OF SILVER-SKINNED FISH.
ARE YOU GOING SOMEWHERE, MAMURA?
TO THE BATH-ROOM.
CLATTER
MANTIS SHRIMP AND ANYTHING WITH A SILVER SKIN? HE HAS RATHER REFINED TASTE.
And he liked the rice ball with seasoned konbu in it.
MS. YOSANO.
THANK YOU FOR JOINING US TODAY.
HUH?

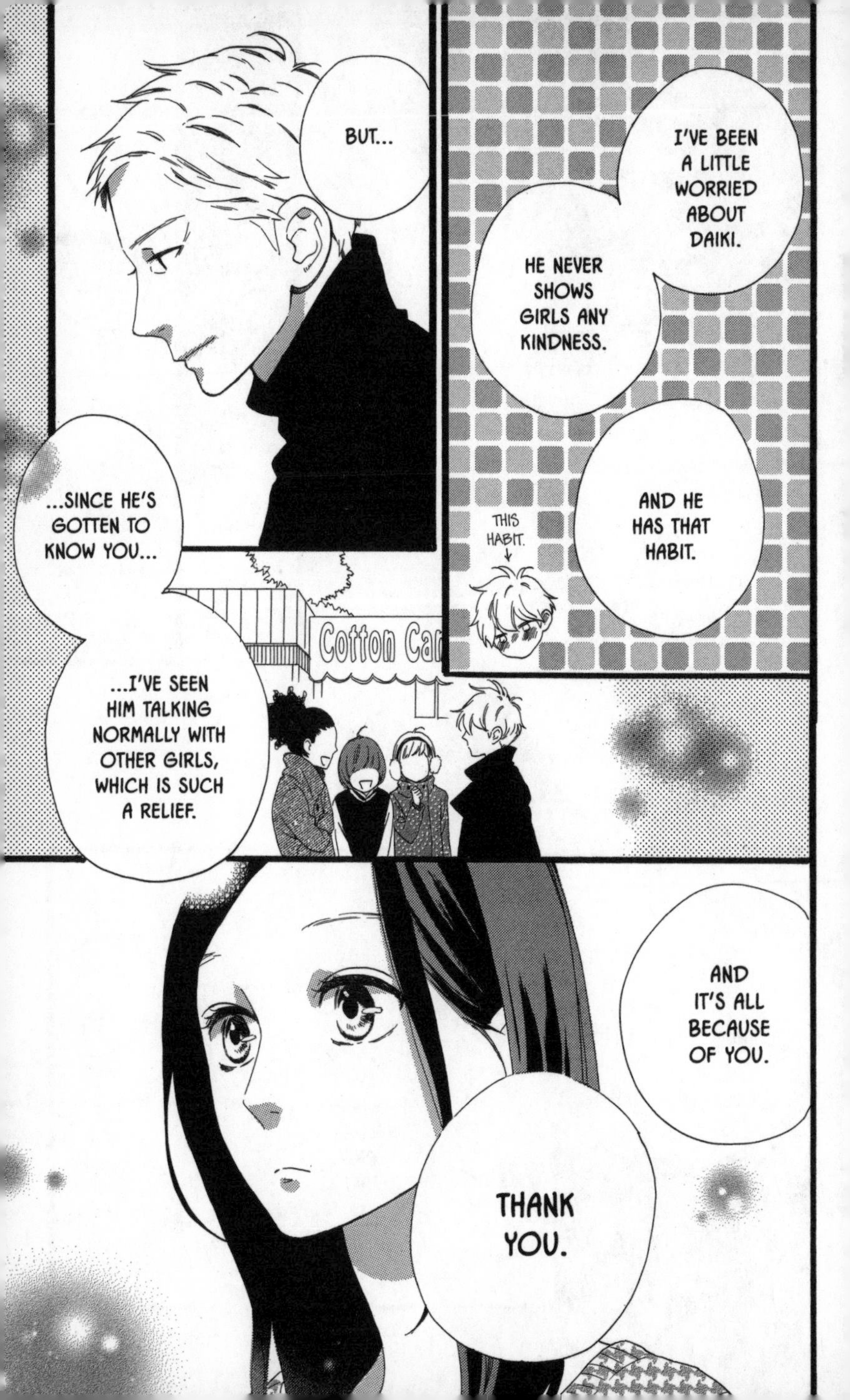
I'VE BEEN A LITTLE WORRIED ABOUT DAIKI.
HE NEVER SHOWS GIRLS ANY KINDNESS.
AND HE HAS THAT HABIT.
THIS HABIT.
BUT...
...SINCE HE'S GOTTEN TO KNOW YOU...
...I'VE SEEN HIM TALKING NORMALLY WITH OTHER GIRLS, WHICH IS SUCH A RELIEF.
AND IT'S ALL BECAUSE OF YOU.
THANK YOU.

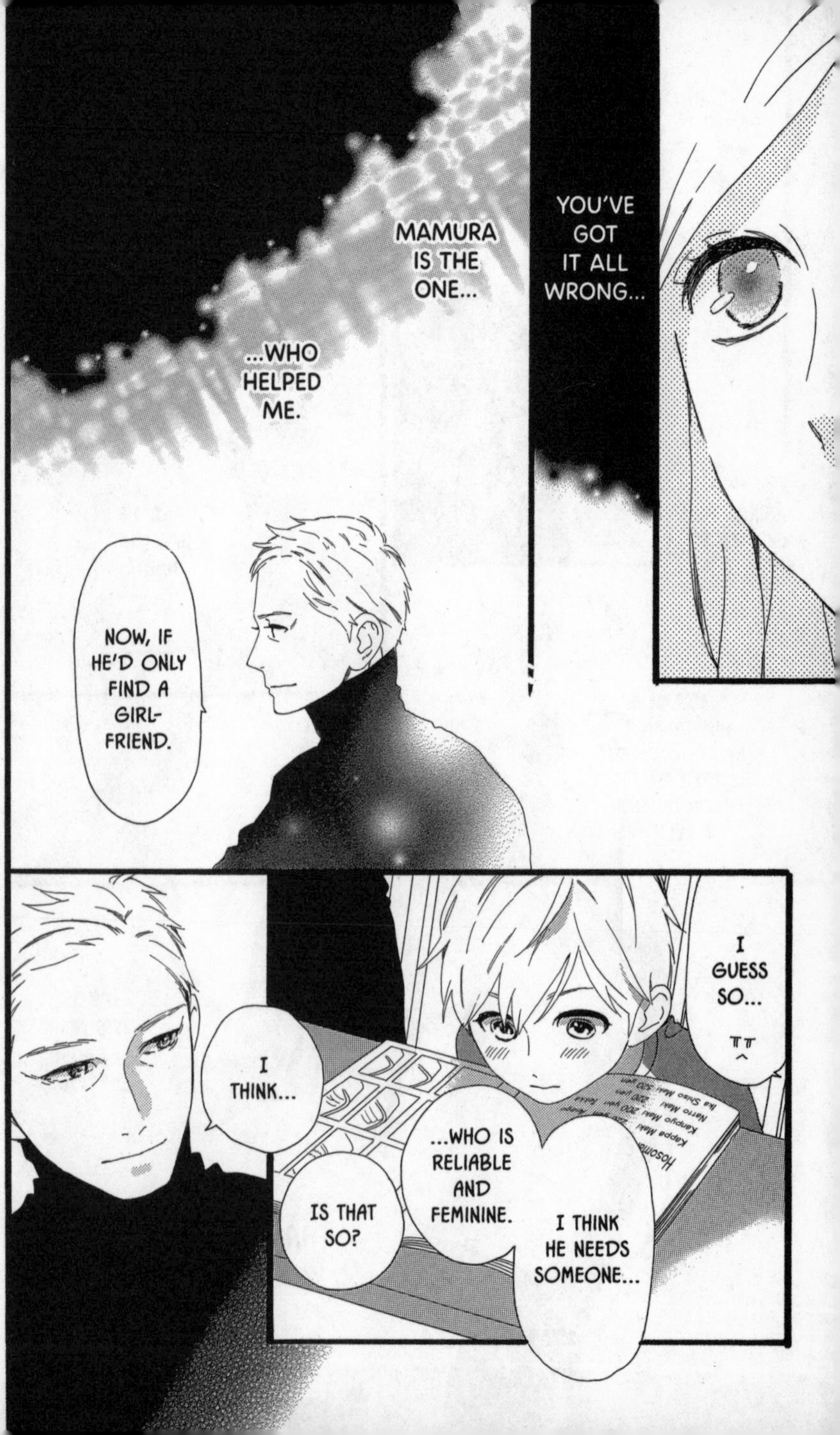
YOU'VE GOT IT ALL WRONG...
MAMURA IS THE ONE...
...WHO HELPED ME.
NOW, IF HE'D ONLY FIND A GIRL-FRIEND.
I GUESS SO...
I THINK...
I THINK HE NEEDS SOMEONE...
...WHO IS RELIABLE AND FEMININE.
IS THAT SO?

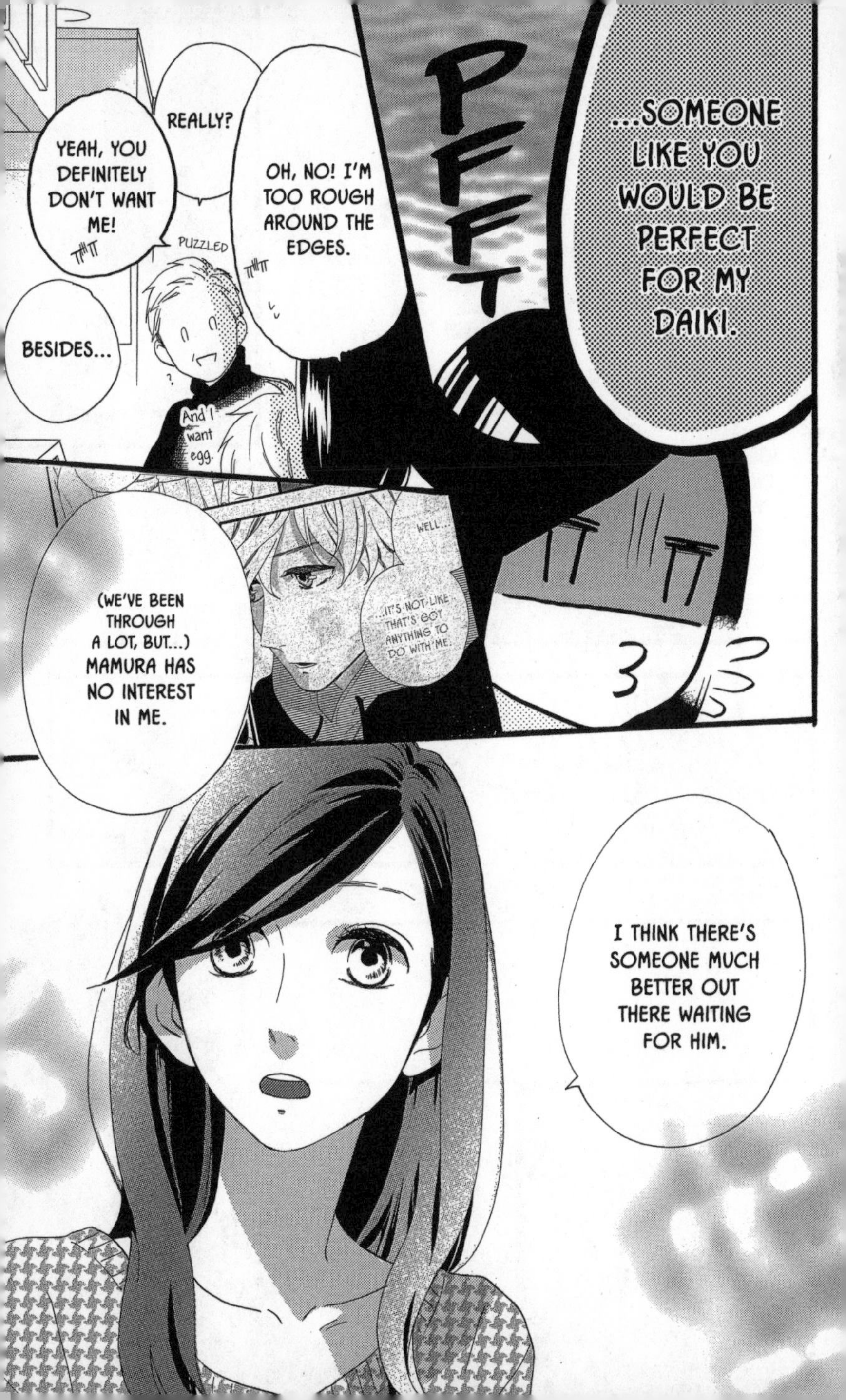
PFFT
...SOMEONE LIKE YOU WOULD BE PERFECT FOR MY DAIKI.
OH, NO! I'M TOO ROUGH AROUND THE EDGES.
REALLY?
YEAH, YOU DEFINITELY DON'T WANT ME!
PUZZLED
BESIDES...
And I want egg.
WELL...
...IT'S NOT LIKE THAT'S GOT ANYTHING TO DO WITH ME.
(WE'VE BEEN THROUGH A LOT, BUT...) MAMURA HAS NO INTEREST IN ME.
I THINK THERE'S SOMEONE MUCH BETTER OUT THERE WAITING FOR HIM.

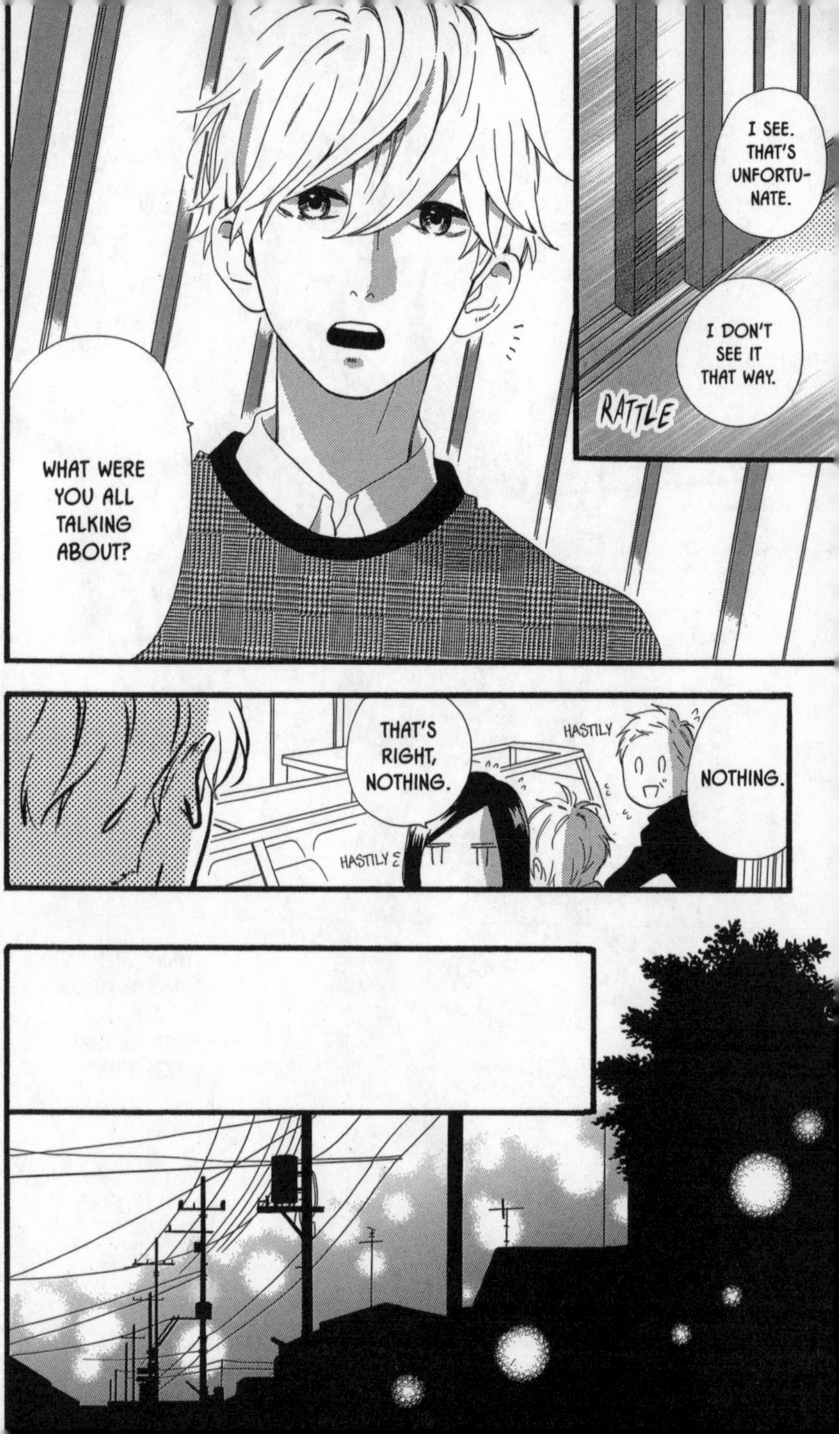
I SEE. THAT'S UNFORTU-NATE.
I DON'T SEE IT THAT WAY.
RATTLE
WHAT WERE YOU ALL TALKING ABOUT?
HASTILY
NOTHING.
THAT'S RIGHT, NOTHING.
HASTILY

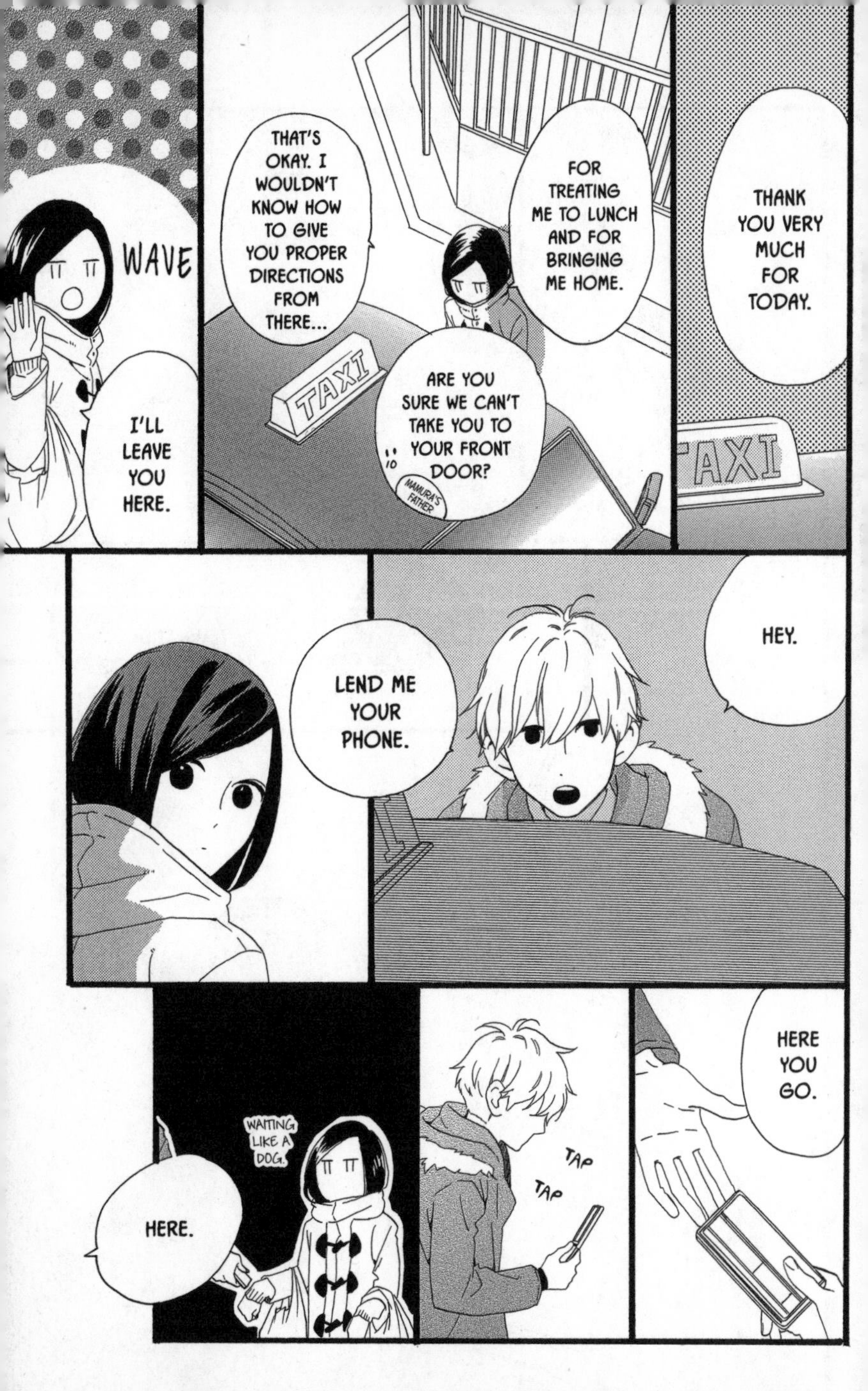
THANK YOU VERY MUCH FOR TODAY.
FOR TREATING ME TO LUNCH AND FOR BRINGING ME HOME.
THAT'S OKAY. I WOULDN'T KNOW HOW TO GIVE YOU PROPER DIRECTIONS FROM THERE...
ARE YOU SURE WE CAN'T TAKE YOU TO YOUR FRONT DOOR?
MAMURA'S FATHER
WAVE
I'LL LEAVE YOU HERE.
HEY.
LEND ME YOUR PHONE.
HERE YOU GO.
TAP
TAP
WAITING LIKE A DOG.
HERE.

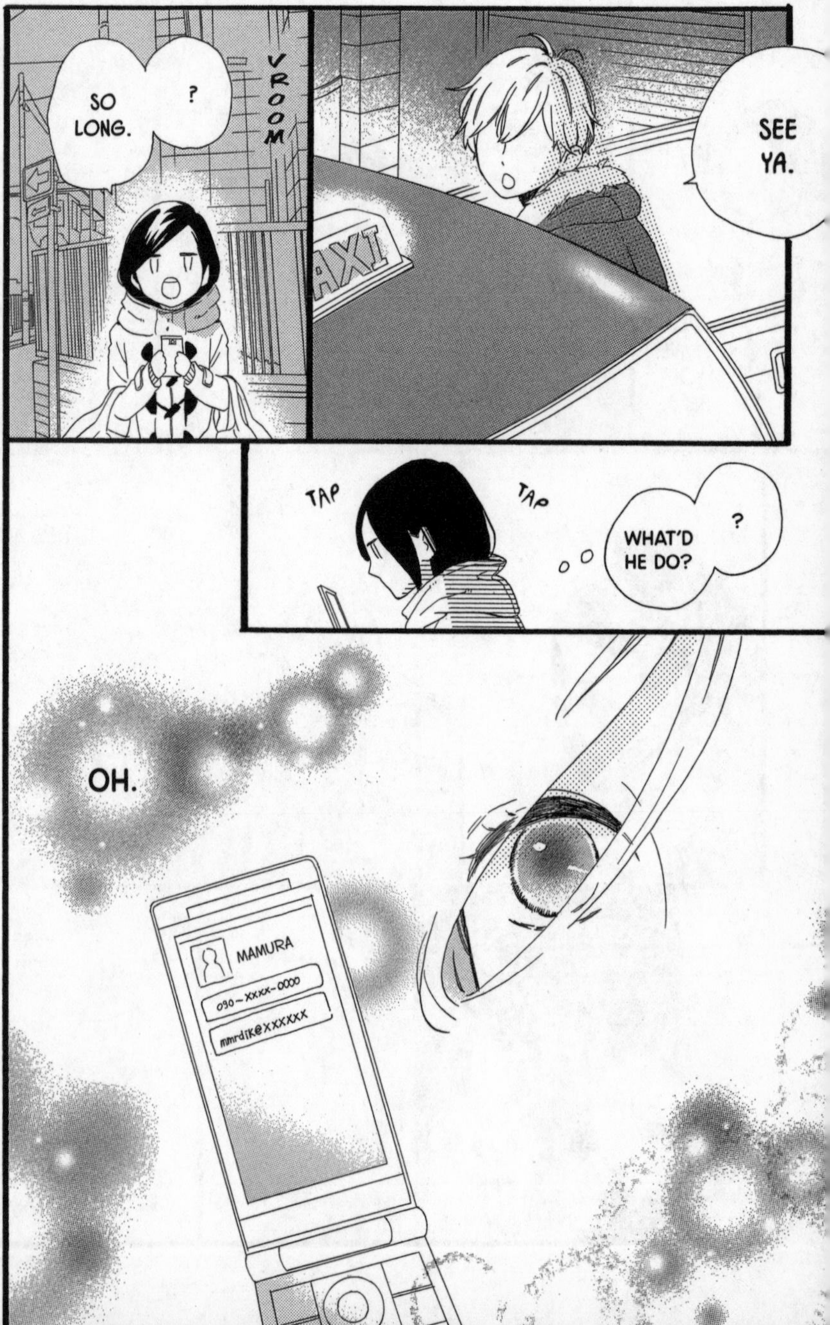
SEE YA.
VROOM
SO LONG. ?
WHAT'D HE DO? ?
TAP TAP
OH.
MAMURA
090-XXXX-0000
mmrdik@XXXXXX

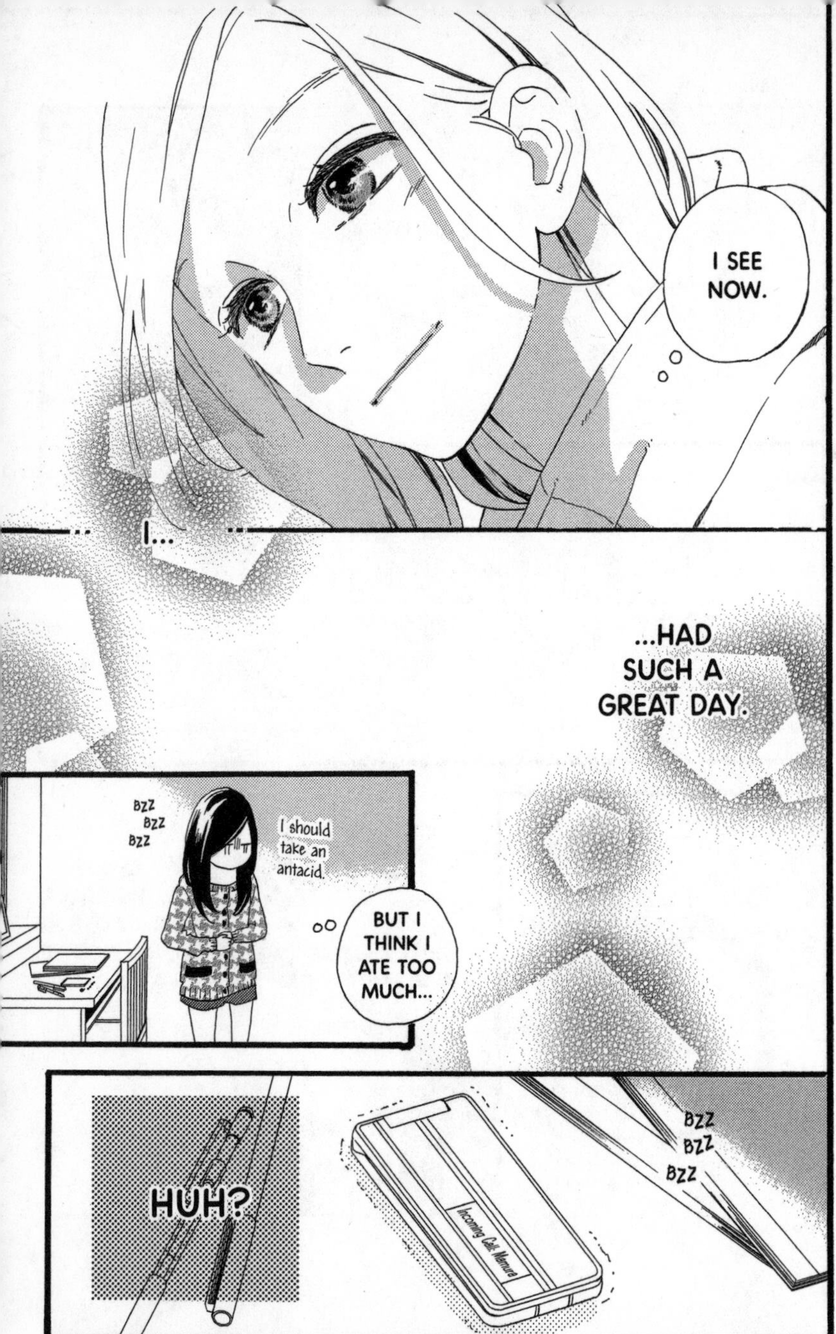
I SEE NOW.
I...
...HAD SUCH A GREAT DAY.
BUT I THINK I ATE TOO MUCH...
I should take an antacid.
BZZ BZZ BZZ
BZZ BZZ BZZ
Incoming Call: Mamura
HUH?

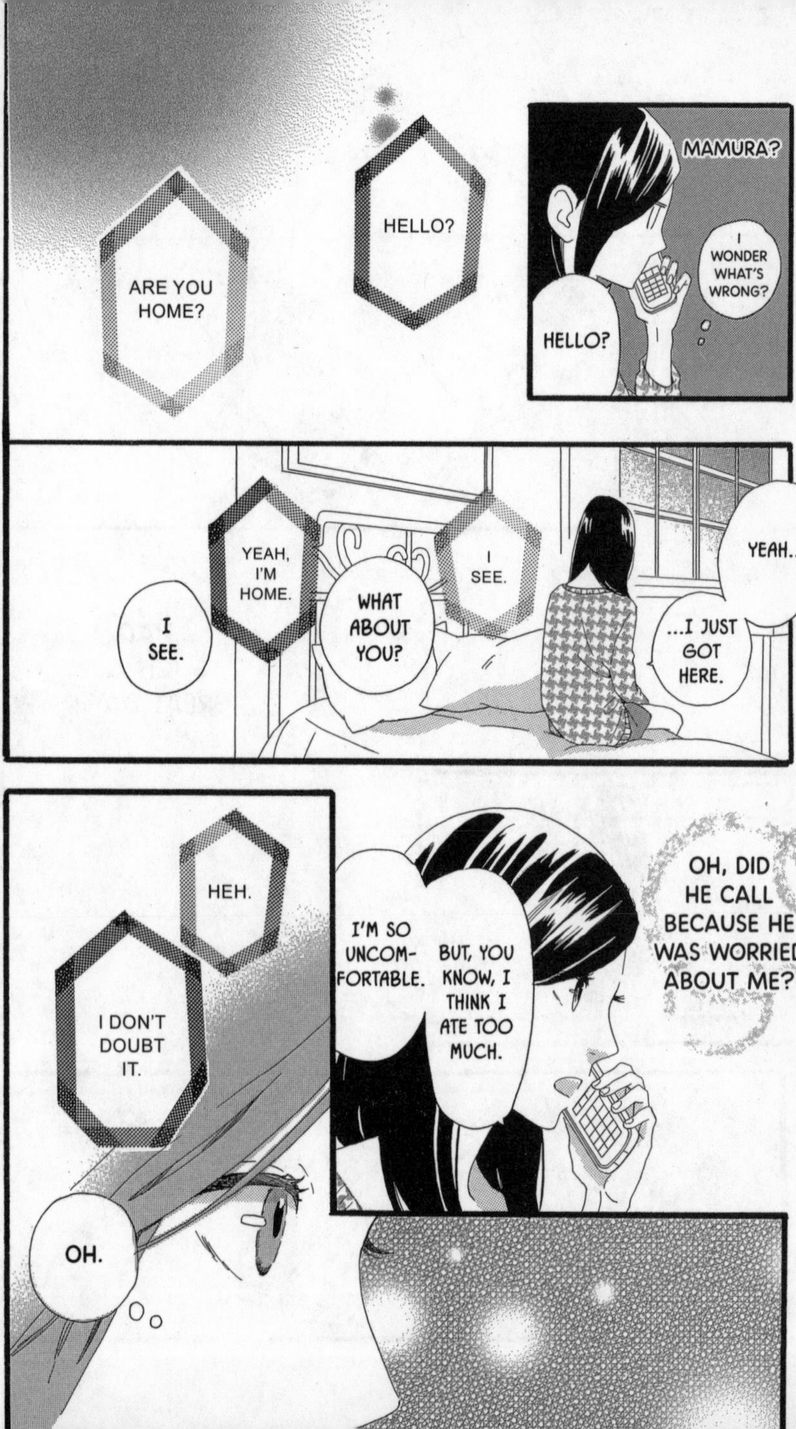
MAMURA?
I WONDER WHAT'S WRONG?
HELLO?
HELLO?
ARE YOU HOME?
YEAH...
...I JUST GOT HERE.
I SEE.
WHAT ABOUT YOU?
YEAH, I'M HOME.
I SEE.
OH, DID HE CALL BECAUSE HE WAS WORRIED ABOUT ME?
BUT, YOU KNOW, I THINK I ATE TOO MUCH.
I'M SO UNCOM-FORTABLE.
HEH.
I DON'T DOUBT IT.
OH.

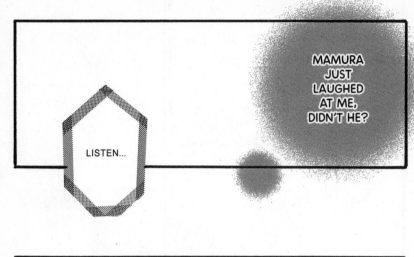

MAMURA JUST LAUGHED AT ME, DIDN'T HE?

LISTEN...

?

YEAH?

WHAT IS IT?

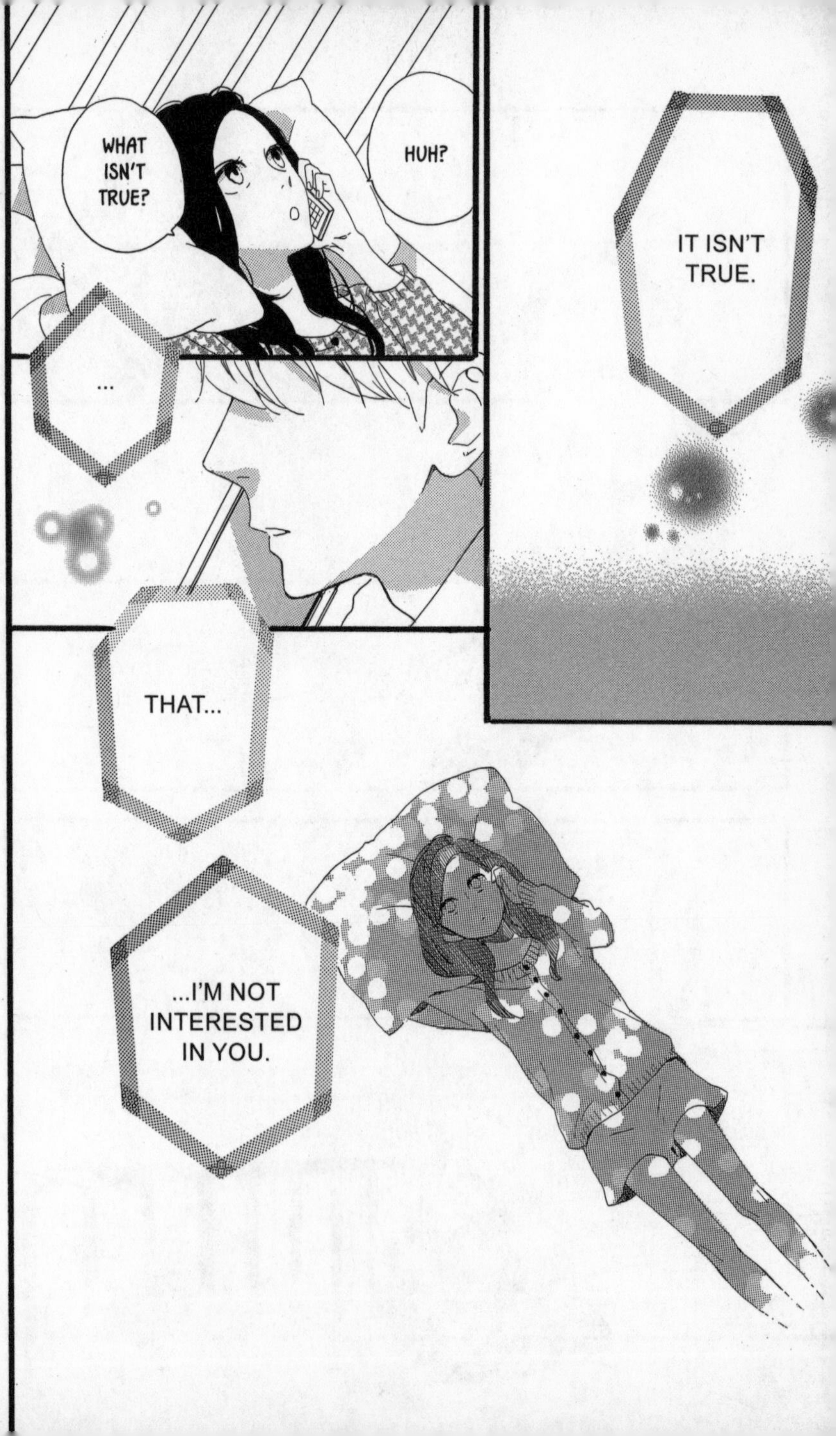
IT ISN'T TRUE.
HUH?
WHAT ISN'T TRUE?
...
THAT...
...I'M NOT INTERESTED IN YOU.

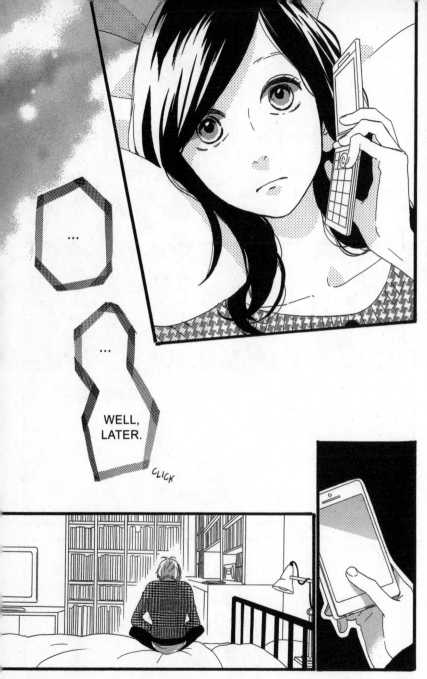

...

...

WELL,
LATER.

CLICK

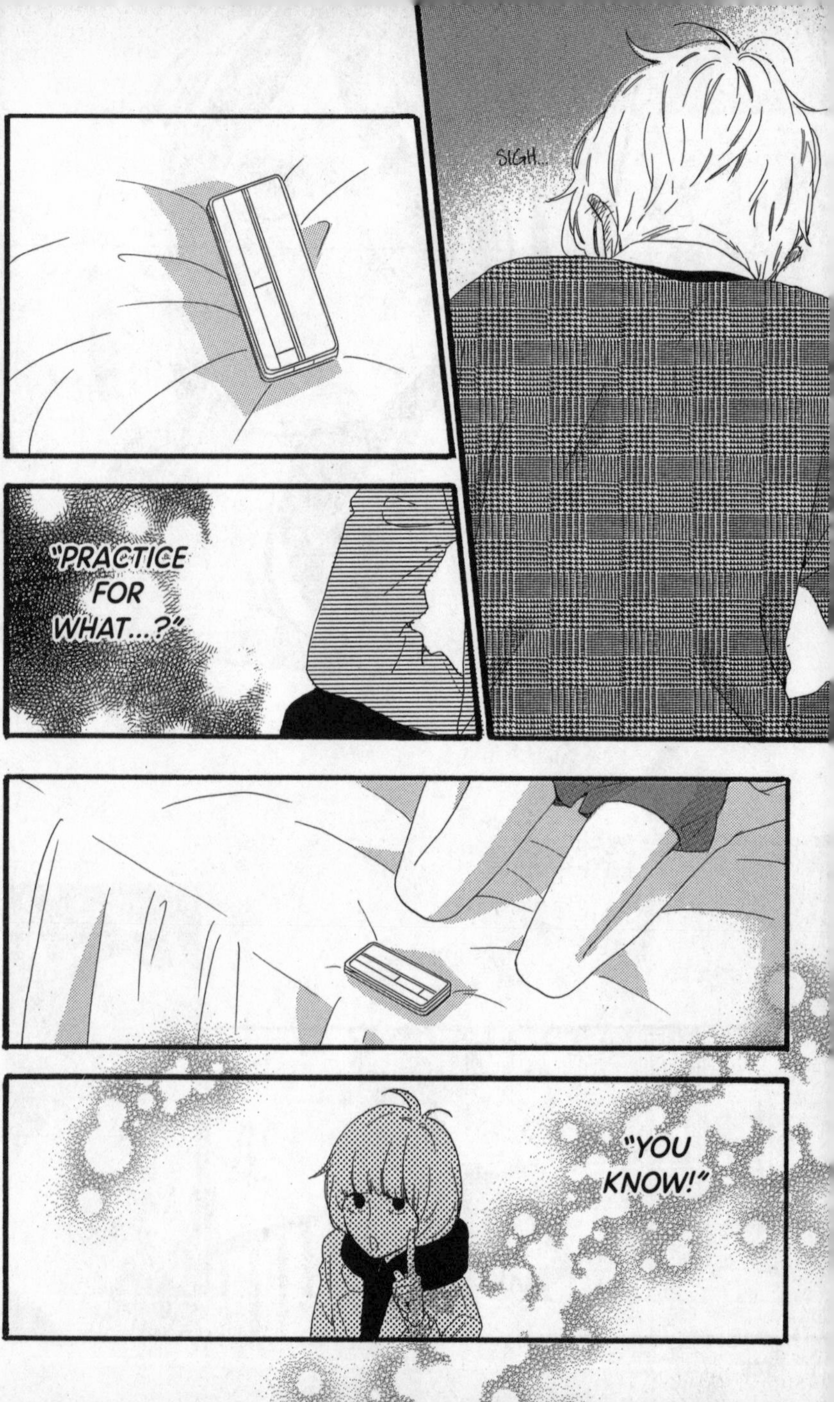
SIGH...
"PRACTICE FOR WHAT...?"
"YOU KNOW!"

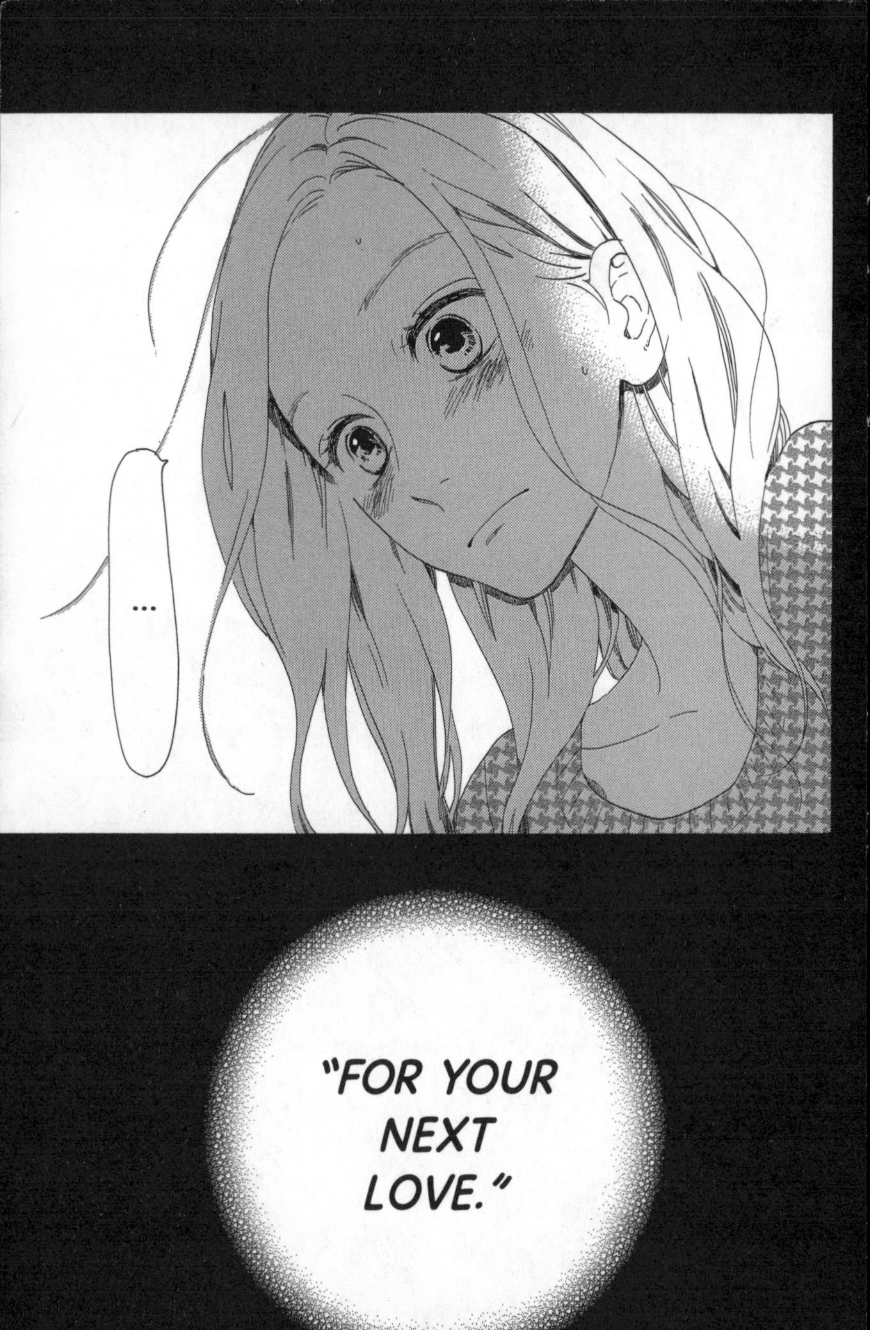
...
"FOR YOUR NEXT LOVE."

Daytime Shooting Star Vol. 8/End

About the time this volume goes on sale, I plan to be on a helicopter with Momoko Koda.

—Mika Yamamori

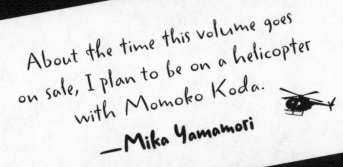

Mika Yamamori is from Ishikawa Prefecture in Japan. She began her professional manga career in 2006 with "Kimi no Kuchibiru kara Mahou" (The Magic from Your Lips) in *The Margaret* magazine. Her other works include *Sugars* and *Tsubaki Cho Lonely Planet*.

★DAYTIME★SHOOTING★STAR★ *8*

SHOJO BEAT EDITION

Story & Art by
Mika Yamamori

Translation ★ **JN Productions**
Touch-Up Art & Lettering ★ **Inori Fukuda Trant**
Design ★ **Francesca Truman**
Editor ★ **Karla Clark**

HIRUNAKA NO RYUSEI © 2011 by Mika Yamamori
All rights reserved.
First published in Japan in 2011 by SHUEISHA Inc., Tokyo.
English translation rights arranged by SHUEISHA Inc.

The stories, characters and incidents mentioned in this
publication are entirely fictional.

Printed in the U.S.A.

Published by VIZ Media, LLC
P.O. Box 77010
San Francisco, CA 94107

10 9 8 7 6 5 4 3 2 1
First printing, September 2020

PARENTAL ADVISORY
DAYTIME SHOOTING STAR is rated T for
Teen and is recommended for ages 13 and
up. This series contains suggestive themes.

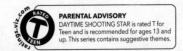

viz.com   shojobeat.com

Honey
So Sweet

Story and Art by *Amu Meguro*

Little did Nao Kogure realize back in middle school that when she left an umbrella and a box of bandages in the rain for injured delinquent Taiga Onise that she would meet him again in high school. Nao wants nothing to do with the gruff and frightening Taiga, but he suddenly presents her with a huge bouquet of flowers and asks her to date him—with marriage in mind! Is Taiga really so scary, or is he a sweetheart in disguise?

Shojo Beat

RATED T TEEN
ratings.viz.com

viz media
viz.com

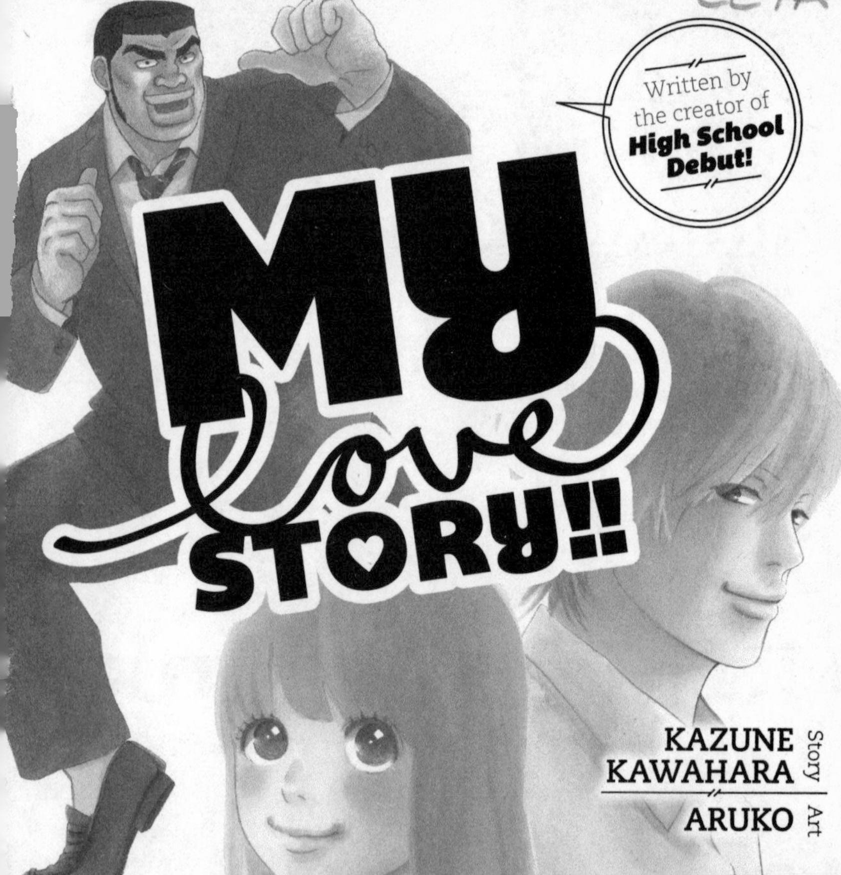

Written by the creator of High School Debut!
MY love STORY!!
KAZUNE KAWAHARA Story
ARUKO Art

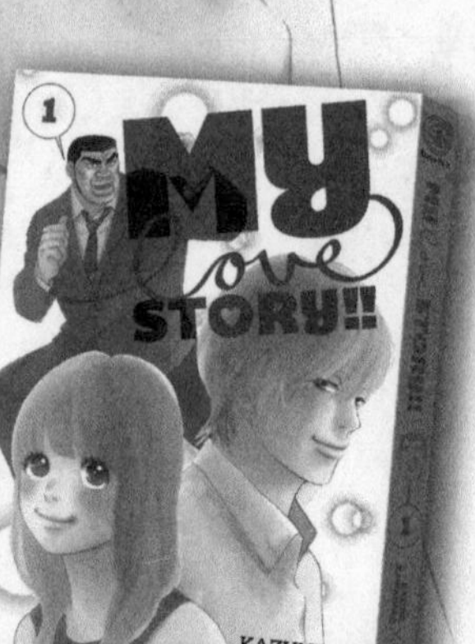

1
MY love STORY!!
KAZUNE KAWAHARA Story
ARUKO Art

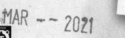